LUCAS:

THE FIRST HUNDRED YEARS

VOL I: THE KING OF THE ROAD

HAROLD NOCKOLDS

DAVID & CHARLES

NEWTON ABBOT   LONDON

NORTH POMFRET (VT)   VANCOUVER

ISBN 0 7153 7306 4
Library of Congress Catalog Card Number 76–19233

Set in 12 on 13pt Aldine Bembo
and printed in Great Britain
by Latimer Trend & Company Ltd Plymouth
for David & Charles (Publishers) Limited
Brunel House   Newton Abbot   Devon

Published in the United States of America
by David & Charles Inc
North Pomfret   Vermont 05053   USA

Published in Canada
by Douglas David & Charles Limited
1875 Welch Street   North Vancouver   BC

CONTENTS

CONTENTS

INTRODUCTION

The idea of publishing a full-scale history of Lucas has often been suggested, but until now it has been firmly resisted. It was always felt that the time was not quite ripe – the organisation was still expanding and its pattern had not fully developed. And there was another, underlying excuse for putting it off. It had become almost a tradition in the company to avoid publicity (much to the despair of successive publicity managers) and the directors shied at the prospect of blowing their own trumpet.

The attitude of the company towards publicity has changed in recent years. In any case these reservations were swept aside when someone reminded us that we had reached our hundredth birthday. There is something about a centenary that is irresistible to British people. At the beginning of every year the reference books are combed to trace centenaries of all kinds – births and deaths of the famous and the infamous, events of historic, dramatic, glamorous and even sordid character – all are seized upon to be recounted in newspapers, books, and on radio and television.

The practice has spread to the industrial and commercial life of the country. Leading British companies have been the subjects of full-length biographies, often linked with their centenaries. Not the least of their uses is that case studies can be based on the successful and unsuccessful episodes in their development and so help the executives and managers of today to learn from the lessons of the past.

Now it is our turn. In these two volumes we present the story of Lucas over the past 100 years – the first 100 years, as we like to think of them, because after allowing ourselves the indulgence of looking over our shoulders we shall be concentrating on the problems that lie ahead.

In fact, 1975 is not strictly the hundredth anniversary of Lucas as a company, for Joseph Lucas, Limited, was not formed until 1897. But 1875 was when the story really began. In that year Joseph Lucas, an independent metal-worker in a red-brick terrace house in Birmingham, patented the Tom Bowling ship lamp and laid the foundations of the company we call Lucas Industries today. From that one-man business has grown an international company with an annual turnover of some £700 million and still growing fast. The direct payroll has grown to some 80,000 people, employed by twenty-six main subsidiaries at home and thirty-six similar companies in nineteen countries all over the world.

How that vast expansion occurred is, I believe, a story that will interest many people for different reasons, because it touches on various aspects of the industrial and commercial life of Great Britain in the last 100 years: the Victorian bicycle boom which was the root of Lucas growth, the Edwardian evolution of the motor-car into the motor industry, the beginning of flying and its rise into the world of aerospace, the 'diesel explosion', and now the exciting prospect of a really practical urban electric vehicle with all its potential benefits to the quality of life in our cities. In all these industrial developments the people of Lucas with their technology and their special production and other manifold skills have played a major role.

But I am not going to try to compress into this short introduction what the author has taken three years and more than 200,000 words to tell. He has been given a free hand to meet people at all levels in the company, including many who have retired, and the inner work-ing of the company has been laid open to him for examination – he has, for example, read the minutes of every board meeting since the company was formed, and much else besides. We have not pulled his punches – indeed he insisted on recording the mistakes along with the successes, for otherwise the book would not have rung true.

The result is an uninhibited chronicle of which we are not ashamed – and which some may think is a cause for pride. I like to think that 'Old Joe' himself, his son Harry and grandson Oliver Lucas might approve our conduct of the great enterprise that they so ably created, and whose great example and spirit we have striven to follow.

BERNARD SCOTT
Chairman

PART ONE

JOSEPH LUCAS...
& SON

CHAPTER ONE

WHO *WAS* JOSEPH LUCAS?

When I began to plan this first chapter of the history of Lucas Industries, Limited, I naturally thought I would be able to start with the birth and parents of the man whose initial enterprise founded the great company that still bears his name today. I quickly discovered it was not going to be as simple as that when I read the opening sentences of the brief histories that had been produced from time to time. 'In 1860 Joseph dealt in buckets . . .' was the starting point for one of these useful documents – but by that time our hero was already 26 years of age. 'One of the first products to come out of the modest little workshop in 1872 . . .' began 'The Early Years', the first section of the *Brief History of the Lucas Organisation*, issued by the company in 1966. Joseph Lucas was by then 38.

But the clearest hint of the difficulties I would meet in reaching back to the early life of the founder was given in the draft of a longer history prepared some years ago, a paper that has been a valuable source of information to me in many other respects. It began: 'Little is known about the family background of Joseph Lucas . . .'

So that was it. Apart from the date of his birth, 12 April 1834, and unconfirmed stories of an apprenticeship that I will come to in due course, the life of Joseph Lucas up to the age of 26 was a blank. Nothing was known, it seemed, about his father, where he lived and what he did, or the environment that influenced Joseph's early years.

The obvious ploy was to get a copy of his birth certificate, which would state the name of his father and his occupation, but the staff of the City of Birmingham Register Office reminded me that birth certificates were not issued until July 1837, by which time Joseph Lucas was 3 years old. This was a setback, but there were still the baptismal registers kept by parish churches – provided, of course, he was baptised. There proved to be eight churches in Birmingham at which baptisms could have taken place in the year 1834, and in the register of one of them, St Philip's, the cathedral church, occurred the following entry: 'Baptised on March 31st, 1834, Joseph, son of Charles and Sarah Lucas, born January 1st, 1834, residing in Tower Street, father's occupation jeweller.'

This was a tantalising discovery, because here was a Joseph Lucas born in Birmingham in 1834, but not on the date that had come to be accepted as the day on which 'our' Joseph came into the world. But the service card at his funeral stated categorically that he was born on 12 April, so there must indeed have been two Joseph Lucases born in the same place within a few months of each other.

I next tried the churches in what were then the outer parts of Birmingham – Edgbaston, Harborne, Handsworth, Moseley, King's Norton – but Joseph Lucas did not appear in their baptismal registers in the 1830s. Having drawn a blank in the registers of the Birmingham non-parish churches and chapels as well, I was left with the conclusion that in all probability his parents did not have him baptised.

Then it occurred to me that I could trace the name of Joseph's father and his occupation through his own marriage certificate. I did not know the date of the marriage, but I could get near it through the birth certificate of his son, Harry, whom I found was born at 86 Carver Street, Birmingham, on 10 February 1855, when Joseph himself was 21. A marriage certificate from the previous year gave Joseph's father's name as Benjamin Lucas and his occupation as plater. Joseph's wife was Emily Stevens, aged 23, and they were married at Edgbaston parish church.

So far, so good, but there was still the unanswered question of Joseph's birthplace. Was he actually born in Birmingham, as was generally thought, or was Benjamin Lucas living somewhere else at the time? The nearest I could get would be a Census Return, in which there is a column headed 'Where born' for each person. The 1861 return, six years after his marriage, might show Joseph still living at Carver Street, in which case it would reveal his place of birth. At the Public Record Office it took only a few minutes to obtain the microfilm I wanted and start examining the census sheets as they slid across the illuminated screen of the viewing machine. At last Carver Street came up . . . No 86 . . . Joseph Lucas, age 27, head of family, where born – Birmingham.

At this stage in my search into Joseph Lucas's origin I spent some time in following up a clue which seemed to be authentic but which eventually proved to be a completely false trail. I will not confuse the reader by tracing every detail of that fruitless search; anyway, it took me to Leamington Spa and the county archives at Warwick, Companies House in London, and brought me one hot July afternoon to the beautiful little graveyard of Elmdon parish church, where I toiled in my shirtsleeves with a borrowed spade at a half-buried family tombstone alongside the churchyard wall. They were Lucases all right, but after more delving among the births and marriages volumes at Somerset House, I found they were not connected with Joseph Lucas in any way whatever.

Then I had another idea, a pretty obvious one, which was that although Joseph Lucas himself was born three years before birth certificates were introduced, he might have had a younger brother or sister, born in or after 1837, for whom a birth certificate was issued. I found that a surprising number of Lucases were born in Birmingham at that time. In 1837 (the year Victoria came to the throne) there were Henry and Joseph George Lucas; in 1838 Eliza, William and Abraham (the last two at Aston), Benjamin, 'a male', Elizabeth, George and 'a female'; and the 1839 crop of Birmingham Lucases were Charles (at Aston), Eliza, Catharine, Sarah, Emily, John and another Sarah.

Looking down this list I plumped for Benjamin ('named after his father') as being the most likely younger brother of Joseph, and rather to my astonishment I proved to be right. A copy of his birth certificate showed that he was indeed the son of Benjamin Lucas, brazier of plated wares, and was born on 15 April 1838 in Carver Street, where Joseph was living when he got married 16 years later. Knowing that Joseph was to describe his father as a plater in later years, it seemed fair to assume that the other details of the younger Benjamin's birth certificate would also apply to Joseph, who was then 4 years of age. So the answer to the question 'Who *was* Joseph Lucas?' emerged as:

> Born: 12 April, 1834
> Father: Benjamin Lucas, plater
> Mother: Catharine, previously Ball
> Place: Dingley's Buildings, Carver Street,
>   Birmingham.

The next step was to find out something about his education and early environment.

CHAPTER TWO

BOY AND MAN

The only positive clue I have found about Joseph Lucas's education occurs in a document that did not appear until after his death. None of the early workpeople who recorded their memories of him made any reference to his schooling, or the extent of it, nor was it mentioned in the obituary notices published at his death.

It was left to Mary Anne Lucas, his third wife and widow, to touch on it in her introduction to a little booklet, *A Fireside Chat on the Commercial Side of Life*, by Joseph Lucas, which she had privately printed in 1906 'in loving memory' of her husband. In this she wrote: 'I have many times heard my husband say that whatever of good was in him was owing to the teaching and ministry of George Dawson, whose school he went to as a young man and whose church later on he was a member of as long as it was in existence as such.'

This is a much more significant revelation than it might seem at first glance, because George Dawson was no ordinary teacher or clergyman. He was, indeed, one of the handful of men in the middle of the last century who had a profound effect on the development of Birmingham into what an American observer called 'the best managed city of the world.' Dawson achieved this by bringing his personality and opinions to bear on the hierarchy of the city; that his influence was equally effective with the ordinary people is shown by the life-long impression he made on Joseph Lucas.

Dawson arrived in Birmingham in 1847 from a small Baptist chapel in Rickmansworth, Hertfordshire, as a handsome young man of 23 to take charge of the Baptist Mount Zion Chapel in Graham Street, a famous place of worship, built 25 years earlier, that could hold 2,500 people. There he immediately made his mark. He had a university MA degree but was never ordained. With his good looks and eloquence (Charles Kingsley called him 'the best public talker in England') Dawson was enormously popular. Three years later, in 1850, after falling out with the administrators over theological differences, in which he was supported by many influential members of the chapel, Dawson broke away and with their financial help built the splendid new Church of the Saviour in Edward Street, off the Parade, which was open to all religious sects. The Mount Zion administrators held that religious teaching should be based on the death of Jesus Christ, whereas Dawson believed it should be based on His life. He consequently preached and lectured with great fervour on the everyday duties of life – the whole of life – including business and trade, and it was no doubt this practical approach to religion that appealed to the young Joseph Lucas. Next to the Church of the Saviour, round the corner in Helena Street, Dawson built a school for boys and girls combined with a lecture room and a library.

This was evidently the school run by Dawson where Joseph Lucas received the teaching he was to remember all his life. It is probable, however, that he attended it only on Sundays, for a reason that will shortly become clear. In Birmingham at that time the Sunday school was an institution for part-time education. In addition to scriptural instruction, the pupils were taught to read (in the hope that they would read the Bible for themselves) and in half the fifty-six Sunday schools writing was taught as well. Some even included grammar, geography and history, and a few taught arithmetic. The Sunday schools were very popular and for at least three-quarters of the pupils they provided the only education they received.

In later years Harry Lucas, Joseph's eldest son, used to rebuke his father sometimes for his erratic spelling, for example: 'Your short note to "The Firs" came this morning. You did not address it right. It should be "The Firs" . . . this is spelt F i r s and not F u r s. The latter kind are those especially interesting to ladies' (Harry Lucas to his father in a letter dated 13 September 1880.) But in fact Joseph Lucas was far from being uneducated by the standard of his time. In a survey carried out by the Statistical Society for the Improvement of Education in 1838 (when Joseph was 4 years of age) it was found that out of 45,000 Birmingham children aged from 5 to 15 years, rather less than half had attended a school of any kind and most of these had 'only a trifle of learning.' Many, for example, were sent to dames' schools, where hardly anything was taught (the main idea was to keep the children off the streets and the dames went on with their housework regardless of their 'pupils', being content to make some easy money). Brought up at a time when more than half the children of Birmingham were completely illiterate, Joseph Lucas was therefore educated to a standard that was a great deal higher than 'rudimentary', as it has sometimes been called. With the same background of widespread illiteracy, which was even more pronounced among girls than boys, it was quite in accordance with the times that Emily, Joseph's first wife, signed the marriage register with a cross as her mark.

Although there is no documentary proof, it has come to be accepted that Joseph Lucas was apprenticed to the famous Birmingham firm of silversmiths, H. & G. R. Elkington. The story is found time and again in the reminiscences of old employees who knew him personally, and they presumably got their information from Joseph himself. Apprenticeships started at the age of 13 or 14, and this is why he probably attended Dawson's school (which opened when he was about that age) only on Sundays.

The firm of Elkingtons is of course still in existence as a subsidiary of the Delta Metal Company, Limited. In 1960 it moved from its historic home in Birmingham to Walsall and the opportunity was taken to donate its archives to the Victoria and Albert Museum. When I called at the Metal Working Department of the Museum to inspect the archives, I was excited to find the heading 'Apprenticeship Indentures' in the list of contents. Unhappily there were only a half-a-dozen and the name Joseph Lucas did not appear among them.

Nevertheless there is some circumstantial evidence. In 1838 the Elkingtons took out a patent for electro-plating copper and brass with zinc. In 1842 Alexander Parkes, who was on their staff, and a medical man, Dr John Wright, patented a method of producing a thick and durable deposit, preferably of silver, by the use of cyanides in the solution of metals, and this came to be recognised as the first practical application of electro-plating. After several years of experiments and trying to exploit their inventions by granting licences for their use, the Elkingtons built a factory in Newhall Street to work the patents on their own account, followed by another in Brearley Street.

What has all this to do with Joseph Lucas? On the birth certificate of Harry, his first child, born in 1855, Joseph Lucas described himself as an 'electro-plater journeyman'. It is most unlikely that he would have used this description loosely, for it was a proud title that no Birmingham man would assume lightly. The word journeyman signified a qualified artisan, someone who had 'finished his time' or completed his apprenticeship, and where else would Joseph Lucas have learnt the trade of electro-plating but at Elkingtons, the firm that had made it a practical proposition? For in 1847 or 1848, when he would have started his 7-year apprenticeship at the age of 13 or 14, Elkingtons had only recently got their new factories into production, and Joseph's father Benjamin, himself a plater, would naturally seek to give his son the most up-to-date training in his own craft.

And so, at the age of 21, married and with his first child, the apprentice had become a journeyman. The boy had become a man. What Joseph Lucas made of his new found independence is another stage in his career.

CHAPTER THREE

TIME AND PLACE

When Joseph Lucas finished his time at Elkingtons and became an electro-plater journeyman, he might well have stayed with the firm or found himself another place elsewhere in the same trade. He had every inducement to do so because journeymen earned good money in Birmingham – anything from 30s to £5 a week – and with rents of houses that cost £60 to build ranging from 2s 6d to 4s a week, the prospects for a hard-working young man in a steady job were not too bad. And a steady job would normally be attractive to a young man who had just got married and was losing no time in raising a family.

That Joseph Lucas eschewed the course of security and launched out on his own was due to a combination of factors of which his own character was but one. There were also the influences of time and place, and it is worth while pausing for a moment in the narrative of his career to see what life in Birmingham in the mid-nineteenth century was like and how it affected Joseph Lucas's attitude to his future.

By that time Birmingham had developed two distinctive features during its growth from a medieval village to a bustling industrial Midlands town (it was not yet a city). The first was its obsession with manufacturing as a way of life and the second was the independent spirit of so many of its inhabitants, which turned them from working as journeymen for masters to setting up as independent 'little masters' producing goods of all kinds in their own homes.

Whether there is any truth in the legend that the knives of Boadicea's chariot wheels were made in Birmingham or not, by the Middle Ages the early hamlet had certainly grown to a village inhabited by craftsmen as well as yeomen. By the fourteenth century Birmingham was well on the way to becoming an industrial village, though its output, of course, was small. A deed of 1448 in the Central Reference Library mentions wholesale merchants known as ironmongers, so Joseph Lucas was following a traditional Birmingham calling when he started selling buckets and shovels some 400 years later. In 1538 John Leland visited it and wrote in his *Itinerary*: 'I came through a pretty street as ever I entered, into Bermingham town. This street, as I remember, is called Dirty. In it dwell smiths and cutlers.'

By the seventeenth century Birmingham had become a small industrial town and Camden described it as 'swarming with inhabitants and echoing with the noise of anvils.' In the early part of the following century swords and guns, for which it was already famous, were supplemented by buttons and buckles, the working of brass and copper being added to the older industries.

The second half of the eighteenth century and the beginning of the nineteenth saw a quickening in the growth of industry in Birmingham, in spite of setbacks caused by wars, bad harvests and even riots. The classic example of this industrial growth was Matthew Boulton's famous Soho Works, built in 1762 at Handsworth on the outskirts of the town, where James Watt perfected his invention of the steam engine – one of the most important events in the history of Birmingham and indeed a milestone of world-wide significance.

Steam power encouraged machine production and with it the beginning of larger factories, but the small domestic workshop, often supplying parts to larger manufacturers, continued to be a central feature of Birmingham life. By the time Joseph Lucas arrived on the scene in the 1850s, the local historian, S. Timmins, went so far as to claim that the trades of Birmingham were 'more numerous than in any single community in the history of the world', and remarked: 'It is easy for a workman to start on his own account as a "little master".'

The tremendous expansion of industry, both large and small, led in turn to a galloping increase in population. In 1660 there had been about 6,000 people in Birmingham; 100 years later there were five times that number. But this was only a beginning. In the next 70 years there was an increase of more than 100,000 to a total of 144,000 in 1831, while between that year and 1871 (roughly the period between Joseph Lucas's birth and his establishment as a 'little master') there was an even more dramatic increase of 200,000 to 344,000, which meant that in 1871 there were nearly two and a half times as many people in Birmingham as there were 40 years earlier.

This population 'explosion', as it would be called in the jargon of 100 years later, created a continuous pressure on housing and a gradual extension of the built-up area of the town. In the 1830s Birmingham was encircled by a natural 'green belt' of small allotment gardens (for example, to the east of Constitution Hill and on each side of Great Hampton Street up to and beyond New John Street, after which there was open country to Aston, where the Hall, church and tavern comprised an isolated community). Hockley Brook was still a country stream. These pleasant and productive gardens were gradually overrun by the construction of a network of streets lined with red-brick terrace houses, many of them back-to-back, with more houses in courts behind.

It was between 1838 and 1855 that the rapid development of the district occurred. The length of Great King Street between Great Hampton Street and New John Street was built up on both sides, whereas from New John Street to Bridge Street there were houses all the way on the right-hand side but none on the left. This meant that Number 209, to which Joseph was to move from Carver Street in 1871, was not built until after 1855. Half-way down there was a side turning marked on the map Accommodation Street. This later became Little King Street. There were a few houses on the left in Great King Street beyond Bridge Street, where the main entrance now stands.

At first the houses in these new streets had a 'clean, neat and cheerful appearance', according to Sir R. Rawlinson's report on public health in Birmingham in 1849, but they were slightly built (the supporting walls were only 4½ in thick) and cracks and leakages and inadequate drainage 'soon dirtied and put them out of condition'. Consequently the streets quickly became slums and 'district after district is vitiated as described'. Living conditions everywhere were such that many people sought solace in drink, and drunkenness was considered 'an infinitely more frequent cause of disease and death amongst the artisans than all the various employments of all the manufactories combined'. (It was a common saying that every third man in the Bull Ring on Saturday night was drunk.)

This was the scene that confronted George Dawson and other ministers when they regarded the lives of their flocks in the 1850s. Dawson was at the head of the sustained campaign to improve their lot, preaching and lecturing in favour of public service as a religious duty. What he urged especially was for more governmental and municipal activity, not merely to administer the town and supply such mundane things as gas and water but to 'shape all the highest, loftiest and truest ends of man's intellectual and moral nature' through the provision of libraries and art galleries, parks and schools. His contemporary, R. W. Dale, summed it up when he said that Dawson was the prophet and Joseph Chamberlain the triumphant leader of the great movement that resulted in Birmingham becoming a model of civic enterprise.

The highlight of Dawson's career came when he was called upon to open the splendid Central Reference Library in 1866. A bust of his handsome figure 'presented by members of his congregation' was placed in the entrance hall to commemorate the event. The library has recently been demolished and rebuilt in a magnificent modern style on a neighbouring site. George Dawson has not been forgotten in the move, and his statue benignly surveys the Social Studies Section.

Joseph Lucas was an ardent member of the congregation that paid for the statue. He was not only a ready listener but also, in his own way, a disciple, as we shall see in due course.

CHAPTER FOUR

THE 'LITTLE MASTER'

In the 1850s and 1860s Carver Street, Birmingham, consisted entirely of red-brick terrace houses, still more or less 'clean, neat and cheerful' when Joseph Lucas was living there with his wife Emily and their little family. Joseph would not recognise it today. Its appearance and character have completely changed; it is no longer a street for living in. Instead, it is typical of those Birmingham streets in what used to be the fringe of the old town, and is flanked by small modern factories engaged in various kinds of light industry.

But one can imagine what it was like in Joseph Lucas's time because one of the old dwelling houses (No 71) still stands in its original form, though disused and sadly derelict. A terrace house of dark red brick, three storeys high, it has a plaque on the front indicating that it was one of a row called Peel Place. (Sir Robert was Prime Minister when it was built.) Alongside is the entrance to No 17 Court, one of 2,000 such places behind the red-brick façades of the residential-cum-working streets of Birmingham in the mid-nineteenth century. These courts – open spaces enclosed by walls and more houses – were smelly and squalid because they were mostly undrained and were beyond the Street Commissioners' jurisdiction, so the municipal scavengers did not clear their rubbish and passed them by.

Where Joseph earned his living at the time of his marriage is not known. One story goes that he worked for a firm of carriage-lamp makers on The Parade called Wisdens, but I have been unable to trace any such firm. The source of this story was an old lady named Emily Prickett who died in 1963, a few months before her hundredth birthday. She used to claim that she worked 'at Wisdens' with Joseph Lucas, and joined him later when he was working on his own account at Great King Street, becoming, as she proudly asserted, 'Little Emmy, his first employee'. She said he taught her to japan lamps.

We can, however, pick up the story of Joseph and his wife Emily a few years after they were married through the words of a friend and neighbour, George Thomas, who later married their eldest daughter, who was also called Emily. Indeed, George Thomas's recollections of Joseph Lucas at this period are the earliest I have been able to trace within the family. George Thomas used to tell his son George and his daughter-in-law how Joseph was out of work for a time and got into

very low water indeed. Like so many of their mid-Victorian con-
temporaries in big towns and cities, he and his wife understandably
sought refuge from their troubles in drink, which was cheap, and for
which they had a liking anyway. But of course it only made things
worse.

So one day he said to himself: 'Joseph, you've got a wife and little
children to feed. You've got to do something about it. You'd better
give up the drink.' Then and there he made a vow never to drink
again (unhappily he could not persuade his wife to follow his
example). He did not make any show of it by joining the temperance
movement or signing the pledge – that would come later – instead he
did something rather more practical. With the little money he had
left he bought a basket skip on wheels and a cask of paraffin (which had
just been invented) and he trundled this round the streets of Hockley.
If no one would offer him a job, he would make one for himself –
Joseph Lucas was cast in the true Birmingham mould of independence.

Where did he get the paraffin? No record survives, but I have an
idea he bought it from a shop on the corner of Great Hampton Street
and Kenyon Street – only a short distance from his home in Carver
Street – that had been started as a drysalter's, druggist and grocer's in
1785. Now, in the mid-1800s, it was owned by a Mr William Canning, who, in addition to being a druggist, imported oil and paraffin
and supplied the early electro-platers in the district with their materials. If this theory is right, there began at that moment an association which was to continue to the present time as the companies
these two pioneers formed grew and developed into the great
enterprises they are today.

One day Joseph Lucas was attacked by hooligans who overturned
his basket, spilling the container into the gutter. While he stood there
dejectedly, a friend (since identified as David Pitcairn Wright) came
up and gave him enough money to replenish his stock. It was Wright's
little joke in later years that he financed the beginning of Joseph Lucas,
Limited.

Shortly afterwards – in 1860 to be exact – Joseph Lucas started
selling various items of holloware, such as buckets, shovels, scoops
and galvanised chamber pots, as well as paraffin. The proof of this is
in front of me as I write in the form of a tattered and disintegrating
notebook in which he began to record his sales in February that year.
Written for the most part in his own handwriting, the book extends
over a period of 12 years, indicating the modest scale of his operations,
but the entries are absorbingly fascinating nevertheless.

In the first month his sales of holloware amounted to £7 15s 9d for 21 dozen buckets and one 'pann' delivered to Messrs Philips & Hill. By May he had achieved a turnover of £22 11s 3d, largely made up of chambers, plus some 'Waterloo' scoops. Other lines he sold were boiler fillers, small cylinders, coal scoops, bowls, cans, cisterns and mysterious objects called 'Dukes'. An early entry, 'Oil on hand £40', shows that he had already built up a small but steady business from his original enterprise. After a while come two pages giving 'A list of customers and persons to be called on'. There are sixty names, and the occupations include 'hotell', 'drugest' and 'gass fitter'. Never mind the spelling; Joseph Lucas was going flat out for business.

He soon became a character in the neighbourhood, and some of the entries provide a partial explanation. Not only did he give credit to his customers but in some cases he helped them with small cash loans, for which he did not apparently charge any interest. Thus a certain Mr Dryhurst's account reads:

Jan 21 Due		£2.	1s. 9d.
28 Paid	1s. 0d.		
Feb 4 ,,	1s. 0d.		
18 ,,	12s. 0d.	14s. 0d.	
		1.	7s. 9d.
20 Lent		8s. 0d.	
Balance		1.	15s. 9d.
25 Paid	2s. 0d.		
Mar 1 ,,	1s. 0d.	3s. 0d.	
Balance		1.	12s. 9d.
18 Lent		8s. 6d.	
Balance		2.	1s. 3d.

Etc, etc, etc.

I am glad to report that this indulgent treatment of customers in difficulties was not abused; only on one page is the list of transactions ended abruptly with the words 'Gone to America' – with £5 6s 9d still owing for paraffin and cans.

He was very methodical – at least in fits and starts – pasting in the book the receipts for parcels sent by the London & North Western and the Midland Railways. Next to them is his own ready-reckoner of weights for quantities of his most popular lines: for example, 'Newcastle shovels, 18 gauge with 14 gauge pockets, 1 dozen 12-inch weight 38 lbs.'

In 1869 Joseph Lucas achieved official recognition as a trader when his name appeared in White's *Birmingham Directory* as a Lamp and Oil Dealer. By then he had moved his family to another house in Carver Street, Number 67, previously occupied by an engraver and almost next door to the derelict house that survives to this day. Lamps were first mentioned in the notebook during this year, bought from the makers and sold wholesale in his capacity as factor.

By now the 'little master' had become firmly established both as a holloware wholesaler and as an oil dealer – one firm alone buying nearly £500 worth of oil from him in 12 months during 1869–70. This growth of business forced him to engage some help, and in 1870 some of the entries in the notebook are written in a beautiful copperplate hand, in contrast to Joseph's own scratchy scrawl. It was in his own hand that he made the most significant entries in the whole book during 1870 and 1871. The first, in pencil, is headed 'The cost of 1 dozen quart oil cans' and goes like this:

Tin	1s. 6d.
Tops	7d.
Making	8d.
Solder	3d.
	3s. 0d.

Sell at 4s. 0d.

Another was for the costing of shovels, 6in 20 gauge with 'holow harlf round handles' at 1s 10½d each, to sell at 2s 4d, and there were many more. Joseph Lucas was taking the momentous road to becoming a manufacturer.

He began to look round for another house where he could carry on his growing business – and expand it. He eventually settled on Number 209, Great King Street, a three-storey terrace house with some buildings behind previously occupied by Thomas Youster, corn chandler. According to the Rate Book, Number 209 consisted of a retail shop, house, wash-house and 'premises'. The estimated rental value was £24 and the rateable value £20, so, with rates at 2s in the pound, Joseph Lucas's rates were £2 a year. The house was near the corner of Great King Street and New John Street, and disappeared in the 1960s when the area was turned into an open space.

The trades carried on by the people in Great King Street in the 1870s were typical of the Hockley district at that time and included gem-setter, pearl-button maker, cooper, cow-keeper, lapidary, black ornament maker, pawnbroker and aquavit maker. In 1872 they were joined by Joseph Lucas, described in the *Post Office Directory* that year as an 'Oil and Colorman.'

CHAPTER FIVE

ENTER TOM BOWLING

Joseph Lucas lost no time in putting his plans for becoming a manufacturer into practice. At first he confined himself to straightforward utility articles like ash-pans, shovels and oil cans, mostly consisting of parts that he assembled himself, but he had some original ideas as well and registered a design (No 5386) for a vegetable boiler and press on 1 July 1872, soon after he had settled into his new premises. This was a sensible kitchen utensil designed to do away with that traditional fault of English cooking, watery vegetables. The vegetable boiler and press has taken its modest place in Lucas history because it marked the first appearance of Harry, Joseph's eldest son, in his father's business. I have a copy of the registration form in front of me and it is made out in his unmistakable handwriting. Harry was then 17, having been a pupil-teacher for a short time after leaving school the previous year. Much better educated than his father, serious-minded and punctilious in matters of detail, he quickly proved a tremendous asset.

In 1873 Joseph Lucas was listed in White's *Directory* as a 'tin-plate worker, ash-pan etc., manufacturer, and lamp and oil dealer.' Selling paraffin was still a useful sideline, and in March that year his notebook listed thirty-eight customers, to whom he had contracted to supply 532 casks or barrels of petroleum. But it was a highly seasonal trade and in August he placed only one contract for four casks.

He was now 39 years of age with a family of six – Harry, born in 1855, followed by Christopher (1857), Emily (1859), Louisa (1861), Ada (1863) and finally Bernard (1865) – and he was gradually maturing into the gruff and kindly figure that many people were to recall when they recounted their memories of him in later years. One Sunday, for example, he came to the rescue of the congregation at the Gospel Hall in New John Street when he found they had no gas lighting for their evening service, which he regularly attended. With the help of some volunteers he fetched lamps and oil from his place at 209 Great King Street, just round the corner, and filled the little chapel with light and warmth. The gas had been cut off, so next day he paid the bill.

In looking around to find more interesting – and profitable – things to make, Joseph Lucas had the vast range of Birmingham products to choose from. Why did he settle primarily on lamps? It was partly due to their being a natural corollary to the lamp oil he was already selling, and partly perhaps because of the experience he had gained in helping to make carriage lamps at Wisdens, if one gives Mrs Prickett's story the benefit of the doubt. He had also been selling lamps as a dealer for the last three years. Lamp-making had of course been a flourishing trade in Birmingham long before the discovery of distilled coal oil in 1850–51 and petroleum and paraffin in 1859 made the old lamps burning fish oil out of date. So great was the demand for new lamps to burn the new fuel that in 1860 one Birmingham firm alone made 375,000 lamps, mostly for domestic use.

Harry was given the job of costing new products that had been started by Joseph in his original notebook, which even then must have been pretty tattered (today it is virtually in pieces). The twopenny memorandum book in which Harry made his calculations has been rebound and preserved. Item No 1 dated 28 June reads:

Candle Hand Lantern
(1 glass, tin fold handles)

	s.	d.
4½ shts tin @ 4½d.	1	8
Japan 1s. glass 4d. Hndles 4d.	1	8
Solder 2d. Clean 1s.	1	2
Making	4	6
Cost per dozen	9s	0d

Altogether some eighty items are costed, most of them lamps of many kinds and for many purposes. Usually they are recosted in foot-notes, apparently written some years later and probably at a time when they were actually put into production, but dates are few and far between. The book was probably in use for about 10 years and includes some attractive little working sketches of lamps to illustrate details of their construction. The costing book was also used for recording notes about materials. An entry dated 4 July 1873, for a stamped flat pocket lantern states: '1 sheet 20 in. by 14 in. cuts 9 bodies, 50 bridges, 52 bottoms, 19 single doors, 60 breakers, 92 cross bars.'

Entry No 79, written by Harry in pencil and headed 'Tom Bowling', was to mark a turning point in Joseph Lucas's progress. This was the name given to a lamp that was being made in small numbers by a man called Isaac Sherwood, lamp and chandelier

May 9/88 T.B. Globe Lp. Brass 8 in

3 lbs Brass. 7½	1	10½
Globe		9
Burner Screw		1½
Union —		1½
Eyelets		1
Polish		3
Stamps . etc.		2
Solder etc.		1
Ears		1½
Hammering Brass		4
Makes 8. & 10% on		9
Guards & fitting up		3
Wrapping up		1
Cost. 4/8 each.		4 8

The twopenny memorandum book, in which Harry Lucas carried on the costing of articles that had been started by his father, contained eighty items – mostly lamps including this entry for the Tom Bowling ship's lamp

The beginning, May 1860. The first page of the notebook in which for twelve years Joseph Lucas recorded his transactions in lamp oil and holloware – buckets, scoops and galvanised chamber pots. To start with he sold the oil from door to door, pushing a basket skip along the street manufacturer, living at 88 Granville Street, Birmingham. It was a ship's lamp, and whether it was already known as the Tom Bowling before Joseph Lucas took it over from Sherwood, or whether he thought of the name himself, is not clear. *Tom Bowling* was the title of a sea-shanty written by Charles Dibdin about 1789 to commemorate the death of his eldest brother, Captain Thomas Dibdin, and was one of several composed by him and sung in *The Oddities* at the Lyceum Theatre, London, in that year. It was still a popular song in the homes and pubs of the 1870s, and survives to this day as a melody in Sir Henry Wood's *Fantasia on British Sea Songs for Orchestra*, which is a traditional favourite at the last night of the Promenade Concerts at the Royal Albert Hall. Dibden composed and wrote over 200 dramatic songs in his lifetime. He was born in Southampton in 1745 and died in London 69 years later. The first verse of *Tom Bowling* was:

> Here, a sheer hulk, lies poor Tom Bowling,
> The darling of our crew.
> No more he'll hear the tempest howling
> For death has broached him to.
> His form was of the manliest beauty,
> His heart was kind and soft,
> Faithful below he did his duty,
> But now he's gone aloft.

At first Joseph Lucas sold the Tom Bowling lamp as a factor; then he found it was so admired by shipowners and chandlers that he was encouraged to try and make it himself. Sherwood was agreeable to parting with it, but Joseph lacked the skill, the labour and the premises to tackle the job. So he decided to consult his friend George Thomas, who had been partly instrumental in setting him on the path of independence (and temperance) in his Carver Street days. George Thomas was a qualified sheet-metal worker and knew something about manufacture. In later years he was fond of telling his son George (Joseph's eldest grandson) and his daughter-in-law, to whom I am indebted for this anecdote, what happened next:

> One day Joseph sent me a message: 'Come down and see me this evening, George, I've got something I think will interest you'. I went to 209 Great King Street and there he showed me a ship's lamp. 'I want to make it', he said, 'but how am I going to get the men to do it?' 'Leave it to me', I replied, and the next Friday I went down to Elkingtons as the staff were leaving and I picked five of their best men. They all agreed to join Joseph Lucas if he could find a workshop. He did, a place round the corner in Little King Street, which he called the Tom Bowling Lamp

Works, after the name of the lamp, and these five men were the first people to work there. I joined him as works foreman.

The year was 1875. From that moment all Joseph Lucas's products, including the shovels and other utensils he was still making, were stamped with the initials 'TBLW'. Before the year was out he put the Tom Bowling lamp on a commercial basis by applying for and being granted his first patent – for 'certain improvements in the manufacture of lamps' relating to 'the mode of constructing them in a portable manner, so that in a case of a breakage of one part that part may be disengaged for repair; hitherto they have been constructed permanently by riveting and soldering.' The part of a ship's lamp most likely to break was the globe, and the patent gave the great advantage that this could now be changed at sea without the delay of waiting to return to port to get the lamp repaired.

The handsome document of the letters patent, with its majestic wording, gave Joseph Lucas enormous satisfaction: *Whereas Her Most Excellent Majesty Queen Victoria, in her Letters Patent, bearing date the Twenty-Eighth day of August, in the year of Our Lord One thousand eight hundred and seventy five, in the thirty-eighth year of Her reign, did, for Herself, Her heirs and successors, give and grant unto me, the said Joseph Lucas . . .* He immediately showed it to his workpeople and added: 'I went home last night and kissed the Missus.'

It might seem odd that a Birmingham manufacturer should try to enter a trade that was more appropriate to a seaport than a Midlands town, but in making ships' lamps Joseph Lucas was carrying on a connection between Birmingham and shipbuilding that had started at the beginning of the century when 'Muntz metal' (developed from an alloy discovered in Birmingham by James Keir and William Collins) was widely adopted for sheathing wooden ships. Birmingham went on to make tubes and marine engine parts for the shipbuilding towns. The extension of rail communications in the 1840s brought manufacturer and customer closer together, and lamps were one of many items that Birmingham could supply readily, along with compasses, quadrants, pumps and bells, to the shipbuilders on the coast.

The Tom Bowling Lamp Works was a small two-storey workshop flanked by shops occupied by James Potts, a coal dealer, on one side and John McKenna, a grocer, on the other. It incorporated an archway on the left-hand side leading into a court which was occasionally flooded when the neighbouring Hockley Brook overflowed. The front door was next to the archway and Joseph Lucas installed himself in an office alongside.

No records – apart from the costing notebook – have survived about the scale of Joseph Lucas's operations in the early years at Little King Street, but it is certain that he was by now employing some female labour (doubtless including 'Little Emmy') and had bought a stamping machine and other equipment and tools. The *Post Office Directory* of 1876–7 listed him as a manufacturer of all kinds of ship, stable, and hand lamps and lanterns, and an oil merchant, at Tom Bowling Lamp Works, while *Kelly's Directory* described him as a mineral oil and lamp dealer, lamp manufacturer and tinplate worker at 209 Great King Street.

All the time he was on the look-out for new products that were suitable for his manufacturing facilities, such as they were (principally the stamping of pieces from metal sheets, finishing them and assembling them with some bought-out parts into various articles). In 1877, for example, he paid an inventor £5 for the registered design of a cash box which Harry proceeded to cost in his notebook in various sizes and models – 'common' and 'best'. A 'common' one cost £1 os od to make and sold for £1 15s od.

Another article mentioned in the notebook at this time was an oval poacher for two eggs, which cost 10s 1d. Harry's costings generally seem to have been precisely calculated, because he goes out of his way to mention that the 9d he put down for making the frames of the poacher was 'guessed at.'

Once again the conjunction of time and place enters the story, for something was happening in the world outside that was to provide the opportunity for the real expansion Joseph was looking for. The bicycle was evolving from an experimental idea into a practical means of transport. So far-reaching were the effects of the bicycle's development on the future course of the little business run by Joseph Lucas and his son in the 1870s that it is worth setting the scene in a separate chapter.

CHAPTER SIX

THE GREAT OPPORTUNITY

Joseph Lucas and the bicycle grew up together. He was a child of 5 when the first experimental pedal-drive bicycle was made in 1839; during his lifetime he witnessed its evolution through the stages of the Vélocipede and the Ordinary to the Safety; and when he died in 1902, cycling was nearing its peak as a national pastime. By then the business of Joseph Lucas, Limited, was wholly devoted to making 'lamps, bells, valves, inflators and other accessories' for the booming cycle trade.

Although the bicycle – unlike the railway locomotive, the motor-car and the aeroplane – did not have to wait upon the development of an appropriate engine for its development, it nevertheless took a long time to become a practical means of transport. It was not until 1790 that the Frenchman de Sivrac made a device, the Célérife or Véloci-fère, consisting of a length of wood with a padded saddle in the middle mounted on two wooden wheels, and proceeded to astonish his neighbours by propelling himself faster than they could walk by thrusting the ground from under his feet. The snag was that he could only do this in a straight line because the front wheel was fixed and he could not steer. And the fixed front wheel made it extremely difficult to balance.

Twenty-eight years were to pass before Charles, Baron von Drais de Sauerbon, a German living in France, produced a steerable 'hobby-horse', which he called the Draisienne. This caught the fancy of the young men of the day on the Continent, in England and the United States. The hobby-horse was promptly dubbed the dandy-horse and was introduced in England by Denis Johnson, who took out a British patent. Johnson was a coachmaker and ran several riding schools in London, which he used for teaching people to ride the hobby-horse.

Another 21 years went by without any advance being made in the design of the hobby-horse until in 1839 a Scottish blacksmith, Kirkpatrick MacMillan of Courthill, Kier, Dumfriesshire, invented the fundamental improvement of enabling the rider to drive the back wheel by the fore-and-aft movement of his legs through a system of cranks and swinging levers. The hobby-horse had become a bicycle.

Joseph Lucas was nearly 30 by the time the next step forward was taken. In 1861 a Frenchman named Pierre Michaux, who made perambulators at 29 Avenue Montaigne, Champs Elysées, Paris, suggested to his son Ernest that he should fit pedals to the front wheel of an old Draisienne hobby-horse he had acquired. Ernest made such a good job of it that in the following year his father started to make similar Vélocipedes and sold 142 of them at about £8 each.

Michaux showed several of his Vélocipedes at the Paris Exhibition of 1867, where they were seen by a young Englishman, Rowley Turner, who was living in Paris as a student. In the following year Turner put up the capital to form a company with Michaux *père et fils* for developing the Vélocipede, building a riding school, stores and a workshop in the rue Bonaparte. They soon had so many orders from all over Europe that they could not hope to supply them, so Rowley Turner took a 36in machine to Coventry and asked his uncle, Josiah Turner, the managing director of the Coventry Sewing Machine Co, whether his company would make 300 Vèlocipedes as sub-contractors. The board agreed and started production in a building at Cheylesmore that was used by the company's direct descendants, Swift of Coventry, Limited, for making bicycles until 1930.

Within the space of less than 10 years, therefore, the bicycle suddenly developed from the individual experimental machine into the Vèlocipede or bone-shaker (as it was called in England), made in small but nevertheless regular numbers both here and abroad. This was exactly the period when Joseph Lucas was beginning to think about manufacturing some products – including lamps – in addition to trading in them. Though he did not realise it, his great opportunity was taking shape, but another 10 years were to pass before the cycle trade grew big enough to provide a worthwhile market.

In the early 1870s, while Joseph Lucas was establishing himself at Great King Street with the Tom Bowling ship's lamp and other articles, the bicycle developed more rapidly in design than it did in numbers. What happened was that inventors in England, France and the United States so changed and refined it that the primitive bone-shaker was superseded by the 'high' bicycle, or what was later called the Ordinary and colloquially the Penny-farthing. The English share of this process was largely due to James Starley, who earned for himself the title of 'the father of the cycle industry.' He made the back wheel smaller and the front wheel much bigger, which made it possible to go faster for the same pedalling speed, and he overcame the effort of hill-climbing with the big front wheel by designing a crank that could be adjusted to various throws. He put all these ideas into a bicycle of his own called the Ariel, which he patented with William Hillman in 1870.

The Ordinary was difficult to mount and ride – you had to be tall and athletic to handle it properly. The roads were appalling by modern standards, especially for Ordinaries, with their tendency to buck their riders off if the front wheel struck a large stone or obstruction. 'The road between Birmingham and Wolverhampton', wrote the author of 'A Text Book for Riders' published in 1874, 'is very bad and wearying; in fact it is full of holes and tramway ruts. The bicyclist had better train this bit.'

About the same time H. J. Lawson made a quite different approach to the problem with an experimental machine built on bone-shaker lines with both wheels only 23in in diameter and chain-drive from the pedals to the back wheel, instead of the pedals driving straight on to the front wheel, as with the Ordinary. Two years later he reverted to lever-drive (similar to MacMillan's) for the big back wheel of another experimental machine, for which he registered the word 'safety' in the patent at the suggestion of his father, who was a clergyman. Lawson finally returned to chain-drive in 1879 for the Bicyclette, which he had made by the Rudge Company, for whom he was then working as manager. The front wheel was bigger than the back, but with its low saddle and pedals the rider could put his feet on the ground at rest and the machine provided a real alternative to the Ordinary. Lawson's Bicyclette was the first rear chain-drive bicycle to go into production.

Another answer to the safety problem was found in the tricycle, which had the great merit of being able to stand up when it was at rest, as well as being much easier to ride than the Ordinary. The tricycle appealed particularly to timid people (including ladies) who disliked the idea of having to balance a two-wheeler.

This was the state of the cycle game when Joseph Lucas decided to make his first cycle lamp in 1878. What finally influenced him was probably the Stanley Bicycle Show – the first of its kind held in Great Britain – at Camden Town, London. Another factor was that byelaws were being passed in many parts of the country requiring lamps to be lit on bicycles at sunset (sometimes earlier, sometimes later). The lamp became an essential accessory because 'cyclers' could not always depend upon getting home before it was dark.

Every year saw more and more of them taking to the roads. By the end of the 1870s there were more than 20,000 members of the Cyclists Touring Club and 230 cycling clubs in Britain. The vast majority of bicycles in use were Ordinaries made by some twenty manufacturers and selling at anything between £6 and £20. The increasing scale of manufacture could be seen in the large new bicycle factory constructed at Beeston, outside Nottingham, by Thomas Humber and his partners. The tricycle was also at the beginning of its boom, which was to last for at least a decade, but as yet only the earliest moves had been made towards the Safety bicycle, which was to replace both the tricycle and the Ordinary and which, together with the arrival of the pneumatic tyre, was to make bicycling the hobby of the masses.

But we are running too far ahead. Let us return to Little King Street and see how Joseph Lucas and his son Harry tackled this new market, the ultimate significance of which they could not be expected to foresee.

CHAPTER SEVEN

GROWING PAINS

So far in this story there has been very little first-hand evidence of what Joseph Lucas and his son Harry thought about running their business. But from 1880 onwards, at any rate for a period of about five years, the curtain is lifted to a large extent by a book containing press copies of Harry's letters, which has been mercifully preserved. Why he came to keep it is worth examining, for it shows how some good can come out of misfortune.

By that time the married life of Joseph Lucas had taken a peculiarly ironic turn: the convert to rigid temperance was having to witness in his own home the effects of the human frailty that he himself had forsworn. The only refuge he could find from the situation in the house at Clifton Road, Moseley, where he was now living with his wife, was to spend a large part of his time travelling the length and breadth of the British Isles seeking orders for the products of his little factory. This meant a constant, almost daily, flow of letters between the father, a middle-aged man of 46, and his 25-year-old eldest son, who had just moved with his younger brothers and sisters to a separate larger house in Stoney Lane, with a garden, a field and a stable. Here they kept two horses, which took turn and turn about in the shafts of the family wagonette in which Harry, Emily and Louisa drove every day to the factory. One side of this correspondence, duplicated in the letter book kept by Harry, provides a vivid record of their fortunes and relationship that would not otherwise be available. The rest of Harry's business correspondence was likewise press–copied, and makes the book doubly valuable.

That was one advantage derived from a sad period in Joseph Lucas's life. Another result was that it threw a heavy responsibility on the shoulders of young Harry, who found himself having to cope with much of the financial and management burden of running the business. Joseph's enforced absences certainly presented Harry with a great challenge and an opportunity to develop his powers of financial and business management, which was all to the good. That he came through it so well was to be a great asset for the future growth of the company.

Joseph Lucas made his first cycle lamp in 1878, about two years before the correspondence starts. The name given to it, the King of the Road, was a brilliant stroke, quickly becoming synonymous with the name of its maker. It was designed to be slung below the hub inside the spokes of the big front wheel of the Ordinary bicycle. In that respect it was not original, because the hub was the most convenient place to carry a lamp on the Penny-farthing and other people were already making similar lamps. The distinction of 'inventing' the hub lamp was actually claimed by the Salsbury Lamp Works, London, one of Joseph's fiercest competitors, who had been in business since the reign of George III, but whether their claim was valid is not clear. In any case the Lucas King of the Road was different from the Salsbury and all others in its construction. And of course it was much better.

The trouble with hub lamps was that their bulk made them difficult to insert between the spokes of the wheel and clamp on the hub. Salsbury patented the idea of swinging the face of the lamp downwards to reduce its size while mounting it, but Joseph Lucas went one better. He split the King of the Road into two parts, front and back, each hinged at the top of the barrel which carried the lamp on the hub. When the lamp was opened lengthwise, it was only half its full width and could be inserted through the spokes quite easily. The two halves were then fastened together by a clip.

Another big advantage of 'the King' over earlier hub lamps was that the oil reservoir could be made much bigger, which meant a longer ride between stops for refilling – 4–5 hours, according to conditions. Perhaps the most serious fault with previous hub lamps had been the soldering of their seams and joints, which softened and broke up under the heat they had to endure. Joseph Lucas overcame this by using copper rivets for all the seams. As Harry pointed out in a letter to the Editor of *The Engineer*: 'Many serious accidents have occurred through lamps coming to pieces, dropping into the wheel and immediately stopping the machine. The King of the Road is perfectly safe; it throws a magnificent light far ahead of the machine and this enables the rider to run with safety over dark roads, while the small lamps now in use are of no real service to the rider and only act as signals to the public.' He added (not for publication) that 'Messrs. Singer & Company, the great Bicycle people, have just given me good orders for it. Mr. Singer has tried the lamp himself and has expressed his approval of it.'

Joseph Lucas was granted a patent for his lamp in 1880, adding to the complete specification as an afterthought a simple means of changing the leather bearings of the barrel – an afterthought that was to cause him some trouble later on. The King of the Road was made in three sizes at first, with front lenses of 3in, 3½in and 4in diameter respectively, but later the smallest size was dropped. The prices varied from time to time, the No 1 being quoted at 12s 6d in 1881 (17s 6d nickel-plated). The German silver reflector at the back had a small hole in the centre which was fitted with a piece of red glass to act as a rear danger light.

To rectify the faults that developed in the King of the Road lamp as it came into service, Harry Lucas asked Mr Hepplethwaite, a leading cyclist of the day, to test one on the long journeys he made on his Ordinary. (Joseph himself is alleged to have ridden an Ordinary repeatedly into a brick wall to see how his hub lamp stood up to it, but there is a touch of unreality about this story.) Mr Hepplethwaite evidently gave some good advice, for Harry sent him a present of a special King of the Road finished in German silver, which he described in an accompanying letter as 'a splendid article, almost a work of art, but of course I am its maker so my opinion is not worth much.'

A month later, in April 1880, he was writing to his father that 'the long chapter of troubles on "his majesty" seems still running, although we flattered ourselves that we had got to the end of it.' This time it was a weakness in the hinge of the barrel, in spite of using thicker wire of better quality, and Harry offered to replace the hasp of any faulty lamps that the readers of the *Cyclist* may have bought. In his letter to the Editor he wrote: 'The lamp has been given a Royal Christening and I am determined it shall not have a pauper's funeral.' By October he was telling Joseph: 'There is a splendid future for "his majesty". In *The Cyclist* this week the Editor says: "Last Saturday evening was exceptionally dark in the Midlands, but we found ourselves travelling from Aston Grounds to Coventry in perfect security and comfort by the light of our King of the Road" . . . Isn't that better', Harry adds, 'than any paid advert?'

In July Harry wrote to a patent agent named Kendrick (who later turned out to be a rascal) saying: 'My father writes from London that he wants the name King of the Road registered with the initials TBLW' (which he intended to use for other products as well). A few months later he wrote to a competitor, Messrs Tongue and Bladon: 'Gentlemen, It has come to my knowledge that you are calling and invoicing lamps under the name "King of the Road". You are aware that my lamp is patented, and I feel that I have only to say that the name is Registered for you to cease using it.' Two days later he was able to report to Joseph: 'Tongue and B. say they would be sorry to give us offence by adopting our name King of the Road and that they will call theirs the Monarch.' Harry rubbed salt into the wound by making them put quarter-page advertisements to that effect in *Bicycling Times* and *Bicycling News*. Not content with that, he suggested to Dearlove, the London factor, that he 'might get an editorial calling attention to the advert.'

From this exchange it can be seen that Harry Lucas was finding his feet as a businessman, and he was now able to take his share of such management decisions as fixing the right prices for their lamps. In September he wrote to Joseph: 'I quite agree with you that we ought to get as much as Salsbury for our patent 90, but although we are getting a name we must not forget we haven't got Salsbury's reputation yet, so don't let us be too hasty in pushing prices up.'

That year (1880) they had a running fight with Salsburys, first over a lamp called the Comet that Lucas made for Dearlove, and then over their own new lamp, the Captain, a variant of the King of the Road. Both had a 'mousetrap' spring for the door which Salsburys claimed was their idea, so they wrote to their dealers and asked them to stop selling Lucas lamps. Harry told Dearlove: 'Directly my father hears of this he will soon settle what must be done;' and to Joseph he wrote: 'Suppose he can claim the spring, we can make our King to fasten with a cotter-pin and the lamp will sell just as well. His lamp is dead and he is evidently finding it out – and don't relish the discovery.'

The Lucases were advised that Salsburys had a poor case, so they went ahead with the Captain regardless. As Harry put it in a letter to Dearlove: '. . . if he makes any noise we can quieten him thus-wise: Look here, S., your patent, as I told you before, is no good and as it happens my registration is as bad. If we keep our mouths shut you can make your lamp and I can make mine and the public will be none the wiser.'

Meanwhile there were the first signs of an export trade developing. A representative of Cunningham & Company, of Boston, USA, turned up at Little King Street to discuss becoming the agent for the King of the Road in America, where the cycling craze was spreading rapidly (it reached its peak at the end of the 1880s, when some 300 factories were making more than a million cycles a year). Joseph liked the idea and wanted to take out an American patent for the lamp, but Harry was against it on the grounds that they would not be able to exploit the patent if they got it. Nevertheless Joseph had his way and by the end of the year Harry was writing to Cunningham: 'I have patented the King of the Road in America' (unhappily this proved to be false, owing to the aforesaid Kendrick's having pocketed the fee and doing nothing about the patent) 'and am therefore determined the sale of it shall be pushed.' The first trial consignment of lamps was sent to the States in the spring of 1881.

They had 'capital' testimonials for the King of the Road from Brussels, which they reprinted, and they had visitors from France (Viennet of Lyons) and Switzerland (Bruel and Delaprez) all wanting lamps with wind-up burners. The Swiss asked for a police lamp that darkened by pressing a 'thumb-bit' at the back. 'It is one of Hopkins,' Harry told Joseph, 'and I saw it illustrated in *The Ironmonger*. I am to get him one for submission to the Geneva police.'

Joseph and Harry Lucas were fiercely proud of their King of the Road lamp and were correspondingly elated or indignant when its merits were either acknowledged or ignored. In May 1881, for example, Harry wrote to Dearlove: 'The "Big King" is ordered from the North to the seat of Royalty . . . It is very pleasant to know that we still reign supreme and that the formidable rivals Guiding Star and Light of the Road are evaporating.'

What a different tone was heard in his letter to Joseph in the following year:

> Don't trust yourself too near the Prince if he should take it into his head to come to the Show. I'm afraid it wouldn't be safe – for the Prince I mean. I suppose you know that he or somebody else for him has ordered his tricycle lamp of Platts, and a notice of it appears in the *Post* today describing it as a very creditable piece of working. I never expected the 'King' would receive the honour because ornament and not utility is required. What would such a useless article and doubtful ornament as a Prince want with anything of a useful nature.

This pride in their product was based on its quality, so they took steps to ensure this not only in their own workmanship but in that of their suppliers, as was shown when Harry warned a firm of nickel-platers: 'Before starting business with you I must impress on you the necessity of seeing that any work I get from you is perfect of its kind.' A few months later he was 'put in County Court' by another nickel-plater for refusing to pay for sub-standard work.

The King of the Road was continually improved. The quick method of changing the leather bearing provided for in the original patent of 1880 was all very well, but this was only necessary because the bearing wore out so quickly. So two years later Joseph filed two alternative specifications for improving the bearing, first by means of anti-friction rollers projecting through holes in the bush (an idea which never came to anything) and more effectually by fixing a tubular collar with a flange each side on to the hub and using the surface for a revolving metal tube on to which the barrel of the lamp was fastened. This killed several birds with one stone – it did not wear out and consequently did not need any attention; it did not rub away the nickel finish of the hub, as the leather bearing had done; and the flanges kept the lamp in a central position and eliminated the need for side check guards (leather spacers or antennae that brushed against the spokes), which were normally used to stop hub lamps shifting from side to side. In the first patent Joseph took the opportunity to include an opening in the side of the lamp, covered by a slide, through which the lamp could be lit without having to open the front. Harry did much of the experimental work on the new bearing himself, including a 40-mile road test at night on his Ordinary bicycle to check its performance. Then he had half-a-dozen lamps made up and sent them to crack riders to report on.

The improvements did not stop there. The later models included a knob protruding from the side for turning the wick up and down, again without opening the front; a brass plate with a rough surface for striking matches; and finally a Lighting Facilitator, Harry's name for a device into which a wax match could be inserted and ignited by pressing a thumb piece at the end.

But Harry realised they needed a wider spread of products to become soundly based and he reminded Joseph: 'We must keep our eyes open to cheap work. It pays best, and I want something for the lads . . . We do nothing with the Coventry (bicycle) manufacturers. I'm afraid some of them connect our name with expensive lamps only, and don't know or forget we do cheap ones too.' His answer was the $48\frac{1}{2}$ model, which hooked on to the hub, and sold at 2s 2d. But for twopence more you could buy the 50, the standard hub lamp with brass barrel axle fitting.

The battle with Salsburys over the Comet and Captain cycle lamps left an uneasy thought in Harry's mind about their own use of the word patent stamped on the Tom Bowling ship's lamp. He confided his feelings to Joseph in a note written in September 1880 beginning: '*Read and destroy this.* You know we have no right to use the label on "T.B." and if Salsbury or anyone else liked we could be made to pay for it. Perhaps the time has come to have a new label like the old one but omitting "Patent".' Since Joseph Lucas had patented the lamp in 1875, the explanation of this quandary would seem to be that he had failed to renew it after the statutory period of four years, which had now lapsed.

In fact Harry did not seem to have his heart in ship's lamps to the same extent that Joseph did (perhaps because his father enjoyed visiting the seaports on his travels) and in 1880 he was complaining: 'You know my opinion is that we have received so little encouragement in our efforts from the shippers that there seems no hope of the expense of advertising being repaid . . . I consider that we are rather deficient in our knowledge of what is required in the ship lamp trade and that there are other things besides side lamps that we can make with profit . . . Can you get to know the kind of anchor and globe lamps that are required? Also speaking trumpets.'

Three months later he had changed his tune and was writing: 'I thought I had finally set my back against all new patterns for this year at least, but the present time above all others is ripe for a smack at ships' lamps by making a *globe* lamp to meet the new regulations. I think I had better make a sample for you to carry to Liverpool, Ireland and Scotland.' But in less than a week he told Joseph: 'Since writing the other day, orders (for other lamps and products) have come in at such a rate that I can see that it will take all our powers inside the factory and all the assistance Bennett [an outside sub-contractor] can give to cope with the work. It's no use pushing the trade in less profitable directions when we can have all we want with plenty of cream on it.'

But Joseph apparently continued to go his own way and two months later he received a lambasting from his son in these forthright terms:

I feel deuced ill-tempered. This is the third letter I have started to you today. I have torn the others up, finding I had said more than I ought. I do feel annoyed that you should pester yourself and me by wasting time and energy in pushing for rivetted globe lamps . . . I don't want ship lamp orders but ship-lamp information . . . I am in constant fear of your running after orders that are no good, and my fears are confirmed by your bothering about globe lamps.

Nevertheless, in spite of Harry's opposition, ships' lamps continued to appear in TBLW catalogues right through the 1880s and into the early 1890s. What helped to sustain interest in them was the award of a bronze medal to the Tom Bowling globe lamp at the International Fisheries Exhibition in London in 1883, an achievement that was proudly mentioned in all advertising and catalogues as long as the lamp was made. It was in fact the only medal awarded to a lamp, and Harry suggested to Joseph that he should send a present to 'the woman at Walker's stand for her successful explanation to the Jury, for without her explanation the medal would not have been given.'

The earliest Lucas catalogue I have been able to discover is not overtly dated but mentions 'improvements for 1883' in the description of the King of the Road. Its ten pages cover everything they made, whereas later on cycle lamps and accessories were given a separate catalogue of their own.

The range of products in the 1883 catalogue sums up the efforts Joseph and Harry had made to diversify their production. It starts with a selection of hand lamps, the cheapest being a candle lantern selling for 10d (1s 2d for oil), a 5s model with wind-up burner being also suitable for carts, and other models for warehouses. A bull's-eye dash lamp sells for 7s 6d, and a registered police lamp for 3s 4d to 6s, according to size. There is also a 'perfectly dark police lamp'. Railway-men's needs are provided for by a ticket lamp and a signalling lamp, while for passengers there is the Edinburgh patent railway reading lamp, comprising a metal candle socket with a built-in rubber sucker for sticking it on the window or any convenient flat surface. This being a time when the horse was a means of transport as well as pleasure, an adjustable lamp is offered for attachment underneath the stirrup iron to horsemen riding after nightfall. A large wall lamp is specially designed to be collapsible, so that it could be packed flat for export (in 1883!), and sells at 15s.

Then come the cycle lamps, led by the King of the Road hub lamp for the Ordinary, though the beginnings of the tricycle and the Safety can be seen in a head-lamp version 'with arrangement at the side for lighting in a wind'. With patent metal bearing, the smallest King of the Road sells at 15s (japanned) or 22s (nickelled tin) and 29s (nickelled brass). The cheapest hub lamp is priced at 3s 6d, and the Captain sells at 8s 6d (japanned) or 14s (nickelled tin). Oil cans seem dirt cheap at 4s a dozen.

The next section of the catalogue illustrates a miscellaneous collection of articles: registered cash boxes, a letter box in japanned oak, a cash till, and two kinds of sugar box 'japanned in colours and ornamented'. Then there are japanned flower-pot covers 'closely resembling china' (2s 4d hand painted, 2s with transfer ornaments), a match box with striker and place for burnt matches, various syringes, and a combined egg whisk and spoon at 5s a dozen. There are also two sizes of 'refrigerator', a round tin which worked by filling the rim with water, thereby keeping the cloth cover wet and the contents cool by evaporation.

Ships' lamps, headed by the Tom Bowling, occupy the last two pages. The Tom Bowling is described as 'very strongly made and will outwear several ordinary lamps'. It comes in several sizes from 6in to 9in, and the price varies from 7s 6d to 16s 6d. Harry's desire for a wider range of ships' lamps has been met by the introduction of engine-room lamps, a hold lamp, a bunker lamp, and a gimbal lamp. The side lamps are still being made, costing no less than 128s for a copper port-and-starboard pair, the same price per lamp as the copper masthead lamp. The catalogue ends with illustrations of an anchor lamp, a flash lamp, and a fishing-boat tricolour lamp selling at 23s japanned.

Altogether, the catalogue is a wonderful testimony to the progress made by Joseph Lucas in the 10 years since he moved from Carver Street to 209 Great King Street, and tentatively started to manufacture simple utensils like shovels and scoops. The wide variety of his products at the end of the decade showed no shortage of ideas or of energy to carry them out.

But something else was lacking.

T. B. L. W.

PATENT "KING OF THE ROAD" HUB LAMPS,

WITH ADJUSTABLE BEARINGS AND ARRANGEMENT FOR LIGHTING IN A WIND.

 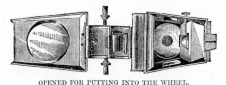 

OPENED FOR PUTTING INTO THE WHEEL.

Improved Pattern for 1883.—No. 112B.—For Bicycles.

	Japanned.	Nickeled Tin.	Nickeled Brass.
Size 0, with 3-inch Front Glass	15/-	22/-	29/-
„ 1, „ 3½ „ „ „	16/-	23/6	30/6
„ 2, „ 4 „ „ „	18/-	27/6	34/6

112T.—For Tricycle axles without Lubricators in the centre, and not requiring Lamps with divided or double barrels, 6d extra to above.

No. 116.

For Tricycle Axles with Lubricators.

			Japanned.	Nickeled Tin.	Nickeled Brass.
Size 0 ..	..	...	16/6	23/-	30/-
„ 1 ..	..	..	17/6	27/-	33/-

When ordering Tricycle Lamps give the name of the Tricycle they are to fit.

LAST YEAR'S PATTERNS, Nos. 54 AND 57, CAN BE HAD AT SAME PRICES AS BEFORE, OR JAPANNED, 6D. LESS, AND NICKELED, 1/- LESS THAN ABOVE PRICES.

As illustrated in the 1883 catalogue. Although the King of the Road hub-lamp was patented, it was widely copied. This involved Joseph Lucas in a successful action which was published in *The Times* Law Reports

CHAPTER EIGHT

'SHORT OF THE NEEDFUL'

In October 1880, five years after he started the Tom Bowling Lamp Works in Little King Street, Joseph Lucas had fifty-eight people on his payroll and the weekly wages amounted to exactly £59 2s 6d, an average of just over a pound a week. Many of the workers, of course, were women and girls, who were paid much less than the men. They were supervised by Polly Clayton, the first forewoman employed by Joseph Lucas.

In that year Harry (who was 25) wrote to Dearlove, the London factor: 'I can only let one or two people work at "his majesty" [the King of the Road bicycle lamp] till I have the various tools and arrangements made for straightforward work. You can hardly credit the amount of forethought and care required to turn out the best lamps. Although I firmly intend cultivating the best trade, I often doubt it being the most profitable.'

The payroll, which was steadily growing larger, nevertheless fluctuated with the state of business, and in the following year Harry was writing to his father: '. . . up till now we have had 83 folks on, but trade has fallen off terribly and today we had to give 9 the tip that they must look out for something else.'

From the beginning Joseph Lucas had taken a fatherly interest in his workers, and Harry was quick to carry on this paternalistic attitude when he found himself virtually in charge. One day he asked Joseph: 'Nellie Heath's sweetheart wants to come and work with her. I think it might cause unpleasantness among the other women. What do you think?' (This is one of the many occasions when it is tantalising not to be able to read Joseph's reply to his son's letters.) The love-life of the women workers evidently caused Harry continual concern, because in another letter he reports: 'Annie Rice has been rather erratic lately. She got her eye blacked the other week by her sweetheart for talking to Cook's chap who did the gas fitting, so she stopped away till it got better, and yesterday and today she is away on the drink.'

The working day was long by modern standards, starting at 8 o'clock and finishing at 7, but in 1880 Harry decided to close the factory at 6 o'clock, arguing that:

Against the hour, we have to place the full half-hour for tea besides the time lost in getting it, and now the dark hours are on we shall save an hour's gas. Of course, we shall have to pay the day workers the same wages for the reduced time, but taking it on the whole there can't be the least doubt of benefit to ourselves and the workpeople, and changes beneficial to both sides are the right sort to make.

By the middle of 1880, as more orders came in, it became clear that the Tom Bowling Lamp Works was not big enough. They were losing the goodwill of some of their customers by late deliveries. Harry wrote to Dearlove: 'I am preparing myself in every form for a big trade and have bought the premises adjoining my place and shall soon have room for a dozen more hands, which will be a good assistance till I can make more extensive alterations.' (That he did not mention his father in these moves can be put down more to Harry's egotism than to any real diminution in Joseph's influence.) He added that the 'shopping' (the workshops) on the ground floor were being used for the women workers.

In one sense Harry was perfectly justified in talking about these plans for a 'big trade' as if they were entirely his own, because it seems to have been left to him to find the money to pay for them. For instance, he borrowed £200 from a Mr Dutton to pay the deposit on the adjoining shops he had bought from Mr Archer, but had to ask for an extension of six months when the time came to repay it. (He was still paying £20 interest two years later.) He was also 'short of the needful' – a phrase he was fond of using when staving off creditors and raising the wind – 12 months later when he wrote to a Mr Jones:

I am desirous of obtaining £200 for 4 to 6 months and beg you will kindly consider if you can advance me this sum. Security is my honour backed by the splendid success I am now enjoying in business . . . I feel confident of repaying the £200 I have had for the past few years. I can prove I am paying in cash for much of my material and getting great advantage by doing so. I simply want the money to assist me in putting in a good stock of finished goods for the busy season.

In fact, at the end of the 1870s, the business was being run on a strictly hand-to-mouth basis, yet somehow it contrived to grow – thanks to the ingenuity and hard work of its remarkable young manager. Various small sums had been put up from time to time by relations, mostly cousins of Joseph – Cousin Harry, for example, had contributed £80 – and they were paid interest at the rate of 5 per cent. Cousin Harry asked for a stamped document in place of the simple IOU he had been given, and was sternly reminded by Harry that 'your real security is in my father's honesty and not in the paper you hold.' In addition, Joseph and Harry had to borrow elsewhere, as we have seen, at the rate of 10 per cent. The result was a continuous headache for Harry, who was so short of money sometimes that he had to pay their bills by cheques postdated by as little as a week. Cousin Bill, who had asked for repayment of £30 of the money he had lent them, was told: 'I can't conveniently send you the money this week. We have spent hundreds of pounds this year, which has made us very short, but our busy season is now on hand and we shall soon have money rolling in.'

Harry summed up his problems, and the scale of the business, in a letter to his father in 1880:

> To assist you in seeing what I have had to cope with, I enclose list of bills I have had to meet, all closely following each other. You see it amounts to £463.13.6d. in a fortnight, without reckoning £60 a week [for wages] and £30 and £40 for various. Now do you see I have had my hands full? This morning 42 letters, which is the most ever by post. Three dozen Kings for Singers and grosses of lanterns, chiefly common, for Treviling & Smith. This will partly assist you to understand why I don't want ships' lamp orders . . . Every bench is full and we are on overtime.

Indeed, the long-term prospects were bright, and in September he was able to tell Joseph: 'Accounts now out reach £1,100, so when we get this in we shall have a bit to go on with. Last month was the best we ever had.'

They were still selling oil and paraffin in bulk – in March 1881 we find Harry asking his father to buy twenty casks of oil for immediate delivery, 'it is much cheaper in London' – but Harry did not want the business and suggested that Christopher, his younger brother, might take it over and run it on his own. In fact Christopher, who did not get on well with his father, set up as an independent maker of lamps, chiefly for the railways, in another house in Great King Street (No 69, between Bridge Street West and New John Street West) which he called the Atlas Lamp Works, before moving on to other fields, and what happened to Joseph's original oil business is not recorded. Christopher was eventually associated with a scheme for developing a housing estate on the outskirts of Birmingham.

About this time Joseph and Harry were approached by James Neale, a maker of carriage lamps in St Paul's Square, to buy his business. Harry turned the offer down, saying: 'I regret I cannot see

(above) Looking ahead with confidence. Joseph Lucas and his first wife, Emily Stevens – daguerreotypes taken after their wedding at Edgbaston parish church in 1854. He was twenty and she was three years older. Their first home was 86, Carver Street, a typical red-brick terrace house of Victorian Birmingham

(below) Looking back in satisfaction. 'Old Joe' – handsome, wise and benevolent – shortly before his death at Naples in 1902 at the age of 68. Five years earlier Joseph Lucas & Son had 'gone public' and become Joseph Lucas Limited, with a capital of £225,000. By then he was living in a large house in Stoney Lane, Moseley

(left) In 1872 Joseph Lucas moved from Carver Street to 209 Great King Street. This is how the little house looked in 1960, shortly before it disappeared without trace in the large open space that now adjoins the Lucas factories. Birmingham plans to commemorate the historic site *(F. R. Logan)*

(below) Builders in Great King Street: the start of the Lucas group of factories in 1889. Joseph wanted the first block built in a hurry and offered the workmen 2d an hour more. The result was disastrous – 'men got drunk, the police were called in to stop fights . . . and so we let the brickwork at piecework and things went swimmingly.'

my way clear to take it up and give it the necessary time and energy to bring it to a successful issue; nor do I see how I could easily bring the two businesses together, and to work them separately would in all probability result in failure to both.'

The day-to-day anxieties and growing responsibilities began to tell on Harry's health, and when he was 26 he thought about going to Scarborough for 'a month's rest and hydropathic treatment'. He actually got as far as writing to Smedley's Hydropathic Establishment for their terms for board and lodging, but somehow could not find the time to go. The hard work seems to have suited him, however, because he had put on a stone in the two years since October 1879, when he had weighed only 8 stone 7 pounds.

It was not until the following year, 1882, that Harry took the plunge and went to Ireland for three weeks' holiday with his brother Christopher. It was typical of him to keep a detailed diary in a black notebook with an elastic band round it (it lies in front of me as I write), starting 'If lost (found?) return to Harry Lucas, The Firs, Stoney Lane, Birmingham. July 20, 1882'. It was only two months since the assassination of Lord Frederick Cavendish and Thomas Henry Burke, so the first thing they did on arriving in Dublin was to go to the fatal spot in Phoenix Park, followed by a macabre visit to Kilmanham Jail. But 'nothing is worthy of note about it', wrote Harry.

The diary is full of picturesque descriptions of what they saw – writing came easily to Harry, as can be seen from his letter book – and the Irish scene gave him plenty of scope. Two examples must suffice:

As we passed Galway the carriage got filled with Irish men and women and I counted nine of the latter without bonnets. Being Saturday afternoon the place seemed full of country women bending under their loads of market stuff – eggs, butter, poultry, etc. – which they carry in baskets on their backs under a thick black woolly cloak of Spanish mantilla pattern, which reaching over their heads also takes the place of a bonnet. Under this black cloak they wear a coarse sort of thick flannel petticoat of a bright red colour, but no shoes or stockings and evidently little or no underclothes to encumber them. These women must be about three women-power at least, and so they should be to endure their elevating occupation of beasts of burden. There were hundreds of them, and while viewing their fate it is difficult for the English tourist to believe he is still within the United Kingdom and has not been transported to faraway Spain. Although we saw so many of these weight-carrying women, not a single man did we see encumbered with a basket or a bundle . . .

At Limerick Station we met with an incident highly illustrative of the ungovernable strength of Irish temperament. A few emigrants to America were going to Cork via our train, and a host of their poor friends had assembled on the platform to bid them their last farewell. What a scene there was among these poor people to be sure! Such hand-shaking, such kissing, such moaning and crying of 'The darlin'! Oh, the darlin'!' repeated again and again that although my sympathies are not easily moved by scenes of this kind I felt the tears coming to my eyes as I looked on this parting of friends and families, a parting which seemed to be the tearing to pieces of their very natures. As the train moved purposely slowly out of the station, the handshaking was renewed with greater vigour and the cry of 'The darlin', Oh, the darlin'!' became more frequent and violent, and it was only with great difficulty the guard could prevent the little crowd, which thronged the carriage window as the train moved, from getting dragged down between the train and the platform.

The green countryside, in such contrast to the red-brick sur-roundings of Little King Street, moved Harry to thoughts of beauty, leisure, and a young man's fancy that found no place in his busy life at the factory. 'I am now in the midst of this beautifully wooded glen,' he wrote, 'seated on the grass with my back against a fallen tree, the delightful murmur of a rippling brook behind and just sufficient sun, cloud and wind to make beauty more beautiful. How much I should like to spend a whole day here with a pleasant com-panion (feminine gender), a nice book and no need for hurry troubling my mind.'

But he did not neglect to record in detail the cost of fares, meals and lodgings, and very expensive these often seemed to his frugal mind. 'We were charged 4s. for a bedroom, the furniture of which could all be bought for the price of a month's lodging at this exorbit-ant rate.' The bill for that night for both of them, incidentally, read: 'Teas 2s. Room 4s. Breakfasts 4s. Attendance 1s.6d. Total 13s.6d.'

Again: 'After dinner we drove to Muckross Abbey, and not having been forewarned that payment would be demanded we were astound-ed to find that a charge of 1s. each is made for all visitors outside the County Kerry . . . this mean charge made by the proprietor, Mr. Herbert – an M.P. too – who we all agreed was no gentleman.'

It was an energetic holiday which no doubt did the town born-and-bred Harry a power of good, for on occasions the two brothers walked up to 30 miles in one day. But the cost of it all was uppermost in Harry's mind when he summed it up: 'This has been the most expensive holiday out we have ever had, costing Chris £15.9s.1½d. and myself £1.1s.7d. extra, that is £16.10s.8½d. I was not mentally prepared for this, although luckily I was in pocket, having provided what I thought would be more than enough. We have been out 21 days and in this time have slept in 16 different places.'

It was now 10 years since Harry had joined his father and he was 27 years of age. Joseph, who was 48, decided the moment had come to take the young man into full partnership. Up till now they had been trading simply as Joseph Lucas, but in September 1882 the name was changed to Joseph Lucas & Son.

Although it was a family business, the partnership needed to be clearly defined – at any rate that seems to have been Harry's opinion. One day in April the following year he took a leaflet illustrating 'Bicycle and Tricycle Lamps – TBLW' and wrote these notes on the back:

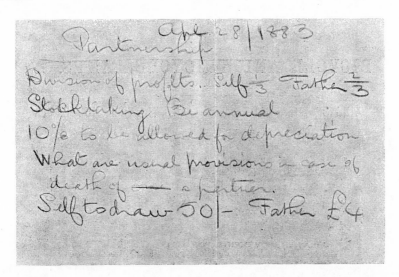

PART TWO

THE MARK OF SUCCESS

CHAPTER ONE

LUCAS v THE REST

The next 15 years were to prove decisive in the history of the company, for if the two partners in Joseph Lucas & Son had not overcome the many obstacles that confronted them, or had failed to grasp their opportunities, they would not have been in a position of sufficient financial strength to register their business as the limited liability company of Joseph Lucas, Limited, in 1897 – the company from which the vast Lucas organisation of today has grown.

When the firm of Joseph Lucas & Son was registered in 1882, the problems facing the two partners were partly financial and partly commercial. The financial difficulties of paying for their labour and materials, waiting for cash from their customers, and at the same time finding the money to add to their factory space and take on extra hands – all within their own resources – were to remain with them throughout the whole period, whereas the commercial problems were varied and intermittent.

The year 1883 opened with a spate of reports of the King of the Road being copied by various other lamp-makers, who sometimes went so far as to use the Lucas illustration and name-block in their catalogues and advertisements. The first case of this piracy had occurred two years earlier, when Harry wrote a letter in Joseph's name to a competitor (Rea, Neale & Bourne) reporting that 'his son' had called at their office to examine a lamp in their window 'similar to my patent King of the Road,' which they had told him was the only one they had made. He supposed that it was their intention to make and sell it, which would be an infringement of his patent, concluding with the menacing remark: 'I should be sorry for anything to occur which would destroy the commercial friendship which has hitherto existed between us.'

This seems to have been the end of that particular incident, but in March 1883 came the first case of the name-block being used by a competitor, Mathews & Bladen. Harry wrote off to Joseph: 'Yesterday Mathews said: "My dear sir, I was bound to use it at a push", when I challenged him about using our headlamp block, and now I find he is still audaciously using it in his advert in *The Cyclist*. Just see it. By jingo, we'll have a smack at him somehow or other. There's no sense of common honesty in the man.'

In the following month he protested to Markham & Brettell about their Victor hub lamp with metal bearing and started an action against Mathews & Bladen for infringement of Joseph's patent for the King of the Road, but the case was settled out of Court 12 months later, which was perhaps just as well, judging by Harry's report to Joseph in March 1884. He wrote:

> Mr. Bladen came this morning with his papers and is to let me have a copy of Counsel's opinion. They know, or have the clue to, more than I like. They have been told that one of our men invented the King, and think his name is Pearce – Pearce and Perry both begin with P. It's evidently good the case took the turn it did. In spite of this I don't think we need hesitate to smack at Millers. They will never fight it like Mathews & Bladen have done, and these people are not likely to assist Millers at all . . . When Bladen talked of a man Pearce having invented it, I told him it was wrong and passed lighter over it than I felt. Burn this as soon as read. Be careful.

This letter probably inferred no more than that in designing the King of the Road lamp Joseph Lucas was greatly helped by having in John Perry, a skilled metal-worker, who could translate his ideas into metal and at the same time offer valuable suggestions of his own. Although there is no reason to believe that it was a case of Joseph simply appropriating Perry's invention as his own, Perry's part in creating the King of the Road was evidently large enough to cause some misgivings in Harry's mind. But since Joseph's absolute personal right to the patent was not questioned in the lawsuit that was fought to the end against Millers (who would certainly have got to know about the doubt hinted at by Mr Bladen) in the following year, it may be assumed that this was a case of there being smoke without any detectable fire.

But the tricky problem of protecting the name of the lamp cropped up again before the year was out when Harry told his father: 'Taylor says Thomas of Newhall Street is starting to make our King of the Road headlamp so I suppose he will put our name and label on. What the devil can we do? We want kicking for not registering the name.' However, a change in the Trade Mark Act, which had previously not recognised words without a design as a trade mark, enabled Harry to apply to the Patent Office for 'King of the Road' to be a trade mark from 1884 onwards.

At about this time Harry, then aged 30, told his father: 'I have been thinking we might manage for you to go to America in August or early September,' but whether Joseph actually made the trip is not clear. Meanwhile they were sending consignments of the King of the Road to Canada, Australia and Constantinople.

Their troubles over patents were not confined to the King of the Road. In September 1883 Harry reported to Joseph: 'As if our cup of bitter doses of competition and piracy were not already full, Mr. Neale walked into our office this morning with a pattern of a globe lamp sent to them to make four dozen of in brass by a London firm whose name he would not disclose. It was our T.B. principle to a T . . . Mr. Neale asked if our patent were up so how could I escape the truth?'

The next case of copying the King of the Road was reported from the United States in the shape of the Maximum hub lamp, which was a dead spit of the King of the Road, but Harry was not unduly worried about the competition from this lamp and wrote to his informant: 'If it were not that we have been shamefully dealt with by a Birmingham patent agent [the rascally Kendrick mentioned in Part One, Chapter 7] the lamp you speak of could not legally have been brought out . . . We have, we think, good cause for believing that we shall not be kicked out of the market. Our lamp is good value, while the Maximum appears by the drawing and price (eight dollars) to be very maximum in price!' A year later, in 1885, he was writing: '. . . a villainous German manufacturer is imitating our lamps and actually advertising them *with our blocks* which he has managed to secure through we-don't-know-who's agency.' He put this right in the following year by applying for a patent for the King of the Road in Germany.

But the *cause célèbre* that was considered to be of sufficient national importance to be reported in *The Times* was the lawsuit brought by Joseph Lucas against one of his most redoubtable competitors, H. Miller & Co, for infringing the patent of the King of the Road. It all began when Harry got to hear that Mathews & Bladen, after the settlement out of court of the Lucas action against them, were going round saying that the Lucases were afraid to go for Millers, who were also selling a copy of the King of the Road. Harry's letter to Mathews is a classic example of the venom with which these Victorian business rivals fought each other:

Dear Sir,
    It's a lie – nothing of the kind has been said by us. The enemy would have heard from us before had we not been so much pressed with so

many matters and our Mr. J.L. had been so poorly that we expect he would have to take a short rest. We shall write to Millers on Monday...

He then wrote to Millers threatening to start an action against them for infringement unless they stopped making their lamp, using such phrases as 'Your shameful attempt to rob me of what you, as much as anyone, know to be my just rights.' But Millers were unmoved, and as the time grew near for the case to be heard Harry wrote to his father: 'I am surprised how cool I feel about it ... I must work up a bit of concern and try to fill my mind with the awfulness of the loss of the suit, because we know it is the unexpected which always happens and realisations belie expectations ... P.S. I heartily hope you are in good form for the fight.' The possible outcome of the case aroused intense excitement among the whole staff at Little King Street, and Harry reported: 'Our men are to hoist a flag I understand they have arranged for if we win – if we lose, blinds will be put up.'

The case of *Lucas v Miller* was heard in the Chancery Division at the Law Courts in London by Mr Justice Kay on Tuesday, 23 June 1885. Mr Bousfield appeared for Lucas's and Mr W. N. Lawton for Millers. The plaintiff's case was that Miller's lamp, called the Monarch of the Road, infringed the Lucas patent for the King of the Road. Miller's defence denied the validity of the patent on the grounds that the provisional specification differed from the complete one, which incorporated an improvement (the method of attaching washers) which Lucas had subsequently discovered, and Miller went on to allege want of utility in the invention and that it had been anticipated by another patent by Henry Salsbury.

Mr Justice Kay, reported *The Times*, delivered judgement at considerable length. He was probably a keen cyclist himself, because in his detailed description of how a hub lamp was fitted to a bicycle he said: '... everybody must have observed that the space between the spokes where they join the hub of the front wheel has been utilized as a convenient place to put in the lamp which is so necessary to prevent all the world being run over.'

The Judge made short work of the argument that the patent was not valid because the provisional specification had not included Lucas's subsequent improvement. 'It could not possibly be claimed in the provisional specification,' he said, 'because it had not been invented.' As to the utility of the invention, 'better evidence cannot possibly be had than the fact that the Defendant has attempted to infringe it'.

Having heard Mr Salsbury give evidence on behalf of Millers to the effect that he and his son had been making lamps in accordance with his patent since 1880, the Judge said he did not think Salsbury's patent anticipated Joseph Lucas's because it only provided for the face of the lamp to be opened and hang downwards whereas Lucas's idea was to open the lamp in two parts by a hinge at the top of the barrel. Lastly, on the point whether or not what Millers were doing was an infringement, Mr Justice Kay said: 'As to that, you have only to put the two things side by side ... to my mind it is most clearly an infringement ... You will take the usual order, with costs.'

> *Bousfield* (for Lucas) – An injunction, an account of profits, and your Lordship will make the usual order to deliver up all infringing lamps. I ask for a certificate that we have proved our breaches, and for a certificate that the validity of the patent has come in question.
> *Kay, J.* – I will give you all of them.

That evening Harry wrote to one of Joseph's cousins: 'Our case against Millers is won and victory is ours. The King still reigns and let us hope he will soon subdue his rebellious, traitorous subjects. A telegram bringing the glad news arrived this afternoon and I have not yet had time to fully realise the great importance of the success.'

And to his father he gave some advice: 'I do not yet know what the terms of the verdict are, but whatever they are let us keep our heads and act in a dignified and reasonable way so that we shall not unnecessarily make enemies. A splendid game is now in our hands and I would rather err on the side of generosity than act in an overbearing manner. Our hands will be wonderfully strengthened, so let us use our power wisely.'

It may well be thought that all this litigation (and there were other cases, including the defence of a complaint that a Lucas lamp lens infringed someone else's patent) must have taken up a great deal of time and energy at the expense of running the small but growing business. Harry thought so, too, and said to his father one day: 'I have been very dissatisfied about our business. I have felt that too much worry has been made over the infringement matters and too little attention to building up a steady trade ... We have been worrying too much about prosecuting other people and are getting punished ourselves in consequence of our paying too little attention to the business.' He summed it up in another letter: 'A little law is all very well – very little, as *Tit Bits* says – in fact the less the better, particularly when legitimate business action is neglected to indulge in legal warfare.'

But when we look at the progress that was being made at Little King Street during this period, it seems that Harry was being unduly self-critical – possibly to compensate for an excessive interest in patent litigation on the part of Joseph. For example, they had sufficient confidence in the growth of their business to make plans to have more factory space available when the state of their order book would require a bigger output. To a customer Harry wrote: 'We have found it impossible to meet all our growing demands and in consequence we have just commenced a range of shopping over 100 feet long and 3 storeys high and this will nearly double our production.' The price was £400 and they borrowed the money on mortgage to pay the owner, Mr Mold. And to his father Harry wrote: 'My imagination already fills the new building to the top.'

Since they were so busy, he told the workpeople that he was going to open the factory at 6 o'clock so that those who were early risers could make overtime. Piece-work was the normal system of wages, but one man who was dissatisfied and wanted to leave was asked what weekly wage he would stay for. He replied 36s or 37s, so Harry gave him 38s and told him, 'I expect you to look after our interests by seeing that the work is properly done and every means used for facilitating it.' To another he delivered a stern warning about his drinking habits:

Sir, although we have several times remonstrated with you and emphatically told you we would not have you here in a state of intoxication, you again chose to appear here in a muddled state and remained in spite of orders to leave. We need not repeat how repugnant anything of this kind is to us. You know it. We have only to say now that we suspend you for the whole of this week, and if you ever again appear here in an intoxicated state we shall feel ourselves compelled to dismiss you lest your bad example weaken our influence in the control of our other employees.

In 1883 Harry wrote: 'We badly want an engine (to drive a lathe) to do all this sort of job for ourselves to save the trouble of educating other people.' But nearly 12 months passed before an Otto engine was installed after a prolonged argument with Tangye about the comparative economy of their engine and the Otto.

Before the bought-out material was used in the factory, it was inspected by 'Louey' (Louisa, Joseph's second daughter), who combined with this job of quality controller the superintendence of the female members of the staff. Quality, on which the Lucas reputation has always rested, was very much in Harry's mind and he told Joseph: 'Our only hope can be in keeping our name good for quality and better for prompt delivery.'

In the summer of 1884 Harry realised they needed to supplement Joseph's single-handed efforts to cover the whole of the United Kingdom trade. He decided the best course would be to 'poach' the salesman from a rival (Snell, whom he despised) thereby achieving the double objective of discomforting the competition and increasing his own sales. C. Hall, who lived at Clifton, Bristol, accordingly joined Joseph Lucas & Son as their first traveller. He quickly proved to be the right man for the job by sending in about £70 worth of orders (very few, unfortunately, for lamps) and Harry sent him a cheque for £7 10s for 'salary and six days' expenses'.

In the following year (1885) it was arranged that Hall should go to Paris, but at the last moment Harry told him: 'Don't go to Paris on Monday. I think I will go with you – "two sheeps heads", you know – and it would do me good physically as well as showing me to my own satisfaction what business we can stand a chance of doing in Paris.' Harry had been learning French for the past three years and had confided in Cousin Walter: 'We have about half-a-dozen French customers and I want to correspond with them in their native tongue – but not just yet awhile.' So this visit to Paris was the fulfilment of a desire to put his French to the test as well as a lesson from 90 years ago to any modern businessman who still insists on corresponding with his French customers in English. But in the autumn of that year they had to put Hall 'on the shelf' until the following year, because business at home was so bad.

Export business was gradually building up and bringing with it the first indication of the problems of competition from local manufacture that would persist until the present day. In discussing with his father the sales of the King of the Road in the United States (where 'stunning lamps' were coming out) Harry made the point: 'I am inclined to think it will be advisable to cut the price fine for the foreigners so as not to offer such a great inducement for them to make.' Father and son were delighted when the Pope Company of America wrote to say they could sell Lucas lamps there as cheaply as they could make them themselves, notwithstanding the cost of freight. In 1884 they received an order from Russia, but Harry was not so keen on it when the customer in St Petersburg wanted six months' credit.

Harry had by this time developed very strong views on what he regarded as the Lucas philosophy of business and he found reason to ram them home to the unfortunate Hall in the following terms:

> For righteousness sake don't attempt to secure trade by any means whatever but only such as are perfectly honest, open and straightforward. Neither can we agree to have our travelling done on the principle of 'forcing trade'. It is repugnant to our principles and contrary to our whole system of business, and we are sorry to know that you have not yet fully appreciated our very definite and oft repeated instructions. We desire, then, that:
>
>   1. No orders are booked from 'shaky people'.
>   2. No order exceeded – or what is as bad forcing or over-persuading a man to order more than you ought to know he can fairly do with.
>   3. All customers are made to know without any doubt the terms on which they are ordering.
>   4. That nothing unfair is said of other people's goods for the purpose of pushing our own.
>   5. That no false inducements of any kind are offered as bait for orders.
>   6. You understand you are not to book orders with unusual conditions, but to submit them for acceptance or refusal.

In the early 1880s their range of products was fairly static, for the real upsurge in cycling had yet to begin, and it was in this area that Harry's complaint about too much time being spent on prosecuting people for infringing their patents was perhaps justified. Being an enthusiastic photographer himself, he tried his hand at making photographic equipment. A dark-room lamp called the Amateur was registered in 1885 and presented no manufacturing problem, but he got into very deep water with a camera and stand specially designed for cyclists, which he patented in 1886. After much correspondence with the makers of lenses here and in France, he produced a prototype camera and stand with the help of the invaluable Perry and sent them to Joseph, who does not seem to have been impressed. Harry himself wrote a few days later: 'I am not so sweet on the camera as I was.' He was annoyed with the man who made the outer case for trying to give it a marble finish – 'It's worse than a pub front.' However, his faith in it returned and he wrote: 'The camera exceeds my expectations in its simplicity and convenience of working. The job has cost a pile of money and I hope and think we shall get it back. It now looks a remarkable success ... P.S. I have heaps of ideas for next year's working.'

The new patent metal camera was called the Cyclocam and sold for

42s. It weighed 22oz, was quarter-plate size and could be had in polished brass or nickel-plated at the same price. The make and size of lens (spelt 'lense' in the advertising leaflet) was not specified, while the focal plane shutter consisted of a strip of thin leather running over a roller and between a metal frame fitting on the lens mount. But the Cyclocam did not take on. The last reference to it in Harry's letter book shows that Joseph's pessimism had rubbed off on to his son, who wrote: 'The little you say about the camera forces the shares below par. If the camera is no good the stand should be some good. I am anxious to hear reasons and then I can settle what is to be done.'

Indeed the introduction of new products was evidently not Harry's strong point, at any rate when they departed from the cycling field. Another of his suggestions bordered on the ridiculous: a combined pipe and whistle. He himself certainly did not smoke, and whistling was hardly in line with his essentially serious nature. Nor is it easy to imagine anyone who would want to whistle and smoke at the same time. What Joseph thought of it is not recorded, which is perhaps just as well.

It was not unusual at that time for manufacturers to factor other people's products and publish them alongside their own in their annual catalogues. A useful example occurred in 1885, when Harry reported to Hall: 'Brooks writes us entirely unsolicited that he has decided to refer all country customers wanting for saddles, etc. to us. This is unexpected and should do us some good.' For many years afterwards Brooks saddles were to be illustrated in the Lucas catalogues for cycle accessories.

For the whole period of 15 years between the registration of Joseph Lucas & Son in 1882 and the formation of Joseph Lucas Ltd in 1897 only two documents about the financial state of the firm have survived. These are a Statement of Affairs dated 31 December 1884 and the Balance Sheet, Trade and Profit & Loss Accounts as at 31 December 1885. Harry's letters to his father contained an occasional reference to financial matters, but the account books have all disappeared, and there are no records of annual production or sales figures of the various lines in the catalogue.

The Balance Sheet at the end of 1885 sums up the methods used by Joseph and Harry to build up the business. The problem was to finance their outstanding accounts (£2,762) and stock in trade (£3,400), and they did this by borrowing from the Bank (£1,270), raising a mortgage on their property (£882) and ploughing back their own profits as Capital Account (Joseph's share then standing at

£4,017 and Harry's at £2,767). They owed their creditors £905 and had £25 cash in hand. The Tom Bowling Works was valued at £2,500 and the adjoining shops at £400 (by this time they had given up 209 Great King Street). Their plant and tools were valued at £1,342. Other facts and figures were that wages and salaries cost £6,455 (there were 140 people on the payroll), purchases £9,286, travelling expenses £382 and advertising £313, while sales brought in £18,102. The Balance Sheet at the end of 1885 showed a profit of £870 14s 8½d, of which Joseph received three-fifths and Harry two-fifths, which were added to their Capital Accounts.

By this time the loans from relations of Joseph amounted to £453, the largest (£150) being from his cousin Maria Tyzack, the widowed daughter of William Lucas, deceased, a brother of Joseph's father, Benjamin. Maria Tyzack was shortly to play a much larger part in Joseph's life.

On 12 February 1885 Joseph's wife Emily died, aged 52, at a little house in Pembroke Road; he was at her bedside when she passed away. He immediately sold the house and went to live at The Firs, Stoney Lane, where Harry was the head of the household with his brothers and sisters. During this difficult period Joseph Lucas had understandably become rather slovenly in his appearance – Nancy Archer, the builder's daughter who acted as his secretary in her father's office across the way in Little King Street, used to tell him he did not dress smartly enough for a man in his position. But during that summer a change came over him and he appeared in smart breeches and stockings with a tassel at the side and a new hat and tie. He was courting. In November he quietly married Maria Tyzack, his cousin, at the Church of the Saviour in Edward Street, where the great George Dawson had been his school-teacher when he was a boy and his minister until Dawson's death in 1876. Bride and bridegroom were the same age, 51, and for a time the whole family (except Louisa, who had married) lived together at Denmark House, Trafalgar Road, Moseley, which Joseph took on a lease at £60 a year.

Marriage was in the air, and a year later, on Christmas Day, 1886, Harry stood at the altar of the Gospel Hall, Great Charles Street, with Kate Steeley, daughter of Joseph Steeley, a School Board officer. Harry was 31, his bride 20.

(*above*) Always wearing a tam-o-shanter, Harry Lucas was an ardent 'cycler', starting with a 52-inch A.1 Ordinary from which he took a header when the front wheel struck a large stone. 'I very seldom ride quick, but at the time of the accident was doing 12 miles an hour'

(*below*) Harry Lucas with cycling friends. His mount is a 42-inch Facile, about which he wrote: 'A fair pace can be got out of it and there is not that feeling of nervous anxiety one must have when riding the Ordinary tall tricky machine over rough roads'

T. B. L. W.
THE PATENT "TOM BOWLING" SHIP'S GLOBE LAMP.

MADE TO UNSCREW FOR CONVENIENCE OF INSERTING A NEW GLOBE IF REQUIRED.

Very strongly made and will outwear several ordinary lamps.

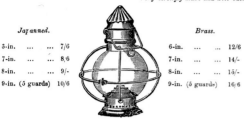
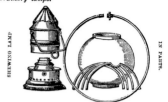

Japanned.		
3-in.	... ...	7/6
7-in.	...	8/6
8-in.	... ...	9/-
9-in. (5 guards)		10/6

Brass.		
6-in.	... ...	12/6
7-in.	... ...	14/-
8-in.	... ...	15/-
9-in. (5 guards)		16/6

Extra Globes should be ordered with Lamps.

Prices, 6-in., 1/8 ; 7-in., 2/- ; 8-in., 2/6 ; 9-in., 3/-

If with Ruby Globes : 6-in., 3/6 ; 7-in., 4/6 ; 8-in., 5/- ; 9-in., 6/- extra.

(above) From the 1883 catalogue: the Tom Bowling was only one of the range of ships' lamps made by Joseph Lucas. Other pages of the 1883 catalogue illustrated a masthead lamp, port and starboard lamps, a bunker lamp, engine room lamps, a hold lamp and a gimbal lamp

(below) The royal wording of his first letters patent – for the Tom Bowling ship's lamp – made Joseph Lucas a very proud man

CHAPTER TWO

FATHER AND SON

Reunited with his father when Joseph was no longer compelled to be anywhere rather than at his own fireside in Birmingham, Harry ceased to correspond with him, and his letter book soon afterwards came to an end. But the 5-year correspondence, one-sided as it is, has left a vivid insight into a father-and-son relationship, which is of deep interest in human terms and of basic importance in the development of Lucas history.

Considering the size of the family and that Joseph spent so much time away from his children travelling, it was remarkable how close Harry was to his father in spirit. In one of the early letters he writes: 'It is only you who can fully understand me, and only I who can understand you.'

In spite of their parent/son relationship (remember this was a Victorian family) and the difference in their ages – Harry was 25 and Joseph 46 when the correspondence started – Harry treated his father as an equal, an attitude that was fully justified in view of the share he took in running the business, but there were times when he lectured his father so sternly that it was almost as though he were addressing his junior. We have already seen him protesting at the waste of time caused by Joseph going after orders for ships' lamps when the little factory was hard pushed to supply orders for other things that were easier and more profitable to make. Here are some more examples:

> If you ever get us into such losses as you have this twelve months or more, I shall go clean off my head. I have often said that you have powerful energies but fail to use them in the right direction. A powerful horse properly directed will do more work than a donkey, but if he is misdirected and runs into a china shop he does a deal more damage than a donkey. See the point?

Four days later he wrote: 'I see with a clearness beyond all dispute that by more steady work we shall accomplish all our aims. We have such splendid business prospects, such capital chances as few people in these times of bad trade have got.' The very next day Joseph received the following:

> You are spoiling us for the future by giving bad impressions. I don't want

to quote recklessly without proper information. Learn what is wanted; tell me and I will soon put the matter in proper shape ... More can be accomplished by judicious thought of a clear head than can ever be done by a random, not-know-where-you-are-going system of working ...

I was surprised to find by your letter this morning that you are getting so near to the North Pole and think you are still acting the part of the powerful but ungovernable horse ... the whole population of Scotland is not so great as London so where is the demand for our stuff likely to come from?

Four days later: 'Make notes of all you want to lecture me on. Don't spare anything and I will do the same. We are on the eve of a revolution.'

These letters were written in 1880, which seems to have been the start of differences between them. Although Harry assured his father in September that 'when your mind is free from knots and mine isn't entangled, we seldom disagree on the best business policy,' five years later he was appealing to Joseph to 'help me build up the business by "slow and slight modifications" instead of going on as we have been without any agreement on policy between us.' Their prolonged failure to agree on policy was largely due to Joseph's enforced absences from the factory and the one-sided nature of the correspondence, Joseph finding letter writing a laborious chore while it came to Harry without any difficulty at all.

At times Harry got very near to breaking point in his irritation with Joseph's attitude to business, and in May 1885 (in between the death of his father's first wife and his marriage to his cousin) he let fly with a long letter in which he gave full vent to his feelings. The burden of his complaint was:

> You have left to me the whole work of directing the course of the business and of watching its every detail, and I have had to make programmes and policy without any assistance or suggestion whatever. Well first I can't, second I won't, bear the strain any longer and I think the time has come for me to say so in unmistakable language.
>
> It has always seemed to me that our position is a somewhat false one – we are credited by many people with extraordinary success, and considerable riches are attributed to us, but you and I know that what success we have acquired is very recent – we have 'gone up like a rocket' and my great fear is that we shall 'come down like a stick'.
>
> My great hope and aim has been to make a comfortable and sound position for you, and afterwards for me, and it grieves me to think that we are not co-operating to bring this about.

Joseph must have taken all this to heart, because two days later Harry writes: 'It does me good to know there is yet hope of your falling into steady work again. Two or three years in intelligent work *must* place us on a sound footing. As yet we are not on safe ground.'

Indeed the vehemence of Harry's reproaches was largely caused by the deep and unalterable affection he had for his father, and he never failed to end his letters 'your loving son'. A more than usually severe rebuke is signed 'your ever loving son', and when his father was under a particular strain, he would end with 'your very loving son'. More explicitly, he once wrote: 'Although I speak thus, my love for you is not one whit the less and is so deep it can never run out this side of the grave.' If these words had ever been spoken, which would have been extremely unlikely, they would have come from a young man with a typically rough 'Brummagem' accent and manner, harsh and brusque, which makes the gentle sentiment and the fluent English in which it is expressed all the more remarkable.

This affection also aroused in Harry the urge to protect his father from the handicaps of his inadequate education. The thought of Joseph struggling with the arithmetic of discounts in front of his customers moved Harry to write: 'You must get a small discount book and if you find it inconvenient to use I must work out the net prices for you.' On their financial prospects he wrote: 'In a little while we shall be free from debt entirely and then all we make will be our very own, as children say, to do as we like with. People may talk as they like about money not bringing happiness. If it doesn't, it is not the fault of the money so much as the possessors.'

Although Harry seemed to find more cause for criticism and exhortation than praise in writing to his father, he was always full of admiration for any useful suggestion put forward by Joseph – for example, when he thought of a new headlamp mount about which he wrote in almost lyrical terms to a cycling magazine. He tried very hard to instil in his father the confidence he himself felt in their future, but did not spare him the realities of their situation when times were bad, as for example: 'Good luck betide your journey, for winter's on us early, and we've little work to do.'

The two men were utterly different in their ways, Harry all neatness and orderly organisation, Joseph evidently casual and lacking in system. 'Much time can be saved by understandable correspondence', Harry wrote. 'I think you will find it a good plan to answer my letter first thing in the morning before your thoughts get confused with your day's work. It is very seldom my letters get properly answered or what you have to say gets properly expressed. I am sure that attention to these matters is wanted on the part of both of us.' But Harry, with a young man's impatience and intolerance, was asking too much of Joseph to change his ways (and to learn to spell properly) at his time of life, and he only showed the rather self-righteous side of his own character when he wrote: 'I again have to speak about loose-ness in names and address. You always spell them wrong. It don't much matter if we know enough to set them right, but it's a lot of time and trouble thrown away when a letter or package goes astray through careless address.'

From the disparate characters revealed in these letters it might be thought that when it came to spending money, Harry would be the cautious one and Joseph inclined to be easy-come, easy-go. On the contrary we find Harry advising his father, 'Nor do you want to be afraid of spending a pound. Well, as to this, I think I have over and over again tried to show you that it is not what you spend so much as what you get that matters. You know perfectly well that my motto has been the contrary to take care of the pence and the pounds will take care of themselves. I don't believe in it.' On another occasion he wrote: 'Don't fidget about spending sixpence, but have a care to make a sovereign' and again: 'It's not what we spend but what we make that tells whether we are extravagent or not,' referring to the wisdom of spending £60 on counsel in a patent infringement case.

Like many Victorians, Harry was fond of propounding aphorisms in his letters, as for instance: 'I want a rest for the head and the best way to get it is to work the legs.' Again: 'Worry kills more men than work, and worry produces no good results like work. Another item to the credit of the Experience Account. Let us profit by it.' In the same letter he shows the fighting spirit that was not the least important of the qualities he brought to the partnership and later to the company in its period of growth. 'If we can't lick any competitor with our facilities we just deserve to be licked . . . you and I ought not to fear any competition if we use our energy and intellect.' Harry was never afraid of competition, wherever it might come from, as was shown when he wrote: 'The Germans for instance may – in fact certainly will – make Cycle Lamps, but why on earth fret over such a thing? We can't control the Germans. The man whose mind is healthfully occupied in his work never regrets the inevitable.'

In reading Harry's long and sometimes opinionated letters it is all too easy to underrate the part played by Joseph Lucas in these forma-tive years and to attribute their success wholly to the son. In spite of his determined views and apparent command of the situation, Harry often ends by asking his father's advice – 'But you know best what to say', 'Now how can I do this?' or 'What had I better say to the Frenchman?' Harry admitted one day: 'I can sometimes see farther ahead in matters of policy than you can but you have infinitely greater power than I have for carrying out a programme.' It is noticeable that Harry is content to let Joseph handle such tricky matters as meetings with lawyers, rival lamp-makers, patentees offering their inventions for Lucas to manufacture, and important customers who want better terms. Perhaps a balanced interpretation of their partnership is that they both contributed vital and compensating qualities which together brought Joseph Lucas & Son through their years of growth in the face of intense competition to a position of overwhelming superiority. It was not the last time in British industry that two such different characters, each insufficient in himself, would prove enormously successful when working as a team.

Inevitably the picture that emerges from these letters is dominated by the writer, Harry Lucas, while Joseph, the recipient, remains in the shadow. Harry was clearly an outstanding young man of strong character who knew exactly where he was going and was determined to get there. 'The course for us to take is so easy', he wrote in 1880, 'so clear and so unmistakably right that why on earth we should go wrong I can't imagine.'

It goes without saying that he was hard-working and conscientious, but that in itself would not have kept the business going, let alone build it up to the success required for its incorporation as a limited liability company. There is no doubt, and the letter book proves it, that Harry Lucas also possessed a brilliant talent for financial and commercial management.

But he did not let work absorb his entire energy. Somehow he found time for all sorts of outside activities as well. He investigated Spiritualism on and off for several years, but while he enjoyed what he called 'the mystic and mystifying art', he never regarded himself as a convinced Spiritualist. (In later years his grandchildren used to 'organise' table-tapping sessions for his benefit and their own amusement.) The occult seemed to fascinate him, and at a demonstration of thought reading at the Town Hall he found himself on the platform being made the butt of the performer's experiments: '. . . after getting a good belting with a banjo I came out of the cabinet with my chain dangling, minus my watch, much to the amusement of the audience, and I had to explain what it felt like inside.'

He was Chairman of the Dawson Society, which held Sunday morning lectures at Nelson Street Board School on varied subjects – political, social, historical, 'anything worth lecturing on'. These drew an attendance of 100–200 people. He also organised lectures for 'young people of the working class' at the Temperance Hall, and to invited speakers he wrote: 'If you can flavour your lectures with some good humoured advice on judicious match-making it would be relevant and received with the deep interest this subject always commands.'

Both father and son, like all good Victorians, were fond of music – as performers, not mere listeners. 'I am going to take my debut as musical conductor tonight', Harry told Joseph when he was 26, 'with what success remains to be seen.' The next day he was able to report: 'We shall be perfection next week. Richard and I pointed out where they were wrong and I gave them notes from my tuning fork so that all started in the same key. I soon began to feel quite at home in conducting.' The only item of their repertoire mentioned is *The Minstrel Boy*, but one would like to think that it included *Tom Bowling*. Harry taught his musical 'folks' to sing the round *A Boat, a boat, haste to the ferry*, and then wrote to a cousin: 'What do you think . . . I made my debut in the singing line a few weeks ago at the People's Chapel schoolroom. Sang the *Gipsy Countess* with a lady pupil of mine. Felt awfully hot and nervous and swigged so hard at the Chairman's water bottle that the teetotal audience must have credited me with having previously had something of a fiery nature and wanted to put it out.'

On top of this he studied in the evenings – French as we have already seen, and geology, in which he 'passed'. But he did not read for pleasure. In a letter to a married woman friend he writes: 'I was in bed most of the time I was at home with a bad cold and read – oh, a lot. Sydney Smith, Channing and Macaulay. I only read when I am *bad* and when my head is unfit for it, and when I can't remember anything of what I have been reading about.' He liked Sydney Smith best – 'I have two of his lives besides his collected works . . . he is rich in humour, sound in reason, formidable in argument and was a great reformer.'

If Joseph and Harry were totally different in most aspects of their characters, they certainly seemed to share a mutual interest in the state of their health. The two men were fundamentally dependent on each other, as was shown when Harry wrote: 'Your health affects my health.' We have seen how Harry had thought of going to Smedley's Hydropathic Establishment at Matlock for a rest, while Joseph was evidently a regular visitor to the same place. Indeed Joseph seems to have become almost a hypochondriac for a time and Harry had to write some strong letters to him about it. In one he says despairingly '... if you have made up your mind you won't get better ...' He went on to describe the stir that was being caused in Boston, USA, by 'the mind cure, a question of faith as well as of physic'.

They also shared a common belief in temperance. How this showed itself in Joseph's conduct at the factory emerged when he returned to Birmingham after his long round of travels. Harry's attitude to it was made clear in a letter he wrote to a prospective cycling tour companion: 'I am a non-smoker and abstainer – not by pledge but by conviction.'

As many who worked at Lucas while he was still alive can testify, this conviction was to make itself felt in the company for many years to come.

CHAPTER THREE

SAFETY FIRST

When Joseph Lucas formally took his son Harry into partnership, the bicycle was still a relatively expensive sporting machine which was difficult to mount and ride. It appealed mainly to athletic young men, and even for them it had to be made to measure by varying the size of the big front wheel to suit the length of their legs. Fifteen years later, when the firm was incorporated as Joseph Lucas, Limited, the bicycle had become a popular – but still quite expensive – means of personal transport that was easy and safe to ride for men and women of all shapes and sizes. In that time the high Ordinary – the Penny-farthing – had given way first to the tricycle and then to the Safety bicycle; and the final step that made cycling a pleasure for everyman and his girl was Mr Dunlop's pneumatic tyre. In the 1890s bone-shaking became a thing of the past, and you did not have to be an athlete in order to explore the country lanes of Britain on two wheels or to meet hundreds, if not thousands, of fellow enthusiasts in such places as Hyde Park or Battersea Park.

In a few years before the first motor-cars appeared the bicycle was also taken up by the well-to-do. All the Royal Princesses rode them, and one observer noted that 'in the marble hall of Chelsea House, in Londonderry House, in Grosvenor House, and most other palatial mansions, the bicycle stand is a matter of course.'

Harry Lucas summed it all up in a little essay on *The Good of Cycling* at the end of one of the Lucas pocket catalogues for 'cyclers'. Under the heading 'Wheeling is the poetry of motion and a transport of joy', he went on to ask 'What, so much as cycling, can take us "out of the hurly-burly" of town life into delightful country lanes or amid in-spiring scenery, and can put fresh life into us as we leisurely glide along or coast down a hill at such a speed that we "seem to cut the wind"? It brings us into contact with many good men and true, takes us out of ourselves, out of our own narrow grooves, and makes us know the world better and think better of it.'

The first significant event in the transformation of the bicycle hap-pened in 1885, by which time there were about 200 firms (most of them one-man or of very small size) making Ordinaries in Britain and the number of cyclists was estimated to be in the region of 400,000. In that year the Stanley Bicycle Show (held in a tent on the Victoria

Embankment near Blackfriars Bridge, London) saw the appearance of the machine that was to give the Safety bicycle the break-through that it needed (Lawson's Bicyclette introduced in 1879 had never really taken on). This was the first prototype of the Rover, invented by James K. Starley, nephew of the great James Starley, and made by his firm, Starley and Sutton, in their Meteor Works at Coventry. (The name Rover was suggested by George Franks, a retired diamond merchant, who put up the money, and it eventually became the name of the company which later made motor cars.) The first Rover, priced at £22, had a 36in front wheel and indirect steering. It was extremely difficult to ride and within a matter of weeks Starley produced a second prototype with sloped forks and direct steering (suggested by a Coventry journalist), which vastly improved its behaviour. Even then the design was not finalised, and it was the third Rover with a diamond frame that was to set the basic pattern of bicycle construction for the next 60 or 70 years. Except for the fact that the front wheel is very slightly larger than the back, and there is no down tube from the saddle to the crank, the Rover Safety in the Herbert Museum at Coventry looks today no more than an old-fashioned machine, whereas the high Ordinary which it replaced seems prehistoric to modern eyes.

But Starley's Rover Safety faced formidable opposition from the diehard makers and riders of the Ordinary. Apart from giving it such derisive nicknames as 'Tortoise', 'Beetle' and 'Crawler', they declared that while it might appeal to old men and invalids, it would never appeal to real masculine men, who would always prefer the challenge of the Ordinary.

While the Ordinary *versus* Safety battle was being waged and new machines were coming on the market, a veterinary surgeon in Belfast (a Scot by birth) was working on an idea to save his young son from the shaking he received while riding his solid-tyred tricycle to school. The primitive pneumatic tyre he fabricated made his son's tricycle not only much more comfortable on the cobbled streets but faster than solid-tyred bicycles ridden by bigger and stronger boys. The pneumatic tyre had been patented as long ago as 1846 by a man named Thompson, but he did not follow it up and it was left to John Boyd Dunlop to produce the first practicable pneumatic tyre, which he patented on 23 July 1888.

From that moment there was no holding the Safety. J. H. Dearlove, the North London agent who had sold Lucas cycle lamps from the beginning, led the last-ditch defence of the Ordinary with a Rational, which itself owed much to the Ariel made by James Starley in 1871. The front forks were raked backwards and the back wheel was made bigger and heavier, making the machine safer to ride but slower. Soon most cycle-makers included a Rational Ordinary in their range, but it was to no avail. The tricycle's popularity waned at the same time, and henceforth it was the Safety all the way.

It did not take Harry Lucas long to realise, after the firm produced the first King of the Road lamp in 1878, that riding a bicycle himself was essential for getting first-hand experience of the fearful pounding their lamps had to endure on the rough roads of the time; and anyway he enjoyed the outdoor physical exercise it provided (he did not play games). The occasional 'header' was an occupational hazard for the rider of an Ordinary, sitting high in the air over its outsize front wheel when it met a stone or some other obstruction on the road, and it inevitably happened to Harry. Recovering at home during a week's absence from the works, he wrote to Dearlove in June 1881: 'My injured limb is nearly well but very weak! It will be a lasting lesson to ride more carefully. I very seldom ride quick but at the time of the accident was doing 12 miles an hour.'

But if he didn't often 'ride quick', he liked to ride far afield, and in April 1883 he wrote to Joseph, who was staying at Smedley's Hydropathic Establishment at Matlock:

> I think of running over next Saturday on my bicycle and if so Chris – and perhaps Harry Clews and Sayer – will come with me. We should I suppose return next day. I believe the road is very good and the journey consequently easy. We should come in short breeches and possibly our appearance at Smedley's in such dress might be horrifying to some of the pious inmates, so perhaps it would be well for you to come out to see us – but this I leave to you.

The first indication of the type of machine Harry used was given in a letter he wrote in August 1884 to a Mr Cherry of Banbury, who had evidently asked for his advice. 'I enclose a list of bicycles made by the man I had mine from', he wrote. 'I know him to be a good maker but stiff in price. Mine was an "A1" 52-inch. He is only a small maker employing one man and a lad and is always busy. Birmingham riders prefer his machines before others.'

But in the following year, 1885, he had bought another machine, a 42in Facile, no doubt influenced by the remarkable performances set up by riders of this machine since its introduction in 1878. (The Facile was the most successful attempt to make a Safety bicycle before

J. K. Starley's Rover finally achieved this objective in 1885. The rider was closer to the ground, the saddle being farther back and the treadle pedals below the height of the hub. In 1884 J. H. Adams beat the Land's End to John o' Groats record with a Facile, completing the distance of 670 miles for the first time in less than 7 days.) Describing the Facile to the man with whom he went on a tour of Scotland, Harry wrote: 'A fair pace can be got out of it and there is not that feeling of nervous anxiety one must have when riding the Ordinary tall, tricky machine over rough roads.'

He was also experienced in riding tricycles – indeed there were several in the family after the move to Denmark House, Trafalgar Road. He had strong and apparently prejudiced views about the relative merits of single-track and two-track tricycles. Writing to an-other friend who asked for his advice, he said:

As to two-track machines, I know nothing by experience ... Two-trackers are not so safe as front-steerers of the Salvo type, but they may be fully safe enough for travelling at comfortable speeds. If I had decided on a two-tracker for my own use I should have a Rotary but my experience is decidedly against this machine if you value a feeling of safety. With a Salvo you can fly a hill and the machine is perfectly under control: you can stop in a surprisingly short space but with a Rotary you daren't risk a high speed ... but really one feels the greatest difficulty in advising about tricycles – it is so very much a matter of fancy. If you were thinking of a Safety bicycle now I could recommend Singer's new one for it *is* a Safety in nature as well as name. At the Speedwell Show it attracted more notice than any other machine – Safetys seemed to monopolise all the attention.

He had apparently got his experience of the Rotary from the tricycle owned by Joseph, which he had advised his father to buy instead of a Humber.

Like most cyclists of his day, Harry was a keen clubman, being a member of the Birmingham Tricycle Club and the Speedwell Club, and helping to organise runs into the country that ended in ham-and-egg or meat teas at Berkswell, Elford, Emscote and other villages. Once they went as far as the Lake District. On these trips Harry practised his photography by taking group pictures which were in great demand among the members, but he gave this up when he found they expected the postage to come out of the cost he charged them for each print.

It was natural that Harry Lucas should want his young wife to share in his enjoyment of these club meetings, and in 1888 he got J. K. Starley to make a bicycle especially for her. It was a man's type Rover with a top tube, so, to get over the difficulty of draping her full skirt over the machine, Mrs Lucas rode in knickerbockers.

Its usefulness for testing lamps was one of cycling's great attractions for Harry, and his letters contain many references to night runs to try out his ideas on new burners and sliding side windows. Although he normally drove down to the factory each morning from Moseley with Louisa and Emily in the family wagonette, he frequently used the journey as a test run for a lamp or accessory on his bicycle. 'I am dressed in my riding suit', he told Joseph, 'and shall come down on Bi every day the weather allows so as to keep trying the lamp.'

Some of the snags he had to contend with were burners that leaked oil inside the lamp or failed to give enough light, lighting the lamp in a high wind, and smoke that tarnished the reflectors, which could lose their lustre through being cleaned too often. The answer was to design his own burner and make it at Little King Street. He tested it on the road himself – 'I tried a headlamp with our new burner on my Facile on the Bristol Road, and although I jolted up to Bournbrook over the granite no oil whatever came out of the burner and I am very pleased with it.' After accusing the wretched supplier of Colza oil burners of 'making vile rubbish', he told him that in future Joseph Lucas & Son would make their own, adding, 'I have often been positively sorry for my sister on account of the extreme care and trouble she has always had to exercise to prevent faulty burners getting passed into use . . . and this at last I am determined to stop.'

They also had a great deal of trouble with lamp hinges that snapped, and bells that came unscrewed and fell off through the vibration caused by the narrow solid tyres of the bicycle and tricycle wheels hammering over the rough stony roads. To get quick controlled results Harry set up a miniature test course in the yard at Little King Street, using wooden planks set at angles to induce the necessary vibrations and shocks. He carried out destruction tests on this course with his own machine, being determined at all costs to achieve the highest quality and reliability in his growing list of cycle products.

CHAPTER FOUR

THE PACE QUICKENS

By now Joseph and Harry Lucas realised that there was far more business to be done than could be supplied by their own manufacturing resources at Little King Street, even with the new extensions they had built. A quick way to take advantage of the situation until they could expand even more was to sell other firms' products in addition to their own lamps and bells and other accessories.

As we have seen, they had already made a start with Brooks' saddles some years earlier, and in 1887 they added saddles made by the Nagel Company of Bielefeld, Germany, and Lamplough & Brown to their trade list. They also advertised Nagel's *Löwenmaul-Schlüssel* wrench – the Lion's Mouth wrench – which sold for 25s a dozen; in return the Nagel catalogue offered the Lucas King of the Road lamp to German cyclists. Other 'outside' items sold by Joseph Lucas & Son at this time were the Boy's and Rucker's patent signal cyclometer, which thoughtfully rang a bell at the completion of every mile; the Hernu patent cyclometer and King of the Road hub lamp combined in one unit, which Harry arranged with the patentee, a man named E. Rusden living in Moscow, through a Baron L. Knoop; and the Underwood odometer.

The range of Lucas products offered in their trade catalogue increased enormously from 1885 onwards. The Coventry oil can, with a pivoting spout that switched off the supply of oil when it was turned alongside the body, was made at Little King Street to a patent granted to James Starley in 1885, and they started to make their own leather saddle-bags and pouches. Lamp wick and King's Own lamp oil (a reminder of Joseph's Carver Street days), enamel, polishing paste, lubricating oil, trouser clips (Lucas-patented), a collapsible drinking cup, a ditto sandwich box, locks and chains – all were grist to the Lucas mill. They were proud of their spanners and wrenches, most of them of Lucas design, which were the only ones they would guarantee.

Joseph had a bigger plan. His aim – though Harry doubtless had a hand in it – was to supply all the needs of the cycle assemblers (which is what many of the so-called 'cycle-makers' were in reality) and the little cycle repairers who were springing up all over the country. And so an extra section was added to the Lucas wholesale list headed 'Cycle Sundries, Fittings and Materials of every Kind', and the 1891 Wholesale Illustrated Catalog [*sic*] of Lucas's Cyclealities ('the Best of Everything') offered bearings, backbones, brake fittings, brackets, chains, chain wheels, cranks, footrests, forks, frames, handlebars, heads and necks (for safeties), mudguards, pedals, tyres, tubing, rims, spokes and wheels – all the bits and pieces to make a complete Lucas bicycle and to repair bicycles that had broken down.

The idea of selling complete bicycles in kit form, as it would be called nowadays, took a little time to organise, but certainly by 1897 the Lucas Cycle Parts Catalog started off with illustrations of sets of parts made up as complete Lucas bicycles – No 1 set for Men and No 2 for Ladies. All the parts could of course be bought separately.

There was nothing static about the range of accessories sold by Joseph and Harry Lucas during this time. If a line failed to catch on, it was dropped from the next catalogue, and new ones were constantly being added. In 1892, for example, they listed the Lucas Military Cyclist's Rifle Clips, which had been 'approved by the Officers and are in use by the Members of the 26th Middlesex (Cyclists) R.V.', price 21s a pair. They also introduced Lucas Inflators.

I have left to the last the two accessories that did most for the Lucas name (and prosperity) – bells and lamps. No bells were shown in the 1883 catalogue, but in the next one I have been able to examine (1887) there is a section on bells headed by Our New Patent Combination Bell No 42. Pulling up a thumb-piece in the centre started the Continuous Ringer, which carried on its jingling warning until the thumb-piece was pushed home again. It cost 2s 8d or 3s, according to size. This was an advance on the earliest cycle bells, which could not be stopped from ringing continuously; they simply consisted of a dome mounted on the handlebar with a loose toggle which was kept ringing by the vibration of the solid-tyred bicycle. The No 42 was made at first for the patentees, Messrs Meeze, Saloman and Phillips, with whom Harry had some tiresome arguments which ended with the patent being transferred to Lucas in 1886.

The selling point of bicycle bells was naturally their power to alert other road users to the bicyclist's approach (though whistles and horns were also sold by Lucas for this purpose). A description of the King of Bells ('the road clearer') in a catalogue issued in the 1890s explains: '*You* press the lever, *the bell* clears the road' with its 'peculiarly imperative tone', price 4s 6d. The Baby Bell 'gives a sharp, shrill tone, much louder than you would expect', while the Challis Alarm ('the loud bell') gives a 'loud, get-out-of-the-way-with-you sort of ring', which must have improved relations between cyclists and elderly pedestrians no end. (The Lucases were not alone in this ruthless attitude towards pedestrians; the makers of the Big Ben tricycle alarm coolly asserted that 'It will make the Deafest Creature Jump'.)

The Challis was the best of the new bells which could be deliberately rung by the cyclist instead of depending on the vibration of the machine on the road to shake the toggle. It had been patented in 1886 by its inventor, a bell-founder and machinist in Hackney, London, named Charles Ebenezer Challis, to whom Lucas & Son paid a royalty for the privilege of making it. Two years later this patent, too, was registered at the Patent Office in the name of Joseph Lucas & Son, thus repeating the tale of the Combination Bell.

But it is the lamps in the early 'catalogs' that are most interesting in showing the Lucas reaction to cycling trends, because they illustrate the gradual shift from hub lamp to headlamp for Ordinaries and tricycles and the eventual supremacy of the headlamp as the Safety took over entirely from the other machines. In the 1887 Lucas catalogue 'our best lamp' is the King of the Road hub lamp for Ordinaries, but a headlamp King for tricycles is shown with the claim that 'it cannot jolt off the bracket', while a King of the Road bicycle (ie Ordinary) headlamp is just mentioned at the bottom of the page. Only three lines are given to the King of the Road for fitting to the footrest of the Rover Safety (which had been introduced two years earlier), and at the very end comes a new King of the Road headlamp for bicycles which are rather contemptuously described as 'Safeties, crippers, and other machines with great vibration'.

Five years later the picture had drastically changed. By then the headlamp had almost completely ousted the hub lamp. The 1892 Lucas catalogue opened with the Holophote King of the Road – the 'great light giver' – which had been put on the market in the previous year. It had a double convex lens and powerful reflectors which had the effect of 'making available all the light of the lamp, as in a light-house' – the phrase used in the Oxford Dictionary to describe the word 'holophote'. In other words, it gave out a beam of light instead of just illumination. Four pages were devoted to headlamps of various models, while hub lamps were relegated to a single page right at the end of the lamp section – including a special model for the narrow hubs of the Rational Ordinary, the final attempt to adapt the High Ordinary to the safety requirements of the man in the street.

Harry Lucas had privately made up his mind that the Ordinary, and with it the hub lamp, was finished when he decided not to pay the annual fee of £10 for renewing the patent of the King of the Road hub lamp in 1890 – the patent that he had defended with such tenacity against all attempts to infringe it only a few years earlier. Such was the rapid development of the bicycle, with which lamp design had perforce to keep pace. The name King of the Road was unaffected, simply being transferred to the best selling headlamp for Safeties.

From the great reputation it acquired it might easily be thought that the King of the Road was the only lamp the Lucases made in the early days of cycling. It was certainly the most prestigious (and the most frequently copied) lamp for the Ordinary bicycle. But there were many other Lucas cycle lamps made at the same time – the Pioneer, the Comet, the Edison, the Club, the Orient, the Popular, the Captain, the Pathfinder and the Planet (the cheapest lamp in the range, selling for 3s 6d, compared with 22s to 30s for the King of the Road). Some of these lamps were much alike both in appearance and price, and the reasoning behind the proliferation of such similar models is difficult to follow today, but Joseph and Harry evidently decided that the market needed them at the time. In 1887 they listed hub lamps and headlamps described simply as 'cheap', selling for half-a-crown.

This is the appropriate time to mention a mysterious lamp bearing the Lucas name-plate that was produced in 1888 but never appeared in a Lucas catalogue. The inscription on it reads: 'J. Lucas & Son's Electric Lamp, Vaughton's Patent (Patent applied for 27 October, 1887 No. 14,622).' This patent was for 'an improved electric accumulator suitable for portable electric lamps and for other purposes', and the Lucas contribution was therefore simply the lamp part. As Vaughton lived in Trinity Road, within walking distance of Little King Street, it was quite possible that Lucas made up a few specimens for him and that the lamp never went into serious production. A fine specimen has recently come into the company's hands, proving its existence, but it is not claimed as a full member of the Lucas lamp family.

This lamp is not the only product with the Lucas name on it that was not included in their catalogue. As I write this chapter, a wooden bicycle rack has been discovered by a collector of cycling relics with a plate carrying the inscription: 'Jos. Lucas & Son. No. 1214. The Whittaker Bicycle Holder. Patented. Birmingham.' This is possibly the holder that was made in considerable numbers by Archers, the builders, towards the end of the last century. But for some reason or other it never appeared in a Lucas catalogue.

Returning to lamps, even the King of the Road was eventually put in the shade by an entirely new Lucas bicycle lamp which was patented in 1895 by Harry Lucas and had its name registered as a trade mark in the same year. This was the legendary Silver King of the Road, as it was called in the catalogue, though it soon became known as the Silver King. This lamp seems to have been designed with the help of a Lucas employee, Thomas Broadbent, to whom Joseph awarded the sum of £25 (which at the contemporary 'rate of exchange' for the pound of 10 to 1 was quite a handsome sum). But Harry played a big part in it, too. Many years later Oliver Lucas used to tell the workpeople that he remembered seeing his father sitting at a stamping machine, his hands all covered in clay through pouring the die from the stamping, until he had solved the problem of making the vessels for the Silver King. His mother, Oliver added, used to bring his tea to him, then his supper – and his breakfast – because Harry Lucas often used to sleep in his office when he was engrossed in a new project.

The Silver King was to be one of the top Lucas cycle-accessory profit-earners for many years to come – as long as cycling continued to be a popular pastime. (Forty years later, in 1936, Harry Lucas celebrated the fact that it was still in production by making a further award to Mr Broadbent.) Harry was so proud of the Silver King when it was introduced that he called it 'the handsomest lamp ever made' – a phrase which no one who remembers it will quarrel with. The barrel shape of the body continued from the front glass to the Mangin silver reflector at the back, which was protected from smoke and grime and the rubbing of continual cleaning by a double convex lens in a nickel mount. When the body of the lamp was swung on its bottom hinge, the lens could be slipped off and wiped clean. The lamp was insulated from road shocks by the Lucas patented spring hinge by which it was attached to the bicycle. Finished in nickel plate the Silver King sold at 15s 6d (cheaper than the King of the Road a few years earlier). An identical model with japanned finish was called the New King of the Road and cost 13s 6d.

Not content with the Silver King, Lucas's produced yet another bicycle lamp in 1896. This was the Microphote, 'our smallest and lightest lamp – just the thing for Lady Cyclers for use on a light machine'. The patentee was Augustine Campbell Davison, a civil engineer in Holloway Road, London, who soon afterwards joined the Lucases at the Tom Bowling Lamp Works in Birmingham as works manager and 'experimentalist'.

But thinking of an idea is one thing, and putting it into execution is another, and it was the invaluable Jack Perry (who, the reader may recall, had played such an important part in producing the original King of the Road lamp) who once more fabricated the prototype. It certainly was a beautiful little job, the body consisting of a hollow sphere which acted as a complete reflector, plated and polished inside as well as outside. To make it possible to clean the inside, the body of the lamp was hinged diagonally into two hemispheres. This delightful lamp was only 4½in high, weighed 9½oz, and sold (nickel-plated) for 14s.

As we shall see later on, the Microphote was destined to repeat the history of the King of the Road hub lamp, and to bring Lucas into legal conflict once again with their constant rivals, H. Miller & Company.

Cycling classic – the Silver King of the Road

CHAPTER FIVE

A TIME FOR IDEAS

From the beginning of their interest in cycling, Joseph and Harry Lucas had been determined to safeguard their ideas for new lamps and accessories, and improvements to them, by taking out patents. In 1882, the first year of their 'official' partnership, they had filed one provisional patent – for a lamp bracket. In 1884 they took out four patents and the same number in the following year (if you include Starley's Coventry Oil Can, which the Lucases manufactured and later patented themselves), but from 1886 onwards the number went up to half-a-dozen or more every year, reaching a peak of ten in 1891. The first United States patent was taken out in 1889.

The earliest patents (the Tom Bowling ships' lamp and the King of the Road hub lamp) had been in Joseph's name, but in later years his name was either joined with Harry's or the patents were granted to Harry alone or in association with someone else. Then of course there were the patents taken over from other people like Starley, Challis, and Messrs Meeze, Saloman & Phillips. One of the early patents (1885, for a combination tool) stood in the name of Joseph Lucas and Charles Hall, the traveller with the neat beard and waxed moustache, and this joint patenting of ideas with members of the staff was to become quite a regular thing later on.

All these early patents described accessories and improvements for velocipedes, and it was not until 1895 that the word cycle began to appear in letters patent.

A milestone in Lucas patent history occurred in 1894, when a patent by Harry Lucas for 'an improved lubricator for Velocipedes and other Vehicles or Machines' was effected through the firm of Marks & Clerk, of Southampton Buildings, London, and Temple Row, Birmingham (a connection that has continued to the present day, when this world-famous firm is handling more than 500 patents a year for the Lucas organisation).

When they first entered the cycle market, Joseph and Harry Lucas naturally concentrated their sales effort on the retail trade through the medium of their one and only traveller, the hard-working and strictly supervised Charles Hall, backed up in the 1880s by annual illustrated trade lists and advertisements in the few cycling papers. But in the 1890s they realised they ought to appeal more directly to their eventual customers, the cyclists or cyclers, as they were variously called, so they started to produce an annual pocket 'catalog'.

The one I have in front of me is dated January 1897 and is quite a little masterpiece. Beautifully bound in dark red calf leather with marbled endpapers, it is something the keen cyclist would have treasured and shown to his friends with pride. They could get it for the price of a postage stamp.

Under the general title 'Lucas Cyclealities' (with a categorical statement that 'all *Good* Cyclers Use Them'), it is divided into sections on lamps and hints on the use of lamps, bells, inflators, clips, tyre repair outfits, toe-clips, wrenches, oilers, locks, stands, sword and rifle clips, the Lucas watch and holder, wallets, tool bags, luggage bags and carriers. Two pages are given to an accessory costing one penny – a combined pocket mirror ('invaluable for locating flies, etc., in one's eye') on one side and the perpetual Time-to-light-up Table on the reverse – 'a *sine qua non* for every good cycler'. It is not difficult to guess which of the partners wrote that piece, or indeed the whole catalogue, for who else but Harry would have included these practical and cautious tips in the list of 'Cyclisms' published, together with other notes on 'The Good of Cycling', 'Wrinkles for Riding' and 'Pneumaticisms' at the end of the catalogue:

Don't lend your cycle or you may regret it. [But see next line!]
Don't learn on a new machine – borrow someone else's.
Don't rush downhill unless you can see the bottom.
Carry a vest for use when you are off your machine.
Don't start a tour unless you are in good riding form. When touring, don't overdo it.

The section of the catalogue on the 'Lucas Valve – you can tell it by the winged piece' announced a new personal service for cyclists. 'If your local cycle agent will not undertake to fit Lucas Valves in your Tyre, send us the Inner Tubes per Parcel Post and we will fit the latest pattern valve for an inclusive charge of 5s. and return promptly by Parcel Post.'

Another idea for direct contact with cyclists was the Lucas Missing Lamp Scheme, which was started in 1893 and continued for several years. Cycle headlamps were all too easy to steal, and for some reason or other cyclists took to reporting their losses of Lucas lamps to the Tom Bowling Lamp Works. The theft of complete bicycles was also becoming prevalent, so Joseph Lucas & Son offered a reward of £5 for the recovery of a stolen 1893 Holophote or Alumophote lamp (each of which was numbered on the nickel part over the sliding side glass) or an 1894 King of the Road lamp (numbered on the top part) – *and the conviction of the thief.* A reward of £10 on similar conditions was offered for the recovery of a stolen cycle fitted with 'one of the said lamps AND one of the Bells mentioned below' (these were the King of the Bells, the Combination, the Challis, the Cyclarm, and the Favourite).

In 1895 Lucas's introduced the Lowest Fixed Prices System 'by which a sure profit is maintained on our Cyclealities for all cycle agents'. In a foreword reproduced in facsimile handwriting Harry explained: 'By lowest fixed prices we mean the lowest price at which an agent can retail the article – but he may charge a higher price if it suits him to do so.' Harry detested price cutting, and he was always harping on it in his letters to Hall and Johnson, the travellers, and to Dearlove and other agents.

Harry had a refreshing disregard for the risks of libel actions in his dealings with the cycle trade, as witness this letter to Iliffe & Sturmey, publishers of the *Cyclist*:

Gentlemen,
   You are advertising a swindle and therefore assisting it. The firm of Abercrombie & Company is a bad lot – a *very* bad lot – full of clever deceit. The writer of this letter called the other evening for the twentieth time or so for a small amount and told the figurehead of the 'firm' he was a humbug and a lying deceiver – rather strong language to use to a *gentleman* but nevertheless truth, and this easily proved. Take advert out of your paper and assist us in slaying the dragon which is ever ready to devour all it can get hold of.

                                        Yours truly,
                                        Joseph Lucas & Son

To a customer he wrote: 'Re Yours of yesterday. Your statement that we are giving higher discounts to other merchants is a lie and we beg you will pardon a plain truth.'

Although the growing cycling market was the main chance that Joseph Lucas & Son kept their eyes on in the 1880s and 1890s, they did not neglect orders for the non-cycling lamps and items that had formed the backbone of the business in the early years. Stable lanterns, for example, were sent abroad in large quantities. These lines were manufactured in one section of the factory and were grouped in a separate catalogue headed simply 'T B L W'. I have one before me, dated as late as April 1892, which includes most of the old favourites

Birmingham
Dec 1/1894.

To our Friends "The Cycle Trade
    Dear Sirs
        We are pleased to say that for
the coming season our numerous
Cyclealities are decidedly better
than ever.
In every Department, we have new
patterns, improvements & better values
which will keep us well to the front.
Our motto is still "Forward" and our
1895 Samples will show it.
Hoping to have the pleasure of your
favors in the future as in the past?

                Yours very truly
                Joseph Lucas & Son

The direct approach – Harry Lucas believed in the value of facsimile hand-
written letters

listed earlier in this narrative, but the refrigerators and flower-pot holders had been dropped.

In 1886, when the firm had their own stand at the National Cycle Show at the Crystal Palace, Joseph Lucas adopted the slogan 'the largest cycle lamp makers in the world'. From the historical point of view it would be nice to know the production figures on which he based this claim (if in fact it was anything more than an impressive sounding sub-title), but, alas, no records survive of the output of the Tom Bowling Lamp Works nor of the various proportions represented by cycle lamps, ships' lamps, and the other products. What we do know is that in 1884 the plant consisted of a 6hp gas engine, a toolmaker's lathe, six brass-workers' lathes, and a few hand presses and vices. All the gauges, dies, taps, drills and jigs were made by the same man who finished the article – the whole process adding up to complete job satisfaction (to use the modern jargon), which is so difficult to find in the repetitive work of machine-minding and assembly necessitated by the mass production methods of today. For certain processes, such as nickel-plating and japanning, the unfinished parts were sent to outside firms for treatment.

An indication of the growth in output can be seen in the increase in personnel. In 1886 there were 150 people employed at Little King Street; five years later twice that number were on the payroll. Most of them were 'set on' by Joseph himself. One old-timer, J. Skeldon, who was engaged as a boy in 1886, recalled many years later that Joseph (who was then 52) had a 'blunt personality' and just asked him how old he was and did he want the job. On being given the right answer, Joseph told him to start work the following Monday at 7s 6d a week.

Harry saw to it that the overheads of the firm were cut to the bone, and it was not until 1889 that he thought they could afford an office boy. G. T. Wilson, who stayed with the company for the next 55 years, answered the advertisement in the *Birmingham Mail* and was set on by Joseph in the usual manner. Joseph apparently made the most of their new acquisition, enjoying opening the office door and shouting 'Boy, fetch me a cab!' Wilson had to run all the way to Hockley Brook to find one. But cabs were only used for business meetings; at other times Joseph walked – indeed he enjoyed walking miles all over Birmingham. One evening he walked to Winson Green to see young Wilson, who had been kept in bed by his mother with a sore throat. There were only five people all told in the office at Little King Street then, comprising the office manager, a day book clerk, a sales ledger clerk and the cashier, Mr Perkins, who married Joseph's youngest daughter, Ada, and later became Secretary of the company – and of course Wilson the office boy. Joseph set them on, but it was Harry who was their real boss in supervising their work.

Harry also took a hand in organising their play and in 1891 he found there were enough keen cyclers on the staff to form a Works cycling club. This was duly reported in *Cycling* in typical Victorian style:

> The opening run of the Tom Bowling Lamp Works Cycling Club was carried out with great *éclat* last week, 20 members facing the camera and afterwards the tea-table at Hampton-in-Arden. The Club, membership in which is confined to the employees of Joseph Lucas & Son, the makers of the King of the Road lamps, has adopted a very distinctive badge bearing the mystic letters 'T.B.L.W.C.C.'

Whatever the output from their plant and personnel was in terms of lamps, bells, and other accessories, Joseph Lucas and Son once again needed more space in which to achieve the rapid increase in its rate demanded by the state of their order book, so in 1890 they built a five-storey factory in Little King Street itself, on the same side as the Tom Bowling Lamp Works. This building was so tall by the standards of those days that people came from the surrounding district just to look at it.

A contemporary report of a visit to 'the famous home of the King of the Road' in the 8 August 1891 issue of *Cycling* shows how far Joseph Lucas had come in the 13 years since he made his first cycle lamp:

> ... and as we watched the varied processes of its manufacture, we only wished it were possible that every cycler could be even slightly acquainted with the scores of operations through which a lamp such as this has to pass before it reaches him in its completed state.
> At present employment is found for

> *over three hundred hands,*

> men, women and lads; and as this is the quiet season, one can form some idea of the magnitude of 'Cycleality' manufacture. As may be imagined, the first absolute necessity for the successful progress of such an establishment is contained in the one word –

> *System,*

> and here it is to perfection. Perhaps the department that struck us most was the stores, and even these are divided into three separate divisions –

namely, what may be termed the raw material, then the 'parts' – that is, the lamp in all its scores of sections – and lastly, the store or stock-room, for the completed work. Here an exceedingly

Smart Young Woman

is in command, and it is her duty to hand out complete sets of parts to the workmen, who then proceed to their respective shops to fit them together and hand them on to the enamelling or painting 'shops' according to instructions.

A very interesting corner of the great factory is the casting shop. Here a host of men are engaged in 'moulding into rough shape' the brass or steel parts

Required for 'Cyclealities'

of all sorts – lamps, bells, spanners, cyclorns and so on. An impression of the necessary article is made in a duplex sand-mould, and when both sides are closed together the molten metal is poured in from white-hot crucibles; it is then allowed to cool, and such things as burners, domes of bells, and nozzles of oil cans begin to take form. These castings then proceed to the different departments to be finished.

In another shop may be seen

The body of a lamp

being stamped out of the sheet, passed through a press, and the air holes perforated; and after passing through dozens of intricate processes, too numerous to detail here, it evolves into the complete and finished article.

It is by a visit to a factory such as this that one realises the tremendous amount of trouble and expense incurred by even the slightest alteration or improvement in a cycle lamp, involving as it often does

An alteration of machinery

in every department. Nevertheless we were obliged to express our astonishment to Mr. Lucas that he was so constantly introducing improvements and novelties. In reply he told us that despite the inconvenience, they 'never failed to keep up with the times', though frequently at a loss to themselves, for just as the machinery is completed to turn an article out by the thousand

Fickle fashion changes,

and a fresh beginning has to be speedily made to gratify her whims.

The writer in *Cycling* would have been even more astonished if he had known that Joseph Lucas was already engrossed in a grand design for the future that was to transform not only his business but the whole locality.

CHAPTER SIX

JOSEPH LUCAS, LIMITED

The grand design hinted at in the previous chapter began to shape one morning towards the end of 1889 when Joseph walked down Great King Street, which was then a miserable slum, to meet John Archer, a builder and fellow temperance worker who had already constructed Joseph's first new factory in Little King Street and had his office opposite. With them was Archer's small son, on whom the incident left such a vivid memory that he was able to describe it in these words some 66 years later:

> Mr. Lucas and my father met outside a Mr. Gilbert's shop which was full of sawdust – a sort of rag-and-bone shop. We went in and there was a scurry of rats everywhere and the smell was awful, and it meant when we got home a bath and a flea hunt!
>
> Mr. Lucas said, 'Well Archer, this is going to be the site of our new factories and we shall build the interior factories first'. You see, he was already planning to buy the property on Great King Street, Burbury Street and Farm Street. What a vision for those days! So he got Ewen Harper and Brother Architects to plan the whole triangle out. Evidently at this time some large orders must have come to Lucases for the old gentleman said, 'Archer, you have got to get a move on, the first factory is wanted at once, so tell your men to get going and I will pay them 2d an hour more'. This was a complete failure; men got drunk, the police were called in to stop fights, and so we had to let the brickwork out piece-work to a 20-stone foreman bricklayer named Kirby who would wring the neck of any man who was awkward, and things went swimmingly!

And so A Block came into being as the nucleus of the present-day group of Great King Street factories. It was not to be expected that its significance would be appreciated at the time – indeed so little was thought of its future that it was locally called 'Joe's Folly'.

Joseph had his own ideas on how buildings should be designed. Mr Archer again: 'I remember his coming into our office one day and he said "Boy, what is the cheapest thing on earth?" I felt like saying "Dirt" but was too frightened. "You don't know" he said, "Well, I'll tell you, and remember if you ever become a builder get plenty of it in your houses and factories, LIGHT!" ' (The firm of John Archer, later changed to W. B. and F. T. Archer and still in existence as

THE TOM BOWLING LAMP WORKS.

Where Messrs. J. Lucas & Son make their "Cyclealities."

The Tom Bowling Lamp Works in Little King Street after it had been enlarged in 1890, as seen by the *Cycling* artist. It was the first five-storey building in the district and people came from miles around just to look at it joiners, made a new addition to Lucas Cyclealities in the form of a beechwood cycle stand, producing thousands by hand in the period 1894–8.)

Joseph's long-term plans for the whole site were evidently much in the minds of the Birmingham authorities. At the Reference Library I have found a street-by-street rating map of 1870–1 which has pencil marks made on it at a later date showing the block of buildings earmarked 'for Joseph Lucas' on one side of Great King Street and along the frontages of Farm Street and Burbury Street, forming the triangle he planned to develop. Inside the triangle, within a broken line, appear the words 'Cycle accessories factory and shopping over scullery'. This was what was to become A Block, the first factory to be built on the site and still standing in 1975.

On the corner of Burbury Street and Farm Street stood the Burbury Arms, which Joseph either could not, or would not, buy (on account of his temperance views), while in Great King Street, between the court leading to the site of the cycle accessories factory and the corner of Farm Street, was a small public house called the Brewers Arms.

Joseph Lucas's grandiose plans for the development of the Great King Street-Farm Street-Burbury Street triangle were not based on daydreams of future prosperity on his part – still less on Harry's. In spite of strong competition from many bicycle-lamp makers in Birmingham and other parts of the country, as well as abroad, in the early 1890s their business was expanding so rapidly that nothing less than a massive building programme would have enabled them to take full advantage of it. The factory in Little King Street was working flat out and could not be enlarged any more.

But this meant finding more capital than could be provided from the Company's earnings, good as these evidently were, and at some point in the mid-1890s they decided the time was ripe to capitalise on the success of Joseph Lucas & Son since its registration in 1882, and to form a company limited by shares in accordance with the Companies Acts 1862–1893.

No correspondence of this period has survived, so it is not known what advice they received in making this decision, but the details were doubtless worked out in conjunction with their bankers, Lloyds (who had provided funds by way of overdrafts for many years); the solicitors, Messrs Johnson, Barclay & Rogers; and the auditors, Messrs Mayo, Powell & Thompson. Nor is it known why or how Joseph Lucas approached Walter Chamberlain of Harborne Hall and Walter W. Wiggin of Forehill House, Kings Norton, to sit on the board of directors of the new company alongside Harry and himself.

Walter Chamberlain was the youngest son of the great Joseph Chamberlain and uncle of Neville Chamberlain, the future Prime Minister. He was chairman of W. & T. Avery and the Soho Trust (the Soho Works at Birmingham, not Soho in London) and a director of Brown Brothers, the cycle factors, the Churchill Machine Tool Company, and the Liverpool, London & Globe Insurance Company. He was regarded as the most athletic member of the Chamberlain family and was fond of hunting.

The other outside director, Walter Wiggin, was the second son of Sir Henry Wiggin, Bart, head of the family nickel-manufacturing business which was later merged with Mond Nickel Company, one of the roots from which Imperial Chemical Industries was to grow. He too was a director of W. & T. Avery. He joined his father's business at the age of 22, and was 42 when he was asked to join the Lucas board. The Wiggins family were friends of the Chamberlains, and Walter Wiggin shared Walter Chamberlain's interest in field sports, later becoming Master of the Devon and Somerset Stag hounds. (He also gave Dunkery Beacon and 800 acres of Exmoor to the National Trust.)

The financial picture of Joseph Lucas & Son in 1897 was outlined in the prospectus of the new company published in November of that year. After describing how 'the demand for the firm's goods has continuously and enormously increased during the last 4 or 5 years necessitating the erection of new and more commodious works in Great King Street, which were commenced about 2 years ago (there are three blocks completed and occupied and a fourth block is nearly finished)', the prospectus went on to say that the average profit for the past three years had been £23,664 3s per annum, without charging interest on the capital employed, income tax, or for partners' services, but after ample provision had been made for depreciation and bad debts. Since the only working capital had been the few hundred pounds borrowed from Joseph's cousins, the money he and Harry ploughed back from their share of the profits, and a bank overdraft, Joseph (and more especially perhaps Harry) had built up an extremely profitable business from scratch, and now they were to reap the harvest that Harry had always claimed was just around the corner.

The freehold land and Tom Bowling Lamp Works in Little King Street, comprising the five-storey block, three houses and range of buildings beyond, were valued at £69,200 6s, and the freehold land

and works at Great King Street stood in the books at the cost price of £24,738 9s 10d. With bad debts and cash in hand at £20,488 6s 11d, the assets acquired from Joseph Lucas & Son by the new company, Joseph Lucas, Limited, amounted to £114,427 2s 9d.

The purchase price paid to the vendors, Joseph and Harry Lucas, was fixed at £170,000, payable as to £100,000 in Ordinary Shares and the balance in cash or shares, or partly in cash and partly in shares at the option of the directors. Father and son agreed to act as joint managing directors for at least five years at 'moderate salaries', and Joseph was also appointed chairman of the board. If one puts the value of the pound in 1975 at one-tenth of what it was in 1897, Joseph and Harry between them had built up a business in the 25 years since they started working together worth at least £1,700,000 in present-day values.

The share capital of the company was £225,000, divided into 20,000 ordinary shares of £5 each, preferred as to capital and dividend, and 25,000 ordinary shares of £5 each. The issue was of 20,000 preference shares of £5 each entitled to a fixed cumulative preferential dividend of £5 per cent per annum, and the registered office was in Little King Street. The physical growth of the firm in the past few years was shown in the statement: 'There are at present nearly 700 employees engaged in the business, that number being largely increased during the season.'

One of the two agreements listed (the other was between Joseph and Harry and the company) was between the Lucases and seven Americans for the establishment of a joint stock corporation with the title the Joseph Lucas and Son Company to manufacture cycle lamps in the United States, with mutual agreement to avoid competition with one another either in the United States or Great Britain.

Finally the memorandum of association stated that the main object for which the company was established was 'to acquire and take over as a going concern the business of makers of lamps, bells, valves, inflators and other cycle accessories carried on by Joseph Lucas and Harry Lucas under the style or firm of Joseph Lucas & Son'. It went on to provide for carrying on 'as ancillary thereto the business of manufacturers of cycles, motors or horseless carriages and all component parts thereof'.

It is intriguing to speculate on what might have happened if the new company of Joseph Lucas, Limited, had decided to follow up this activity provided for in the memorandum of association and had produced a Lucas motor-car. But the disruption of the top management that was to occur within a few years prevented any time being given to considering such possibilities in the Edwardian years, and after that the company had all it could handle in coping with the development of business as suppliers to the cycle and motor industries. In any case, their position as major suppliers would have been jeopardised by setting up as rival manufacturers to their customers, so the provision to build motor-cars in the memorandum of association was never really more than an academic exercise.

All the 20,000 preference shares of £5 offered for sale had been applied for when the list was closed on Thursday, 25 November 1897 – indeed the list was oversubscribed. Only five of the 144 subscribers applied for 1,000 or more, these being Joseph Lucas (2,000), Harry Lucas (1,805), Walter Chamberlain, Herbert Chamberlain, and George Dickson (1,000 each). Walter Wiggin bought 500 £5 Ordinary shares from the Lucases after the issue, and his father and brother each bought 100. Joseph and Harry seem to have disposed of many of the 20,000 Ordinary shares given to them as a part of the purchase price, and in a list of Ordinary shareholders issued in the following September Joseph was shown as holding 4,151 shares and Harry 4,195. Among the original Lucas preference share subscribers were Brown Brothers Ltd (both as a company and as individual directors), Thomas Canning, and the traveller Harold Johnson.

Joseph Lucas showed his satisfaction with the successful formation of the company by a characteristic gesture. He went out and bought a magnificent diamond bracelet for Louisa, the hard-working, reliable daughter who had helped him and Harry to run the business, had supervised the women and girls, and had visited them and cared for them when they were ill.

As for Harry, he now had enough money to realise the home of his dreams, taking until 1900 to complete it. On a site of two acres in St Agnes Road, Moseley, he built a comfortable red-brick Tudor-style house which he helped to design himself – as he did the gardens. Although he had never had much use for organised religion, Harry Lucas was a firm believer in the institution of family prayers, and so half-way up the staircase the carved wooden banisters were interrupted by a projecting miniature pulpit from which he carried out the daily patriarchal reading from the Bible to his family and servants assembled below in the hall.

Naming the house gave him a splendid opportunity to exercise his talent for meaningful word building: he called it 'Hilver', a compound of Hilda and Oliver, his only children.

JOSEPH LUCAS LIMITED.

SHARE CAPITAL, £225,000.

Issue of 20,000 5 per cent. Cumulative Preference Shares of £5 each.

𝔓rospectus.

Directors—

JOSEPH LUCAS, Little King Street, Birmingham.
(Chairman & Joint Managing Director.)

WALTER CHAMBERLAIN, Harborne Hall, nr. Birmingham.

WALTER W. WIGGIN, Forehill House, Kings Norton.

HARRY LUCAS, Little King Street, Birmingham.
(Joint Managing Director.)

Thos. Hillman & Co., Typs., 1, Lionel St, Birmingham.

The offer of 20,000 preference shares of £5 each was oversubscribed when the list closed on 25 November 1897. Only five of the 144 subscribers applied for 1,000 or more shares

CHAPTER SEVEN

LIFE AT LITTLE KING STREET

All these financial and legal arrangements made at offices in 'Town' were barely noticed at Little King Street, which continued to be the headquarters of the firm in spite of the new factory blocks springing up round the corner in Great King Street. It was still essentially a family business, with its roots in the Birmingham tradition of the home workshop, and it was vividly described by an old employee, Mr Twist, when he recalled in later life how he was 'set on' by Joseph Lucas as a young man in July 1898. He had heard from a post-man in Great Hampton Street that there was a job to be had at the Tom Bowling Lamp Works, so he went along to try his luck. He found a group of unemployed men hanging round the door who told him that the vacancies had just been filled. Just as he was turning away, Joseph Lucas appeared and beckoned Twist forward (he got the impression that this was because he was the only one who was not smoking). Inside the little factory he was taken into a kitchen with a red-tiled floor, a fire with a hob each side, and a white scrubbed kitchen table over which hung a brightly polished Tom Bowling ship's lamp. (Here, every day, Louisa cooked 'dinner' for Joseph and Harry, in between managing the warehouse staff of about a dozen men and girls and inspecting all incoming parts and materials.)

Twist recounted how Joseph Lucas, on finding out about his family situation – he had a widowed mother and two young sisters to support – said he would find him work somewhere, and told him to report the following Tuesday morning after the August Bank Holiday. He was given a job as a toolmaker; toolmaking in those days consisting of drawing blanks from the stores, the turning, drill-ing, milling, shaping and grinding all being done from raw metal without blueprints. There was only one 2in micrometer (which could be converted to 1in), three lathes, one drilling machine, a shaping machine, a grinding machine and a gas muffle for hardening tools, forging and so on. All the lathes were belt-driven, so that if the belt broke, the whole lot was out of action while it was repaired. The toolmakers were their own blacksmiths and worked in pairs, one holding the piece on the anvil and the other acting as striker. No eating was allowed in the factory on pain of the sack, but the toolmakers used to brew tea secretly by heating a piece of steel in the muffle, putting it into the tea-can till the water boiled and then dropping in the tea.

Soon after the formation of the company, Harry began to spend a lot of time in the factory with Augustine Davison working on the introduction of acetylene headlamps. Acetylene gas had become available as an illuminant a few years earlier through the discovery of the electric-furnace method of producing calcium carbide from the combination of coal and lime by Willson and Moorehead in 1892. Willson followed this up in the same year by demonstrating in the United States that the right amount of air mixed with acetylene gas obtained by immersing calcium carbide in water produced a white light so intense that it was the nearest known artificial approach to sunlight. The first practical acetylene bicycle lamp is believed to have been made by the Badger Brass Manufacturing Co of Kenosha, Wisconsin, USA, and was appropriately called the Solar. The Lucas Acetylator headlamp, patented jointly in the names of Harry Lucas and Augustine Davison in 1898 and exhibited at the National Cycle Show at the Crystal Palace, was therefore not the first in the field, and this was made clear in the provisional specification, which stated: 'The invention (consists of) improvements relating to acetylene lamps, our object being to construct a lamp with its complete gas generating apparatus in a simple, compact, and convenient form suitable for attachment to cycles and other services.' Unhappily the Acetylator was not a success, because the water container was on top of the flame and the water boiled away. This fault was remedied in the Luminator, which was patented by Davison in 1899 and had a detachable carbide holder at the bottom of the lamp with the water vessel just above it. The body of the Luminator was made with the press used for the Microphote, so it benefited from that lamp's attractive appearance as well as its improved design. It was to stay in production for eight years and was joined by the Acetyphote, while the Acetylator was dropped in spite of being improved.

The Lucas candle bicycle lamp produced in 1900 seems to have been a backward step after these acetylene lamps, because its light must have been feeble by comparison. Candle lamps had been made by Riemann of Germany, Asp of Denmark, and several small British firms before Lucas produced their pretty little design, which looked like a miniature carriage lamp with a long stem containing the candle.

While these new lamps were being put into production, Joseph and Harry found themselves at war once more with Millers. The Microphote had been exhibited at the National Cycle Show in 1897 and had been greatly admired. As orders poured into Little King Street and the lamp became a best-seller, Millers brought out the Miniature Lito lamp, which was so similar in design and construction that Joseph Lucas, Limited, and Harry Lucas (the patentee) immediately slapped down a writ for infringement and passing off.

The case was heard at Birmingham Autumn Assizes before Mr Justice Matthews and a special jury just before Christmas 1899. Millers, of course, tried to argue that there was nothing new about the Microphote, which indeed was largely true (it was the way the various parts were combined that mattered), but, as the judge remarked, the fact remained that nobody had produced as good a lamp before. 'Certain it is,' he added, 'that the lamp produced by the Plaintiffs at the Show was immediately afterwards copied, it is agreed, by the Defendants. Now, why did they copy it? – and copy it they did.'

On the jury's answers to the questions put to him, his Lordship granted an injunction to restrain Millers from infringing the patent, and certificates that the validity thereof came in question and that the particulars of breaches were reasonable and proper. But he acquitted Millers of any intention of passing off their lamps as being of Lucas manufacture. Millers appealed, but the original judgement was confirmed.

A few days before the first meeting of shareholders the company, coupled with Joseph and Harry Lucas, were granted a perpetual injunction in the High Court against A. W. Gamage, Limited, for selling unlicensed American-made rotary action bicycle bells of Lucas-patented design. The result was advertised in the cycling papers with the ominous footnote: 'We have brought other actions, which are now pending.'

In the summer of that year (1898) Joseph went to Paris to settle some matter connected with the patent of a bell, and at a subsequent board meeting it was decided to have a Lucas stand at the Paris Exhibition, a decision on which he no doubt had the final word. As we have seen, he had always enjoyed travelling for its own sake, and he was not in the least daunted by his lack of foreign languages when he ventured farther afield. On his first visit to Paris several years earlier he had got round this handicap by arranging with the Lucas agent, Lewis Barnascone, for a bilingual 16-year-old youth named Henri Rousseau (who later became manager) to be attached to him and to do all the talking. Their first meeting took place one afternoon after lunch, and Joseph was scandalised to notice that the boy's breath smelt quite strongly of drink. In his direct Birmingham way he challenged him about it immediately. 'Why, of course,' replied the boy, 'I always drink wine with my meals – we all do.' And Joseph had to swallow his Temperance Society principle ('I will discountenance its use by others') and be content with Rousseau's frank answer. He was not in Great King Street now.

He also crossed the Atlantic several times, visiting Canada as well as the United States. In 1896 the American cycle industry had persuaded the Government to impose severe customs duties on imports, to which Joseph Lucas replied by arranging with the New Departure Bell Company of Bristol, Conn, to make Lucas bells and other accessories for sale in the American market. W. H. Egginton, later to become one of the most prolific inventors of new Lucas products and modifications, was sent to America to represent the firm at the factory, staying on for several years. He thus became the first overseas staff representative in Lucas history. The Bristol, Conn, operation was also the first attempt by Lucas to establish manufacture overseas, but it was not a success and came to an end in 1901.

Joseph's last visit to North America was in 1899, when he made the journey in company with a party of young lads who were emigrating to Canada from the Middlemore Homes in Birmingham. From the Hotel Victoria, Quebec, he wrote to Lear Caton, secretary of the Birmingham Temperance Society, on 8 July 1899, with his characteristic wry sense of humour:

Dear Caton,
   I am going well – and so is the money.

This is the only letter I have been able to trace in Joseph's handwriting. It contains words like 'allso' and 'som' that show his spelling had not improved with the passage of time. He had never been at ease with a pen. He once sent a message to someone saying 'he could talk his letter better than he could write it so he would bring it with him on his next visit'.

Joseph Lucas had by now become a father figure within the factory, admired and respected for his kindness and consideration. Little acts of thoughtfulness, unimportant in themselves, grew in significance when they were retold in the works and were quoted as typical of his character. For example, one day he saw one of his men, Fred Ansell, who had just been discharged from hospital, walking on the other side of the street. Joseph immediately crossed over, shook him by the hand, said how glad he was to see him looking better, gave his regards to his wife – and slipped a sovereign into his hand. If a girl turned up with a shabby pinafore he would give her the money to buy a new one. He knew all his workpeople by name.

But he expected a certain standard of decent behaviour in return. Once a workman received a rise in wages but said nothing about it. After a fortnight Joseph not only stopped the rise but deducted the two weeks' extra pay from the man's wages. The workman immediately asked why. Joseph told him that as he had said nothing, he thought he had not noticed it, and when the man tried to make an excuse he gruffly added: '. . . you'll have to wait to get it back now.'

In his sixties Joseph Lucas was described by one of his workpeople as a benevolent looking man of medium height, broad-shouldered, bearded, and seldom seen wearing a hat. Every Saturday (the factory worked a six-day week of course) he appeared in a 'clerical grey' knickerbocker suit, grey stockings and black shoes.

He carried his benevolence beyond the Tom Bowling Works into the neighbouring streets, where he was widely known as 'Joe'. He was fond of giving lectures at such places as the People's Hall and Lozell's Street Chapel. Before one of the Pleasant Sunday Afternoons for young people that were popular in those days he got a rather impish satisfaction by scandalising the regular chapel-goers with the announcement that the subject of his next lecture would be 'Tops and Bottoms'. Bottom was definitely a rude word in polite circles, but Joseph blandly explained that he was referring to the tops and bottoms of round loaves, and he went on to claim that if only two-thirds of the thousands of families in Birmingham wasted the top and bottom crust of each loaf once in 12 months, this would amount to x number of loaves which would feed y number of families. He ended with the grim warning that the working population of this country were the most wasteful in the world, and before they departed this life they would most surely want.

Careful with money himself (though he could be generous with others, as we have seen), Joseph Lucas disliked any sign of improvidence in his workpeople. He would not tolerate gambling. One unforgettable day he saw the name of a racehorse on a shop wall. He called a meeting of the entire staff to lecture them – and no one dared to stay away.

He lived in an age of texts, sayings and mottoes, his favourite becoming a watchword in the factory: 'Look after the complaints, the compliments will take care of themselves.' Others that he was fond of bringing out to drive home a point were:

No one can get the best out of others who is not himself doing his best.
Do the duty that lies nearest to you.
If you are at fault acknowledge it; this will gain respect from all.
Let the bank be your servant not your master.
The use of the present opportunity will decide your future.

Joseph Lucas had been a member of the Birmingham Temperance Society since 1877, when he paid a subscription of 5s and signed the society's pledge 'To abstain from all Intoxicating Liquor as a beverage and to discountenance its use by others'. Two years later he was elected to the committee and in 1888 he was put on the board of directors of the Temperance Hall Company, which helped to finance the Society as well as provide a home for their lectures and concerts. But Joseph was too busy to attend many meetings, and his name appeared mostly under the 'apologies for absence' heading in the Minute Book until 1898, when he tried to promote a scheme for a new headquarters of all temperance bodies in the centre of Birmingham. Now that Joseph Lucas, Limited, had been formed, he had more time for such outside interests.

Two years later he threw his weight behind a proposition to rebuild the Temperance Hall in Temple Street, canvassing prominent people in Birmingham for contributions after heading the list himself with a personal donation of £1,000. Even so, the target of close on £5,000 was not reached without Joseph giving an extra £250 to pay for a tiled dado in the entrance hall, and coming to the rescue at the last minute with a second mortgage of £1,000 on the old building.

The opening ceremony on 14 October 1901 was probably the most important public event in his life. Although the Lord Mayor, Alderman S. Edwards, presided, and the building was declared open by none other than the Rt Hon Joseph Chamberlain, MP, HM Secretary of State for the Colonies and Chancellor of Birmingham University, it was Joseph Lucas who was the real star of the day. His was the first portrait in the 36-page souvenir programme (price 3d), which began with the words: 'The work of rebuilding the Temperance Hall has been largely due in the first instance to the munificence of Mr. Joseph Lucas, and in the second to the generous donations of the other donors who have supplemented his effort.' The list published at the end, headed by the donation of £1,000 from Joseph, was followed by 100 guineas from Mr Ewen Harper, the architect, £100 from Anon J. C. (a fairly obvious pseudonym) and another £100 from Mr W. Houghton, with all the rest less than 50 guineas, and proved that this tribute to Joseph's generosity was no more than just. At the preliminary reception Joseph and his new wife, Mary Anne, accompanied the Lord Mayor and Lady Mayoress in token of his being Chairman of the Birmingham Temperance Hall Company Ltd and President of the Temperance Society. (Joseph's second wife, his cousin Maria, had died in July of the previous year, aged 67, and he was married for the third and last time to Mary Anne Owen, aged 50, spinster daughter of Samuel Owen, gentleman, at Yardley Wood Parish Church on 30 July 1901.)

After Joseph Chamberlain had opened the building with a special presentation key, the whole party adjourned to the Town Hall, where Joseph Lucas took the chair and gave an address. The audience included many of his workers, and they were delighted to see him on the platform – 'our Jo by the side of our Jo'. Then Joseph Chamberlain rose to give his address – which went on and on for $2\frac{3}{4}$ hours – and he was followed by a succession of people jumping up and down to move and second various votes of thanks.

Then began the Grand Temperance Week, with lectures and musical interludes every evening, Joseph being chairman of the In-augural Pleasant Saturday Evening when the programme included soprano and violin solos, an elocutionist, and the Clarion Glee Union. Admission, front row gallery, was 6d, gallery 3d, floor 2d.

It goes without saying that strict temperance was the order of the day at Little King Street and Great King Street – as was no smoking. It was fatal for any unfortunate worker to be seen emerging from the Burbury Arms or one of the other pubs in the neighbourhood. If he were spotted he would be followed back to his workshop. There Joseph would ask the foreman: 'Does that man work for you?' 'Yes'. 'Well, he don't no longer. I just met him coming out of the pub and anyone who thinks he can go drinking in his lunchtime don't work at Joseph Lucas. Finish him off.'

It was an old-established tradition in Birmingham for clubs and associations to hold their meetings in public houses, and it can be imagined how Joseph Lucas detested it. 'There's too much club business done in pubs,' he complained, and he arranged for the meetings of members of the Tin-Plate Workers Society to be held at the People's Hall in Hurst Street so that there would be no temptation for them to drink. It is only fair to point out that this dictatorial step was practicable because so many of the men in his employ were members of the Temperance Society. What, if any, pressure he put on them to join is not recorded.

But it should not be thought that being a teetoller detracted from Joseph's natural ebullience. As Harry wrote to a certain Mr Renouf: 'Our Mr. J.L. has dropped the blue ribbon but not his temperance principles, and if you could have seen him leading the entertainment at our Temperance Hall on the last Saturday of the old year you would have thought he needed no hard spirits from where to draw his inspiration.'

CHAPTER EIGHT

'THE KING' COMES HOME

From time to time after the formation of the company Joseph Lucas had bouts of illness. He could not attend the board meeting on 2 January 1899, and 18 months later he had to leave a meeting because he felt unwell. Nevertheless, he had every reason to feel satisfied with life as he sat back in his chair and surveyed the handful of shareholders who turned up for the fourth Annual General Meeting of the Company in the Great King Street offices on Monday, 3 November 1902. He began his own speech on an equivocal note. 'The remarks I am going to make are neither of an optimistic nor pessimistic nature,' he said, explaining that 'we are passing just now through the early experiences of the cycle trade in reference to the motor trade, and we are trying to follow as far as possible the same policy as we did then in producing articles of a reliable character.' Once again the Lucas policy boiled down to one word, quality.

Through charging all the costs of developing 'the Motoralities business' (horns, pumps, lamps and various articles for motor-cars) against the year's profits instead of spreading them over a period, they had had to reduce the dividend on the Ordinary Shares from 6 to 5 per cent, but, as Walter Chamberlain reminded the meeting from the Chair: 'We are in a very sound financial position indeed – there is a sum at the Bankers of £17,000 and £3,000 invested in Lancashire & Yorkshire Railway stock, money that we were able to put on one side.'

Not even Harry's usual wet-blanket speech could damp Joseph's sense of well-being – 'I am not going to prophesy because I do not know. I simply said last year that we would promise to do our best, and I can repeat that promise. This is all that I think I can safely say; we are hoping, more than that we do not know.' What was sending a glow of anticipatory pleasure through Joseph was the thought that in a few days' time he would be leaving the November skies of Great King Street and Moseley for a combined holiday and business journey to the Mediterranean with his newly married wife, Mary Anne, his youngest son, Bernard, and his daughter-in-law.

His little party left England on Thursday, 6 November. After calling at various ports in the Mediterranean, they visited Egypt, where they spent some time before starting the voyage home. Just before Christmas 1902 the steamer called at Naples, and a few days later Harry and the family in Birmingham were alarmed to receive a telegram from the Hotel Bristol in that city telling them that Joseph had been taken ill. This was followed by another on Saturday, 27 December, giving them the brief but tragic news that he had died that day of typhoid fever. Upholding his pledge to abstain from taking intoxicating drink as a beverage, Joseph Lucas had shunned the customary wine and had drunk the local water – in a city where typhoid fever was endemic.

There could be no question of his being buried in Italy. Plans were put in hand for a great funeral and interment at Moseley Parish Church, where he would be buried in a coffin and with a service both worthy of his position. Meanwhile a temporary coffin had to be provided for the return of the body to its native land. The story is still told in at least one part of the Lucas family (whether it is apocryphal or not I cannot say) that a large packing case used for carrying samples of the King of the Road and the Silver King – for Joseph Lucas was not the man to spend all that money on pleasure travelling without doing some commercial travelling as well – was adapted for the purpose. And thus, according to this family legend, the 'King of the Road' himself came home, in a style of which I like to think he himself would have approved with a chuckle – economically, slightly shockingly, and advertising his famous cycle lamps on his last earthly journey.

In contrast to the life and bustle around them, the red-brick factories of Joseph Lucas, Limited, in Little King Street and Great King Street were as still and silent as if it had been the Sabbath on Wednesday, 14 January 1903. All were closed so that the workpeople could pay their last respects to 'Old Joe' – and nobody lost any wages.

In order to accommodate as many people as possible, the Church of England funeral service was held in the New Temperance Hall in the centre of the city. The place was crammed – there were deputations from the various societies and institutions Joseph had been connected with, as well as many of his workpeople – and Chopin's Funeral March was played as they took their places. To the dismay of the family, Harry Lucas turned up wearing a red tie. ('Mourning won't help,' he said afterwards – he had always considered it sheer waste for poor people to spend money they could ill afford on lavish funerals and mourning, and this was his chance to rub the lesson home.)

Then came the first hymn, 'Tell me not in mournful numbers,

Life is but an empty dream!' with the verse that all present regarded as the appropriate epitaph for Joseph Lucas:

> Lives of great men all remind us
> We can make our lives sublime,
> And, departing, leave behind us
> Footprints on the sands of time.

Joseph Lucas had shared the Victorian love of church music, so the service included his favourite hymns: 'He liveth long who liveth well' (sung to the tune of 'Old Hundredth') and 'Lead, Kindly Light'. Then Miss Nellie Pritchard, the soprano who had sung so often at his Pleasant Saturday Evenings, sang 'O Rest in the Lord' and was followed by the Birmingham Temperance Philharmonic Choir rendering 'No Shadows Beyond'. And as the bier was carried from the Hall the organ intoned the Dead March in 'Saul'.

The family mourners were followed to their waiting carriages by the deputations and the rest of the congregation. The long *cortège* then set off through the streets of Birmingham for Moseley Parish Church and the interment.

The dark-red granite tomb is one of the largest in the old churchyard. The main inscription reads: 'In ever loving memory of Joseph Lucas of Moseley who passed away at Naples December 27th 1902 and was buried here January 14th 1903 aged 68 years. O Rest in the Lord. Do noble things, not dream them, all day long, and so make life, death and that vast forever one grand sweet song.'

In his 41-page will Joseph Lucas left the sum of £4,000 to three special trustees to form the Joseph Lucas Trust with the object of maintaining the Birmingham Temperance Hall and 'towards the expenses incurred in the diffusion of the principles and practice of total abstinence from alcoholic liquors among the inhabitants of the city of Birmingham and its neighbourhood . . .' He also gave £200 each to officials of the Temperance Society and of such organisations as the Birmingham Band of Hope Union.

But he did not forget his faithful friends among his workpeople, and to each of the following he left £50:

John Perry, the elder
John Perry, the younger, lampmaker
– Midgeley, order clerk and warehouseman

E. Danks, toolmaker
George Vickery, press toolmaker
Charles Hopkins, machinist
Lucy Medcraft, warehousewoman
Emily Innes, manageress of the rough warehouse of the said Company
James Parsons, metal spinner
Thomas Randall, foreman
William Pearce
William Broadbent
George Taylor, foreman
John Skeldon
– Jackson, foreman of shop formerly under supervision of Albert Greaves
George Richards, invoice clerk

To Roland Atkins, order clerk, he left £100, and he even remembered the chaplain of Smedley's Hydropathic Establishment at Matlock, where he had been a frequent visitor for so many years, with a legacy of £200.

The major part of his £92,000 estate went to his family – his wife, sons, daughters, grandchildren, nephews and nieces.

When Joseph Lucas died, he was publicly mourned as the figurehead of a small but famous Birmingham company and as a worthy citizen of that city and all it stood for. A plaque was put up in the new Temperance Hall by his workpeople 'as a token of the respect and high esteem in which he was held by them'. But that was all. The passage of time – and the subsequent enormous growth of the company (still bearing his name) he formed with such enterprise and wisdom – have increased his stature to that of an archetypal Victorian manufacturer.

Born three years before the young Victoria came to the throne in 1837, Joseph Lucas spent the whole of his lifetime under her reign, outliving his Queen by only one year. When her Golden and Diamond Jubilees were celebrated in 1887 and 1897 (the year of his own modest maturity, when Joseph Lucas, Limited, was incorporated as a company), he could look back at the changes in the condition of the people brought about since the 'hungry forties' he remembered as a child. Some of these changes had their origins in the improvements in civic enterprise propagated by the hero of his boyhood and youth, George Dawson, and enacted by Joseph Chamberlain in the 1870s with such effect that Birmingham became an example to the rest of the country – and to the world. Others lay in the more humane outlook towards the working people that now prevailed, a change in which he himself played a small but significant part. Life, though still hard for many, was vastly improved for most, compared with the early years of Victoria's reign. There was more food, more clothing, more furniture, while household amenities were improving – though very slowly – as oil and gas lighting gave way to electricity, as there was more gas for cooking, and sanitation was modernised.

Finally, in the 1890s had come the boom in bicycling as the replacement of the high Ordinary by the Safety had sent thousands of people – men and women – into the great countryside in search of adventure, exercise and the pleasure of discovering a new world. Their arrival did not disturb the peace and slow tempo of country lanes and roads. The noise and speed of cars, motor-cycles, lorries, buses, coaches – and their convenience – would not be seen in Queen Victoria's reign, nor in Joseph Lucas's lifetime.

But the internal combustion engine was to be at the root of his company's future growth.

The Lucas stand at the 1896 Cycle Show

A FIRE-SIDE CHAT

COMMERCIAL SIDE OF LIFE.

———————

TO-NIGHT I purpose giving you a free-and-easy fireside sort of chat, which I intend mainly for you young men and women who have just started or are about to start in life.

While what I have to say is chiefly on the commercial side, I trust I am sufficiently well known to you for it to be understood that I do not undervalue the religious side, but

———————

To my mind, the most contemptible persons to do business with are those who *can* pay, but who mean to sweat out the last fraction of interest before they will give you their cheque. I used to do business with a man of this character, whose name was Potter. He would go away on a holiday, and leave all accounts till he came back. On one occasion he found on his return several applications from me, and as it was St. Valentine's Eve, he coolly wrote thus :—

> " The man who craves for cash of mine
> Must not hope to be my trade's Valentine."

I answered :—

> " A man for his wit may be admired,
> But he should pay for work that has tired ;
> For puns or wit, whate'er their rank,
> Won't pass for credit at the Bank.
> The lack of this puts me about,
> So now shut up, and potter out."

Mary Lucas, Joseph's widow, published his 'Fireside Chat' privately a few years after his death (*extracts*)

PART THREE

PEACE AND WAR

LUCAS'S
✢ MISSING LAMP SCHEME. ✢

LUCKY MAN!

"Hallo, old chap! Off for a holiday?"
"Yes" I've just landed a fiver in Lucas's
Missing Lamp Scheme.   "*Cycling*."

We launched this Scheme after the publication of our Catalogs last season, and consequently too late to be widely known and understood.

We shall continue it for 1894 as described below, and believe it will materially assist in the recovery of Stolen Lamps and Cycles.

During the past season several losses of Lamps and Cycles have been reported to us, and in one instance a Lamp was recovered, although the thief was not found.

We hope to have the pleasure, during 1894, of paying out some rewards, as well as being the means of recovering the stolen property.

→✥·✥←

FIRSTLY AS TO STOLEN LAMPS:—

Our 1894 pattern "KING OF THE ROAD" is numbered on the top part of the Lamp and our 1893 pattern "HOLOPHOTE" and "ALUMOPHOTE" Lamps, are numbered on the nickeled part over the sliding side glass, for the purpose of identification.

If one of these is stolen, either from or with a Cycle, we shall offer—

A REWARD OF FIVE POUNDS

for the recovery of the Lamp and conviction of the thief.

SECONDLY AS TO STOLEN CYCLES:—

In the case of the theft of a Cycle fitted with one of the said Lamps, AND one of the Bells mentioned below, we offer—

A REWARD OF TEN POUNDS

for the recovery of the property and conviction of the thief.

The Bells we refer to are—The "King of Bells," No. 60   The "Combination," No. 42c; The "Challis," No. 50c; The "Cyclarm," No. 53; and The "Favorite," No. 58.

The owner of the stolen Lamp or Cycle must have previously filled up the form supplied with the above-mentioned articles and send it to us when a theft is reported,
If the owner discovers the thief himself, we shall pay him the whole of the £5 or £10 Reward, on satisfactory proof to us of the conviction. But when another person is the means of bringing the thief to justice, we shall pay half the amount to him, and half to the owner.
We reserve to ourselves the right of deciding to whom the money shall be paid.
This scheme relates only to Lamps and Cycles in use in Great Britain and Ireland, and not when stolen from an Agent's or Dealer's stock.
In case we find it necessary or desirable to alter or cancel this scheme, we shall do so by advertisement in some or all of the Cycle Papers, in which our advertisements usually appear.

JOS. LUCAS & SON, Little King Street, BIRMINGHAM.

Publicity in 1894. The Lucas Missing Lamp Scheme became a talking point
with cyclists throughout the country

CHAPTER ONE

'MOTORALITIES'

Although Joseph Lucas only lived to see the very early days of motoring, he had something to say about the company's prospects in this new market at the annual general meeting in November 1902, a month before he died: 'As far as we can see before us,' he said, 'we have every reason to believe that we shall have a fair share of the Motoralities business as it develops, and it is our duty to follow that business as closely as possible as it runs in the same groove as the cycle trade, and we do not want to follow anything outside our own business but to follow closely anything that will lead up in the same tenor.'

The Motoralities business at that time was of course very small – in fact the company had only just gone into it when Joseph died – because motor-cars were still very thin on the ground. To put the scene in perspective, it is worthwhile glancing briefly at the development of the motor-car up to this point.

From its beginning as the steam coach in the first part of the nineteenth century the self-propelled road vehicle had always been opposed by vested interests in Britain. First the landed gentry, through their control of the Turnpike Trusts, imposed a discriminatory toll of £2 on steam coaches compared with only 3s for a horse-drawn coach. Then, when the tolls were equalised in 1860, the railways (through the Locomotive Act) succeeded in restricting the speed of road vehicles to a miserable 4mph in the country and 2mph in the towns. Even when the need for a man with a red flag to walk in front of the road vehicle was abolished in 1878, the same deliberately crippling speed limits were continued until 1896, when the limit was raised to 14mph (which local authorities could, and did, reduce to 12mph).

The result was that in the formative years of the motor-car from 1860 to 1890 most British engineers were so inhibited by legislation that all the real progress in producing practical motor-cars was made abroad, particularly in Germany and France. Fortunately Britain had a few irrepressibly inventive men like Frederick Lanchester, who made the first all-British four-wheel petrol-driven motor-car in 1894–5, and Herbert Austin, who turned from making Wolseley sheep-shearing machines to the prototype Wolseley three-wheeler in 1894. But they did not make much progress in terms of production, and efforts to make British cars in the last few years of the nineteenth century were overshadowed by a new threat, this time from lawsuits resulting from the attempted monopoly of motor-car patents by H. J. Lawson and his associates in the British Motor Syndicate. It was not surprising that most of the motor-cars in use at this time were imported from the Continent. But there were not very many of them – the first one, a Benz, was imported in 1894 – and this was evident at the inaugural meeting of the Automobile Club of Great Britain and Ireland (the nucleus of the Royal Automobile Club) in 1897, which was attended by 163 people, who probably comprised most of the motor-car owners in the land. The founder of the club was F. R. Simms, whose name was to be linked with Lucas long after his death.

The motor-car first became a topic of national discussion in Britain in 1896, when hopes of the speed limit being increased to 12 or 14mph were raised by the Light (Road) Locomotives Bill. In May that year two rival shows were put on – an International Horseless Carriage Exhibition by the ambitious Lawson at the Imperial Institute, London, and a demonstration of motor-cars organised at the Crystal Palace by Sir David Salomans, an amateur whose only object was to spread the gospel of automobilism (he had already held an exhibition of motor-cars at Tunbridge Wells the year before).

The Bill became an Act of Parliament on 4 November 1896, and Lawson, always the opportunist, immediately organised the Motor Car Tour from London to Brighton, which was described as the First Meet of the Motor Car Club (a euphemism for his British Motor Syndicate, Limited). Motor-cars were still regarded as horseless carriages, so the word 'Meet' was not out of context.

There were so few motor-cars available in Britain to take part in the run that Lawson had to get H. O. Duncan, an Englishman living in Paris, to bring over some of the leading French automobilists to swell the field. Even so, only thirty-two vehicles assembled on the damp and foggy morning of 14 November outside the Hotel Metropole in Northumberland Avenue, London, where the drivers fortified themselves with a 'récherché luncheon' before setting off at 10 o'clock. Nevertheless it was the biggest collection of horseless carriages ever seen on the roads of England, and they were watched by a large and excited crowd. The Brighton road was rough and muddy and it rained all day, but the event was a propaganda triumph and the motor-car was talked about as never before. By the turn of the century Riley, Lagonda, Humber, Napier and Sunbeam had joined Lanchester and Wolseley as makers of British motor-cars, and the number of cars in use had grown to about 2,000. Among the pioneers was Harry Lucas, who bought his first car – one of the first twenty in Birmingham – in 1899. I have not been able to trace the make.

But whereas the Emancipation Run, as the London to Brighton event came to be called, was something of a publicity stunt, the 1,000 Miles Trial organised by the Automobile Club in 1900 was a controlled test of speed, hill-climbing capacity and reliability that demonstrated the real capabilities of the motor-car as a serious form of transport.

The 1,000-mile route took the competitors all over the country from London to Bristol, Birmingham (where their passing was doubtless noted with keen interest by Joseph and Harry Lucas), Manchester, Kendal (with an optional attempt to climb Shap Fell), Carlisle, Edinburgh (the turning point), Newcastle, Leeds, Sheffield, Nottingham, and so back to London. Of the sixty-five cars that started, thirty-five returned to Marble Arch nearly three weeks later (there were rest days *en route*, when the cars were exhibited to the public), and the event was voted an enormous success, even if it had little effect on the lamentably slow development of the entirely British designed motor-car.

Joseph and Harry Lucas, ever on the look-out for new markets, were quick to spot the potentialities of the horseless carriage as a vehicle for their lamps and other accessories. As Joseph had told the shareholders at the annual general meeting in 1902, it was the experimental costs of developing the Motoralities business that were to a large extent responsible for the reduction in profits and the drop in the dividend.

What did this new business consist of? In his speech Joseph had mentioned horns, pumps, lamps, etc, under the collective term Motoralities, 'our registered word'. (To digress for a moment, this was obviously another of Harry's rather laborious inventions. He had registered 'Cyclealities' as a trade mark in 1897 – it had already been in use for some time – followed by 'Autocalities' and 'Motoralities' in March 1901. Several years later, in 1910, he was to register the word 'Electricalities' to cover the complete electrical lighting sets that superseded petroleum and acetylene lamps, and in the 1920s the word 'Batteryalities' was invented. Although not normally given to seeing the humorous side of things, especially when it concerned himself, Harry did poke fun at his obsession for coining elaborate trade names by producing a leaflet in 1896 headed 'All Good VELOCIPED-ESTRIANISTICALARIANS use Lucas Cyclealities'.)

Motoralities were first offered for sale in the Lucas catalogue for

1902, but they naturally took second place to the cycle accessories and were put at the back of the book. The first Lucas motor headlight burned petroleum and all the lamps were called simply 'Lucas', but in 1903 the King of the Road label was given to a new headlight burning acetylene gas and having other improvements 'which make all other Motor Head Lamps old-fashioned'. There was also the acetylene Motor Luminator, introduced the previous year for motor-cycles and *voiturettes*, or light cars, while conservative motor-cyclists could still buy an oil-burning Holophote King of the Road. The motor horns were all of the bugle type, with a loop between the bulb and the mouth. Then there were several models of motor pumps, a girder wrench, tyre repair outfits, tyre valves, lifting jacks, Wells-Lucas Motoil ('no gum, no char, no stick, no acid, no dirt') manufactured by the Henry Wells Oil Company of Manchester, for whom Lucas were sole agents, lubricators of various sizes, oilers, and sundries, including a grease injector. The jingle for Motoil was inspired by George Johnston's slogan a few years earlier for the Arrol-Johnston car (one of the first cars owned by Harry Lucas) – 'No noise, no smell, no dirt and no vibration'.

The 1903 catalogue appeared in January, just as the thoughts of everyone at the factory were fixed on the funeral of Joseph Lucas. But business had to go on, including the preparations for the Lucas stand in the China Court at Crystal Palace, where the newly formed Society of Motor Manufacturers & Traders were about to stage their first London Motor Show from 30 January to 7 February. It was an ambitious undertaking, twice the area of the Paris Salon de l'Automobile and with more than 200 exhibitors. A large fleet of demonstration cars gave trial runs to prospective customers round the grounds of the Crystal Palace.

Motor-cycling, too, was becoming increasingly popular, forming an additional market for Joseph Lucas in between the bicycle and the motor-car. In the five years from 1898 to 1903 no fewer than fifty-five separate makes of motor-cycle were advertised from time to time, though some of them of course were short-lived.

The beginning of 1903 was therefore a climacteric in the history of Joseph Lucas, Limited. It saw the change from a business wholly based on the cycle trade into one in which Motoralities and Motor-cyclealities would play an increasing part. It saw the death of the founder, and the end of his shrewd and pervading influence on policy and people.

And it left Harry very much on his own.

CHAPTER TWO

HARRY AT THE WHEEL

When Harry Lucas returned to Great King Street on the day after his father's funeral, he was faced with the prospect of controlling the company virtually single-handed, for he was now the only executive director. This did not worry him much, because he had been running the place largely on his own for some time, though he would miss the discussions with his father on the overall strategy of the company and the innate wisdom and experience that Joseph had brought to them. And of course he had lost the man for whom he had felt a life-long affection of peculiar intensity. But the ultimate responsibility for the company had rested more and more on his shoulders as Joseph – understandably in a man approaching three score years and ten – had taken life easier and become more involved in such practical good works as serving on the Board of Guardians of the Poor and opening a cabmen's shelter near his home at Moseley, which he donated to the City Mission – his last official appearance. 'Gaffer Harry', as Harry was called in the factory at this time, was described by one of his workmen as 'a tall, ascetic-looking man, bearded, with a twitch in his right eye'. He was 48.

The company's dependence on Harry Lucas could not be allowed to go on for long, so in the spring of 1903 he was made chairman and managing director and Bernard Steeley, his brother-in-law, who had been working in the company for some time, was appointed to the board as his assistant managing director. The two Walters, Chamberlain and Wiggin, completed the board as non-executive directors. This was the team that was to run the company throughout the Edwardian years and up to the outbreak of and during World War I. It was a time of steady, then accelerated growth, and for the purposes of this history it will be convenient to deal in turn with the various aspects of the company during the whole of this period.

Having started at board level, so to speak, let us see first of all how the young company was faring financially. The guarded statements made by Joseph and Harry at the annual general meeting at the end of 1902 indicated that it was not exactly bounding ahead. Indeed, since the first balance sheet for the financial year ending 31 July 1898, the nett profit and the dividend on the ordinary shares had shown an overall downward trend from £27,129 and 7½ per cent respectively to a nett profit of £11,009 and a dividend of 5 per cent in 1902. Since the sales were almost the same in both years (the figures were actually £97,000-odd, but they were not disclosed in the annual company reports in those days), this cut of nearly 60 per cent in the nett profit might have been viewed with some alarm if it had been purely a reflection of the state of the cycle trade (cycling was in fact still booming, the membership of the Cyclists Touring Club having reached a peak of 60,499 in 1899). But though more intense competition – and leaner profit margins – in the cycle trade probably played a part in reducing the Lucas profit in 1902, the major cause was undoubtedly the decision to write off all the development costs of the Motoralities which were launched in that year, instead of spreading them over a period.

From the beginning the board were concerned about widening the influence of the company, which tended to be too concentrated on Birmingham and the Midlands. The first step was to open an office in London at No 1 Dyers Buildings, Holborn, in 1898, and this was followed soon after Joseph's death in 1902 by a London showroom at No 224 Shaftesbury Avenue (which cost £300 a year for a seven-year lease) to expand the Motoralities business. These locations were not chosen haphazardly. The London office in Holborn was next to Holborn Viaduct, where nearly every other showroom was the London depot of Coventry and Birmingham cycle-makers. The Motoralities showroom in Shaftesbury Avenue was in a new building nearly opposite the splendid showrooms of the Daimler Company, and only 200yd from Long Acre, where every available shop was occupied by London agents of French motor-car makers. (Long Acre had also been the centre of the coach-building trade for 200 years).

In 1904 the company's sales and profits started to climb sharply and continued to do so until 1907. By that time the sales had soared from just under £100,000 in 1903 to nearly £174,000, and the profit had doubled from £11,000 to £23,000, encouraging the ever cautious board to raise the dividend on the ordinary shares to 7½ per cent. (An incidental event at this time was the granting of an official quotation on the company's ordinary shares on the London Stock Exchange at the end of 1906.)

These were crucial years in the trading history of the company, because they marked simultaneous changes in the two main markets for its goods. The overall position was clarified by Harry Lucas at the annual general meeting in 1906 when he said: 'We have now practically *two* businesses, one which we call the Cyclealities business and the other, the newer development, the Motoralities business', and Walter Chamberlain went so far as to prophesy that 'the Motoralities business may increase to a considerable extent' – which with hindsight would seem to have been the understatement of the year.

What in fact was happening in 1906–7 was that the popularity of cycling as a pastime had reached a plateau from which it would gradually fall away (membership of the Cyclists Touring Club was going to drop to 40,000 by 1910), while the motor-car had gained a firm place in the life of the nation. After the long years of repression at the end of the century motoring had been encouraged by the Motor Car Act of 1903, which raised the speed limit to 20mph while stipulating that every car must be registered with the County Council and carry number plates (illuminated at the rear). By 1904 several British makers were turning out five or six cars a week each, and there were 8,500 cars on the roads. In 1905 the Motor Show was held at Olympia for the first time, and there were 434 different models of private cars on display.

In the following year a young Member of Parliament named Winston Churchill was moved to say at a public dinner that one of the most striking things to his mind was the extraordinary rapidity with which automobilism had overspread the national life since the start of the century. 'Five years ago', he said, 'a motor-car was an object of derision if it stopped for one moment; now the horses have got used to them, the asses have got used to them, and we see them on every road.'

The motor-car was seen to be really accepted in 1906 when it was used almost universally as transport in the General Election. That summer it was possible for the first time to hire a chauffeur-driven car and tour any part of the British Isles (for £5 a day plus the chauffeur's meals). The number of cars on the road rose to 45,000 and the Motor Show held at Olympia at the end of the year was attended by nearly 200,000 people. The rapid progress noted by Winston Churchill in 1905 continued in 1906 and 1907, when several motoring events of historic importance took place – the opening of Brooklands Track and S. F. Edge's 24-hour run there at 60mph, the Pekin-to-Paris motor tour, and the appearance of the fabulous Rolls-Royce Silver Ghost, which set a new standard of superlative quality and effortless motoring. By now there were some 60,000 cars in use and an Act was passed compelling them to carry lights at night – cars were not supplied with lights by their makers so this was good for the sale of Lucas lamps. In that year the British cycle factories produced 624,000 machines. And so, with a strong business in the still prosperous cycle trade, the growing motor-cycle trade and the booming motor-car trade, the company was sitting pretty in 1907.

Harry's firm control of the company's finances (based on his experience in building up the business of Joseph Lucas & Son) was made abundantly clear to the shareholders every year. In 1907, for example, he told them: 'From the very commencement we have exercised a stringently sound and careful financial policy, never giving away today what we might want tomorrow.' Twelve months later (10 years after the formation of the company) he was able to announce '... our solid assets, without reckoning the item set down for goodwill, are now sufficient to account for the whole of our capital', and three years later (1911), when the profit was £28,179 and the sales were £220,488, he had the satisfaction of telling the shareholders that the £55,572 allowed for the goodwill of the business had been wiped out. In the following year the profit reached a peak of £31,472, but by the time war broke out a few weeks after the 1914 financial year ended it had dropped to £25,628 – less than the profit achieved in the first year of the company's existence in 1898 – from sales amounting to £289,933.

A valuable result of this careful husbanding of resources was the ability to pay for new factory buildings with their own money without increasing the authorised capital of the company. With the growth in motoring the demand for motor-car lamps and accessories could only be met by building more factory space, and throughout the Edwardian years the Great King Street-Burbury Street-Farm Street triangle continued to be developed. The interior factories were put up first, followed by the Burbury Street factory, then Great King Street on the side adjoining the triangle, and the casting shop with its 100ft chimney. Then came Farm Street, of which Mr Archer, the builder, was particularly proud. 'I contend it was the quickest job ever done in Birmingham', he said, remembering the event in 1955. 'Four months to take down thirty slums and build a factory of 54,000 sq. ft. with a million bricks.' That was in 1910. Some of the buildings were six storeys high.

In time Harry Lucas was able to report that the company owned the whole of the land forming the triangle

... with the exception of the bit on which the public house [the Burbury Arms] stands at the corner of Burbury Street and Farm Street, and we

The Lucas Portrait Gallery: Joseph and Harry were great believers in teamwork and never kept the limelight to themselves

Jobs at Joseph Lucas & Son were eagerly sought by men and women alike because the firm was regarded as a reliable and considerate employer. Points of interest in these photographs taken in 1893 are the timekeeping discs which indicate the size of the payroll and the wagonette in which Harry and his sister, Louisa, drove to the works from their house in Stoney Lane

A NEW FOREST HOSTELRY.

(above) Cyclists at play in the 1880s. The Lucas King of the Road lamp, introduced in 1878, can be seen slung below the hub of the Ordinary, or penny-farthing. In this position the light was kept near the road

(below) Harry Lucas (seated on the ground at the extreme left) was a keen member of the Birmingham Tricycle Club, pictured here at a social meet

own practically all the property, which includes a pawn shop, but the fates have so far saved us from the ownership of either the Public House or the Beer Shop. In addition to this triangle, we now hold a large block of freehold small house property on the other side of this street (Great King Street) ... We have bought these properties because we have faced the possibility of wanting land for extensions which could not be provided for in the triangle, and it seemed to us that it would be unwise to use up all our available land before making sure that further extensions are possible in case they prove to be required.

Little did he know then how soon those extensions would be needed.

Harry Lucas used the annual general meetings and the printed reports of them to press home his views on national problems. Pages of the reports were devoted to the evils of Free Trade and the need for Tariff Reform, especially as they affected the competition the company experienced from foreign-made goods (often copied from Lucas designs), which were unashamedly dumped in Britain and sold without profit when the demand for them in their home countries slackened. He backed his general complaint with specific examples, as in this case:

A few years ago a foreign firm put a competitive line of goods on the English market at such exceedingly low prices that made us, in this business, wonder at them. We got into communication with the firm, and they then offered the goods to us on condition that we took the lot. Here are their letters, and this is what they say: 'We are willing to admit that we overproduced quite largely on certain lines last season, and as so many of the manufacturers on this side are in the habit of doing, we intended using your market for our surplus stock. We take the liberty of sending you a few samples, with prices marked, thinking it might be more to your interest to take these goods at these figures than to make them in your own plant. We believe any manufacturer would find these prices below the actual cost of production'. The firm concluded their very candid letters and very remarkable admissions with the threat that they would have to break the market with the goods if we did not take them ourselves. It is not our policy to buy foreign goods such as we ought to make ourselves, so they were, as the firm threatened, dumped on the English market. I know that free traders generally like this sort of thing, because they say that the country gets the benefit of it, so I make them a present of the facts. But I think the employed, as well as the unemployed, will see in these letters some very suggestive food for thought. They will see that our very-open-door policy allows foreign manufacturers to do just what they like with our home market. It encourages them in speculative over-production, because they know they can dump when it suits them, or break our market with unfair prices, and they can harass British manufacturers generally. And it must be plain that this sort of thing, which in the first instance hits manufacturers, must sooner or later be bad for work people, this is why our foreign competitors protect themselves against such unfair competition.

He also protested against the introduction of the Insurance Bill, declaring that 'it will not reduce poverty, but it will make many people more dependable [dependent?], less inclined to be self-reliant, and in this alone the effect will be very, very bad indeed . . . we have a most useful combined Sick & Benevolent Society which is excellently managed by the work people themselves.' One wonders what he would have said about some of the workings of the Welfare State.

It is time we moved away from the boardroom and shareholders' meetings to take a closer look at the products of the company in these pre-World War I years and the conditions in which they were made.

CHAPTER THREE

OIL . . . ACETYLENE . . . ELECTRICITY

In the same way that the bicycle had settled down to the basic (Safety) design, so the Cyclealities that Lucas sold for it showed little change in the dozen years between Joseph Lucas's death in 1902 and the outbreak of World War I. Some of the Lucas cycle lamps – the Acetyphote (introduced in 1903), the Silver King (with its large brother the Holophote), the Lucent, and the Pathfinder – continued throughout the period, and were joined by such new models as the acetylene Calcia and Calcia King, Colonia and Colonia King, Aceta and Aceta Major, Lucia and Lustra, and the oil-burning Leader; but some old favourites like the Luminator, the Microphote, the Pioneer, the Club and the Planet dropped out of the catalogue. The acetylene King of the Road was called the KORA from 1909 onwards.

'Progressive' cyclers were all for acetylene lamps, others clung firmly to oil, so Lucas obligingly made a full range of both kinds. A special model of the Silver King was made for petroleum, which had the great advantage of burning for a long time. Some diehards even persisted in demanding candle lamps, so Lucas supplied these, too, until 1912. Rear lamps and reflectors appeared for the first time in the 1909 catalogue, their purpose being 'to protect Cyclers from being run down by Motorists'. One of them, the Rubia, mounted on the front fork, burned acetylene and combined the function of a headlight and a rearlight in one lamp. It seems to have been dropped after a couple of years, but was revived after the war. The Motor Acetyphote for motor-cycles was produced in the early part of the decade.

Thanks to some notes (possibly by Bernard Steeley) in the margins of a 1907 catalogue that has survived, we know the number of cycle lamps produced in the seven months from 1 September 1906 to 6 April 1907. Looking at the list below, what seems odd today is the large number of models supplied, but this of course was in the days of batch production, before assembly line production took over and the need for standardisation subordinated the individual preferences of customers.

Nevertheless the figures were evidently closely watched, for alongside some of the lamps with poor sales were pencilled the ominous comments 'out', 'omit', 'exit', and 'to die'. The same decisions must have been made about other Cyclealities that disappeared from the

Lamp	Price	Quantity
Silver King of the Road	10s 0d	14,131
King of the Road	8s 6d–10s 6d	5,402
New Holophote	12s 6d	2,084
Petroleum Silver King	10s 6d	1,277
Mediophote	7s 6d	1,507
Pioneer	7s 0d	2,026
Club	5s 6d	4,505
Captain	5s 0d	15,037
Kinglet	4s 0d–5s 0d	7,406
Leader	3s 0d	11,481
Pathfinder	3s 6d	9,247
Lucent	2s 0d–2s 6d	20,152
Candle lamp	8s 6d	1,434
Keros (petroleum)	9s 6d	505
Total cycle lamps		96,194

Lucas catalogues during the Edwardian period. Brooks' saddles, factored for over 20 years, were dropped in 1907, and other long-established lines that were quietly allowed to go were tyre valves, puncture repair outfits, toolbags, enamel, toe clips, trouser clips, and rifle clips. Celluloid mudguards were tried for a time, and a front-rim brake that lasted only a year. Only the range of bicycle bells continued almost unchanged, but with an important addition that will 'ring a bell' in some older readers' minds – the revolving dome bell which the present writer can clearly recall as a boyhood memory more than half-a-century ago, so insistent was its silvery jingling. Other accessories that sold consistently throughout were pumps, carriers, girder wrenches, oil cans, lubricating and lamp oil, lamp wick and carbide.

More important changes – and what mainly occupied Harry Lucas's mind during this time – occurred in the design of motor-car lamps. As we have seen, the first Lucas headlamps for cars in 1902 burned petroleum (though there was also the acetylene Luminator for motorcycles and *voiturettes*), but in the following year the pattern was set of acetylene for headlamps and petroleum for side and back lights that was to last for several years. The King of the Road headlamp burned coated carbide 'to moderate the gas production' and lasted 5–8 hours on one charge, according to model. The cheapest sold for £12 5s 0d and the most expensive cost £15 10s 0d. As the pound of 1900 was worth about ten times as much as the pound of 1975, it is clear that these lamps were luxuries.

The first headlamps were made like cycle lamps in one unit with the acetylene generator. The next step was to sell a pair of 'projectors' burning ordinary carbide connected by rubber tubing to a separate generator mounted on the running board. These projectors appeared in 1905 as an alternative to the headlamps, which now included a new model, the Autolite, for small cars. The set of two Lucas projectors and a generator cost £9 (all brass) or £10 (all plated).

But the self-contained headlamp was by no means finished, and in 1907 the King of the Road Duplex headlight was announced with a double carbide chamber which provided 'a reserve charge to meet the emergency of an extra long run or unexpected exhaustion of the charge in use, the second charge being instantly available'. There were more than 400 separate parts in this massive headlamp. Behind the statement that 'an extended series of experiments has enabled us to receive several patents for the improvements which we embody in this new model' lay the testing of prototype lamps carried out by Harry Lucas in which he not unnaturally sought to involve the company in paying something towards the considerable sum of money he spent on his motor-car. This was only right and proper – as the board readily agreed – because without Harry's personal testing of lamps on night runs the company would never have been able to market a substantial range of headlights and projectors at the critical moment when the motor-car was gaining popularity.

The double carbide chamber idea of the Duplex headlamp was extended to the separate generator supplied with two projectors in 1908, and in the same year a Mangin lens mirror was fitted to both the projectors and the self-contained headlamps. This improvement was claimed 'to provide the motorist with a sufficiency of light and avoid the terrible glare from the car which dazzles cyclists and pedestrians and frightens horses.'

The marked catalogue gives us the production figures of these lamps for the seven months from September 1906 to April 1907:

Lamp	Price range	Quantity
King of the Road Duplex headlight	£7 to £10 10 0d	1,312
King of the Road projectors and separate generator	£10 to £10 15 0d	328
Autolite headlight	£4 10 0d to £5	871
King of the Road side lamps (pair)	£2 2 0d to £4 10 0d	6,248
King of the Road tail light	19s 0d to £1 15 0d	3,543

Lamp	Price range	Quantity
King of the Road Commercial		
Vehicle lamp	£1 10 0d	86
Ditto tail lamp	£1 1 0d	64

The high proportion of motorists who apparently contented themselves with buying side lamps is interesting. Whatever their reasons
may have been, what is beyond doubt is that in 1907 Lucas made no
fewer than five different ranges of side lamps with twenty different
models. They were all large and handsome lamps between 10 and
12in tall, with handles on top, and they were carried on standard
brackets on each side of the scuttle, clear of the windscreen. With 4½
or 5¼in glasses, some with lenses, their petroleum burners gave a light
which many motorists found sufficient for the low speeds at which
they were prepared to travel on the rare occasions they were caught
out at night. In other words, acetylene headlights were bought only
by motorists who contemplated long runs at night and extended tours.

Harry Lucas was particularly proud of the King of the Road side
lamp he introduced in 1907 'for cars of the highest class ... Every
detail is of the best. Special tools have been designed for the construction of the component parts, which are built up mechanically, no
connection being dependent on solder [just like the original King of
the Road hub lamp 30 years earlier]. This system gives a combination
of strength, good outline and high finish not otherwise attainable, and
makes the lamp an ornament to any car.'

The competition from rival manufacturers in the expanding motor
trade was as fierce as it had been in the cycle world, and in 1908
Harry came out with a powerful piece 'Concerning Lucas Head
Lights and Projectors' written in the stern and straightforward style
in which he excelled:

> We prefer to give a few plain facts about our Lamps and Projectors,
> rather than talk about their Candle Power, which can have little or no
> meaning to the average Motorist. Our Lamps and Projectors are the
> result of our actual Motor Car driving Experience, and are designed to
> meet all modern requirements. MISLEADING STATEMENTS, which
> are nevertheless literally true, can easily be made. For instance, it is a fact
> that the time can be read on an ordinary watch held in the hand 350
> yards away from our large size King of the Road Projectors ... But any
> Lamp or Projector which gives merely a narrow pencil of bright light
> will serve for the watch test but be practically useless for driving.
> Of course, THE MOTORIST REALLY REQUIRES a Lamp or

Projector which will give a sufficiently *wide beam* of bright light to show up the various objects he meets on the road, under the varying conditions, so as to make night driving not merely safe but even pleasurable. Our King of the Road Projectors are designed to give sufficient light to show up the hedges or borders of the road, but with a broad beam of the greatest intensity straight ahead, so that the path of the car is strongly and evenly illuminated.

THE DRIVER CAN ACTUALLY SEE light objects, such as light-coloured cottages, walls, gates, posts, etc., fully 200 yards away and vehicles, pedestrians and cyclists at about 150 yards. We have proved this under fair average conditions, but it is only right to say that these distances would be considerably reduced in the case of dark objects on a dark, muddy road.

In the same year, 1908, the company stopped selling Wells-Lucas motor oil and grease (leaving only the cycle lubricating and lamp oils to continue the link with Joseph's early days of paraffin-selling in Carver Street), while tyre valves, puncture repair outfits and funnels all disappeared from the catalogue at about this time. (A Lucas steering wheel had been tried and dropped in 1903.)

Motor bulb horns, on the other hand, continued to be in demand, but presented a production problem. In Joseph Lucas's time each horn had to be tuned individually, and this was done in a small shop in Little King Street, where a reed voicer, or tuner, named Mann worked with a row of horns in front of him, all apparently identical but no two of them alike in tone. The method of working was for Mann to insert the reed, adjust its length and tune it, and then solder it into the horn. As Joseph Lucas had pointed out: 'If a customer in Timbuctoo damages the reed, the whole horn has to be returned to us for a new reed. What can be done about it?' The answer was the standardisation of a replaceable reed, but this took some years to perfect. In 1907 a new post-horn was produced which was claimed to be acoustically correct so that 'the resulting tone, while not too loud, reaches the slow traffic in time to allow of its clearing the road before being overtaken, and is especially useful at cross-roads and corners.'

The pace of improvements to the acetylene lamps did not slacken in 1909. A small-size King of the Road projector was added to the large and medium sizes previously listed, and the widening range of motor-cars now being offered was seen in a new projector set suggested as suitable for small cars. The Motorlite was also introduced as a medium-priced lamp for the popular car. An entirely new separating generator was put on the market which enabled the used-up carbide to be separated from the unused, with various advantages such as steady lighting and easier cleaning.

But the most significant improvement was tucked away on page 40 of the catalogue. This was a set of King of the Road electric side and tail lamps which, it was claimed, 'will be recognised as a great advance in design, style and finish on those already on the market'. They were supplied complete with bulbs for 4-volt current and three yards of wire, but nothing was said as yet about an accumulator. In addition, electrical bulb holders and bulbs were offered at 7s 6d each for screwing into the back light of existing side and tail lamps as an alternative method of illumination. The petroleum burner was left in place while the electric light was used, and it was only necessary to remove the bulb in order to convert the lamp back to petroleum burning.

At the board meeting on 14 March 1910 Harry Lucas, in a review of the future, pointed out that 'the importance of expansion in the electric lighting branch could hardly be over-rated if we are to maintain any position in it at all'. He mentioned that they were making experiments with electrically controlled dynamos but that so much had already been done and so many patents taken out that 'there is little room left for a new thing'. C. A. Vandervell & Co announced their 'new and improved system of lighting by dynamo' in August that year and there were others (Peto & Radford, Blériot, Ducellier, etc) already on the market, whereas Joseph Lucas were only able to exhibit at the 1910 Olympia Motor Show a dynamo lighting system which was still in the experimental stage and was not for immediate sale.

Harry then referred to a development in the motor business that was bound to take place sooner or later and had already started in the United States. A great number of American cars were being sent to the United Kingdom and the Colonies fitted 'free' with acetylene generators and projectors, and Harry emphasised that their own sales of acetylene motor lamps to motorists were consequently affected by this trend as well as by the growth of electric lighting. So began the first signs of the 'original equipment' market for accessories that was to assume such importance later on.

Although Harry Lucas was by now convinced that the long-term future of motor-car lighting lay in electricity, the process had to be accomplished gradually, and in the meantime there was still scope for improving the acetylene lamps which most motorists seemed to want. In 1910 he even produced an entirely new petroleum side lamp, square in shape, and specially designed to harmonise with the body of closed carriages. This was patented jointly by Harry Lucas and Egginton.

The simultaneous development of acetylene and electric lighting was seen at its height in 1911. On the acetylene side several new lamps were introduced – the medium-priced Kinglite with Mangin mirror lens in four models selling at around a fiver each; the Landlite, a small headlight suitable for small cars, slightly cheaper; and the Lorilite, a strong headlight for commercial vehicles, again at about £5. But it was with the electric lamps that most progress was made. New electric projectors were announced, supplied by a King of the Road accumulator – the first Lucas battery – sold in two sizes, the 8-volt being able to light two 8cp projectors and four 4cp side and tail lights for about 12 hours, while the 4-volt size would run side and tail lights for about 16 hours. Since no dynamo was yet provided, motorists were advised to carry a spare accumulator in addition to the one in use. This early accumulator consisted of tubular lead plates wrapped in perforated Ebonite separators in a transparent celluloid container, which was carried in either a tin case or a teak box 'acid-proofed, stained walnut and polished'. The two sizes cost £4 10s to £5 10s in tin cases or £8 10s to £9 15s in teak boxes. The company now felt itself in a position to recommend the Lucas King of the Road Electric Lighting Set 'for the Professional man or Owner-Driver preferring Electric Lamps' – all for £24 13s 6d (brass) or £25 11s 6d (plated). But the set lacked the vital component, the dynamo, which was still not ready for general sale.

The provision of an accumulator made it possible to supply the first Lucas electric horn, which was 'believed to be ahead of all others yet placed on the Market'. It may have been noticed that the company seem to have made a habit of being rather slow in bringing out the latest devices, but when they did, it was with the confidence that they were doing it rather better than anyone else. In this case they had stated publicly in their catalogue three years earlier that 'We do not make electric horns because we have not found any of them so reliable and durable, and always ready for use, as our standard (bulb) horns.' This hostage to fortune was prudently excised from the catalogue of 1909, by which time they were hard at work experimenting with a suitable design, but it was not until 1911 that they felt ready to market an electric horn priced at £4 10s. In case this seemed rather steep, the point was made that 'as in all electrical apparatus, the best will always in the long run be found the cheapest'.

By the end of that year there were 72,000 cars in England, but the

motor-car was still a long way from matching the horse-drawn vehicle in popularity. It was reckoned that there was one motor-car for
every 570 inhabitants compared with one private carriage for
every 140.

And so we come to 1912, when the company were able at last to
announce that the dynamo lighting system exhibited at Olympia in
1910 had been further developed and improved and had been tested
for many thousands of miles in its own cars. A certain number of sets
(two a week) had been sold to selected customers and were giving
complete satisfaction, so the King of the Road Dynamo Lighting
System was now listed at £16 for the G80 model (100-Watt) and
£18 10s for the G90 (200-Watt). These dynamos were very heavy
by modern standards, the 100-Watt model weighing 25lb and the
200-Watt 35lb. The design incorporated a clutch which automatically began to slip when the dynamo reached a speed of 1,500rpm,
and the switchbox included a cut-out to disconnect the dynamo from
the accumulator when the dynamo stopped running, and so prevent
the accumulator running down through trying to motor the dynamo.
The switchbox included a 'charge' switch and a 'tell-tale' that lit up
automatically when the tail light failed, and a two-pin plug adaptor
for an inspection lamp (an expensive job, selling for £6 10s od
with 16ft of cable).

That was not the whole story. The clutch-type dynamo was only a
temporary measure to keep the company abreast of the tide of
electric-lighting development which was flowing strongly in the
motor trade both here and abroad. What Harry Lucas was aiming at
was the dynamo with electrically controlled output (third brush
control) which he had mentioned two years previously. At a board
meeting in June 1912 he was able to report that as a result of experiments they had made, a patent had been applied for after a considerable search had been made by Marks & Clerk. He pointed out that it
was impossible to tell whether there was any anticipating application
for a like patent until publication, but he considered it important that
the new dynamo should be on the market at or before the next Motor
Show. In fact the new dynamo (the E40, 8-volt 6-amp) was not
produced until the next year, selling at £9 10s od.

The number of motor-cars continued to increase year by year –
24,000 more came on the roads between 1910 and 1912, and in 1913
alone there were 26,238 new registrations. At Olympia that year no
fewer than sixty-five makes were exhibited at the Motor Show. Another significant trend for the future of Lucas was the rapid increase

in motor-cycle production, which grew from 3,800 in 1907 to 37,600 in 1912. Perhaps the most important development of 1913 was that William R. Morris produced his Oxford model chassis with White & Poppe engine for £175 (standard) and £195 (de luxe), with all the consequences for the British motor industry which that event portended. The early Morris Oxfords did not have any Lucas components or accessories, but in 1913 and 1914 Morris was also designing and ordering parts for the prototype of the Morris Cowley, which was to appear in April 1915, during the war. For this car, which had a Continental 'Red Seal' engine made in the United States, Morris came to Lucas for the 6-volt dynamo and a set of three lamps (two combined head and side lamps fitted on brackets on the windscreen and a tail light). The dynamo was mounted on the cylinder head by means of a steel bracket and was driven by a flat belt from the fan pulley.

In July 1913 Harry Lucas returned to his survey of the motor-car business and told his fellow directors that since his last board statement on these lines there had been the change from acetylene and petroleum lighting for motor-cars to electric lighting, and now a further change was taking place – to electric starting as well as lighting. (I believe the first car to have an electric starter as standard equipment was the 1912 model Cadillac, though it had been an expensive optional extra on various cars since about 1910.) Harry went on to estimate what he called the 'loss' on experimental work, tools, etc, in connection with electric lighting at £10,000 (at least), adding that a very large expenditure was still necessary for the company to keep their chance in the combined lighting and starting business. On top of that they had to take into account the depreciation, practically to nil, which was taking place in the value of their tools for acetylene and petroleum lighting.

Development work continued at Great King Street and on the road, and in the months before the outbreak of World War I Harry Lucas saw his plans of a complete Lucas dynamo lighting system for motor-cars finally realised. Actually there were six different sets listed in the 1914 catalogue, and illustrations of typical cars (none of them specified by make) for which they were suitable showed the vast progress made in motor-car design in the 12 years since Lucas Motoralities were first introduced. Each set comprised a dynamo, switchbox, battery (the new term for accumulator), a pair of projectors, a pair of side lamps, a tail lamp, a complete set of sundries (cable, clips, screws), and a Vee driving belt. There were four dynamo models (E20, 40, 50 and 60), the smallest being 8-volt 6-amp and the rest being 12-volt 8- to 12-amp. Three alternative drives for the dynamo were suggested – from a pulley on the clutch shaft, by extension of the water pump shaft, or belt drive from the magneto shaft. The set for small cars up to 12hp (Sunbeam and Rover were illustrated) cost £32 10s od. The next set cost £40 and was for medium-powered touring cars, as illustrated by the 25hp Lanchester and 24–30hp Wolseley. Set 'C' for medium-sized covered cars cost £42 15s od and was shown installed on 25hp Vauxhall and 18–24hp Deasy landaulettes. The fast powerful touring cars for which the £49 10s od Set 'D' was designed were typified by the 38hp Daimler and 45hp Napier, while the next set for large covered cars like the 35hp Renault cost £51 4s 6d. Finally came the Set 'R.R.' for Rolls-Royce cars costing £49 10s od. The extras available included an electric horn, an inspection lamp, and various interior lamps for closed cars. A dynamo set for motor-cycles and sidecars was also offered with a special small dynamo (the E10).

Harry Lucas had always realised that all their efforts to make lighting sets of the highest quality and reliability could be undone by slipshod installation of the equipment, which of course was still the responsibility of the motorist, because motor manufacturers did not normally supply electric lighting sets with their cars. Motor manufacturers were astonishingly slow in appreciating the possibilities of improved car lighting made possible by the introduction of the tungsten filament lamp, which could withstand the shaking of the car. The Lucas company therefore offered to fit the lighting sets to customers' cars at their works or at the London and Manchester depots at a cost ranging from £6 5s od to £7 15s od for ordinary cars, but 13 guineas for a Rolls-Royce, including special fittings supplied by the makers. The company also offered to send skilled workmen to motorists' houses in any part of the country, charging the return railway fare, 1s 6d an hour travelling time and 4s od a day expenses on top of the fitting charge.

Electrical equipment brought with it the need for repair facilities. A yard behind the Shaftesbury Avenue sales depot in London was used for this purpose, while at the factory dynamo lighting sets were fitted to individual customer's cars and afterwards serviced in a building in Farm Street which had been used by the Daimler company as a service depot but was too small for the number of cars requiring attention. A sales office had been opened in Manchester in 1908, followed by similar depots in Glasgow and Bristol in 1910. But there were no proper service facilities in the modern sense of the term.

In November 1913, just as the 1914 Lucas leatherbound catalogue was going to press, the motoring world was stirred by a new 'record' of 26 hours 4 minutes for the drive from London to Monte Carlo. The car was an open Rolls-Royce and the driver James Radley, a dashing amateur who had made a name for himself in the Austrian Alpine Trials. On his arrival at the Hotel de Paris in Monte Carlo, Radley wrote a letter to Harry Lucas that was rushed into the catalogue at the last minute. Headed 'An Appreciation of the Lucas electrical lighting system from an Experienced Motorist', it read:

> You would perhaps like to know something about a recent experience of mine with your Electric outfit. On my London–Monte Carlo run it was only your Lamps that made it possible to average more than 37 m.p.h. for 12 hours of night, including passing through many miles of thick fog. Owing to striking a *caniveau* at high speed one of the head-lamps jumped off the car altogether, so therefore for the seven hours of night I had only the light of one, but still was able to drive from Boulogne to Lyons, a distance of 728 kilometres, in 12 hours of pitch dark night and fog, averaging over 60 kilometres per hour. I don't think I need to try any other outfit.

One of Radley's companions on that carefree adventure was Billy Rhodes-Moorhouse, who was to die, Britain's first airman VC, only 18 months later.

Until the moment when war engulfed Europe and all normal business planning became pointless, Harry Lucas continued to look ahead. He was particularly concerned about expanding the production of batteries. He began in April 1914 by fixing up a licence for making wood separators with the Chloride Electric Storage Company, who held various patents. The fee was the enormous sum of £50 a year for the unexpired term of about eight years of the patent. Then, after explaining to the board in May that the company could not hope to obtain any worthwhile increase in its electrical business with its present accumulator shop, he got them to agree to the construction of an entirely new block in Farm Street which would comprise an assembly shop, warehouse and packing room, offices and stores. This was exactly three months before war was declared, and the building was put in hand immediately.

Two electrical components were still lacking before the company could be said to offer a comprehensive electrical equipment service to motorists – and ultimately to manufacturers. The self-starter, as we know, was already in Harry Lucas's mind and may well have been in the course of design and experiment. The high-tension magneto had been in fairly general use in motor-cars since about 1909, but so far it had been left to specialist magneto firms to make, dominated by Robert Bosch in Germany.

Before we see how the war brought about a revolution in the British attitude to the magneto, and the part Joseph Lucas, Limited, played in its subsequent development, let us see something of the people at Great King Street and Little King Street and the conditions they worked in there while the bicycle and motor-car trades were jointly building up the company's reputation in the Edwardian years.

CHAPTER FOUR

A HARD LIFE - BUT A HAPPY ONE

There is probably no more striking difference between life at Great King Street today and as it was in Edwardian times than in the way people used to arrive at the factory in the morning. In 1906, for example, of the two executive directors Harry Lucas was ahead of his time in driving himself to the works in his two-cylinder Lanchester motor-car, and so too was the general manager, Mr Jackson, who arrived in a single-cylinder Wolseley with 54in front wheels and 24in wheels at the back. The other executive director, Bernard Steeley, rode up to the directors' entrance on horseback, dismounted, and handed the reins to a waiting boy, who led the horse away to a stable in Little King Street where Strawberry, the roan mare for the company's single delivery cart, was also kept.

The 1,000 or so workpeople got to Great King Street by tram or on foot – usually the latter for the sake of economy. (L. Boughton, for instance, has told me how he walked to work from the other side of the Bull Ring when he was 14 because he could not afford the tram fare out of his 4s 6d a week wages.) Those who came long distances either walked or used bicycles. Many of the workpeople, of course, lived in the neighbouring streets. They all had to be inside the factory by 8 o'clock, come foul weather or broken-down tram, for the gates were then shut by Mr Davis, the martinet timekeeper, until lunchtime at 12.30. For the unfortunates who were late this meant hanging about in Burbury Park until the afternoon, or even suspension for a fortnight if Mr Davis was in a bad mood. Being late twice in a month meant the sack. The day's work officially ended at 6 pm but most people worked overtime until 8 o'clock at night, regarding the bonus as pocket money.

Some of the girls had to walk or cycle all the way from the Black Country, and they were not allowed to eat or drink in the factory before lunchtime. One day Harry Lucas caught a girl taking a drink of tea from a flask she kept hidden under her capstan lathe. He wanted to give her the sack, but was persuaded not to by the foreman, who explained that she had to leave her home at Hints, near Tamworth, at 6.30 am to cycle to work.

Not that all the foremen were so humane. Listen to Alice Bosworth, who joined the company as a solderer in 1909:

Mr. Johnson, the foreman of our shop, was in complete control; he was a small dictator. He could suspend workers for anything from half-a-day to a month for very trivial matters (like singing after an outing to a pantomime). There was no redress, no-one to appeal to. Any attempt to reach management always came back to the foreman, who could then take it out of you in many ways. I once organised a collection for a man who was away sick; Mr. Johnson made me return the money. If you tried to justify yourself for any action it was labelled 'cheek' and treated accordingly. Mr. Johnson wouldn't allow any eating of apples or oranges – because he didn't like the smell. In any case if you were caught eating you could be sent home for a day. But that didn't stop us making tea and toast and even cooking eggs on the coke stove when he was out of the way. If he saw a magazine on a bench he would tear it up and throw it into a bin.

In fact Harry Lucas used to walk round the factory twice a day, stopping to talk to workpeople and asking the foremen, 'Got anything for me today?' since he was always on the lookout for new products and ideas.

Working conditions at Joseph Lucas were no worse – very often better – than in most Birmingham factories, but in some shops the standards fell far below what they are today, partly because operations that used to impose great hardship on the workers who did them by hand are now done automatically. The plating shop was perhaps the worst. Elsie Walker worked there as a girl for 8s 6d a week, underground, with poor lighting and wet floors, stooping over the hot vapours of a plating tank. Mr Archer, the builder, has recalled: 'What used to worry me was the dipping shed and plating shop in those days; strong men and women working in the fumes of sulphuric acid, and we had to lead-line the floors every two years. In the fogs of November the fumes hung around and to me this was a terrible sight.' Fortunately this was not allowed to continue for long, and such innovations as the issue of clogs as protection from damp feet, waterproof aprons, better ventilation and afternoon tea-breaks all helped to improve the conditions in keeping with the spirit of the times.

Throughout the factory the women and girls scrubbed their benches every Saturday morning, and took it in turns to blacklead the grates and go down on their hands and knees to scrub the floors of the workshops with paraffin. The toilets were pretty foul by modern standards: a continuous bench with partitions and an automatic flushing system that worked only at set intervals. Even so, they were used by the girls as a refuge in which to snatch a bite of food. This led to half-doors being fitted, so that the dame put in charge to stop the practice, nicknamed 'Polly Closet', could spot them and haul them out. Harry Lucas himself was known to have stormed into the place on several occasions, regardless of the impropriety of his action, if he thought the privacy of the toilets was being abused by malingerers.

The men and boys seem to have got on a good deal better with their foremen. Jack Orme, who joined the company as a lad in 1906, benefited by coming under a foreman named Phillips who was very exacting but used to encourage him by saying 'Try and do it a little better' – which of course he did. The foreman had to be a man of manufacturing experience and responsibility, and he was an important link in the organisation of the factory. When he received an order to make a batch of, say, 5 gross of bells or lamps he had to calculate his own quantities of materials, decide the quality of material for each part, write out his orders and send them to the Buying Office. The suppliers were often interviewed in the shop and the foreman checked that the quality specified was delivered by a 'trial through the tools', which were designed and made in the tool section of the production shop. The prices of piece-work were fixed by the foreman with the help of a stopwatch and the Taylor time and motion study principle; and the work was then put in progress. A man was given a bunch of templates and a stack of metal and told to make, say, twenty lamps; there was no allowance for scrap. Tools were taken from Stores and returned after each job, no man being allowed to keep company tools. The only tool normally provided by the company was a boxwood mallet, but sometimes men were given a file, which had to be worn out completely before it was replaced. Any other tools the men wanted they had to buy themselves. Emery cloth was issued by the strip. Inspection at various stages was the foreman's responsibility.

Toolmakers were, of course, relatively highly paid, and a good toolmaker could earn £2 2s od for a 50-hour week at Lucas before 1914, compared with only 37s for a 53-hour week elsewhere. The company's policy was to get the best people and to keep them by paying them well.

There was no canteen before World War I, but there was a little shop on the other side of Great King Street where a meat and potato pie could be bought for 1½d. Most of the workpeople either went home or brought sandwiches or their midday meal in the traditional basin wrapped in a cloth, warming it up in a little gas oven provided for the purpose. Harry Lucas never really liked people eating and drinking tea on the premises, and occasionally he gave vent to his feelings in a quite alarming way. One day he came into a workshop and picked up ten tea mugs off the benches, took them to the far end of the room and smashed them. 'They're made of my metal', he said. 'Don't use it again.' The reason for this outburst was that he had noticed that the mugs were all square, having been made specially by the men to fit the top of the dampers on the furnaces.

Nevertheless the Lucas workpeople – men and women, boys and girls – were on the whole happy and contented. The companionship of working together making complete articles overcame petty tyrannies and hardships. Lucas's were regarded as good and considerate employers; they planned the work to avoid laying people off, building up stocks in the winter for sale in the summer, and if forced to lay people off by circumstances, they would give a few days' notice compared with the two hours in other factories. And having worked at Lucas was the best recommendation for another job anywhere, especially in sheet metal working.

At first the factory was lit by gas lamps, with the incandescent mantles mounted on springs to absorb the vibration of the machinery. Power for the lathes and other machines was provided by gas engines fed by a gasometer of town gas on the premises. When the engines broke down, Harry Lucas hired steam traction engines to drive the shafting by long belts running through the windows. Sometimes the traction engines were standing on floors over basements, and Mr Archer used to warn Harry that they were never intended to take such a load. Harry would smile and say, 'Well, we can't stop them now, can we?'

The old shafting had wooden cog wheels at the bends which were always causing trouble. The engines, too, were unreliable and in the month of February 1906 the following stoppages were recorded:

Cause	Delay (Minutes)
Engine stoppages	35
Belt repairs	50
Insufficient gas	180
Engine bearings overheating	195
Valve stuck	120
Water in cylinder	120

The average delay of 21 minutes a day galled Harry Lucas, and he was relieved when the Birmingham Electricity Supply Company opened its power station in 1906 and offered to supply current to the factory on good terms. In due course electric motors were installed to replace wooden cogs at bends in the shafting, and electric lighting was put in alongside the gas lamps, which nevertheless still had to be called upon when the electric bulbs failed to stand up to the vibration of the factory. As a long stop, three Tom Bowling ships' lamps were kept in the gatehouse for use in an emergency.

The horse-drawn delivery cart mentioned earlier was supplemented by errand boys with box tricycles. Between them they covered deliveries to shops and railway stations over a fairly wide area. The cart also collected coke for the foundry. In 1910 the railways started to collect long-distance consignments from the factories themselves. Horse transport and tricycles were used until 1914, when an old Tilling-Stevens London bus was acquired with an open top and reversing seats. In trying to drive it through the archway in Little King Street, the driver ripped the top off, so it was cut down to window level and converted to a proper lorry. But it was not nearly so reliable as the horse and cart. A light Austin van was also bought, and a very smart chauffeur with breeches and leggings was put in charge of it.

Harry Lucas, of course, had a hand in all these affairs, and much more besides. Like his father, he was fond of and proud of his workpeople. It seemed natural that he should entertain them at local Church Halls with magic lantern lectures with his own slides of his visits to Turkey and Italy and Joseph's trip to Canada before he died. He gave Dickens readings, delighting especially in *A Christmas Carol*, and used these occasions to tell his people about the company's plans for the next 12 months.

In these contacts he was sorely handicapped by his deafness, which by middle-age (he was 50 in 1905) had become acute. He offered a reward of £1,000 to anyone who could cure him, and got the experimental department to make him a telescopic ear trumpet, which he conveniently forgot to pick up when he did not want to hear. He went to Switzerland for treatment and possibly an operation, and came back with a little black box hearing aid instead. This had a 4½-volt battery and a cable with an earpiece at the end made of soft material, which Harry pressed to his ear. It was essential to speak very slowly, loudly and deliberately when he was using the box, otherwise the words became blurred for him. Fortunately he had good eyesight and was in sound health.

For several years he nursed the idea of starting a savings bank in connection with the factory, being constantly worried by the apparent improvidence of his workpeople. Shortly before the annual meeting of the Sick Society on 20 February 1907, the company distributed a leaflet expressing Harry Lucas's belief that the time was ripe for this to be done. 'Once the habit of saving is acquired', he said, 'it will become a pleasure.' On 16 March (less than a month later) the Lucas Works Savings Bank was in operation, being one of the first, if not the very first, of its kind in the country. Saving stamps for 1d, 3d or 6d were available from foremen and forewomen, and stuck into a book (price 1d) which was handed in once a month for the audited amount to be transferred to the Bank ledger. Interest at 2½ per cent was paid half-yearly on all deposits over 10s. (Later on stamps of a higher denomination were issued, and in 1921 the use of stamps was dropped and substituted by cash payments.)

The simultaneous manufacture and improvement of cycle, motorcycle and motor-car lamps burning oil, petroleum, acetylene – and later electricity – meant a busy programme of road testing for Harry Lucas and the experimental staff. To get the cycle lamps right, three or four of them were mounted on the handlebar of a bicycle and sent out on test. Jack Orme recalls that his usual test run was from Birmingham to Worcester and back. For trying out the first motor-cycle headlamp produced in 1904 Harry bought an Enfield motorbike. But it was the motor-car lamps that required most testing, which was done entirely by Harry Lucas with various motor-cars he owned in the six years between 1899, when he bought his first horseless carriage, and 1906 when he was certainly running a Lanchester with an open body, tiller steering, no windscreen and only a leather apron to protect the driver and passenger from rain and wind. With his trim pointed beard, and wearing a black leather coat and cap, he was a familiar character at the wheel of this Lanchester, driving through Moseley village to and from his home. It was with this car that the Duplex King of the Road lamp was developed on long night runs in 1906, when Harry was accompanied by W. H. Egginton, with whom he had jointly patented it the year before. In 1907 Harry is reported as having a Wolseley of unspecified model, which soon afterwards became a company car, as was an Austin 18/24hp purchased for him to carry on lamp-testing in 1909. Meanwhile he seems to have had a 25/30hp Austin of his own.

It was Jack Orme's job to start the 18/24hp Austin every evening. Harry had got tired of hand-starting it, and had made up his own self-starter consisting of a cylinder 12in in diameter and about 15in long containing springs which were wound up by a handle like clockwork. This device was mounted in place of the starting handle. The controls of the car were set, petrol pumped up by hand, the ignition switched on, and the lever of the starter was then pulled to release the springs. If the engine started – as it usually did – it rewound the springs.

It was not long before Harry had another companion on these drives, someone who was to follow in his path as the head of the company, as he himself had followed his father, Joseph. Oliver, his only son, born in 1891, had taken to visiting the factory in the holidays as a schoolboy to get his various models repaired and maintained. He spent hours on the bench with Jack Orme, a born craft metal-worker, who was much the same age and with whom he formed an instant understanding that was to last his lifetime. It was therefore not surprising that when he left King Edward's School, Birmingham, Oliver Lucas went straight into the 'family' business instead of going on to university. His first job was in the experimental department, working with Egginton on lamp design. After a while he seems to have been sent round some of the motor factories, such as Austin and Rover, to study their engineering operations, and when he returned to Great King Street he was given an office of his own next to 'The Gaffer'. But this was only a base from which he ranged all over the factory. He was in his element there, working on the bench and learning practical engineering. Small for his age, with an open direct manner, he got on well with the workpeople, who had taken to him as a rather pathetic boy whose clothes were always too big for him – a deliberate economy move on the part of his parents, who believed he would 'grow into them', which of course he never did.

On his seventeenth birthday Oliver Lucas arrived at the factory at the wheel of the family 25/30hp Austin, and it was said that his father had given it to him as a birthday present. (This seems rather difficult, but not impossible, to reconcile with the fact that he had only 5s a week pocket money until he was nearly 21.) He quickly became an enthusiastic motorist, finding full scope for his enthusiasm in the development of lamps and other products in the pipe-line. Before that, he had been riding a bicycle for testing lamps for some time. Oliver Lucas had arrived on the scene at the very moment when the company was preparing for the introduction of electric lighting for motor-cars, and this required continual tests of lamps and in due course dynamos and batteries, in which he played a leading part. J. H. Tansey recalled later how the young man – not yet 21 – 'used to proceed along the roughest roads at breakneck speed with the embryo lighting set attached to his car to test its efficiency and durability.'

Oliver's 21st birthday in 1912 was marked in a manner that befitted Joseph Lucas's grandson and Harry's son. The directors recorded their pleasure that two of the sons of directors (Bernard Steeley's son being the other) were now working in the company and would thus ensure the continuity of its successful management, and on a more practical note Harry gave him a 38hp Daimler motor-car. A memorable day was rounded off by the foremen presenting 'Master Oliver' with a gold watch – a gesture that must have touched him deeply. There was still a strong family feeling in the business, and Oliver and his sister, Hilda, were popular for their 'renderings of musical items' at works concerts when they were in their 'teens.

Oliver turned his Daimler into a mobile test bed, rigging up as many as four dynamos at a time for comparative testing, which he did mostly with a clever engineer in the experimental department named Handley, with whom he became very friendly. The favourite test run was from Birmingham to Bournemouth. When the first car switchbox was being designed with great urgency, Oliver Lucas and Handley decided to speed up their part of the job by taking their drawing board and instruments to the Cotswolds one Sunday evening. So little traffic was about in those days that they were able to work with great concentration at the side of Fish Hill, near Broadway, and when it got dark, they trained the acetylene lamps of the Daimler on their drawing board to finish the job.

A few years before the war Oliver Lucas was given an assistant, Carl Breeden, who was later to make his million in the motor components business he started with a Birmingham hardware manufacturer named Wilmot. (He was also to marry Oliver's sister Hilda.) They worked together in the experimental department with W. H. Edwards on dynamos, switchboxes, and motor-cycle electrical equipment, all of which had to be tried out on the road. Breeden had his own Hillman car, which was also used for testing. Outside the factory the two young men shared the same tastes in being smartly dressed, always in the height of fashion (Oliver evidently compensating for the badly fitting clothes of his boyhood).

Meanwhile Oliver Lucas had become respected as a fast and experienced driver. A. E. Noakes has remembered how Oliver used to stop and pick him up sometimes when he was waiting on Colmore Row for a tramcar to take him to the factory. As they drove down Snow Hill one day, Noakes was rather disturbed to notice that between Great Charles Street and Constitution Hill the speedometer needle touched 65mph – and there was a policeman at the bottom. To his astonishment the constable saluted as they passed and Oliver remarked: 'Nice chap, that, always gives me a salute when he's on duty.'

CHAPTER FIVE

WAR - AND A MOMENTOUS ACQUISITION

When war was declared on 4 August 1914 normal business virtually dried up, so Harry Lucas (now in his 59th year) turned his mind to developing some new line of manufacture which would be required by the Government for the Armed Services and would preferably be suitable for continuing afterwards as a peacetime product. It did not take him long to decide what this should be. He knew that the country would soon be facing a crisis in making engines for aeroplanes and motor vehicles because 98 per cent of the magnetos used in Britain came from Robert Bosch of Germany. If Lucas could meet this need, at any rate in part, it would be a vital contribution to the war effort and at the same time improve the company's position in the growing motor industry when peace returned.

Having found an electrical expert (his name is not recorded) who could provide the technical background the company lacked, Harry put his plan for making magnetos to his directors at a board meeting on 14 September 1914. The issue was so important that Oliver Lucas (now 23), Carl Breeden and Mr Jackson were asked to come into the room and give their views. Walter Wiggin, one of the two non-executive directors, was a Territorial Army Officer and had rejoined his regiment immediately the war started, so the other directors present, apart from Harry, were Bernard Steeley, assistant managing director, and the non-executive Walter Chamberlain. All agreed that they should go ahead.

A month later Harry had to report back that for various reasons it had not been possible to come to terms with the expert and he had opened negotiations to buy the manufacturing side of a company called Thomson-Bennett, Limited, who had a little factory in Cheapside, Birmingham, where they were making about twenty-five magnetos a week for agricultural, marine and industrial engines. Harry Lucas had been introduced to them by Dr J. D. Morgan, who ran the Temple Street, Birmingham, office and basement-laboratory of Marks & Clerk, the consultants who were retained by Lucas as patent agents. They also acted for a firm called Morris & Lister, of whom we shall be hearing more. Morgan may well have been the expert whom Harry had hoped to engage in the first place. The purchase was approved by the Lucas board for the sum of £9,000, and in December 1914 a new company, Thomson-Bennett (Magnetos) Limited, was formed with a capital of £5,000. Harry Lucas and Bernard Steeley were the first directors. The factoring side of Thomson-Bennett was transferred to another company, James Thomson & Son, run by one of the partners.

The acquisition of Thomson-Bennett was to be of great significance to Joseph Lucas. Apart from the value of the magneto 'know-how', with all that this was to mean in opening up the supply of ignition equipment to motor and motor-cycle manufacturers after the war, one of the two shareholders of the little company was a man who was to wield considerable power at Great King Street when peace returned and would eventually become the Lucas chairman. Meanwhile he was appointed manager and secretary of Thomson-Bennett (Magnetos).

Born in 1880 and educated at King Edward's School, Peter Frederick Blaker Bennett was a Band-of-Hope teetotaller (which would have appealed to Joseph Lucas), a religious man and a superintendent of Sunday schools at Acocks Green. In 1903 he had joined the Electrical Ignition Company at Sparkbrook, a small company making a mica sparking plug which became very popular as a result of being used by S. F. Edge in the Napier he drove to victory in the 1902 Gordon Bennett motor race. EIC went on to make trembler coils, contact breakers and switches, but had no success with their batteries. Two years later, in 1905, when he was sales manager, Bennett met James Albert Thomson, a motor factor in Scotland, when he came to ask for the agency for EIC plugs North of the Border. (Thomson's company, James Thomson & Son, started in Edinburgh and grew to have branches in Scotland, England and Ireland. In 1919 it was amalgamated with Brown Brothers of London as the nucleus of a chain of branches serving every part of the United Kingdom, and Thomson became managing director.)

Two years after Bennett first met Thomson the Electrical Ignition Company went into liquidation, from which it was later resuscitated. Meanwhile Bennett, having already lost faith in the management, had decided to strike out on his own. Thomson backed him in a new company registered in their joint names to make the same lines as EIC except that they bought batteries from C. A. Vandervell & Co and sparking plugs from the old Sphinx company. They introduced a dual coil and magneto system with an outside distributor, using a

Bosch single-cylinder magneto and then a Fischer, which was cheaper. They started making magnetos of various types themselves in place of the dual system, but Bosch had a virtual monopoly of the motor-car business so they turned to the agricultural, marine and industrial engine markets, where they managed to get a foothold with a trip-type magneto and a simple single-cylinder rotating machine that was also suitable for motor-cycles. Nevertheless they were still in a small way of business when they moved the company from Heaneage Street to the grandly named Arden Works in Cheapside, Birmingham, a few years before the war, and their entire effects, including machinery, went into one furniture van.

Peter Bennett recalled later that making 'magnetos was a heart-breaking business and time after time we faced the question whether it was worth going on or not.' He reckoned that the three companies that tried to fight the Bosch monopoly in Britain before 1914 must have lost £100,000 between them.

When the war started, Thomson-Bennett were the only British company actually making magnetos, but very soon afterwards a few others, among them BTH and Morris & Lister (ML), started to make good the deficiency in magneto production. The Government seemed to be quite unconcerned at the position and the War Office told Peter Bennett that though they would not be able to import Bosch mag-netos from Germany, they foresaw no difficulty in getting them from the German-owned and controlled Bosch-USA Company! (This de-lusion lasted a year.) So the British companies decided to go ahead on their own. ML, for example, made an exact copy of the Bosch single-cylinder magneto for Triumph motor-cycles used by Army despatch riders. The job of finding out how the Bosch magneto worked and how all the materials, components and the finished article could be tested was given to a brilliant young engineer, Ernest Wat-son, who had studied mechanical and electrical engineering at Bir-mingham University and went on to specialise in high-voltage problems at Liverpool University, where he gained his MSc in 1909. For his work on improving magneto design, particularly for aero-engines, Watson was awarded the OBE at the end of the war. (Years later Dr Watson was to become Technical Director of Joseph Lucas, Limited, and his name will figure prominently in the account of the company's most important work in World War II.)

Thomson-Bennett supplied large numbers of hand-starting mag-netos to the French Gnome Le Rhône company for their aero-engines by converting one of their single-cylinder motor-cycle engine magnetos, and this was widely used on British aero-engines as well.

Nothing more was heard from the Government about magnetos until July 1915, when the Admiralty suddenly woke up to the fact that they were needed urgently for the new engines being developed for the aircraft for the Royal Naval Air Service. This led to the timely appointment of Lieutenant (later Lieutenant-Commander) Bristow, RNVR, an engineer in civil life, to investigate the position. Bristow carried out his task with tremendous energy and efficiency. He went round the magneto factories, put them under Admiralty control, and apportioned the manufacture of various types to each. Thomson-Bennett, being in a more advanced state of production than the others, were given the magnetos for some motor-cycles, including V-twins, the six-cylinder tank engine, and four-cylinder engines for transport vehicles, these magnetos being used also in the early aero-engines of orthodox design. BTH, ML and North (who made the Watford magneto) had the more difficult task of making magnetos for the new aero-engines and EIC were kept on simple motor-cycle types. Eventually Bristow was instrumental in forming two associations – the Aero Magneto Manufacturers Association and the British Ignition Apparatus Association – and Peter Bennett was appointed chairman of both.

Harry Lucas could not move Thomson-Bennett (Magnetos) from Cheapside immediately Lucas's took over because there was no room at Great King Street for the expanded plant that he and Peter Bennett agreed they would require. Work on clearing away the old houses and erecting the new seven-storey building (G Block) on the right-hand side of Great King Street had been stopped by the Government on the outbreak of war because Lucas had no vital war material orders that could not be made in the existing buildings. The purchase of Thomson-Bennett enabled Harry to get the Government decision reversed, but it would take some time to get the new building completed.

Harry used to visit the site every day to watch its progress. One day he turned to Mr Podbury, the works electrician, who was walking round with him, and said: 'This taking on Thomson-Bennett – I don't know whether I'm doing the right thing.' Podbury replied that he firmly believed that he was, but this did not seem to lessen 'The Gaffer's' anxiety. The next day Harry Lucas said to Podbury: 'Do you know what par means?', to which Podbury replied that he did. At that Harry took out his chequebook and gave the astonished

Podbury a cheque for £100, telling him to go to Mr Slade, the registrar, and buy himself shares in the company for that amount.

The magneto company finally moved from Cheapside to Great King Street in 1916. In the interval they continued to make single-cylinder and two-cylinder magnetos and developed the first four-cylinder magneto, machining the parts on the ground floor and assembling them on the first floor of the Cheapside works. Peter Bennett had a small shop on the ground floor which was virtually the experimental shop. He often worked at a bench in the machine shop dressed in an overall or 'cowgown', teasing the other turners that he was working more quickly than they were – and so getting them unconsciously to speed up their output. George Winnall was one of them, and he recalled later what happy days they were – in spite of working from 6 am to 9 pm on weekdays, 6 am to 5 pm on Saturdays, and 6 am to 4 pm on Sundays. To paraphrase an old song: the rest of the week was their own.

When the little company moved into the Great King Street factory Peter Bennett was made a director, and so too was Carl Breeden. The trading figures of Thomson-Bennett (Magnetos) were noted at the Lucas board meetings, but otherwise the company was run quite separately under Peter Bennett's control as managing director. To begin with, his most pressing problem was to make good the lack of materials – 'as a country,' he said later, 'we had been depending on American and German supplies for practically all the raw materials used in magnetos, as well as magnetos themselves.' Vulcanite for electrical purposes had been imported from Hamburg, and the manufacture of enamelled wire was still in its infancy. The special ball bearings and magnets were also made in Germany. But British companies were found to meet the demands: the Indiarubber Company made mouldings, the London Electric Wire Company expanded their output, and Hoffmans produced the Norma type bearings. The lack of magnets was met in the first place by Swift, Levick of Sheffield, who had the extraordinary foresight to bring over some artisans from Germany in the summer of 1914 and get them to start up production on a pilot scale before war was declared. Shortly afterwards another Sheffield firm, James Neill & Co, began to make magnets and ensured their future supply. Insulating materials – tapes and paper and varnish used in the windings – were provided by the British branch of the Sterling Varnish Company of Pittsburgh. Workpeople, of course, had to be trained to operate the bigger production plant at Great King Street.

One of these newcomers was a man of such experience and knowledge that he was put to work at first with Dr Morgan in the Marks &
Clerk laboratory in Temple Street, until the beginnings of a laboratory and experimental shop took shape at the Thomson-Bennett
factory in Great King Street. His name was J. L. (Jock) Miller, and he
soon took on the major share of responsibility for magneto development and service. Miller had started as an apprentice in the Glasgow
instrument factory of Lord Kelvin's company, Kelvin & White, in
1892, when he was 15. Seven years later the early growth of the
motor industry attracted him and he joined Arrol-Johnston, moving
to the Argyll company in 1908, where he was put in charge of
engine-testing. In the course of this job he had tried out every magneto
on the market against the all-conquering Bosch.

While getting into production themselves, Thomson-Bennett undertook the repair and maintenance of Bosch magnetos in use on
service vehicles. Once production started, it went rapidly ahead and
by the end of the war the company were turning out magnetos at the
rate of 2,000 a week. The 130,000 Thomson-Bennett magnetos supplied were more than half the total number of magnetos produced in
Britain during the war.

Meanwhile the parent company had been getting on with its own
war work after a slow start. The Government commandeered all the
stocks at the outset ('commandeer' was of course a military term of the
South African war that was normally used in World War I; by World
War II it had fallen into disuse and its place had been taken by the
bureaucratic 'requisition'). Then the company was made a controlled
establishment by the Munitions of War Act and was given War
Department contracts for cycle lamps, carriers and bells – the Army
used thousands of bicycles – and for a special King of the Road lamp
adapted for paraffin. Another order was for acetylene lamps for
Douglas motor-cycles carrying machine guns. Everything was painted
a drab green. A minor crisis arose in getting red and green glass for
the side windows of the lamps – it had all come from Austria-
Hungary. One of the men, S. Roberts, asked his foreman whether
he would like to go round the glassworks of John Walsh in Lodge
Road, where his father was head glass mixer. The result was a new
department at Great King Street equipped with small furnaces so
that Lucas could produce the glasses themselves. But coloured glass-
making is a technique that is not learnt in a day, and they could
not get the colours right. While experiments went on, the glasses had
to be painted, which was considered rather shaming. Harry Lucas

came every day to see how they were getting on and once remarked: 'You know, I'd sooner pawn my shirt than buy any more foreign glasses.' The technique was mastered in the end, but after the war it was decided that it was more sensible to resume importing supplies from the traditional glassmakers of central Europe.

One of the earliest Government contracts was for the development of the Aldis signalling lamp. Lucas designed the trigger mechanism while Aldis made the telescope and the Mangin mirrors, the two companies working in close collaboration. A special Aldis lamp made of aluminium was produced for the Royal Navy, and another with rubber sheathing of the terminals for use in airships. The Aldis lamp could be read 10 miles away.

Lots of the men went off to the war. Harry promised them all that they would have their jobs back afterwards, and to every one he gave a personal parting gift. F. C. S. Coe told me how the routine went when he himself joined the Duke of Cornwall's Light Infantry on 31 August 1914, being then 17 years of age. 'I hear you've joined the Army,' Harry Lucas said, with his ear to the black box. 'Do you speak any foreign languages?' 'I'm afraid not, sir,' replied Coe. 'Well, I expect you'll go abroad eventually so I'll give you something that speaks the same language the whole World over.' And he gave the lad a golden sovereign.

To H. G. Emmett, who was taken to see 'The Gaffer' by R. Instone, his boss, with the remark 'Here's another of my staff off,' Harry Lucas said: 'You ain't big enough. Why don't you let the big'uns go first? Our Oliver wants to go too, but he's too small.'

Emmett got his sovereign, but it is not recorded whether Oliver got his too when he joined up shortly afterwards. He was soon commissioned in the Royal Naval Air Service and went to France in February 1915 with a section of the Royal Naval Armoured Car Division. At the beginning of the war armoured cars had been found to be extremely useful in Belgium for conveying vital information about German troop movements, spotted by the RNAS pilots, to the staff at Ostend, being able to deal with any roaming Uhlans encountered on the way. But by the Spring of 1915 the war had settled down to more clearly defined territories and the armoured car squadrons were taken over by the Army. Oliver Lucas was transferred to Mechanical Transport, working with caterpillar tractors and heavy howitzers. He came home on a short leave and had his Daimler car repainted in camouflage.

He was in France again at the first battle of the Somme. In planning the attack General Gough was worried about the difficulty of keeping in touch with the advance troops because the field telephone wires would be wrecked in the initial artillery barrage. He called for signalling lamps, but the trouble with those the Army had was that the enemy could read the signals as they were transmitted. One of his staff suggested calling in 'young Lucas', as he might be able to help. Oliver had seen the Aldis signalling lamp for the Royal Navy which the company was making and immediately got to work on a lamp suitable for Army use. He went to Paris for parts and produced in the Base workshop a number of lamps which were rushed to the Front with the paint hardly dry. These were used with great success in the advance. The messages from them could not be seen from the German lines as it was necessary to bend down almost to ground level to see their flashes. When he was asked to produce the lamps in quantity Oliver suggested that it would be much better if he could get them made at the Lucas works. This was agreed. He was attached to the Munitions Invention Board in London and spent much of his time during the rest of the war superintending the production of the OL Daylight Signalling Lamp, of which many thousands were made. As a reward he was allowed to license the French authorities to use his patent.

The energy Oliver Lucas put into starting up production of his signalling lamp left a lasting impression on the people who helped him. He was a wiry young man, very fit and smart, and would vault over a bench to speak to someone as he walked round the works. P. S. Kemsley, who made the jigs, Sid Corbett, who did the preliminary lamp work, and Alice Bosworth, who did the soldering of the prototypes and helped with the focusing – all became devoted to him. The production lamps were made by women, and the first batch to be sent to France very nearly missed the boat. At one o'clock on a Saturday the company's one and only lorry failed to turn up – the driver had forgotten and had left his lorry at the back of the factory and gone home. No one else could drive it (very few people could drive a motor-car in those days) and the train was due to leave at 4.20 pm. A frantic telephone call to his home brought Oliver Lucas to the scene. All hands loaded the lorry, Oliver climbed into the cab, and the consignment caught the train at Hockley Station.

The working hours were long – 12 hours a day and nearly as long on Saturdays – and conditions were hard. Zeppelin raids began, and there were no lights in the streets. There was no canteen at first (a small one was started later) and the workpeople depended as usual on their own sandwiches and food brought in basins and warmed up, supplemented by snacks from the little shop in Great King Street – pigs pudding, bread and lard, suet pudding, salad, all cost 1d each. There was still a ban on any hot drink in the morning, so one day one of the foremen, 'Pony' Moore, asked to see Harry Lucas in his office, where he could hear what was said to him through the black box, and give him what Moore described afterwards as 'a bit of plausibility.'

'How would you like to come from the Black Country and get here by hook or by crook at 8 o'clock,' he said, 'and carry on till lunch time without a cup of anything?' 'Well', Harry replied, 'I don't suppose I ever had to.' Moore proposed that the workpeople should be allowed to have a drop of tea from an urn at 9 o'clock, breaking off for 10 minutes. 'Well, that's not a bad suggestion. Let's try it in your own shop, on one condition – if they don't behave themselves the thing will be taken away.' They did behave themselves and it was not taken away; indeed the idea spread to the other shops and thus was born, at any rate at Joseph Lucas, the institution of the morning tea-break.

Women were exploited in those days – in industry as a whole, not only at Joseph Lucas. Girls under 18 were employed where possible, because they were paid at a low rate; when they reached 18, they were sacked. Married women were not taken on ('You can't depend on them'), so they took off their wedding rings when they applied for work and did not wear them if they got married while they were working. And women had to do the dirty job of scrubbing the workshops and benches before leaving at 4 pm on Saturdays. But they were happy in their work, and those who got the top wages of 32s a week felt themselves well off.

Nevertheless on one occasion the women and girls in the lamp shop said they were going on strike for a bonus. Let Miss N. Rowe (then 19) tell the story in her own words: 'Some gentleman came to talk to us about how the men were suffering at the Front, it was wrong to strike at that time. Mr. Harry was with him. All of a sudden Mr. Harry shouted "Now Yo wenches Yo go back to your work". We did go back – we also got our bonus.'

But it did not need the threat of a strike for Harry Lucas to have greater influence on his workpeople than the public figure who had come to address them; he could be just as effective in a quiet vein. Soon after the war started, the staff were called together to hear a well-known MP tell them how serious the position was and how much the country needed their best efforts. When the MP had finished his routine piece, Harry got up and 'said a few words'. Someone who was there recalls that 'the commonsense of his remarks, the directness of his appeal, his obvious sincerity and the manner in which he was received by the audience must, in contrast, have made the M.P. feel how weak his effort had been.' An unfair comparison, perhaps, but nonetheless a telling description of Harry's leadership.

The Lucas factory also turned out vast quantities of repetition parts like shell fuse covers and rings. On the electrical side, batteries and dynamos were made not only for lorries, armoured cars and ambulances, but for tanks and aeroplanes as well. The lighting sets for tanks consisted of a belt-driven dynamo, 12-volt battery, two headlamps, a tail light, and five 'festoon' interior lamps for the crew. For a bomber aircraft the company were asked to supply two dynamos driven by small 18in wooden propellers attached to the struts of the wings. These were required for the aeroplane's lighting and to warm the flying suits of the crew. The 4in dynamos provided all the current needed – 18 to 20 amps – because they were kept so cool by the air flow. These dynamos were also used on airships.

Another aircraft commission was the landing light system called the Orford Ness, consisting of a set of four powerful projectors mounted on the undercarriage. It was tried out on a Handley-Page at Upavon, and the beam stretched for a mile ahead of the aeroplane as it came in to land.

A much more difficult order to fulfil was for a self-starter for a 240hp twelve-cylinder Sunbeam seaplane engine. Although self-starters were not in regular production at Great King Street before 1914, a few experimental motor-car starters were made during the war – one was fitted to Harry Lucas's Argyll and another to Bernard Steeley's Albion – so they knew what was required. These starters were operated by a pinion on a toothed ring which was bolted or shrunk on to the flywheel. The yoke of the first prototype for the aero-engine starter was turned out of the solid metal, 5in in diameter, and all the metal inside was bored out until the carcass was only 5/16in thick. 'Pony' Moore made the whole thing, machining, armature winding, steel coils and all the necessary outputs. The most critical part of the programme was the cold test for high altitude and Arctic operation, for which there were no facilities at the factory. So arrangements were made with the Air Inspection Department for the engine to be set up in the cold storage room at the Birmingham Meat Market in Bradford Street and dropped to the stipulated temperature for 24 hours. Wearing four blanket coats, Moore pressed the starter button; the great engine turned, and in a moment it fired. Afterwards the engine was brought along to the factory and started up with a roar in the quadrangle between A, B, C and D Blocks, causing a tremendous stir among the workpeople.

Then they had an order for self-starters for tank engines. The armatures for some of these dynamos and starters were wound with exceptionally stiff wire (912 gauge ·104 square) and they had to be wound by hand. No one at Lucas could do it, so they advertised in the Birmingham papers. Two girls applied, saying they had been working on fan armatures at the GEC with a very small wire. 'Pony' Moore described what happened: 'They said, Well, one of the first prominent questions is what's the wages? I said, Ah, I thought you'd come onto that, so I told them (it was quite a good wage). They both looked at each other and they said, Well, we're going to have a go at that. I said, Right, that's all I want you to do, have a go.' He went on:

> So anyway those two sisters, they were by the name of Ward, we called them the Ward Sisters. I brought them a tank armature and they simply watched me for about two days. I wound them in front of them until one said to me one day, I'd like to have a go at that. I said, That's the idea, that's just what I wanted you to say, have a go. So the one started off alright and the other one seemed to be a bit jealous, so she had a go, in fact those two sisters became so proficient in the winding of these tank armatures that they set out to beat each other. How many have you done today, Elsie? Oh I've done 10. Have you? Yes. Oh I haven't. She starts off next day to beat her sister, which was what we required. Now eventually these two girls were given the charge of half-a-dozen other girls who also knew nothing about it. They were worth in those days, as the saying goes, 'their weight in gold'.

After two years of war, in August 1916, so many changes had happened at the factory that Harry Lucas raised the question of increasing the capital of the company to £500,000. This was sanctioned at two extraordinary meetings of the shareholders in the following February 1917, when it was decided to divide each of the existing £5 shares into £1 shares and to create 275,000 new £1 shares.

At the beginning of 1918 it was clear to Harry Lucas that something would have to be done about the shortage of space at the factory if they were to provide for the electric lighting and starting business as well as magnetos they would have to handle after the war, in addition to the full range of Cyclealities and Motoralities. He told the board at a meeting in January: 'We have almost reached a criminal stage of risk in not being prepared to meet the coming requirements of the trade.'

No decision was reached then, but he returned to the subject at the July board meeting, by which time the whole problem had become complicated by fresh demands from the Government. (The background was that the American magnetos coming over with the Liberty aero-engines were not considered reliable enough, and British-made magnetos were called for; secondly, the military setback caused by the German push in the Spring of 1918 was thought to have placed Paris in jeopardy and plans were being laid to supply the French need for magnetos if it was found necessary to evacuate the city.) Harry Lucas reported that the officials consequently wanted to commandeer the whole of the new block used for Thomson-Bennett magnetos in Great King Street, and this had forced him to make a compromise in return for which a permit was to be granted for another building to be erected on another site already cleared in Well Street. He went on to emphasise that the worst of all this pressure was that it prevented their completing the experimental work necessary for after-war business (for example, a combined dynamo and magneto had been registered as the Magdyno in 1915).

Only the framework of the building had been erected when the Armistice was signed and Lucas were instructed to stop work on it. This order was later revoked and the building went ahead. The buildings put up during the war were of great benefit to Lucas, of course, because they qualified for Government financial assistance. This took the form of permission to write off large parts of the expenditure on both buildings and plant out of excess profits.

During the war the profits of the company increased with the greater volume of work done and were 80 per cent higher in 1918 than they were at the beginning of the war. The sales figures, on the other hand (which were not disclosed at the time) were more than three and a half times bigger by the end of 1918. The payroll had grown from about 600 to 4,000 people, of whom 1,200 were employed by Thomson-Bennett. In assessing the profits, provision had to be made for the payment of excess profit duty on Government contracts and special allowances on plant. The annual figures were as follows:

Year	Profit £	Sales £	Dividend (Ordinary) %
1914	25,628	289,993	10
1915	39,675	383,725	10
1916	} 70,165	500,955	10
1917		832,624	10
1918	47,279	1,082,731	10

The end of those four years of human toil, hardship, deprivation and bereavement were greeted on 11 November 1918 with the same outburst of relief at the Lucas factory as in every part of the United Kingdom. The emotions of that morning were remembered many years later by Miss N. Rowe, who was 21 and working in the block making lamps in Great King Street at the time. Her simple words give an extraordinarily vivid impression of the scene:

I Remember the day when the war ended 1918, we had been warned that if Peace came Maroons would be sounded between Half Past ten-Eleven. Everybody was sought of in stait of Expecting and when we heard the Maroons we stopped work and we went out onto the Balcony and waiting all of a sudden Mr. Oliver came from our side of the road to Thomson-Bennett side. You never heard such Cheering that went up when we saw Him. We started to sing. Then the Union Jack was shot up into Position. We stood quietly while that . . . Then again another Shout went up. After that we walked through all Departments singing anything that came into our minds, after we had sung ourselves dry we were told to go home. Several of us went down Farm Street with Union Jack on the end of our Umbrella, even the foremen became human beings.

PART FOUR

THE NINETEEN-TWENTIES

CHAPTER ONE

A NEW TEAM

Ironically, the return of peace was followed by an outburst of hostilities among the Lucas directors after 20 years of untroubled co-operation in the boardroom. Privately it was a family quarrel between Harry Lucas and his brother-in-law and assistant managing director, Bernard Steeley, the details of which do not concern us. Outwardly it resulted in Steeley tendering his resignation, which was not accepted; and a long resolution proposed by Walter Chamberlain and seconded by Walter Wiggin at the March 1919 board meeting, which was carried with Harry Lucas dissenting (and no wonder) made Steeley managing director in sole charge of the commercial side of the business and of production, except for electrical matters. Chamberlain also wanted to have a staff committee nominated by the managing directors to meet the directors before each board meeting (an early attempt at 'participation') and the Thomson-Bennett company, which was run almost autonomously by Peter Bennett, brought more under the control of the main board.

At the next meeting Chamberlain had to explain that after talking to Harry Lucas and Steeley it was necessary to modify the resolution, which now made Steeley managing director of the commercial side only while Harry Lucas remained managing director in sole charge of the production side and continued as before to deal with financial questions in conjunction with the board. An important addition was that Peter Bennett was to attend all board meetings so that he could help on the production side. All this was not completed, however, without the confirmation of a noisy shareholders meeting.

In September Harry Lucas (now 64) stood down as chairman, and the board agreed with his proposal that Walter Chamberlain should take his place. Three months later Peter Bennett was at last appointed an additional director, and his further advancement was made possible shortly afterwards when Bernard Steeley, after three months leave of absence, asked to be relieved of his position as managing director while keeping his seat on the board. This left the way open for Bennett to be made one of the two managing directors, Harry Lucas being the other.

No sooner had this been accomplished than Walter Chamberlain and Walter Wiggin both resigned from the board in July 1920 after

22 years' service, their places as non-executive directors being taken by Alderman J. Sayer, an old cycling friend of Harry's and the head of a Birmingham company making steel pens (a traditional Birmingham trade), who was appointed chairman, and J. Albert Thomson, Peter Bennett's old associate in Thomson-Bennett (and chairman and managing director of Brown Brothers, the factors), who therefore nicely balanced the new intake on his side. A month later Walter Chamberlain died.

The changes did not stop there. In the following year Bernard Steeley gave up his seat on the board so that Oliver Lucas, now 30, could become a director, and two years later, in 1923, the new team was finally completed when Oliver was made joint managing director with Peter Bennett. Harry himself took the non-executive title of consultant director, which meant that, though virtually retired, he would be able to come to the factory every day and wander about wherever he pleased.

While these boardroom manoeuvres were going on, the factory was getting back to production of its three peacetime ranges of products. The bicycle-makers were soon back in business, so we will start with Lucas Cyclealities, going on to Motor-Cyclealities, which held great promise for the future because so many servicemen had got used to riding motorbikes during the war, and leaving Motoralities for the next chapter, while the motor manufacturers sort out their problems.

Life had been too grim and earnest during World War I for much cycling to be done for pleasure, and the membership of the Cyclists Touring Club had dropped from 40,000 in 1914 to 8,500 by the time the Armistice was signed (many members, of course, gave their lives during the war). But the mere thought of the peaceful English countryside sent people back to the bicycle, and, with public transport in poor shape, it was bought in large numbers for its sheer utility as well.

Most of the pre-war Lucas Cyclealities were continued, with lamps (both oil and acetylene) and bells as the best-sellers. Two new lamps were introduced: a new model of the acetylene King of the Road, and a projector supplied by a separate generator clipped to the down tube, which was also connected to the tail light (the arrangement that had been used successfully for cars and motor-cycles).

The nationwide slump which started during 1920 and went on throughout 1921 knocked the bottom out of the market for bicycles – and accessories. Orders for bells fell away to such an extent that the company were obliged to hold up production for a time. At one stage they had a quarter of a million bells in stock. Fortunately they had built up a strong export trade in good quality bells which outsold cheaper American and German bells all over the world, and production was resumed at the rate of 20,000 a week. The sales of bicycle lamps were also affected by the Government's decision to continue 'Summer Time', which had been introduced as a temporary wartime measure in 1916. The saving of 150 hours of extra daylight meant that many cyclists found they did not need lamps in the evening, and Peter Bennett gloomily reminded the board: 'We must face the fact that "Summer Time" has caused a permanent reduction in the number of cycle lamps sold.'

When trade began to pick up after the slump, Bennett decided to make a strong bid to capture a bigger share of the world market for cycle lamps – which meant cheap lamps. 'Instead of attempting to cheapen our existing lamps,' he said, 'we have redesigned them completely from the beginning and as a result have been able to put on the market lamps at prices very much lower than ever before.' That Lucas were able to do this was due to that master-craftsman in metal-working, W. H. Egginton, who worked out a method of pressing the lamp bodies instead of spinning them. This did not suit some of the agents, because it involved Lucas dropping other more expensive models. They admitted they had sold only a few of them, but were quite happy to regard Lucas as high-class manufacturers of high-class goods and to fill up their stocks with cheap lamps from Lucas's competitors at home and abroad.

The Lucas reputation was firmly based on quality, and this began with the materials used. W. I. Shaw, who joined the buying office as a young man in 1919 after serving in the Royal Flying Corps (and retired in 1967 as group chief buyer) has told me how Harry Lucas made certain of this basic quality:

There were no specifications to work to in the old cycle days, no material specifications – I'm speaking from the purchasing point of view – and the materials that came in were understood by the suppliers to be exactly as Lucas required. If it was brass it was the Birmingham Mint or Whitfields, if it was nickel silver it was Headley Birch or Barker & Allen, if it was burners for the acetylene lamp it would be George Bray of Leeds, if it was wicks for lamps it had got to be Morgan Crossley. They had earned their passage, you see, and they held it to quality as Harry Lucas needed it.

The latest Lucas lamps brought in big orders when they were introduced at the Cycle Show at the end of 1922: over 30,000 for a new Planet oil lamp selling at 2s, 20,000 for the new cheap acetylene lamp called the Calcia Cadet and 10,000 for the larger Calcia Club. Good export orders were received from Australia, India and Japan. Two years later exports of cycle accessories to Japan fell sharply after the great earthquake of 1924, which destroyed all the trade-mark records. Local manufacturers took advantage of this to produce articles with the Lucas trade mark and Lucas name without payment, and the company had to ask the Department of Overseas Trade to apply diplomatic pressure in Tokio to get it stopped. Meanwhile the cycle bell business had recovered so well that output reached 40,000 a week in 1923, and £11,000 had to be spent on new plant to avoid the slow deliveries which were upsetting the cycle trade at home.

In the range of Motor-Cyclealities the most important change after the war was the introduction of the Magdyno as an alternative to the separate magneto and dynamo for ignition and lighting. Many motor-cyclists still distrusted electricity for lighting, however, so Lucas had to continue marketing a full range of projectors and separate acetylene generators.

The word Magdyno had been registered as a trade mark for dynamo electric machines on 23 October 1915, but it was not until 23 April 1917 that the patent for such a machine was taken out in the joint names of Harry Lucas, Carl Breeden and the company. It consisted of a magneto and a small dynamo mounted above it in one compact unit driven by gears from the magneto shaft. This was considered to be an improvement on having a separate dynamo, which needed its own pulley and a belt, but it was to have problems of its own. Lucas produced a battery and lamps to go with it. The development of the Magdyno was done partly on the private motor-cycles owned by members of the staff and partly on machines on loan from the manufacturers. Arnold Egginton claims that he had the first Magdyno to be fitted on a motor-cycle, an ex-WD Sunbeam he bought after the war for £90 with his demobilisation gratuity. It was a chain-cum-belt model made for the French Army and was used in the Alps. He and his father, W. H. Egginton, E. J. B. Danks and W. H. Edwards used to have various pieces of electrical equipment fitted to their motor-cycles and go out testing them at weekends after the war. 'I remember once I was testing the Magdyno with Danks,' he told me, 'and the fibre gears weren't working properly. We had this thing taken down and laid out on a sheet of paper all over the road. Oh, we had some fun with it . . . The ladies used to sit around while we worked eating ice cream and one thing and another.' Summer in the early 1920s . . . .

Where the Magdyno could be fitted in place of a magneto, some sets were sold to convert existing motor-cycles, but for new machines Lucas canvassed the public and the motor-cycle dealers to specify the Magdyno when ordering a new motor-cycle, in which case the manufacturer fitted it as an extra and the price was fixed by Lucas, including the retail figure and the trade discount. A thorough marketing job was done on the Magdyno, with models available for single-cylinder, horizontally-opposed, Vee-twin and four-cylinder engines, each costing about £20 retail. A Magdyno lighting and ignition set for a single-cylinder solo machine complete with battery, switchbox, head and tail lamps cost £27 10s.

A good business was also done in selling separate magnetos, dynamos, batteries and lighting sets. By the end of 1919 Thomson-Bennett magnetos were being fitted by twenty-five motor-cycle manufacturers, including such well-known firms as Triumph, Sunbeam, Enfield, James, Matchless, New Hudson, AJS, Scott and Zenith. But these were only intermittent orders for batches of 50 or 100 magnetos, each one having to be competed for with rival magneto manufacturers. For road-testing the post-war Thomson-Bennett motor-cycle magnetos a typical route was up Sunrising Hill and down Edge Hill, then in reverse, continuing all day. Another took the testers to the West Country for four days during which they climbed all the well-known test hills used for the Motor Cycling Club's reliability trials.

The motor-cycle firms did not get into sizeable production until after the slump, and by 1922 Lucas were making over 1,000 Magdynos a week. A member of the staff who was employed on the motor-cycle side at this time was a young man named Jack Masterton, who had been introduced to Lucas in 1920 by his uncle, J. Albert Thomson, straight from the RNAS and was destined to have a distinguished career in the company. After spells at the works and the Willesden service depot he began selling magnetos to the small engine manufacturers and motor-cycle manufacturers, many of whom used proprietary engines in their machines. Then he turned his attention to persuading the bigger manufacturers to list the Magdyno as an extra at a reasonable price. Masterton got Norton and BSA to agree to this policy, but the biggest 'scoop' was achieved by Peter Bennett with Triumph, who 'accepted his suggestion' (as he modestly put it) to fit the Magdyno (and a Lucas bulb horn) as standard equipment on a new machine they were planning for 1923, for which they expected an output of 10,000 a year.

All this was achieved in the face of keen competition. Robert Bosch had made a strong recovery from the war, with their reputation for engineering quality untarnished, and this was reflected in demands from export markets for British motor-cycles (21,000 were exported in 1920) to be fitted with Bosch magnetos. Bosch also produced their own version of the combined magneto/dynamo, and it was this that led Lucas to start negotiating with the motor-cycle manufacturers to fit Lucas Magdynos and magnetos as initial equipment.

The popularity of the Lucas Magdyno became such that every motor-cycle manufacturer, whether he fitted a Lucas/Thomson-Bennett magneto or not, had to provide for a Lucas Magdyno to be fitted to special order. Apart from Bosch, there was strong competition from home suppliers like ML, who brought out a smaller combined lighting and ignition set called the Maglita which did not have a gear drive (a feature that gave Lucas a lot of service trouble with the Magdyno, because most of the gears were made of a fibre composition for the sake of quietness and were prone to strip their teeth). Lucas replied with a cheaper and smaller Magdyno on the same lines as the Maglita called the Magdynette, which overcame the gear troubles but multiplied the electrical ones. BTH got together with Powell & Hanmer and Chloride to produce a competitive Mag-Generator set, and the old Lucas rivals, Millers, sold separate dynamo sets with separate drives.

The competition in selling magnetos was perhaps even fiercer because an important criterion was the success obtained in motor-cycle trials and races, above all in the annual Tourist Trophy races in the Isle of Man. A Lucas Electrical Company advertisement in *Motor Cycling* on 23 June 1920 stating that Thomson-Bennett magnetos were fitted to the first three finishers in the Junior TT is the first indication that the company had become aware of the importance of racing successes (though the earliest advertisement of this kind I have been able to trace was in the same magazine on 8 August 1911, announcing that John Guzzwell had used a Lucas King of the Road acetylene projector with separate generator for his record ride of 2,801 miles in six days). Three months later they were proudly advertising that out of eighty-eight machines awarded gold medals in the 1920 ACU Six-Days reliability trial, twenty-five were fitted with

Thomson-Bennett magnetos and seven with Lucas Magdyno sets. By June in the following year there had come a change of emphasis in nomenclature, for the AJS motor-cycles ridden by Howard Davies and Eric Williams which won the 1921 Senior and Junior Tourist Trophies that year were advertised as being fitted with 'Lucas magnetos (formerly Thomson-Bennett)'.

This change in name of the magneto was a belated result of the change in name of Thomson-Bennett (Magnetos) to the Lucas Electrical Company, which had taken place in October 1919. But loyalties die hard, and the magneto continued to be called the Thomson-Bennett for over a year. It was now described as being manufactured throughout by Joseph Lucas, while the Lucas Electrical Company was referred to as the sales company. The Magdyno, though developed in the Thomson-Bennett days, seems always to have been attributed to Lucas. In fact a sense of division persisted among the staff, many continuing to think of themselves as 'T-B people' and the rest 'Lucas'. After the Thomson-Bennett name disappeared, the company remained in two camps on each side of Great King Street – the Electrical Company (with Thomson-Bennett overtones), who regarded themselves as technically superior with their dynamos and magnetos on one side of the road and in Well Street, and what Peter Bennett himself described as 'the JL side', which made the common-or-garden lamps, horns, bells and other cycle, motor-cycle and motor-car accessories, on the other side adjoining Burbury Street and Farm Street.

Although not connected with any contemporary products, both sides of the company took pride in the part played by Lucas in two national achievements after the war. The Vickers-Vimy biplane that made the first direct Trans-Atlantic flight in June 1919 was fitted with Lucas aero-dynamos to provide current for lamps, flares, horn, wireless and for heating the airmen's clothes, and the R34 airship that made the first double crossing of the Atlantic in the same year was equipped with Lucas self-starters for its 275hp Sunbeam engines.

But to return to the Tourist Trophy races. It was quickly realised that some practical help would have to be provided for the racing motor-cyclists whose successes were so valuable for advertising the magnetos (by whatever name they were called). In keeping with the times the organisation was minimal, and this is how it was described to me by one of its early members:

The Lucas team that went to the Isle of Man in those days was very different from what it would be today. I remember there was one bloke with a motor-cycle and sidecar – Jock Miller, he was our chief magneto engineer with The Electrical Company – myself and another bloke. That was the whole team, you see, and that's how things were done. I had my own motor-bike with me and we just went round the island with this motor-cycle and sidecar with a few spares in the back.

The speaker was Robert Neill, who was to spend his life with the company after joining straight from school in 1922 and eventually became vice-chairman of Butlers, the Lucas lamp subsidiary, before he retired in 1969. His father was James Neill, head of the Sheffield steel company, which the reader may remember as coming to the rescue with supplies of magnets for Thomson-Bennett magnetos in 1914 when Britain had to depend on her own resources for these essential components. James Neill and Peter Bennett became life-long friends.

Another Lucas visitor to the island was Masterton, who went to the TT races regularly with his friend Gilbert Smith, of the Norton company. Nortons dominated the TT races at that time and, although they bought some Lucas magnetos and Magdynos for their standard machines, they used BTH magnetos for their racing motor-cycles. Masterton eventually persuaded them to change to Lucas magnetos, whereupon BTH gave up the business. This was particularly gratifying because Nortons were controlled by Charles Vandervell of CAV, who was a long-standing rival of Lucas. He had gained a controlling interest in the Norton Manufacturing Company in 1913 through R. J. Shelley, Ltd, a CAV associate manufacturing tools and fixtures. Vandervell became chairman and renamed the company Norton Motors, Limited.

The biggest prize in the motor-cycle field was BSA, who surpassed even Triumph and became the leading firm in the British industry. They were a challenge to Lucas because, although they specified the Magdyno in a few cases, they were inclined to prefer other competitors' sets. In 1923 Masterton persuaded them to order half their requirements from Lucas (the other half being supplied by BTH) but three years were to pass before Bennett was able to report that arrangements had been made to meet the whole of BSA's requirements for the next year.

Making magnetos had become an extremely cut-throat business, so much so that some of the firms engaged in it were reported to be getting into financial trouble. Peter Bennett, who probably knew more about the subject than anyone, remarked: 'How much longer

THIS IS INCORRECT

this will go on we cannot say, but of course it is perfectly ridiculous that one of the most delicate parts of the mechanism of the petrol vehicle should be called for at an absolutely uneconomical price, and it is a position that cannot permanently go on without injury to all parties concerned.'

EIC Magnetos in particular, though they had contracts with a score or more well-known motor-cycle firms, including Douglas, Rudge, Ariel, ABC, Dunelt, P & M, Levis, Scott, JAP and Sunbeam, and claimed to be supplying about 80 per cent of the motor-cycle market, were short of money. They tried to sell a 'magdyno' of their own without much success, and were working on a new small dynamo. To cope with their increased business they had bought some land at Shaftmoor Lane, Birmingham, for a new factory which became essential when they got a contract for a four-cylinder magneto for the Clyno car, which was intended to attack the Morris Cowley's grip on the low-price car market. At this point W. T. Turner, the managing director, approached Peter Bennett to discuss selling the company to Joseph Lucas, but no progress could be made because of the attitude of A. J. Ash, who had acquired control of the old Electric Ignition Company from the founders, the Hall family, when it ran into difficulties before World War I. Bennett and Oliver Lucas went to see Ash without success, but a few weeks later Ash died. Turner offered the business to Lucas once more, with the agreement of the executors, and a purchase price of about £35,000 was settled. And so in August 1925 Peter Bennett found himself in control of the company that he had left 20 years earlier in order to start Thomson-Bennett. Meanwhile the original makers of ML magnetos, Morris & Lister, had sold this side of their business to S. Smith & Sons, the motor accessories company, immediately after the war.

EIC was not the first Lucas post-war acquisition. Twelve months earlier, in 1924, the directors of Brolt, Limited, a small firm in Oldbury, north of Birmingham, had found themselves in financial straits. After making several approaches, they insisted on Lucas taking them over to save them from collapse, and the business changed hands for £50,000. It had been formed in 1911 by two men, H. B. Brooks (one of the bicycle-saddle making family) and Holt – hence the name Brolt – to manufacture and factor electrical equipment. They were early in the field with an electric starter before the war, and later built up some electrical equipment business with the makers of commercial vehicles (notably Albion, Beardmore and Jowett) and a few motor-car firms like Rhode, Star, Hampton and Calcott. This was useful, but what really decided Lucas to buy Brolt was the fear that if they did not take over the company, someone else might do so, to their possible disadvantage in the future.

In both these approaches by competitive firms that were finding the going too rough could be discerned the growing commercial as well as financial strength of Joseph Lucas in the motor components industry. This strength was not fortuitous; it was the result of Lucas's noticing signs of the 1920–1 slump before it came, and retrenching in time. When the slump finally hit the economy, Lucas were only working hand-to-mouth and had no stocks to be written down or scrapped, whereas some of their competitors, who were unprepared for the slump, were faced with over-production problems and made heavy financial losses.

The picture was therefore the reverse of what was commonly supposed at the time – that Lucas sought to expand by absorbing competitors. Instead, as in the case of Brolt and EIC, it was the competitors who approached Lucas. As we shall see in due course, these two were only a foretaste of something very much bigger to come.

A Lucas 'Motor-Cycleality' – the Magdyno

CHAPTER TWO

THE IMPORTANCE OF WILLIAM MORRIS

Now let us return to Motoralities. The sale of Lucas ignition, starting and lighting equipment and other motor accessories after World War I was bound up with the progress made by those hopeful companies, old and new, which set out to make their fortunes in motor-car manufacture when peace returned. The output of cars had reached only a modest scale when war broke out – the number produced in 1913 was 26,238, Ford with about 6,000, Wolseley between 2,000 and 3,000, and Morris, Austin, Singer and Rover about 1,000 each, being the leading makers. Very few cars were made for private use during the war, and it was reckoned that there were about 100,000 cars (including many imported from the Continent) on the road after the Armistice was signed on 11 November 1918. In the next four years this number was to grow to 500,000.

More than forty new makes appeared in the first two years after the war, and there were some 100 British car manufacturers at the 1920 Motor Show, which was held in two sections at Olympia and White City, compared with sixty-five at the 1913 Show. Customers for Thomson-Bennett magnetos among the newcomers included Cubitts, the building contractors; Angus-Sanderson; Ruston & Hornsby, who made farm tractors; and Leyland, the commercial vehicle manufacturers. They were all encouraged to enter the motor-car industry by the $33\frac{1}{3}$ per cent McKenna duty on imported cars imposed in 1915. Then there were the pre-war firms, in addition to those I have mentioned, who reconverted their factories back from armaments and munitions to making motor-cars: Standard, Crossley (who had done good business with a staff car and a tender during the war), Clement-Talbot, Vulcan, Calcott, Humber, Arrol-Johnston, GWK, Sunbeam, Jowett, Deemster, Belsize and Straker-Squire. All fitted Thomson-Bennett magnetos to some of their cars – as soon as they could make any.

The key man in the whole business was William Morris, who was aiming to be the Henry Ford of Great Britain with his Morris Cowley, made by mass-production assembly line methods using as many bought-out components as possible. As one of the leading component suppliers, Lucas had been close to Morris since the beginning of the war, when he was working on the first Morris Cowley, which he showed to the editors of the motoring magazines early in 1915. Morris had fitted a Lucas 6-volt dynamo and Lucas electric head, side and tail lights (price £10 10s) as standard equipment. This was the first proper contract received by Lucas from a motor manufacturer – orders were usually placed for batches of items – so it was a landmark at Great King Street. The quantity, fifty sets a week, was considered enormous, and some people even thought it was beyond the factory's capacity. Lucas lighting was to remain standard equipment on the Morris Cowley throughout its whole life. At first it was a three-lamp set (two combined head-and-side lights and a tail light) until in 1923 Oliver Lucas persuaded Morris that the 1924 Cowley ought to have the full five-lamp set with separate side lamps that was already fitted to the Morris Oxford.

The position with magnetos was somewhat different. In 1915 Morris had specified a Thomson-Bennett as one of three optional magnetos for the Continental Red Seal engine which he imported from America. When he changed to the Hotchkiss engine made in Coventry from 1919 onwards (when the car really got into production), he continued to use a Thomson-Bennett magneto at first. But the magneto, produced at a low price in quantities which the factory was not accustomed to, gave so much trouble that the Lucas directors decided on the drastic step of voluntarily withdrawing it, asking Morris for six months' respite in which to put it right, during which time he would be free to buy his magnetos elsewhere. Morris, greatly impressed by this courageous admission, fell in with the request and ordered a supply of magnetos from BTH. At the end of that time he offered the Morris Cowley with the option of a Lucas Magdyno or a BTH Mag-generator, neither of which was really satisfactory.

The Lucas Magdyno was originally designed for single-cylinder and twin-cylinder motor-cycles, and it was adapted for use on a four-cylinder car by means of a split slip-ring and four leads to the plugs. There was no earth return in the ignition circuit, this being completed in each case by firing on another plug and the lead back to the Magdyno. In those days a magneto was considered to be working satisfactorily if it produced a spark – any spark – and the Magdyno modified for the Morris Cowley gave a thin spark that did not do its job properly. It was not a success and had its share of gear failures and troubles with the high tension windings in the armatures and with condensers.

After another 12 months Lucas had developed a smaller magneto, the G4M, which they could supply at a price that suited Morris if they put it into volume production. Unhappily they went too far, making it too small and too light, and it gave a good deal of trouble until it was improved by strengthening it here and there and fitting bigger electrodes. Magnetos that gave trouble were immediately replaced, and this generous policy was inevitably abused by the trade and the public. In fact, a large proportion of the alleged 'faulty' magnetos returned to the factory were found to be perfectly all right. This was not the first time that complaints about equipment were to prove to be exaggerated, some motorists – and others – being always on the look-out for a stick with which to beat Joseph Lucas.

The 1915 Morris Cowley had no self-starter, but the French-designed Hotchkiss engine which Morris took over for the 1919 production model incorporated a combined dynamo and starter called a dynamotor, which was used on several cars on the Continent. As no dynamotor was available in England, Morris asked Lucas to produce one. Meanwhile the new Morris Cowley went into production without a self-starter for the first two years. This continued until the Lucas 12-volt dynamotor began to be supplied in 1922 as an optional extra, and from 1924 onwards all Morris Cowleys were to be fitted with it. Morris wanted it in such a hurry to begin with that it was put into production straight off the drawing board, without any development testing, yet it turned out to be reasonably reliable in service.

The dynamotor, combining the functions of dynamo and self-starter in one unit, had the great advantage of being silent when starting because it was chain-driven. Mechanically it was a compromise, because the right gear ratio for starting resulted in the dynamo being driven rather fast, which entailed using an excessively large dynamo with an unnecessarily big output. A 'half-charge' switch (demanding some discretion on the part of the driver) was provided to avoid overloading the small battery on the running-board, but the large dynamo was nevertheless the source of battery overcharging and short life. Other firms that ordered the Lucas dynamotor were Humber and Hillman, which were independent companies in those days (but Oliver Lucas was going to have to fight hard to keep the Hillman business from going to Delco-Remy after the McKenna import duties came off in 1924).

A separate electric starter designed specifically for its job was required for other cars. In the United States the Eclipse Machine

Company had produced a form of starter drive by means of a pinion driving a toothed ring on the flywheel that was a great advance on the friction drive previously used for most starters. Vincent Bendix got control of Eclipse and bought up other manufacturers until he obtained a monopoly, and the Bendix became the accepted form of starter drive in America. In England it was made under licence by Rotax and used by CAV, but because of internal dissension at Bendix they were never called upon to pay any royalties. Joseph Lucas produced their own version of it, with a compression spring instead of the torsion spring employed by Bendix, and they patented it in the belief that it was secure (it was not until many years later, when the Bendix patents had expired, that they found out that Bendix had earlier patents which could be claimed to have anticipated the Lucas ones). The Lucas electric starter had two important advantages: it was more compact and the spring very rarely broke, and when it did, the broken spring would not put the starter out of action, as was the case with the Bendix. On the other hand it gave a somewhat harsher engagement and was noisier. The arguments for and against it were to continue for many years both inside and outside the factory, but it was to survive and give satisfactory, if noisy, service in millions of cars.

The euphoria of 1919 gave way to the slump of 1921, which sent some motor firms to the wall – orders for Lucas electrical equipment dropped from £874,346 in December 1920 to £514,461 in the following May. Morris shocked his rivals by a series of cuts in the prices of his cars that were more drastic than anything they envisaged for themselves, and by cutting his prices before they did. The Morris Cowley two-seater had cost £465 when it was put on the market in 1919, but when the slump started at the end of 1920 Morris slashed it to £375 to stimulate demand (his sales had dropped from 276 cars in September 1920 to 74 in the following January). That year he produced 1,932 cars out of a total UK output of 60,000. At the 1921 Motor Show he cut the price again to £299 with the result that, whereas the total output of the industry in 1921 fell by a third to 40,000, Morris increased his sales by 50 per cent to 3,076 cars. The price of the Morris Cowley went down again in 1922 (when he made 6,956 cars and took the lead in the industry), dropping to £225 at the Motor Show in October, but this time Morris had a specific target – to match the price of the new Austin Seven.

This enormously successful little car was designed to take the place of the cycle-car, which had been popular before the war (there had been twenty-one makes in 1914) and was revived by a number of firms in 1919. Most cycle-cars were noisy, uncomfortable and unreliable, whereas the Austin Seven was a 'proper' motor-car scaled down to miniature proportions. Austin was also said to have introduced it as an alternative to the motor-cycle and sidecar, used by many young family men, and its track was no wider so that it could be parked in the same area in a suburban front garden. The Seven was introduced in the nick of time to save Sir Herbert Austin from disaster. The company was in financial difficulty (a receiver had just been appointed) caused by trying to sell one model, the Twenty, in too large quantities at a price that was too competitive to be economic.

Lucas did no electrical business with Austin at that time; it was said that Harry had fallen out with 'Pa' Austin, but whether this was true or not Austin certainly got all his requirements from C. A. Vandervell, for whose electrical equipment Lucas had a healthy respect. But they had the important Morris contract and for a couple of years before the Austin Seven appeared they had done almost as much business with Rover, who had produced the Rover 8 from a design they had acquired from Jack Sangster, whose father had been a pioneer manufacturer with the Ariel car in the 1890s and had later bought Swift. The Rover company advertised in the daily press inviting tenders for the supply of components for this important new model, and they were quoted prices so much lower than anything Lucas could offer that they had practically decided to give half the orders for ignition and lighting equipment to Rotax Motor Accessories. For the past three years Lucas had had a very influential agent in Coventry named Alfred Bednell, and it was probably due to his efforts that Peter Bennett was able to report to the board that 'by judicious handling the whole business has been secured and at a price which is quite favourable.' The Rover 8 got away to a very good start – Rover took 630 Lucas sets in May 1921 compared with Morris's 100–120 a week. 'As this is one of the cars which is selling in quantity,' Peter Bennett added, 'it is extremely satisfactory to have established this position.' In his view the Morris Cowley and the Rover 8 were the outstanding cars of the 1921 Motor Show, and Lucas were fortunate in having their equipment fitted on both.

With so much depending on the Morris contract, it was perhaps unwise for Lucas to leave the arrangements with William Morris almost entirely in the hands of one man, Carl Breeden, the sales director of the Electrical Company. So it was hardly surprising that there was consternation in the boardroom in January 1922 when a quarrel involving the Lucas family (Breeden, it will be recalled, was married to Oliver's sister Hilda) resulted in Breeden immediately leaving the company. With no one else on close terms with Morris, who was very friendly with Breeden but was not an easy man to get on with, the business with their biggest customer could be in jeopardy. A replacement for Breeden had to be found – quickly.

Fortunately a candidate was ready at hand, having just joined the company. Shortly before the Breeden *contretemps* Oliver Lucas had been approached by a young man named Frederick Thacker, who worked for Rolls-Royce and used to visit the Lucas factory occasionally to discuss problems with Harold Ireland, the chief engineer of the Lucas Electrical Company, about the E575 dynamo and switchgear Lucas supplied for the 'best car in the world' (Rolls-Royce made their own coil and distributor and starter). Thacker, wanting a change after 17 years on the drawing board, first at BTH and then at Rolls-Royce, had got his release from Henry Royce himself, on whose personal staff he was working at West Wittering as electrical assistant. Oliver Lucas, who had met Thacker during his visits to Birmingham, shared the universal veneration of Rolls-Royce, and the chance of employing a Rolls-Royce technician at Great King Street greatly attracted him. Thacker had therefore found a ready response to his enquiry about a job at Lucas and he was just the man, Oliver now thought, to handle William Morris. Thacker was thereupon sent off to Cowley in a company car, while Peter Bennett and Oliver Lucas anxiously waited for his return.

In the event there was nothing to worry about. Thacker spent about half an hour with Morris, who told him what he knew about the Lucas-Breeden conflict, and when Thacker tentatively remarked that he hoped to be the Lucas liaison man with Cowley in future, Morris simply said: 'Well, that's all right.' Before leaving Oxford, Thacker took the precaution of meeting Breeden at the Morris Garages showrooms in Queen Street, where Morris had given him the job of manager, and got his good wishes for success in his new appointment. When he arrived back at Great King Street, his report was received with noticeable relief. One consequence of Breeden's departure was that Alfred Bednell was given his seat on the board of the Lucas Electrical Company with a nominal shareholding. About this time the commission basis on which Bednell had been working seems to have changed because of the greatly increased sales figures in the motor industry, and this was probably linked with his being given a directorship.

As a result of the policy of closer liaison with William Morris, Oliver Lucas succeeded in getting an order for the whole of his 1923 requirements for starting, ignition and lighting equipment (Thacker providing the continuous liaison), an event that was reported with considerable satisfaction at the next Lucas board meeting. Oliver also acquired a Morris Cowley for his own use. As he drove it, he instinctively thought of ways in which it might be improved, and during a talk with Morris he suggested having the ignition advance-and-retard and hand throttle controls operated by rods and levers alongside the steering column. Morris jumped at the idea, and Jack Orme was asked to work it out in detail with a draughtsman named Slater. (Orme had made the lamp brackets for the prototype Cowley produced during the war.) The Morris steering column control rods were made complete in one shop at Great King Street – all the pressed parts were made there, and they did their own brazing – and they were assembled at the rate of 2,000 a week. The young man in charge of assembly was Arnold Egginton, son of the inventive W. H. Egginton, thus carrying on a Lucas father-to-son tradition which was to be seen in all parts of the factory.

Another addition to the Morris Cowley suggested by Oliver Lucas was the scuttle ventilator. Orme and Slater were sent on detachment to Cowley, where they worked with Morris and his chief engineer, a man called Seddon, whom Orme has described to me as being 'much given to cursing blindly'. Orme thought William Morris was a 'clinking fellow'. If any trouble occurred in the works, he asked the men to go to the canteen and join him in a cup of tea, over which everything was settled. He used to keep three or four bicycles at various parts of the factory so that he could make a quick tour of the workshops at any time (he had started, of course, as a cycle-maker and had won cycle-racing championships). Having Orme designing parts on the car itself, as it were, meant that they could be put in hand at the Lucas factory exactly as they were wanted. And if there was a crisis in getting sufficient cars out on time while they were at Oxford, Orme and Slater used to help the Morris men to finish the job – a point that was not lost on William Morris and did much to build up goodwill for Lucas.

At the beginning of 1922 Lucas succeeded in getting the first order for 500 sets for the new 8hp Standard. 'As in the past we have never had any lighting and starting business from them,' reported Peter Bennett, 'this is very gratifying.' Other orders were for the Hillman, Vauxhall (500 sets for the Fourteen), and the Buckingham light car 'which is very well thought of in Coventry' (an opinion that was not justified by events, for the Buckingham company folded in 1923, but its founder, T. G. John, went on to achieve success with Alvis). Angus-Sanderson, a company that Lucas had co-operated with in producing its first car after the war, had been revived after going into liquidation and naturally ordered equipment from Great King Street. Triumph, too, placed an order in connection with their first 8hp car. Other car firms Lucas were supplying included Armstrong-Siddeley, Crouch, Calcott, Cluley, Galloway (an offshoot of Arrol-Johnston), Airedale, Vulcan and Talbot-Darracq. In August 1923 Lucas were asked for the first time to quote for Ford lamps (for the Model T). They put in a quotation as a matter of form while realising that they lacked sufficient factory capacity at that moment to take on another really big customer. They did not get the order, but the initial contact was historically interesting.

In the summer of 1922 Rover were working on their new 12hp model and Alfred Bednell was able to report that they were going to standardise Lucas equipment, including horns, on all their 1923 range. Considering their price was £2 more than the Rotax price, this was a tribute to Lucas quality – and salesmanship. Bednell, who had been the Ministry of Munitions representative in Coventry during the war and knew everybody worth knowing in the district, operated largely from the bar at the County Club, which was the unofficial head-quarters of the motor industry in Coventry and was where all the real business was done between the manufacturers and their suppliers. Thacker was introduced by him to this inner circle and was im-mediately accepted. One result was that Thacker found out that Rovers were saving up a number of small points about Lucas equip-ment which the factory were then able to deal with straight away, thereby improving the efficiency of the equipment and removing possible causes of complaint in the future. This action opened the way for the new contract. They also got the contract for the new 9hp four-cylinder model which Rover had to produce in a hurry when they found that their two-cylinder Rover 8 could not compete with the four-cylinder Austin Seven.

Two early signs of changes that were to take place later in the design of electrical equipment occurred in 1922. In the spring Oliver Lucas went to Switzerland, where he found that the Lucas dynamo with its third brush control (which was also used by American manu-facturers) was meeting strong competition from the German Bosch dynamo with a system of voltage regulation. If Bosch had tried to

(right) Magnetos made by Thomson-Bennett (acquired by Lucas in 1914) were successful in motor-cycle racing after the Great War, starting with the 1920 Junior TT in which they were fitted to the first three finishers. Here is C. J. Williams (AJS) nearing the winning post to win by ten minutes after 'pushing in' from Creg-ny-Baa with gear trouble. *(National Motor Museum)*

(below) Oliver Lucas was a motoring enthusiast throughout his life. Here he drives a 15.9hp Daracq of 1912 vintage

(left) When the company was formed in 1898, Harry Lucas built himself a house in Moseley which he
called 'Hilver' after his children,
Hilda and Oliver, shown in this contemporary photograph
(below) Three Lucas generations.
Harry Lucas and his son Oliver with
their wives and grandson, John. A
picture taken at a Lucas sports day in
the 1930s *(Harry E. King)*

make such a dynamo in England, they would have been priced out of the market, but the exchange rate of the German mark made it possible for them to sell their dynamos in neutral countries at competitive prices. Peter Bennett suggested that Lucas should get some experience of the voltage regulator by making special dynamos for Switzerland, and use that country as an experimental ground. (Whether this idea ever came to anything is not recorded, but the voltage-regulator dynamo did not become a standard Lucas product for another 10 years.)

Then, a few months later, Bennett reported that the Humber company were going to use coil and distributor ignition instead of a magneto for their new 8hp car, and that Lucas had secured the first order for it, as well as for the lighting and starting equipment. (Again, this development was ahead of its time, for Lucas coil and distributor ignition did not take over from the magneto as original equipment for cars on a wide scale until 1928.)

The sales technique employed in getting the car manufacturers to fit Lucas magnetos, starters, dynamos, batteries and lights as 'initial equipment' was also used to develop the sales of horns, observation mirrors, and other accessories. The essential point was to keep in close touch with the manufacturers in the planning of new models from the drawing-board stage onwards. As Peter Bennett said: 'Once our models are designed into the car we can hold the business, and it is part of our principle to push wherever we can for any of the general lines as soon as we have fixed up the contract for lighting and starting, or magnetos.'

They were also doing a big business, of course, in the sale of ignition, starting, and lighting equipment and other motor accessories through wholesalers, retailers and shippers. In addition to magnetos, impulse starters, self-starters, Magdynos, dynamos, dynamotors and batteries, the Lucas catalogues of the early 1920s listed a whole range of electric projectors (what we call headlights nowadays), combined head and side lamps for small cars, electric driving side lamps ('giving a soft, pleasant light good enough for moderate night driving'), and ordinary side and tail lights – as well as electric bulbs. There was also a headlight dimmer.

But in the early 1920s electric lighting was by no means everyone's choice. They were also selling oil and acetylene motor-car lamps, which Peter Bennett thought was 'a marvel, considering the amount of electrical equipment that is being sold.' The pre-war electrical attachment for screwing into the back of petroleum side and tail lights continued to be offered as a belt-and-braces safeguard for cautious drivers who disliked relying on one form of illumination. For really determined die-hards Lucas supplied an acetylene projector and separate generator for small cars and a self-contained acetylene head-lamp for lorries. A minor headlamp development in 1923 that brought back echoes from the bitter legal battles of the past was the granting of a licence to their old rivals, H. Miller & Company, for the manufacture of a motor vehicle lamp incorporating a method of ad-justable attachment that had been patented by Harry Lucas and W. H. Egginton in 1921. The fee charged for this licence was £10 a year. The general accessories included girder wrenches, screwdrivers, oil cans and lifting jacks.

It is necessary to emphasise the wide extent of Lucas business at this time in order to put into perspective the claim sometimes put for-ward that Joseph Lucas, along with several other suppliers of com-ponents for the Morris Cowley, really developed their business on the strength of Morris orders. The biographers of Lord Nuffield went so far as to say:

> These are 'household names' now, but in those days the specialisation among motor industry suppliers was far less advanced than it has since become . . . Lucas's, for instance, got their first bulk order, which was from Morris, in 1914 . . . at that time they were a relatively small con-cern, only just embarking on the supply of electrical equipment for cars . . . Morris men are probably not in error when they think that the award of the first contract for lighting sets to Lucas and for speedom-eters to Smiths led to the specialist development of these particular firms, which resulted in their present peculiar importance in their lines of industry.

Against this it can be claimed that Morris was enabled to produce the Morris Cowley largely because of the help he got from Lucas and other suppliers by such good credit terms that he was able to assemble, dispatch and get paid for cars with their components before he paid their bills.

Nevertheless, it was perfectly true that by 1923 over half the Lucas output of starting and lighting equipment was being supplied to Morris. What counted even more was the volume, and this can be judged by the fact that in the five years from 1921 to 1925 the sales of Morris vehicles went up from 3,000 to 55,000 a year (out of a total output of 132,000 British cars). In the same period the Lucas sales to Morris increased on the following scale:

	£
1921	94,725
1922	135,217
1923	372,358
1924	504,411
1925	907,860

(In 1919 the sales to Morris amounted to £6,288!)

The preponderance of Morris business in their turnover was closely watched by the Lucas directors, but in fact the proportion of Lucas output of starting and lighting equipment taken by Morris dropped as the sales of Morris cars and commercial vehicles continued to rise, and it was to fall to one-third by 1926. This was because, as we have seen, Lucas were very wisely increasing their business with other motor manufacturers at the same time; for example, the increase in Lucas business in the six months to February 1924 was more than the total supplied to Morris, which meant that even if they had lost the Morris account, they would still have been better off than in the same period the previous year. Nevertheless the importance of Morris to Lucas contract business at this time was undeniable, as the figures for the top ten annual contracts for 1924-5 show:

	£
Morris (car)	840,550
(commercial)	67,310
Triumph	98,467
Rover	95,538
Standard	88,806
AJS	45,597
Humber	44,759
BSA	44,445
Armstrong-Siddeley	42,404
Wolseley	32,122
Jowett	23,188

The rapid increase in Lucas sales from 1920 to 1925 was inevitably accompanied by production problems, notably in designing machines for winding armatures (and later coils). This in turn led to an increasing number of complaints about faulty components, especially magnetos. Complaints from Morris owners were very carefully watched, because of the importance of the Morris contract, and at the beginning of 1924 Lucas organised a special visit of service engineers to all the main Morris agents to explain the action that was being taken to put the matter right. They were surprised to find the understanding way in which the agents had accepted and dealt with the complaints. Trouble had also been experienced with the magnetos supplied to Ford for their industrial engines and Fordson tractors, but as they were also having difficulty with carburation and some poor sparking plugs as well, the Lucas magneto was having to cope with exceptional conditions in this case.

Nevertheless this did not exonerate the magneto, and as the failures persisted, some radical treatment was obviously required. The cause had to be tracked down before a cure could be provided, so in 1925 Oliver Lucas arranged for a system of detailed report cards to be introduced in order that a complete case history could be built up. He himself took the chair at a meeting every Monday morning to discuss progress. In between he spent hours at the electrical laboratory in Well Street with a young technical recruit named Herbert Astbury (later to become commercial director of CAV) who has told me what happened: 'We found that the trouble was mainly due to the magneto armatures having a very low level of reliability, so once a week Oliver Lucas, Dr. E. O. Turner, Freddie Brown (from the service organisation) and I sat down and stripped, layer by layer, armature windings of various types endeavouring to find out the cause of failure and then jointly work out a solution.' The armature windings of various types referred to by Astbury included all the important makes of magneto available. A standard test was set, equivalent to 50,000 miles at 60mph (at that time more severe than the user was able to equal), and Oliver Lucas told the annual meeting of shareholders in October that whereas all the latest Lucas magnetos had withstood the test, 'a world famous foreign make failed to stay the course on more than one occasion.'

The company were then faced with the problem of restoring the confidence of the motor trade and the motoring public in the Lucas magneto. At the 1926 Motor Show they announced a unique magneto guarantee, covering all electrical and mechanical breakdowns, burning of contact-breaker points, and all wear and tear for a period of two years. To give the GA4 magneto every appearance of new construction the contacts were labelled L26 (26 for 1926), but in fact they were made of the same material (tungsten) as before, though slightly different in shape. An extraneous cause of magneto failure was the unreliability of condensers. 'They gave a lot of trouble in those days,' Roy Harrison told me, with the experience of having run the Acton depot in 1926 with a daily throughput of 100 cars sent in with electrical trouble. 'They were made with plates of mica and tinfoil laboriously stuck together,' he said, adding reflectively, 'They were Turks . . .'

The magneto crisis produced a development which was to grow in time into a much wider part of Lucas service, under a different name. It was realised that people for whom their vehicles were essential – farmers and their tractors were a good example – could not be expected to wait for a magneto to be repaired at the factory and sent back; they had to have another one straight away. And so the RBA (Replacement Before Arrival) scheme was started, and this helped the factory staff, too, because they were able to arrange for the repair of magnetos in bulk.

CHAPTER THREE

ORGANISING FOR GROWTH

The end of 1925 is a convenient time at which to pause and look at the state of the Lucas company, for it marked the culmination of seven years of rapid growth since the end of World War I – growth in output, sales, profits, factory buildings, plant, and company organisation.

First let us glance at the overall figures:

Year	Profit £	Sales £	Dividend on Ordinary Shares %
1919	44,545	972,607	10
1920	57,844	1,331,658	10 (plus 5% bonus)
1921	66,586	1,366,110	10 (plus 5% bonus)
1922	73,298	1,082,572	10 (plus 5% bonus)
1923	128,812	1,514,863	15 (plus 5% bonus)
1924	137,584	1,831,669	15 (plus 5% bonus)
1925	164,850	2,421,691	15 (plus 2s)

What was the basis of this steady progress? In tracing the broad sweep of Lucas history we have seen how the business was developed on the cycling boom in the closing years of the nineteenth century and how it expanded with the early growth of motoring and motor-cycling in the Edwardian period before World War I. When normal business was resumed in 1919 it was at first divided fairly evenly between the electrical and non-electrical sides, but in the next seven years the motor-car and motor-cycle industries made rapid strides, altering the composition of Lucas's trade. The sales figures for the financial year ended 31 August 1925 show the general picture and emphasise the emergence of electrical components for cars and motor-cycles as the dominant part of the company's business:

	£
Cycle accessories	225,479
Motor-cycle accessories (non-electrical)	131,670
Car lamps and non-electrical accessories	148,651

Electrical components (car and	
motor-cycle)	1,670,296
Spares and repairs	27,366

Exports were a very small part of the total by modern standards, being in direct proportion to the size of the car and motor-cycle industries' export trades, which were still small. In 1924–5 Lucas export sales brought in £177,911, mostly from Far Eastern countries (£117,911), followed by Europe (£32,322) and Colonial, etc (£27,678).

During these seven post-war years the sales of the company increased by two-and-a-half times in value but profits were nearly four times as big, indicating both the benefits of large-scale manufacture and the introduction of more efficient methods of production. This was Oliver Lucas's particular interest, and at every board meeting he presented a list of new machines and plant for sanction by the board. The technical effort of the company was concentrated not so much on the design of the products, which had become fairly standardised by then, as on the machinery and methods required to manufacture them economically, and it was this effort that enabled Lucas to maintain their superiority over their competitors.

Peter Bennett told the board in March 1921 that he thought someone from the factory ought to visit America with the special object of investigating manufacturing processes there. Oliver Lucas, who was on the point of being appointed to the board, was the obvious man to go. And so began the series of visits that were to continue for the rest of Oliver Lucas's life. He sailed in the old *Mauretania* in April 1921 and stayed for a month, visiting seventeen factories, including Bosch Magneto, Westinghouse, Rolls-Royce (Springfield), Delco Light, Electric Auto-Lite, Packard, Gabriel, Edmunds & Jones (the largest makers of electrical car lamps in the world), the Willard Storage Battery Company (the largest makers of small storage batteries in the world), and the Canada Cycle Co.

On his return he reported that he had received 'a broad-minded welcome without exception, although in every case I made my business clear ... I was greatly impressed by the apparent intimate terms between managers and the workpeople who called out "Hallo" to each other in their Christian names right and left on walking through the shops, and in certain cases sit down to meals together in a common mess room.' A subject he noted for further study was the economy and planning of internal transport by travelling belts and gravity conveyer systems (still practically unknown in Britain) to ensure a steady flow of parts. 'I think we could do much in the factory by adopting similar measures, though we are restricted by our many varied productions and the erratic manner in which they have to be sanctioned.' (Thus early were sown the seeds of that drive for rationalisation and standardisation of parts and components by the motor industry in which Oliver Lucas was to play a leading part in later years.) He also brought back some useful ideas on the manufacture and finish of Bakelite mouldings, reflectors for electric lamps, and the winding of magneto and dynamo armatures. A final point that impressed him, and which was to influence his own future policy, was that the American managers were very much younger than men in similar positions in this country. He himself was exactly 30 at this time.

A year later the Lucas factory was saving 7s on each pair of lamp reflectors and had installed an armature winding machine which, by increasing the efficiency of the small E3 dynamo, had saved the order for the Rover 8, which would otherwise have been lost.

The bigger scale of operations inevitably brought changes in the management and organisation of the company. At the same meeting in April 1921 when Oliver Lucas was brought on to the board, commercial managers were appointed on the electrical side (F. H. Walker) and the non-electrical (A. Paddon Smith, who later became Lord Mayor of Birmingham). After serving in the Coldstream Guards during the war, Walker took a job for a short time with a trade protection company before joining Thomson-Bennett at Well Street in 1919. He quickly became an expert in the pricing of electrical equipment, and his experience with the trade protection people was to prove useful when some of the weaker motor-car firms began to falter and credit control had to be exercised with discernment.

Soon after Fred Thacker joined the staff in 1922 the procedure of negotiating contracts with the motor and motor-cycle manufacturers for the supply of electrical equipment was changed when Peter Bennett suggested that the time had come for this to be done by engineers instead of by non-technical salesmen, as had been the case up till then. This was Oliver Lucas's belief, too, and thus came into being the technical sales or sales engineering department with Thacker at its head because of his experience with electrical equipment at Rolls-Royce. Thacker continued to handle the important motor-car firms himself, with the help of W. E. Robinson (who had followed him to Lucas from Rolls-Royce), while Masterton was responsible to Thacker for the motor-cycle companies. None of them were given any formal titles. It was the job of the technical sales department to discuss the fitting of the electrical equipment on a car or motor-cycle as well as its price and specification, so much of Thacker's time among the car firms was spent with the chief engineers, such as Vic Oak of Morris Motors. For the crucial pricing discussion of major contracts Thacker would arrange for Oliver Lucas to accompany him, but as the contracts grew larger Oliver Lucas took on this task alone with his opposite numbers at the motor factories because they were yearly contracts and the quantities got bigger and bigger as the factories were enlarged.

At the same time the Lucas Electrical Company was strengthened by the appointment of Dr E. O. Turner as technical chief. Turner had started life as a teacher at the Birmingham Technical College and had left to join the BLIC company, makers of magnetos and other electrical equipment. His move to Lucas was a severe loss for BLIC and may have contributed to the events which followed his departure and have a later place in this history.

On the organisational plane the formation of an Improvements Committee on the non-electrical side of the business to exchange ideas on design and manufacture was a more radical step than it might seem, for it marked the beginning of the end of the autocratic rule of foremen over their respective domains. At this time all but directors and a favoured few were told to keep out of the shops – and in the plainest possible language. Peter Bennett explained the position in his monthly report in July 1921:

> As we have so very many greatly varying classes of production being carried on in the same organisation and each line is being attacked independently by specialised competitors, the writer feels that our only chance to carry on the business successfully will be by becoming 'a family of specialists', and we are re-organising all the time with this end in view.

Bennett elaborated on this point a few months later when he told the directors: 'We are now considering embarking on a large scheme which will alter our works procedure. For years we have felt the need of a proper planning and progress department so that various heads may be able to devote themselves properly to their own work.' A consultant named Stelling was engaged to prepare data for introducing the scheme.

It was in 1923 that a minor but significant flaw in the Lucas technical organisation became apparent, largely because of the interfering ways of a young man named John Morley (destined to have a distinguished career in the company), who had just been given a job in the Lucas garage. Morley was a rabid motor-cycle enthusiast who could do any repair on his machine and even make the tools for the job. He had an annoying habit of telling the fitters: 'It's no good changing the magneto on that engine, or changing that on that, because the engine's clapped out anyway, the valves have gone.' He was promptly made a chargehand, but what was more important, he made the Lucas managers realise that whereas they had plenty of skilled electrical fitters, they had practically no one who really understood the motor-car and motor-cycle engine as well. This deficiency was quickly made good.

The first conveyer at Great King Street was installed in 1924 – a simple Ewart Chainbelt tray conveyer to feed the first automatic silver-plating plant in A-Block with headlamp reflectors from the polishing shops above. The plating plant was put in by Lucas's neighbours, William Canning & Co, and was the first of its kind to be supplied by Cannings or anyone else in Britain. The demand for lamps soon outran the scope of the old A-Block, so the polishing and plating shops were moved to the newly erected S-Block in Farm Street. They had to be fed with parts from the main blocks in Great King Street, so permission was obtained from the City Council to build a tunnel under Farm Street in which another conveyer was installed. F. A. Jones, the works engineer, designed a special tray for this conveyer which could be set to empty itself automatically at any given floor. This was followed by steel band conveyers for switchbox assembly and test and the dynamo slat conveyer for yoke assembly and test. Many of these new production methods were developed in the factory by a new department of methods engineers started by R. G. Purcell, adding up to the beginning of mass production of components to keep pace with the expanding motor industry.

The increased demand for the company's products (once the slump of 1921–2 was out of the way) continually outran their manufacturing facilities, and at times Lucas definitely lost business through not being able to keep to delivery schedules. Peter Bennett told the board that for the first time in its history the company were not looking for new business because they would not be able to cope with it if they got it. Extra floors were hurriedly added to existing buildings in the Great King Street area, a factory used for making cash boxes on the corner of Burbury Street and Farm Street was bought, empty corners were filled in by new blocks, old brick-built buildings were torn down and new and bigger steel-frame buildings put up in their place. Still the pressure continued, until in May 1923 they found a factory at Formans Road, Sparkhill, Birmingham, that had been used by the Lanchester Motor Company during the war for making cartridge cases and later Rudge-Whitworth wheels. This was snapped up for £45,000, and after some alterations had been made to some of the shops the manufacture of batteries was moved there in January 1924. Lucas had opened their first branch factory. Harry Lucas celebrated the occasion by giving the new department one of his special brand-names, Lucas Batteryalities, which was painted on the sides of the vans allotted to Formans Road.

The wisdom with which staff appointments were now being made (and which has been an outstanding feature of Lucas policy ever since) was seen when R. D. Paterson was put in charge of the new factory. Nowadays, when Joseph Lucas are in the forefront of graduate employers, it is strange to recall that Paterson was the only university graduate on the Lucas payroll of 5,000 people at that time, including the directors. Paterson was an engineer, and he was backed up by a strong team of young chemists, electrical engineers and draughtsmen.

One of the objects of the bigger output obtainable from the new factory was to make batteries capable of operating the electric starters that were now becoming standard equipment on most cars. So far Lucas batteries had been primarily for lighting, and little was known about the different techniques required for starter batteries, which had been developed in the United States. Chloride, the makers of Exide batteries, had access to this know-how through their parent, the Electric Storage Company of America, and offered to supply Lucas with starter batteries for resale. Lucas declined and were going ahead on their own. To make up for their lack of elementary research and development they hired one of Chloride's bright young chemists, John Merrick, who knew all about starter battery technology, and in due course he became technical manager at Formans Road. In later years Merrick was to become director and general manager of Joseph Lucas (Batteries) and a director of Joseph Lucas (Electrical) Ltd.

The move to Formans Road was a timely decision – apart from the need for more factory space – because the conditions in which batteries were made at Great King Street were far from satisfactory, and indeed would not have met the new Home Office regulations for lead factories that were just coming into force. The manufacturing processes at Formans Road – 'the factory in the country' as it was called – remained much the same as they were at Great King Street, and were crude by modern standards. F. W. Wells, who later became personnel manager of the factory, has recalled:

> No machinery was used. Lead casting was done by pouring from ladles into hand-held moulds and surfacing the moulds with chalk dust, which gave the casting shop the appearance of a very dirty bakery. Pasting was all done by hand and the plates were dried in ovens, in racks which were filled by hand, de-crated by hand, put one by one into acid by hand, and taken out of acid by hand. Conveyers were unknown.

Where the new regulations made their mark was in the provision of baths and shower baths, protective clothing, a works canteen, free milk, enforced breaks from work, and medical inspections. Discipline was strict, and the 300 employees were forbidden to smoke or eat anywhere in the offices or factory except the canteen. They worked hard – 12 hours a day – and there were the usual rows about the productive workers being paid at piece-work rates (which were disputed) and the non-productive workers by day rates, which always seemed lower. Eventually there was a strike in the pasting shop, during which plates were 'imported' from another firm to keep the factory going, but Oliver Lucas with his rational influence put everything right in the end.

The great worry, of course, was the risk of lead-poisoning, and the management were kept on their toes by a very active factory inspector, the Hon Miriam Pease, who later became chief factory inspector for Wolverhampton. Her method was to put her head into the time office and shout: 'Tell the manager I'm in the pasting shop!' This effectively forestalled any delaying tactics by the management while the lead departments were hurriedly hosed down before she inspected them.

The medical department consisted of one untrained VAD nurse and a weekly visit from an elderly doctor in accordance with the new regulations. His inspection took the form of looking at each worker, examining his gums for a 'blue line', and asking him if he felt all right. There was no blood test.

In spite of its shortcomings as seen in retrospect, Formans Road under Paterson's initial direction evidently met the requirements of the new regulations with something in hand. When the Home Office representatives checked it up for the first time, they gave it a clean bill of health – and learned some useful lessons from various procedures that Paterson had introduced. No serious cases of lead-poisoning had occurred.

But Formans Road provided only a temporary relief, and in January 1925 the board sanctioned the purchase of a factory in Great Hampton Street that had come on the market. Previously used for making domestic paraffin lamps and chandeliers by a firm called Hinks Brothers (who were friends of Peter Bennett), the old building had stood empty for years and was now derelict and rat-infested. A good deal of work had to be done on it before it could be occupied – indeed Harry Lucas, after walking round it in gloomy silence, finally growled: 'We'd better pull it down' – but in a few months the spare parts and service departments were installed there, and this gave more manufacturing space at Great King Street. The move was very carefully thought out, chalk marks on the floor indicating exactly where every piece of equipment and furniture was to stand, and the operation went off so smoothly that letters dictated at Farm Street before 10.30 am were signed and posted at Great Hampton Street by 12.30 pm. A few months later another building was put up alongside at a cost of £31,000.

Service had come to be recognised as an essential function of the company, and the first Lucas service depot was established at Scrubbs Lane, Willesden, London, soon after World War I. (There were already sales depots in London, Manchester, Glasgow and Bristol.) It had a garage that could take about twenty cars, a battery repair shop, an electrical repair shop, and a lamp repair shop, as well as stores and offices. In Birmingham the overloading of Farm Street garage was relieved by the move to Great Hampton Street, where there was room for holding bulk stocks of spares, workshops for various repairs, and garage facilities for customers' cars. Henry Urquhart, who was put in charge of Great Hampton Street, was also appointed Service Manager, largely as a result of drawing Peter Bennett's attention to the lack of a central service department. Urquhart had joined Lucas from Siemens, where he had done a similar job. At Siemens Harold Ireland was in charge of the experimental department and was a magneto specialist, having been given the job of making a good copy of the Bosch magneto towards the end of the war. When Ireland left Siemens to join Lucas he asked Urquhart to go with him as an experimental engineer specialising in examining and reporting on defective units in the electrical laboratory.

Urquhart's pleading for a service department had an unexpected sequel. In September 1924 he was sent for by F. H. Walker, who asked him if he would like to go to Australia, at which Urquhart felt that only one answer was expected of him. Walker went on to explain that the joint managing directors had decided that having focused attention on service facilities at home, Urquhart had better go round the world to organise and report on the Lucas service facilities overseas, which had only recently been started.

He went *via* South Africa, where the Lucas agents, Ratcliffes, took him up Table Mountain in a Morris Cowley fitted with a Magdyno, for which they had nothing good to say. Half-way up, the engine petered out. 'What did we tell you!' they said grimly. After much tinkering and checking they had to admit, with rather red faces, that they had run out of petrol!

In Australia, where Lucas were represented by various agents in the different states, Urquhart came to the conclusion that what Lucas needed was their own representative to co-ordinate their efforts. On his return – after an absence of 12 months and visits to New Zealand, South Africa (again), India, Burma, Singapore, Japan and Canada – his recommendation was acted upon and Jack Masterton was sent out to become the first Lucas manager in Australia.

Meanwhile at home it became apparent that more service depots were needed to deal with the vastly bigger numbers of Lucas electrical units now in use in cars and motor-cycles. This was all the more necessary because Lucas products were being adversely compared with those of competitors, in particular Bosch magnetos, Delco coils, CAV dynamos and starters, and Exide batteries. Many of these complaints were justified, sometimes because of faults in the products themselves (as with magnetos), sometimes because they were wrongly designed for the conditions of use (the Magdyno in cars), but often because of ignorance on the part of motorists and the motor trade in diagnosing and treating troubles. But whatever the reason, the effect on the Lucas reputation was bad.

The initial defence lay in good – and more generous – service, and it was decided to cover the whole country with Lucas depots. In due course service depots were opened at Manchester, Glasgow, Edinburgh, Newcastle-upon-Tyne, Liverpool, Bristol, Leeds, Coventry, Brighton, Cardiff, Dublin and Belfast. And two more London depots were added, one at Wandsworth, the other at Leyton. For the first few years after the war the Lucas service depots helped to recondition many pre-war cars for their owners by replacing oil and acetylene lamps with dynamo lighting sets, and by adding electric starters. Some new imported cars had electric lighting equipment but no starters, and these were added to Itala cars, for example, for Malcolm Campbell, the concessionaire, at the Lucas Willesden depot.

As Peter Bennett pointed out, batteries were almost the only item of a replacement nature that the company supplied. Their reputation had suffered to some extent from the inevitable troubles experienced by new motorists in the early lives of their cars, when they had difficulty in starting the engine for various reasons. When this happened, the battery came in for a good deal of ill-treatment and was often blamed for faults that were not really its own. Lucas got most of the blame because they had most of the initial equipment battery business, and their competitors not unnaturally took advantage of this. Denigration of the Lucas battery became a popular gambit which they did nothing to discourage. Lucas hit back with a sales drive through the service agents.

Cycle accessories were still being repaired at Great King Street, but these accessories were so long-lasting that in the mid-1920s the company reluctantly had to make it a rule not to undertake repairs of any made before the beginning of the century. This was rather hard on some of the old hands, who got a great thrill when they came across lamps that they had made themselves 30 or 40 years earlier. They were able to tell they were theirs because the operator's number was stamped on a part and hidden under a lead seal. But in those early days this could work against them. If a lamp came back that had been badly made, the lead seal was knocked out and the operator's name was traced from the number underneath. As an old pensioner at the Lucas Social Club told me: 'You couldn't say it wasn't yours, so you were for the high jump. It was just a matter of having your cards. There was no inspection in those days, you see.' Another pensioner recalled that when an article came back for repair, it would be deliberately left under the bench for 24 hours because it was thought that if the customer got it back by return he would not want to pay the price of the repair.

It came quite naturally to Peter Bennett and Oliver Lucas to show the same concern for the welfare of their workpeople that had existed in the company since Joseph's early days in Little King Street. And after all, Harry Lucas was still around as the symbol of that paternalism. This humane spirit came through in various ways, some of them quite orthodox, such as the provision of three tennis-courts and a bowling green, and another canteen, others of a more distinctive pattern, such as the Common Good Fund, which was a permanent item on the board meeting agenda. In 1925 the Lucas Sports Club was formed and a 30-acre sports ground was opened at Moor Lane by the Lord Mayor of Birmingham.

Two incidents taken at random from those reported show that in spite of the pressure they were constantly submitted to in coping with the rapid growth of the company, both managing directors found time to deal with the problems of individual employees. In the first Peter Bennett arranged for an ex-soldier in the works who had developed tuberculosis as a result of his war service to be sent to a convalescent home, and Oliver Lucas saw to it that the daughter of an employee who had been drowned was taken away from the job she was doing in the factory and sent to a training college so that she could qualify for better-paid work in the office. The expense of these arrangements was met by the Common Good Fund.

On a more cheerful note the company began to organise works outings, the first being for foremen and departmental managers, who went to Dovedale on a pouring wet day in 1922. Outings and social events were of course 'dry' because of Harry's strict temperance principles (as all Lucas functions were to be as long as he lived), but a concerted dash to the nearest pub after the party officially broke up on the return to Birmingham was the usual ending to a happy and instructive day. The old man occupied himself for weeks in advance preparing attractive little monographs of the places they were going to visit. On a much larger scale was the excursion for employees and families to the British Empire Exhibition at Wembley in 1924, for which the management organised special trains to London. Actually it did not cost the company any money, for the workpeople paid for their own much-reduced railway fares.

Ever since the days when 'Miss Louey' ministered to the sick and injured at the Tom Bowling Lamp Works, before Joseph Lucas & Son became Joseph Lucas Limited, the Lucas employees had enjoyed the benefit of some help of this kind, if only of a very elementary nature. Up to about 1917 this was limited to a first-aid box and one worker skilled in putting on bandages in each department. First aid was done from the Time Office until the first ambulance room was opened in the early 1920s, followed by others in various parts of the factory. When the workpeople numbered about 3,000 the medical staff consisted of one nurse, but a night nurse was taken on when an extra shift was worked in the press shop. To begin with there was only a visiting doctor. The company welfare officer visited the sick at home and reported to the Welfare Committee. At the beginning of 1924 a safety superintendent was appointed, and in October it was decided

(above) Sir Herbert Austin in his famous 'Seven', which he produced in 1922. He bought his electrical equipment from C. A. Vandervell & Company until 1926, when Lucas acquired CAV and transferred the car equipment side of the business to Great King Street. Austin was 'most resistant and awkward' about having to deal with the same company that supplied William Morris, at that time his bitterest enemy. *(National Motor Museum)*

(below) William Morris (later Viscount Nuffield) was Lucas's biggest customer for car equipment in the early 1920s. He is seen *(left)* alongside a 'bull-nose' Morris Oxford in 1924 with Mr Tozer of Tozer, Kemsley & Millbourne, the exporters, and Miles Thomas (later Lord Thomas) who had just joined Morris as publicity adviser. The car was about to start a non-stop engine run from Land's End to John-o-Groats *(British Leyland)*

The inseparables: Oliver Lucas *(left)* and Peter Bennett, the joint managing directors who contributed vastly different but complementary qualities in building up the company between the wars

to report the number of accidents and illnesses dealt with by the ambulance rooms at the monthly board meetings. The figures given for the main works in October were 580 accidents, 605 illnesses, 2,010 redressings and 359 outside cases. At Formans Road there were 134 accidents, two illnesses, 574 redressings and 12 from outside. Compensation cases were two accidents and three septic cases. The total workforce at that time was about 6,000.

Most of the accidents seem to have been caused by people knocking themselves against tools and bits of machinery, and by the lack of safety guards and other devices that were gradually introduced in the light of experience. The only serious injuries from fire at this time were self-inflicted as a result of panic when a row of stoves caught fire and the man in charge fled through an adjacent door. Some girls on the other side rushed through the flames to follow him, instead of leaving by other doors on their own side of the room. Happily the three girls who were more or less seriously burnt all recovered in the course of time and were able to return to work, being helped in the meantime by the Hospital Committee and the Benevolent Fund.

The endowment of two beds at the Queen's Hospital and two more at the General Hospital was a useful addition to the medical arrangements, especially for cases of injury requiring full hospital treatment. This endowment was announced by Alderman Sayer, the Chairman, at the shareholders' meeting in 1925.

Writing in the 1970s, after British industry has been reduced to a three-day working week for a time because of the need to conserve electric power during the miners' strike, there is a sense of historic irony in recording that more than 50 years ago, in 1921, the Lucas factory was asked to reduce its consumption of electric power by half and was running its machine shops in the mornings only – because of a strike by the coalminers. And the 1974 dispute with tool-setters at Lucas factories had its own precedent half a century ago in the engineers' lock-out of 1922, which caused 167 Lucas toolmakers and tool-setters to stop work.

But labour relations remained remarkably good at Great King Street and were helped by such innovations as the workpeople's suggestion scheme, introduced by Oliver Lucas in 1921. Awards were given for acceptable ideas and designs for products, saving of materials and labour, prevention of waste and finding use for waste, improved production methods, saving of power, light, gas and water, prevention of accidents, and economy in internal transport. A feature of the scheme was that each suggestion was distinguished by a numbered stamp (the worker retaining a counterfoil) instead of a name to ensure that the idea would be judged impartially. It was not long before suggestions started to come in, the most promising being for sinking an artesian well in the Great King Street triangle. The well was successfully sunk to a depth of 500ft and gave an ample supply of water.

The physical growth of the company after the war naturally necessitated some increases in capital, notwithstanding the ploughing back of profits made possible by the conservative dividend policy. In 1920 the authorised capital of the company was increased from £500,000 to £800,000, while rights issues in 1919 and 1920 added to the issued capital until it reached £700,000 in July 1920. Four years later, when Brolt was purchased, a further 50,000 ordinary shares were issued to the shareholders of that company, bringing the issued capital up to £750,000. The growth in the company's output required not only new buildings and plant but more workpeople, and this was reflected in the increase in the payroll from 2,800 in 1919 (after the reduction from 4,000 when the wartime contracts abruptly ended in November 1918) to 7,000 by the end of 1925.

The annual report and balance sheet for the financial year ended 31 August 1924 was signed by a new secretary, whose name was to have great significance in the years to come. Walter J. Perkins, who had been secretary of the company since its formation in 1898 and had married Joseph Lucas's youngest daughter, Ada, had retired during the financial year and had been succeeded by Arthur Bertram Waring, who had joined the company as its first qualified accountant in 1922.

Waring had been caught by the outbreak of war in the middle of his training as a chartered accountant in Manchester. He joined the Lancashire Fusiliers, was commissioned in the field and served as a captain in the 29th Division at Gallipoli. After six years in the Army – an experience that was to bear fruit in his later flair for the human side of industrial management at all levels – he went home to Manchester to finish his articles. He qualified, but – as he described it to me:

> Though I had every prospect of becoming a partner, I came to the conclusion subconsciously that I didn't have the makings of a professional man. I decided I would like to get into business or industry and find out what it was all about. I thought I would go to America.
>
> In the meantime I saw an advertisement for a job as assistant secretary of a foundry company in Derby – this would be about 1920. I took the job, thinking in the back of my mind that it wasn't of vital importance because if I didn't like it I could always go to America. Then the firm

got into difficulties – there was a depression at the time – and I became redundant.

So then I answered advertisements again and one of them was with Joseph Lucas. When I arrived here and walked down Great King Street I thought I had entered a chasm – vast buildings on each side – and I thought it was the last place where I could serve any useful purpose. I still had the thought that if I didn't like it I would go to America.

Looking back at the beneficent influence Bertram Waring exercised on the progress of Joseph Lucas – in time he was to become a director, then chief executive director, joint managing director, chairman and managing director, and on his retirement the company's first honorary president – one can only be thankful that he found inside the 'chasm' a challenge that put all thought of going to America out of his mind.

CHAPTER FOUR

THE BIG DEAL

By 1925 the annual output of motor-cars in Britain had increased by two and a half times compared with 1920 and reached nearly 580,000. This prompted Harry Lucas to say at the annual meeting: 'Here at home we see that every week brings more cars on the roads and at present there is no sign of slowing down. Naturally we ask whether and how long the pace can last.' He went on to draw this picture of the progress of motoring in the United States and its moral for Britain:

> We are told that there are already more cars than garage accommodation and that in one city alone there are many thousands of cars which are left in the roads all the time because the owners have nowhere else to put them. This is an astonishing state of affairs and obviously one to be noted seriously. It looks very much as if the saturation point has nearly been reached in America, and it makes one wonder what will become of the surplus production.

The immediate problem facing Lucas was the competition for supplying ignition, starting and lighting equipment to the manufacturers, which had become intense. Lucas's chief competitors were C. A. Vandervell and Rotax.

Charles Anthony Vandervell was born in London in 1871, and as a boy was fascinated by electricity, his first job being with the Lithanode Battery Company in Horseferry Road, Westminster. By the time he was 21 he thought he knew enough about the subject to rent a small workshop from a jobmaster in Thorpe Mews, North Kensington, where he started making portable batteries with the aid of his brothers, Percy and Frank, trading as C. A. Vandervell & Company. (Percy and Frank later left the company but they joined forces again in 1920 when Charles Vandervell helped to finance them in starting Vandys, Ltd, which made Vandy cars with mostly American components at Pembridge Villas, Notting Hill Gate.)

In 1902 Charles moved to larger premises in Chapel Road, Willesden, by which time he was making all sorts of electrical products as well as batteries – X-ray and cautery sets, ammeters and voltmeters, trembler coils for motor cars, lamps, electrical tie-pins and brooches for actors and actresses, and electrical lighting sets for horse-drawn vehicles. His 1902 catalogue described and illustrated a lighting set for a brougham consisting of a pair of traditional carriage-lamps fitted with electric bulbs, an interior light and a battery. If required, the set could be adapted to provide lamps for the horses' heads! (In 1975 the principal royal state coaches and the Lord Mayor of London's coach all had CAV equipment for battery-operated fluorescent lighting.) In 1903 he added switchboards and panels to his range of products.

Vandervell soon outgrew the little works at Willesden and in 1904 he moved to Warple Way, Acton, where CAV have stayed to this day. A new factory was built on the site in 1913 and another two years later. During the Edwardian years C. A. Vandervell & Co led the way in the production of batteries and dynamo lighting sets for cars, and they were making magnetos and electric starters before World War I. In 1904 Vandervell produced a variable speed dynamo which had a revolving field system as well as a revolving armature, with a brake on the field system creating a predetermined slip between the two to give controlled generation at varying speeds. This was followed by the Leitner dynamo, which he marketed for a time, until he was joined by A. H. Midgley, who became chief engineer. Midgley had patented a dynamo which had main and auxiliary fields, and Vandervell arranged for this to be made for him by a small firm near Birmingham run by H. B. Brooks. The magneto showed promise, so in 1911 Vandervell decided to make it himself. Brooks retaliated by poaching one of Vandervell's best men, a Mr Holt, and between them they put on the market a car ignition and lighting set they called the Brolt. As we have seen, this company was acquired by Lucas in 1924.

For ignition equipment Vandervell had turned to Germany, and in 1904 he started to import the Ruthart magneto. At the same time he began to develop an electric motor for engine-starting – a series wound machine with epicyclic reduction gear. It was engaged by means of canvas/metal/rubber discs, which were brought into contact with the flywheel by a pedal.

Perhaps the most important Vandervell development before World War I was the production of commercial vehicle dynamo lighting sets. This began in 1911 and coincided with the arrival of E. L. Cadwallader as foreman of the winding and assembly shops. In the next 50 years 'Caddy' was to play a major part in the success of the company, eventually becoming joint general manager. One of his early jobs in 1911 was to supervise the fitting of the first dynamo lighting set to a London & General Omnibus Company B-type double-deck open-top bus. Most manufacturers sent their vehicles to the little factory at Acton for the equipment to be fitted. The lorries and buses overflowed into the street, so the fitters took their tools outside and worked on them there to save time. Long arguments with the police ensued. (Lucas did not get a foothold in the commercial vehicle market until the end of 1922, when they supplied forty dynamo sets to Tilling Stevens for a bus service in Madrid – an order that was regarded as 'a definite start'.)

The peacetime products of Vandervell & Co continued to be in demand for lorries and buses during the 1914–18 war, but they were also called upon to make large quantities of armaments including hand grenades and the Allways fuse designed by Midgeley for Stokes mortars. Charles Vandervell now decided that the time had come to incorporate the business as C. A. Vandervell & Company Limited, and this was done on 1 January 1916, with a share capital of £350,000.

The only other event of importance during those war years was the introduction of the original axial starter, called the 'Z' starter, in 1917. This starter developed the very heavy torques required to crank the big engines used in buses and lorries, and its main feature was that the complete armature assembly and pinion moved forward axially to enable the pinion to engage with the flywheel gear. This movement was effected electrically by current flowing in the auxiliary field windings. Only when the engagement was completed was the main supply to the motor switched on and full power output obtained. 'Holding on' windings were incorporated to prevent the risk of the pinion being thrown out of engagement too soon through spasmodic firing before the engine was running properly, and a multi-plate clutch provided an effective safeguard against damage caused by overloading.

After the war advantage was taken of the boom in the motor industry to make the company a public one, this being accomplished in 1919. A large expansion programme was planned, including the production of the CAV-Willard storage battery with threaded rubber separators, but its realisation was overtaken by the slump which set in at the end of 1920. A new multi-storey factory which was built at Acton, nearly doubling the production space, stood unused for many years and was eventually let as a warehouse to Parfumeries de Paris and to Daniel Neal's for storing children's clothing.

Nevertheless technical work continued and in 1922 a voltage regulator system for dynamos with large output was introduced. The engineering ability of C. A. Vandervell did not escape the notice of Robert Bosch AG in Germany, and in 1924 an agreement was made between the two concerns for the exchange and use of patents. Specifically, Bosch were to use the CAV axial starter patents and CAV the Bosch drum-type voltage regulator patents.

By this time C. A. Vandervell had developed such a strong connection with the commercial vehicle firms that the company enjoyed almost a monopoly in that market, having contracts for the supply of ignition and lighting equipment to Leyland, AEC, Thornycroft and the London & General Omnibus Company. This was largely due to Cadwallader, who used the tactics of cultivating the operators of vehicles – people like Midland Red and Tillings – and getting them to specify CAV equipment when they ordered new vehicles from the manufacturers. He also had first-class products to sell.

C. A. Vandervell were quite strong in the car industry, with a contract for the whole of the Austin lighting and starting business as well as orders from Clyno, Lea & Francis, and others. (CAV never made motor-car lamps themselves; they got them at first from a firm called Worsnop and later from Samuel Heath of Birmingham, who were referred to within the company as the Lamp Works.) CAV magnetos were popular with the motor-cycle manufacturers, and as a sideline the company started making radio batteries and complete radio receivers. By 1925 they were employing about 1,400 people.

But financially the company was in a critical state. Sales fell from a peak of £1,030,000 in 1920–1 to figures below £700,000 in the three following years and reached a low point of £601,000 in 1922–3. Such was the slump in the motor industry as a whole that in December 1922 Charles Vandervell estimated that the actual value of £96,000 debentures given by the Austin Motor Company in payment of debts was no more than £20–25,000. The year to March 1921 ended with a devastating loss of £251,000, almost 75 per cent of the company's issued capital, and in the following year the loss was £206,000. There was talk of a reduction of share capital, but this was deferred when the results to 31 March 1923 showed a loss of only £18,000. But by 1924, with a further loss of £134,000, the share capital of the company was no longer represented by tangible assets. With its office block and factory mortgaged, large debentures outstanding and £70,000 due to the founder for loans, the company was offered (not for the first time) for sale to Joseph Lucas by Clarence Hatry, the City financier, towards the end of 1925. Lucas thought very highly of the C. A. Vandervell products – their electrical quality was admittedly superior – but their opinion of the management was inevitably coloured by the parlous state of the company's finances.

With Rotax it was the reverse: Lucas respected the shrewd management of the company but did not have a particularly high opinion of its products. (Rotax, for their part, thought that their equipment was rather superior to the Lucas stuff on the grounds that Lucas supplied the mass-produced cars like Morris – they conveniently overlooked Rolls-Royce – while they supplied such high-class firms as Daimler, Sunbeam, Clement-Talbot and Riley. This juxtaposition of views is not uncommon in the companies involved in a take-over.) The roots of the business went back to 1902, when Eugen Aron started up as a manufacturers' agent in a few rooms at 22 Long Lane, in the city of London. By the following year he was doing so well that he took the whole of the premises and brought in his brothers, Albert and Hermann, to form the Continental Hardware & Cycle Company. They opened an office at 20 rue Brunel, Paris, to handle a variety of Continental goods – phonographs, footballs, electric toys, and a small range of motor and cycle accessories which turned out to be their best selling lines. By 1905 they had to move into larger premises with showrooms and offices in Great Eastern Street and a warehouse at 60 Curtain Road, London EC.

At this point the brothers decided to concentrate on the motor and cycle accessory business, and even to start manufacture on a small scale, so they changed their business name to the Rotax Motor & Cycle Company. Electric head, side and tail lamps appeared for the first time in the Rotax catalogue in 1906. Manufacture began at Curtain Road with trembler coils, steering column switches, car jacks and some interior car fittings, including speaking tubes, followed by the assembly of accumulators in celluloid containers. In 1909 they expanded the manufacturing side by renting a brass works in Landor Street, Birmingham, to make lamps, horns and other brass motor accessories. The motor-car had now become so well established that the Arons decided to drop the cycle part of their business, necessitating yet another change of name to the Rotax Motor Accessories Company. In 1910 they expanded the manufacture of accessories in London by taking over additional premises in Holywell Lane, EC, but the main business of the company was still as wholesale agents, their stock including voltmeters, ammeters, speedometers, clocks, magnetos, sparking plugs, electric generators and transformers, motor clothing, lathes, drilling machines and tools.

In 1910 they also took on the Leitner dynamo, the invention of Henry Leitner, the managing director of Accumulator Industries, of Woking, from whom they obtained the plates for the accumulators they assembled. The dynamo, which C. A. Vandervell had been selling, was made by a subsidiary company bearing Leitner's name. It was of the 'third brush' type and had the merit of being self-regulating. Rotax were given the concession for marketing and fitting it to motor-cars, advertising it as the Rotax Leitner dynamo. Among its earliest users were Daimler and Standard. By 1913 their business had grown to such an extent that a large factory belonging to the Edison Phonograph Company had to be acquired at Willesden, London, with the intention of manufacturing on a large scale not only dynamo lighting sets but also a full range of accessories for motor-cars. Sales and service depots for the dynamo lighting sets were opened at Deansgate, Manchester, and the Faubourg St Honoré in Paris. Just as production was about to start at Willesden, World War I broke out and the factory was immediately changed over to the manufacture of 4.5 howitzer shell and hand grenade cases, aero-engine carburettors, aeroplane wing bracing wires, soldiers' packs and electrical switch panels. The most important order was to adapt their car generator to be driven by a small wooden propeller in order to provide electrical power for aircraft, which up till then had relied on batteries. The early 'windmill dynamo' produced 36 watts, but by the end of the war 100-watt generators were being made. The first recorded installation of a Rotax dynamo was on the Sopwith Pup, powered by an 80hp Le Rhône rotary engine, and 1,300 of these successful biplanes were built.

The scale of aviation in those days was the subject of a favourite anecdote told in later years by Bill Summerfield, then a foreman in the Rotax experimental shop and afterwards factory manager at Chase Road. Trouble was being experienced with an aeroplane fitted with a wind-driven generator at Hendon aerodrome. Summerfield was sent over to make adjustments but found that he would have to go back to Willesden by tramcar to collect a tachometer. The pilot suggested they should fly over to the aerodrome near Chase Road, now the site of the Renault factory on Western Avenue. As they were making their approach the propeller of the aeroplane flew off and windmilled safely down to the ground. They glided in and Summerfield walked the half-mile to the Rotax works, collected some nuts, a spanner and his tachometer, and walked back, by which time the pilot had retrieved the propeller. Summerfield secured it to the aeroplane and adjusted the dynamo, whereupon the pilot took off for Hendon and Summerfield returned to Chase Road on foot.

During the war Eugen and Hermann Aron reorganised the company as an essentially manufacturing concern, and in 1917 they liquidated the Rotax Motor Accessories Company and re-formed it as a private limited liability company. In the same year they acquired the business of H. T. Saunders & Company, of Birmingham. When peace returned, they set to work to rebuild their motor-car business mainly on the Rotax-Leitner dynamo lighting set, which was chosen as standard equipment by Daimler, Crossley, Sunbeam, Coventry-Simplex, Riley, Singer and Belsize. It was also supplied to Cubitts, the building contractors, for the car with which they hoped to compete in the post-war motor industry. It was typical of the ingenious business methods used by the Aron brothers that they arranged for Cubitts to build a lead-melting shop and a three-storey block in exchange for the electrical equipment Rotax supplied for the Cubitt car. The dynamo lighting set was backed up by batteries and the range of accessories made before the war, to which was now added an electric starter with the Bendix pinion engagement of the flywheel by arrangement with the American company.

In 1921 the Arons expanded their horizon once more by gaining control of Newtons Electrical Works Ltd, an old-established electrical engineering firm at Taunton in which they already had a small interest. The Rotax Motor Accessories Company was liquidated, amalgamated with Newtons, and a new company, Rotax (Motor Accessories) Ltd, was formed. Newtons made industrial motors, transformers and switchboards, and the Leitner dynamo under licence for railway lighting. They also supplied some lighting equipment for ships. Rotax activity in the West was also expanded at this time by the opening of a sales and service depot at Bristol. By this time they also had depots in Glasgow, Newcastle, Manchester, Leeds, Birmingham and Brighton.

Although the company was now primarily a manufacturing one, the opportunity to become agents for Jaeger, the Swiss makers of speedometers, clocks and other instruments held in high esteem by motorists, was too good to miss. A special department was set up at Willesden to handle this business.

It was in 1921 that Kynochs, Limited (a subsidiary of Nobel Industries) acquired one-third of the issued capital of Rotax and Sir Harry McGowan (later Lord McGowan) joined the board as their nominee. Two years later McGowan got in touch with Lucas and offered to sell Rotax to them. Instead, some form of working arrangement between the two companies was arrived at (the details do not seem to have survived).

At the end of 1925 the Arons had another idea – that Lucas and Rotax should jointly take over and manage the ailing C. A. Vandervell company, which they said was being hawked around the City. The suggestion somehow leaked to the motor industry and gave rise to rumours that Nobel Industries (and through them General Motors) were going to get a very large interest – even a controlling interest – in Joseph Lucas as a result of the plan. Oliver Lucas did his best to calm the fears of the industry and trade by seeing some of the leading car manufacturers and making statements to press representatives which were published in the weekend papers, but the Lucas customers remained on edge throughout the whole negotiations.

In the New Year Sir Harry McGowan made a formal offer to Charles Vandervell on behalf of Lucas. The offer – £321,745 in cash – was accepted, but then came a decision by Lucas that changed the whole project. Thinking it over, they realised that joint management of C. A. Vandervell with Rotax was not really practicable; it would be much better to take over Rotax as well, giving Lucas complete control of all three companies.

The Lucas position was put to the shareholders in the following terms:

> The products of the three companies are to a large extent complementary, and it will therefore be apparent that by co-operation, considerable economies can be effected in management, research and organisation. It will also be possible to develop more fully your directors' policy of standardisation and the elimination of unnecessary duplication, which they believe will lead ultimately to a reduction in costs and selling prices ... A united scheme will offer more comprehensive after-sales service facilities, and can be undertaken on a more economical basis than by independent effort.

The Aron brothers were quite happy to accept the Lucas offer, which was understandable in view of the purchase consideration they received for their company – £707,217, payable partly in cash and partly by the issue of 130,000 Lucas ordinary £1 shares. For this purpose there was a rights issue of one new ordinary share for every five shares held, bringing the authorised capital up to £1,100,000 and the issued capital to £1,006,500. Looking back on the deal in recent times, Sir Bertram Waring told me: 'We got CAV at a bargain price, but we paid in full for Rotax.'

C. A. Vandervell was a bargain partly because of the Austin contract, and a minute of the Lucas board meeting held on 25 August 1926, after recording that 'we have successfully arranged for the whole of next year's business with the Austin Company for all their models,' went on to say: 'This is very gratifying, as it will be remembered this was the one place where there was a possibility of our having difficulty, due to their attitude over amalgamations. We have completely changed this, and have shown that we are able, by co-operative action, to put forward reduced prices for a composite Set, when CAV alone would have been quite unable to meet them.'

In reality the deal did not go off quite as smoothly as the minute might indicate. Years later, in evidence to the Monopolies Commission, Lucas admitted 'Austins were the most resistant and most awkward about it. Their bitterest enemies in those days, Morris, were entirely in the Lucas camp, and Austins didn't welcome it at all. Sir Herbert Austin was a very bitter man about it.' Austin was not alone in disliking what amounted to Lucas getting a monopoly of the starting, lighting and ignition initial equipment business; the whole motor industry and motor trade shared his feelings to some extent.

These broad questions of monopoly will be dealt with in a later chapter, when the Monopolies Commission's report on the supply of electrical equipment for mechanically propelled vehicles is discussed. It is enough to say here that Oliver Lucas was able to go round and reassure the manufacturers that Lucas would be able to give them the benefits of the amalgamation, which meant benefits of price reduction. And that was what mattered to motor-car manufacturers who were fighting against rising costs while having to keep their own prices down, and were now having to contend with competition from more foreign cars since the import duty had been lifted for a short period in 1924. (Peter Bennett was a member of the six-man delegation from the motor industry that represented the case for the restoration of the duties to the Financial Secretary to the Treasury.)

Oliver Lucas's message was not just a catchphrase designed to placate hostile feelings among restless customers; he meant what he said. In the years immediately following the CAV-Rotax take-over the benefits of increased scale of production so reduced Lucas's costs that they had 'money to give away at the end of the year.' This was passed on to their customers, the method of doing so being a matter of individual negotiation – it could be either by rebates or by overall cuts in prices, as agreed.

Even though Lucas now had a virtual monopoly in the supply of lighting, starting and ignition sets as initial equipment for motor-cars (a monopoly that was to last until after the end of World War II), the negotiation of prices was still a tricky business. It was of course done individually on a 'catch as catch can' basis, and the Lucas policy was to try and make each of the big manufacturers feel he was receiving 'most favoured nation treatment'. The negotiations started with a bargain being struck on the comprehensive price for the set of equip-ment for a particular car; but the set was never delivered as a set but in its constituent parts. For invoicing these parts the contract price of the comprehensive set was broken down more or less arbitrarily and the invoices were stamped 'nominal prices for invoicing purposes only'. This was not a very satisfactory system and gave rise to all sorts of trouble. There was always the possibility of an invoice going astray, which would necessitate an embarrassing explanation of differ-ent prices being charged to different customers, so as far as possible the nominal prices on the invoices were kept constant. But the system did have the advantage that if a discrepancy in price was discovered, Lucas were able to point out that the invoice prices were purely nominal and were only a part of the overall contract price for the comprehensive set.

But of course the very use of the word nominal left room for further bargaining over a confidential rebate or allowance. This was only right and proper, because it enabled Lucas to recognise the in-dividual claims for special treatment by manufacturers who were offering them a bigger volume of business by increasing their produc-tion of cars, or who were facing the expense of introducing a new popular model with a big sale. The rebates allowed were round sums deducted from the price of each set, but occasionally a percentage reduction would be made at the end of the year according to the number of sets supplied.

Contracts with the big manufacturers were negotiated individually mainly by Oliver Lucas as joint managing director of Lucas talking direct with his opposite numbers in the motor factories. Contracts with smaller firms and minor variations of the contracts with the big companies were handled by Thacker, who had developed relations of confidence and goodwill with individuals throughout the industry since his successful initiation over the Morris contract.

The Lucas policy of selling electrical equipment in 'sets' rather than as individual components was to have far-reaching effects; it is not too much to say that it has been one of the roots of Lucas success. The idea was probably conceived by Peter Bennett and Oliver Lucas acting together from their different points of view – Bennett seeing it as a means of maximising the business with each manufacturer and Oliver Lucas advocating it because it was technically sound for the design of the various components to be inter-related. Selling 'sets' was so much a part of Lucas philosophy that 20 years later it came as a matter of course to John Morley to talk about sets of fuel and combustion systems for gas-turbine engines when he was making arrangements with Hooker and Lombard to do this or that for a new Rolls-Royce jet engine. 'I think that was where we were successful,' he added. 'They saw the benefit of it being a tidy piece. You could draw a line down there and say "That's Lucas's responsibility".'

Unlike the previously acquired companies, Brolt and EIC, which were totally absorbed by Joseph Lucas and disappeared, C. A. Vandervell and Rotax continued to operate as separate companies with separate accounts in order to benefit from the goodwill each company had created. Oliver Lucas joined their respective boards and Waring was sent to CAV for a short time to reorganise their administration. The job of rationalising the CAV products in relation to the Lucas range was given to Hubert Mason, who was transferred from the magneto sales department at Well Street to Acton. His subsequent work as commercial sales director was to be largely responsible for establishing CAV as the leading manufacturers of electrical equipment for commercial and passenger service vehicles.

Charles Vandervell stayed on as a director of his company, but his elder son Guy Anthony (Tony) Vandervell, who had joined him at Acton on being demobilised from the Army after the war, was sent up to Birmingham to work on the motor-cycle side of Lucas. Tony Vandervell was a boisterous extrovert (he had raced cars and motor-cycles with some success at Brooklands) and it was not surprising that he did not take kindly to the discipline of a big Midlands factory. It was not long before he left to join his father in the O & S Oilless Bearing Company at Willesden, which Charles Vandervell had just bought. The name was changed to Vandervell Products, Ltd, in 1933 when Tony secured the UK licence for the thin-wall bearing from the Cleveland Graphite Bronze Co of America. With the help of £400,000 invested by Charles Vandervell to pay for the tooling costs, Tony Vandervell built up the company into an international concern, which after his death was acquired by GKN. Tony Vandervell made his mark in motor-racing history by producing the Vanwall racing car, which won the world's motor-racing championship in 1958.

On the manufacturing side Lucas transferred all the CAV motor-car electrics and lamp and battery business to Birmingham, leaving CAV to concentrate on the manufacture of starters, dynamos and switchgear for the commercial vehicle market in which it had such a strong position. The lamps, batteries and other electrical equipment for commercial vehicles were manufactured by Lucas and sold to CAV for resale to their customers. This was called 'factored business' in the accounts.

At Rotax the Aron brothers withdrew from active participation in the company (though they still came in occasionally), and the powerful manager, Arthur Gerald Benstead, stayed on as general manager of the new Lucas subsidiary. Benstead, who will appear from time to time in connection with various events as they are described in this chronicle, was a remarkable character who never really entered the Lucas circle. His early employment by the Aron brothers seems to have been in the nature of driver-cum-confidential assistant. Whether he actually wore a chauffeur's cap originally may be no more than a question of gossip; certainly the Arons introduced him to all the managing directors in the motor industry and the aeroplane firms – and Benstead had an astonishing memory for names and faces which was to be a valuable part of his stock-in-trade. Lucas gave Rotax a fair amount of autonomy; Oliver Lucas went to meetings and Peter Bennett visited them occasionally, but they were largely left to get on with the job.

One of C.A.V.'s first ventures in the vehicle lighting field. The illustration and following descriptions are taken from the 1902 catalogue.

"The advantages of lighting all kinds of vehicles by means of electricity are obvious; it can be adapted to light the Interior, Exterior, and even the Heads of the Horses. The illustration shows a complete set for lighting a Brougham."

CHAPTER FIVE

'THREE CHEERS FOR THE MANAGEMENT!'

In the spring of 1926, while Lucas were still digesting the sudden acquisition of their two main competitors, the social and economic troubles that had been brewing since World War I came to a head in the calling of Britain's first General Strike. Actually it was not intended to be general – the TUC called it a National Strike and restricted it at first to the railways and transport, most of the printers, the builders, and gas and electricity workers. The rest were held back in the 'second line'.

The strike began at midnight on 3 May, but the effect on Lucas was negligible. On the first morning most of the workpeople managed to reach Great King Street, though some of them were late, and for the rest of the strike arrangements were made to fetch the 500 or so who lived some distance away in the company's vehicles and a few hired char-à-bancs. Production was barely affected. Apart from a few carpenters who were subject to building restrictions, no labour was lost. When the news came that the engineers were also going to be called out, the company took steps to strengthen the decision of those who might wish to stop in, at the same time enrolling special constables to give adequate protection if picketing took place. In fact 495 men failed to clock in, but they made it known that it was entirely against their own wish that they did so – even the union secretaries in some cases said how sorry they were that the men had to be called out. As Peter Bennett reported: 'There was no heart in it.'

The general strike collapsed on the same day and 'it was a very shamefaced crowd that presented itself next morning'. They were addressed by Normansell, the works manager, who read a letter from Oliver Lucas which contained some phrases that were characteristic of the relationship between the company and its workpeople at the time:

Your Directors listened last night, as we hope that many of you did, to the Prime Minister's message to the country with profound appreciation and respect. We are sure we all have a great deal to thank him for in his sane and masterful leadership of the nation during this difficult time. We hope that this will mark the beginning of a new era of

sympathy, understanding and trust between master and man. This is not
time for recrimination or allocating blame. It has been a victory for
common sense. We must all look to the future with the hopefulness that
a better spirit of co-operation will bring the nation back to prosperity,
without which no one can benefit. If we work to this end we shall have
a common goal and be able to pull together with the will and determina-
tion to win through. All men can return to work immediately and will
be paid as from 8 o'clock today.

Master and man – an echo of the Victorian spirit of patriarchy in
which Joseph Lucas built up his business can clearly be heard, and so
too can the voice of Harry. For there is little doubt that Oliver sought
the help of his father, still a consultant director of the company, in
drafting this message. People present at the meeting reported that
'the relief of the strikers was intense,' finding expression in 'Three
Cheers for the Management.' (It is not recorded whether Normansell
had his hat on when he addressed the men. It was a saying in the works
that if he walked through the shops hatless he was in a good mood,
but if he had his hat on, it meant he was coming to check up on
something he had heard.)

At Acton, even then a centre of militancy, the CAV and Rotax
men were all called out by the engineers in the neighbouring Napier
factory, who had immediately struck work, and production was
disrupted until they gradually got a few men back. The General Strike
was called off on 12 May.

As we have seen, the loyalty of the Lucas staff and workpeople had
a practical basis of fair treatment, and this was expanded by the setting
up of the Pension Fund and the Work People's Dependants' Benefit
Fund in July 1928. Bertram Waring played a big part in both, preparing an explanatory booklet on the Pension Fund which saved the
staff meeting at which Sir John Burn, a leading actuary, talked down
to his audience to such an extent that without Waring's booklet the
employees would have been left without any of the details they
naturally wanted to know.

Other welfare schemes largely initiated by Waring (both in 1927)
were a girls' rest home at Weston-super-Mare, which was an immediate success, and a new ambulance room in which a dental department was installed with a full-time dentist in attendance. To
begin with, dental examination was made compulsory for all newcomers under the age of 18, the intention being to bring all the
employees under that age under examination and treatment. The
idea was to concentrate on the younger employees.

By this time the installation of safety guards on machines had become widespread, and their use was strictly enforced. Even so, Waring had to report the case of a girl working a press without the guard in position. It cost her three fingers. The tool-setter and charge-hand were instantly dismissed 'as we feel we must take every disciplinary measure possible to ensure that the safety devices are used and the rigid rules laid down are carried out.' Safety rules were not so easy to define at Formans Road battery factory, and the risk of lead-poisoning was still present in spite of Paterson's efforts, three cases being reported in one month in 1927.

Bertram Waring was now concerning himself more and more with the treatment of the Lucas workpeople. Like many men who had commanded troops in World War I, he returned to civilian life with humanitarian views which were left of centre (Harold Macmillan felt the same), as he explained to me in his office at Great King Street shortly before he died: 'Some of the people here were not well paid, especially the girls. When I came here they earned 24 shillings a week and I felt this dreadfully, being brought up in a socialist atmosphere, and I got them up to 30 bob a week without any piecework system or anything else. I think it was one of the best things I ever did – I didn't even consult my managing director – but I got them up to 30 bob by stages and we got the best girls in Birmingham.'

He went on to start various works committees dealing with such matters as health and canteens, and even effluent, and one of these committees reported to the board each month, providing shop-floor experience on each subject. In the offices Waring swept away the small rooms with old sloping desks and a brass rail for the ledgers and replaced them by an open-plan office with light oak furniture. He said to Coe, his general office assistant: 'You know the way to get the best out of this place is to run some bonus schemes,' and introduced Veeda counters on the typewriter keys and a method of counting the number of ledger postings. According to Coe 'it was very, very successful; everyone on the staff was pleased because they got extra money – and we got the output.'

In walking round the various workshops, Oliver Lucas could not fail to notice the difference in tempo, as well as production techniques, between the British and American factories he had visited. He decided that others ought to share the same experience. At the end of 1928 Turner, works manager of the Electrical Company, and Jones, head of the cost office, were sent to the States to investigate new methods with a view to throwing out much more of the old Lucas plant and bringing it up-to-date. Among the places they visited was the Delco-Remy factory, which was a parallel with Lucas in that it made lighting, starting and ignition equipment (it was also said to be the most highly organised factory in America). Their comment was that they had never seen anything like it as regards speed of work – 'They don't work like men, but like devils' reported Jones on his return. Jones was himself a fierce character who was feared and at the same time liked by workpeople. As a result he got things done. His assistant, Jack Smith, was made in the same mould and has been described to me as 'a proper Brummie who could go right off the handle and within the next five minutes put his arm round you.' Many Lucas veterans today believe that it was characters like Jones and Smith who (at their level) earned for the factory organisation its reputation for efficiency – and good works relations. But they used methods that could not be used today.

A series of visits to the States by members of the staff was planned for 1927 so that they could study American methods. One of the leading machine-shop foremen was included, while Peter Bennett himself went to Virginia as one of the delegates in a British industry party, going on to visit the organising side of General Motors through an introduction from Sir Harry McGowan. In April 1927 Bennett was appointed deputy chairman of the company in recognition of the fact that he invariably took the chair when Sayer, the chairman, could not attend board meetings.

Now that Joseph Lucas (together with CAV and Rotax) had a virtual monopoly of the supply of ignition, starting and lighting equipment to the motor industry, sales interest shifted to the motor-cycle field, where they still had competitors. Not that they wanted the business at any price. In 1926 they deliberately sacrificed part of the Raleigh account because they refused to cut their prices to the figure demanded. Against this, useful orders for magnetos were coming in from motor-cycle manufacturers on the Continent – FN, Sarolea and Gillette in Belgium, and Peugeot in France. These sales had to be backed up with service, so in 1928 Henry Mayer was given the responsibility (under Urquhart) of visiting the agents and appointing new ones in the whole of Europe from the Arctic Circle to the Mediterranean, and from the Russian frontier to the Atlantic, travelling everywhere by train. The agents were given a stock of spares in a cupboard, on sale or return, and the visiting representative had to make sure the cupboard was kept topped up.

Meanwhile, on the other side of the world, John Morley was doing the same sort of job in China, Japan and the Far East generally. The big business there was in the cycle trade – Lucas sold over a million bicycle bells in Japan in one year – and although there were very few motor-cars (because the roads were only the width of a rickshaw), there were lots of motor-cycles. In those days the Japanese were imitators rather than creators, and they started making a JAP motor-cycle engine which was attributed not to J. A. Prestwich but to the Japanese Automotive Product Company. Morley had to contend with a 'Lukas' Magdyno which was a carbon copy of the Birmingham article. Nevertheless the Lucas Magdyno was much in demand as an accessory.

In terms of individual orders some of the British motor-cycle firms ranked high in the Lucas list of contracts in 1928, when production of motor-cycles reached the record number of 146,000. BSA and Ariel were only surpassed by Morris at the top of the list, while AJS were taking more from Lucas than Vauxhall, Hillman and Armstrong-Siddeley, and Matchless and Raleigh were ahead of Humber and Standard as Lucas contract customers. The picture was distorted by the fact that the car-makers as a whole bought £180,324 worth of equipment on contract while the motor-cycle total was only £56,090. But £94,461 of the car supplies went to Morris alone. The import-ance of Morris Motors, now supplemented by Morris Commercial Cars and Wolseley (which William Morris had bought personally from the liquidator) was seen in the 1928 Morris balance sheet, which showed a trading profit of £1,334,907. The Lucas reaction to this news was that it would have been much more difficult to negotiate the annual contract with Morris if his balance sheet had shown any sign of going backwards while Lucas were maintaining their own profits (the Lucas profit in 1928 was £220,660). The Morris propor-tion of Lucas contract sales now stood at 30.4 per cent. By the end of 1928 it was down to 26.8 per cent, the smallest figure recorded since the growth of the Morris business.

By now, of course, Lucas also had the Austin contract (the first order for 'season's requirements' coming through in 1926 soon after CAV were taken over), and the comparative figures of Morris and Austin sales were available. For the eight months from September to April, 1927-8, Morris Motors and Morris Commercial Cars took £606,383 of Lucas equipment while Austin orders were £82,163 from Lucas and £187,372 from CAV, a total of £269,535. Morris also spent £54,648 with Lucas for Wolseley, so altogether he was a long way ahead of Austin at this time.

Indeed William Morris set a cruel pace. Frank Smith of Clyno, Lucas's second-best customer since EIC had been taken over, had put up a brave fight to match the Morris-Cowley's sales but had never been able to retain a sufficient profit margin on his cars. Bennett and Waring went to see Clyno and decided that if honesty and hard work would pull them through they would make a success of it yet. A new 9hp car was introduced as a last throw, but it could not stave off creditors' meetings in August 1928, followed by the appointment of a receiver in February 1929. The Lucas loss after a final payment of 10s in the £ was relatively small at £16,797.

The Clyno failure was only one in a list that had been lengthening rapidly, and by 1929 the number of British car companies had dwindled from its post-war peak of around 100 to about thirty. Of these, Morris and Austin accounted for about three-fifths of the total output, their flow-production methods enabling them to sell at much lower prices than the small-volume makers. The big component firms like Lucas helped by keeping their own prices down.

During the late 1920s the trend towards coil-and-distributor ignition gained ground, and there was growing controversy about the relative merits of 6-volt and 12-volt electrical equipment – controversy that was to continue until after World War II. Coil ignition had the attraction of being cheaper than the magneto, but its dependence on the battery was held against it at first by its opponents. Provided the battery was in good condition, it gave easier starting, but it was not so efficient as a magneto for the high speeds required for sports cars and motor-cycles. Magnetos were also preferred in remote districts abroad, where battery failure was feared and service facilities were sparse.

The argument became particularly fierce in Australia, where the Morris, with its magneto ignition and 12-volt Lucas lighting, was challenging the American cars, which usually had coil ignition and 6-volt lighting (significantly, the most popular American cars, the Dodge and Chevrolet, had magnetos on their Australian models). The Lucas lamps were better than the American anyway. Jack Masterton was called upon by the distributors of British cars to give lectures to combat the American propaganda denigrating magneto ignition and 12-volt lighting. Then General Motors decided to establish their own assembly plant and distribution to dealers. Their chief distributor, finding himself sidetracked, took up the Morris with such success that for a month or two Morris headed the list of new car registrations.

By 1927 Joseph Lucas, always closely in touch with American

motor industry thinking, realised that the magneto had had its day as initial equipment for motor-cars. Experimental work had been going for some time at the electrical laboratory in Well Street, where young Herbert Astbury's Austin Seven was converted from its original magneto ignition to coil and distributor for use as a mobile test bed. Coil ignition meant that starting depended on the battery, and batteries – while still far from being completely reliable – had improved so much that the advantages of coil and distributor ignition (especially its lower cost) could no longer be ignored. Peter Bennett and Oliver Lucas decided to take the bold step of killing the magneto as initial equipment and offering coil ignition to manufacturers at a considerable saving in price. The move was so successful that practically the whole British motor industry switched to coil ignition for their next season's requirements. For Lucas this meant not only a change in manufacturing arrangements but also a smaller profit on the cheaper equipment, but in the circumstances this had to be accepted. The new coil and distributor ignition had the useful improvement of a centrifugal automatic advance-and-retard mechanism for controlling the timing in relation to engine speed.

As we have seen, the improvement in battery design had come about largely as a result of the need for it to operate the electric starter as well as the lights. When John Merrick arrived at Formans Road at the beginning of 1924, the Lucas battery had earned a rather poor reputation because of its inability to cope with the additional load. The containers were made from pieces of celluloid sheet stuck together with amyl acetate, and were sometimes attacked by the electrolyte, which caused frothing and other troubles. The first step was to discard the old celluloid container in favour of a monobloc one made with a composition of coal tar pitch and asbestos which was developed at Formans Road in the same year and was called MILAM (Moulded In Lucas Acidproof Material). Other people were also making moulded containers: Chloride used a hard rubber composition, while Rotax, still a separate company, made Ebonite containers in a little factory at Willesden which later became the Lucas Ebonite Works. (Two years later Lucas had talks with Pritchett & Gold, in which Chloride had a controlling interest, and a French company who were said to have developed an improved composition, but nothing transpired.)

Lucas batteries were still not very good, and did not compare well with the Exide batteries made by Chloride, with their wealth of American experience behind them. Merrick, having worked at

Chloride, was in a position to point out that the plates in the Lucas battery were too thick and consequently shed their paste easily if they were overcharged, as often happened with the dynamotor fitted to the Morris Cowley. Following Exide practice, the plates were made thinner, the greater number in the same space improving the output of the battery for starting. Then the Lucas separators were made of corrugated perforated ebonite, and when they vibrated they were liable to rub the plates. Chloride used wooden separators, so these too were adopted.

But the complaints about Lucas batteries were not yet finished. The usual location of the battery at that time was on the running-board. The MILAM cases were made with a fairly low melting point to prevent them being brittle, and service reports began to come in of batteries sagging and distorting when exposed to hot sunshine for any length of time. It was decided to forgo the risk of brittleness and make them harder, which cured the trouble but not before further damage was done to the reputation of the battery, particularly abroad. This added fuel to the belief (which their competitors were certainly not loath to encourage) that all Lucas products were cheap and shoddy because they had to be made down to a price – which was of course quite unfounded.

The new batteries required new manufacturing techniques as well as new materials. Robert Neill, who was Paterson's assistant in running the factory at that time, recalls a rather terrifying piece of electrical apparatus which was used to test the containers to make sure there were no leakages between the cell partitions: 'It sent a very high voltage spark through the whole thing, and if the case was all right the spark went up all round the outside but didn't go through the MILAM, but if there was a blow-hole or weakness anywhere it used to break down and a spark went through the weak spot and the case was rejected.' Then there were the new separators made of wood – 'it had to be a particular type of cedar wood that we bought I can't remember where from, but the separators had to be treated and tested and we had all sorts of troubles before we got them right.'

Leakage between the cells and cracks in the partitions gave rise to some criticism of the MILAM container in service, which the testing procedure described by Neill helped to mitigate, but the main remedy lay in moulding a rubber insert on the top of each partition to strengthen it. While this was being developed some pressure was put on the company by various people in the motor industry and trade · to go over to hard rubber containers. This found an echo in some quarters inside the factory because of the danger of losing the original equipment business if the trouble was allowed to persist. Once the cure was found, Lucas held a series of conferences to demonstrate to agents and trade customers the steps taken to exploit the advantages of the MILAM container, and all talk of going over to hard rubber containers died out.

Although the MILAM integral container enabled the traditional wooden battery box to be dispensed with, boxes were still required sometimes for special purposes. For instance, an Indian maharajah (either the Gaekwar of Baroda or the Maharajah of Mysore) ordered outsize batteries in teak boxes for the caravans he used for tiger shoots. The batteries were five times as big as any previous battery made at Formans Road, and it took four men to lift them by their rope handles.

MILAM was a feature of the wireless batteries which the company started to produce in 1925. In reporting their introduction to the shareholders Peter Bennett gave an insight into the state of home radio at the time: 'They are made on similar lines to the ones which you will see on the running boards of the latest cars,' he said. 'The cases are of a special material of our own, known as MILAM, and their handsome ebony appearance is greatly admired. They look well on a car, but how much more important is this high-grade finish in a drawing-room in place of the crude workshop batteries which are so commonly in use.'

The die-casting of lead plates, connectors and other parts led to Formans Road becoming the die-casting department of Joseph Lucas. Pressure die-casting of zinc and aluminium, as Wells remembers it, was a dangerous and uncomfortable job:

> The danger was of burns from splashes of hot liquid metal, which under pressure would suddenly fly up to the roof and all over the shop. It was to the credit of the shop management, works engineers and safety people that the hazard was gradually overcome. The first step was to isolate each machine in a cubicle, which limited the danger to one man – the machine operator – but complete safety was only achieved by enclosing all working parts of the machines and the pots of metal, which took several years of experiment.

After the take-over, the production of CAV and Rotax batteries was moved from London to Birmingham, and Formans Road became the battery factory for the whole group. To avoid any labour opposition, the CAV and Rotax battery workers in London were offered jobs at Formans Road if they were prepared to move to Birmingham. Many of them did so, and Formans Road was faced with the difficulty of having three people for every job – with a million unemployed outside – until production could be reorganised to supply the increased demand. Then a night shift was started for the whole factory, and the rat-race for jobs came to an end.

Special service arrangements were needed for batteries, which were now being sold in large numbers not only to the car manufacturers to fit as original equipment but also to the motor trade as replacements. After the CAV-Rotax take-over in 1926, a Battery Service Agency Agreement was introduced as a part of the United Service Scheme, which covered the products of all three companies. The agents were for the most part wholesale stockists and repairers of electrical equipment, many of them motor-car distributors as well. They were prohibited from selling other batteries, and Lucas laid down the prices and discounts they received. They also had to provide a specified service. The battery service agents did most of their business with garages and repairers, but they did some retail trade themselves.

CAV and Rotax continued to operate as separate companies under the general direction of Joseph Lucas for some years and at the end of 1927 it was possible to get the following picture of their respective sales for 12 months:

Lucas	£3,149,525
CAV	846,307
Rotax	673,988

Afterwards the sales became confused by inter-company trading and the respective contributions of the three companies were never quite so clear.

In London the Lucas Willesden service depot was closed down and combined with the CAV depot in larger premises at Acton. After giving it a run, Lucas decided to get out of the radio business done by CAV and Rotax, except for batteries, with which the company had wider interests. When Lucas took over, Rotax had just started to make a range of radio sets designed by Professor A. M. Low of London University under the brand name Rotola, while CAV had been making radio receivers and HT and LT batteries in celluloid or glass containers since 1921. At first the radio business of the two companies was concentrated at Acton, but it was soon realised that it was not worth continuing as a side-line when other people were devoting their whole energies to it, so production was stopped in 1927. But for CAV, at any rate, this was only to be a temporary decision.

CHAPTER SIX

GAINING STRENGTH—IN SECRET

Although the question was never debated – or at any rate recorded – at board meetings, it is clear that Peter Bennett and Oliver Lucas saw the future expansion of Joseph Lucas more in terms of acquiring other companies and in making other people's products under licence than in the research and development of entirely new products of their own. Of course research was not neglected. The 'New Joseph Lucas Research Laboratories' were opened in 1926 in their own three-storey building in Well Street. 'It is here,' Oliver Lucas told the shareholders, 'that our technical staff are continuously at work sifting fact from fancy, getting down to the fundamental principles controlling the problem, preparing new specifications and designs, and testing all materials; in other words, cutting out rule of thumb and introducing an exact science.'

The key to their future in the motor industry, as Bennett and Lucas saw it, was to achieve the highest possible volume of production and so keep down their prices. The urgency to do so arose from the threat of competition from the United States. Ford had always had their own British factory, and in 1925 General Motors acquired a controlling interest in Vauxhall. For the time being both bought a considerable amount of equipment from Lucas, but there was always the possibility of Auto-Lite, who supplied Ford in America, and Delco-Remy, the electrical equipment subsidiary of General Motors in the States, opening factories in the United Kingdom to meet their British companies' needs. And they might not stop at Ford and Vauxhall – they could compete with Lucas for supplying Morris, Austin and the rest of the British manufacturers. Oliver had seen enough on his visit to American factories in 1921 to appreciate their enormous superiority in engineering techniques, based on volume production far in excess of British and Continental demand. Bennett shared his view that Lucas's best hope was to keep their prices low enough to discourage the Americans from entering the market, and they could only do so by raising their production to the highest possible volume. This in turn depended on capturing the largest possible share of the market in advance. The acquisition of Brolt, EIC, C. A. Vandervell and Rotax had shown them the way, and now they devoted a great deal of their time to similar opportunities and to manufacturing licence agreements.

A few months after the completion of the CAV-Rotax take-over in 1926, Bennett was in touch with Peto & Radford about the possibility of getting the selling rights of Nife alkaline batteries for lighting purposes on commercial vehicles. These worked on a different chemical basis from the normal lead-acid battery, using a steel case and an alkaline electrolyte, which made them very robust and suitable for commercial vehicles. The Post Office liked them for their motor-cycles, and so too did the Automobile Association. They could withstand being run right down (as, for instance, when a vehicle was laid up for a time) and charged up again without damage, and were altogether less sensitive than lead-acid batteries. Against this they lacked the same capacity and voltage, and required nine cells in a 12-volt battery instead of six. Peto & Radford had the selling rights for Nife batteries for railway lighting from the makers, Batteries Ltd, of Redditch, who were an offshoot of the Swedish company Jungner. The agreement for Lucas to have the sole selling rights of the Nife battery for commercial vehicles in the United Kingdom and British Dominions was signed in July 1926.

In the following spring Bennett made an offer of £9,000 for the tools, patents, trade name and stock of magnetos, lighting and starting sets and parts of the British Lighting and Ignition Company (commonly called BLIC), a subsidiary of Vickers. He told the board that there would probably be a loss of £2,000 or £3,000 when these assets were realised, but this would be money well spent in keeping any other company from obtaining possession of the trade (they had developed the first British rotating magnet magneto) and possibly becoming a competitor to a small but irritating extent. The Lucas offer was accepted, and BLIC disappeared from the scene. Wolseley was also owned by Vickers and naturally fitted electrical equipment made by BLIC, a sister company. It had come as a surprise, therefore, when Lucas got the order for equipping a new 11hp Wolseley shortly before they took over BLIC. When the enquiry came through, Walker said to Robinson: 'I think they only want a check quotation but we had better deal with it as though we want the business,' so they went down to the Wolseley factory at Adderley Park together. There they saw the two joint general managers, Oliver Boden (who later became vice-chairman of Morris Motors) and a man named Dallow (who was afterwards managing director of British Timken). But to Robinson the most fascinating figure in that dark office was a portly gentleman of rather more than middle-age wearing a velvet smoking jacket and a brocaded velvet smoking cap. He sat in a corner, listened to the discussion, but took no part in it. He was the consultant to Wolseley, and turned out to be none other than the great Dr Frederick Lanchester, who with his brother George had made the first full-size four-wheeled car of purely British origin in 1894–5.

Relations with Robert Bosch AG, already established at one remove in 1924 by the agreement between the German company and C. A. Vandervell for the exchange of patent rights, were put on a direct footing for the first time when Bennett and Oliver Lucas called at Stuttgart during a visit to Germany in April 1927. The excuse for this visit to their great European competitor was that they had been asked to quote for the electrical equipment on the Austin Seven that was to be made under licence as the Dixi in Germany, and that before doing so they wanted to find out what chance they had of obtaining the business in competition with Bosch. Dr Rassbach (technical sales), Karl Wildt (manufacturing) and Dr Felmett, the lawyer, received them most courteously and showed them round the works, but it soon became clear that there was no hope of getting the Dixi order. The Germans added that they had often toyed with the idea of manufacturing in Britain themselves but felt that competition from Lucas would make it almost hopeless, except for replacement work. They gave the impression that they had practically abandoned the idea of manufacturing in Britain but were quite willing to co-operate in a scheme for using each other's service agents in non-manufacturing countries. Bennett and Lucas agreed to think this over.

Bennett then went off to America, and while he was away, plans for making under licence car door-locks and window-winding mechanism that Oliver Lucas had brought back from America went ahead with the sanctioning of four new bays at the Shaftmoor Lane works (the old EIC factory) after a pilot run of 1,000 sets had been made at Great King Street. A new spot-welding machine was purchased for their manufacture.

At the same board meeting in July 1927 it was reported that an agreement had been signed with the Auto-Research Corporation, a Canadian company, for the manufacturing rights in the British Empire, excluding Canada, of the chassis lubricating system invented by Mr Bijur, the president. This was given to CAV to make and was fitted to two cars at the 1928 Motor Show, being called the Bijur-Luvax central chassis lubricating system. In the following year it was taken up by Rolls-Royce and was fitted to certain Sunbeam and

Singer models. The idea of lubricating all the chassis points by the single operation of a lever instead of going round them one by one with a grease gun was admirable from the motorist's point of view, but the motor manufacturers never widely utilised it, probably because of its extra cost.

Up to this time some motor manufacturers were still fitting bulb horns to their cheap models, but in the spring of 1928 there were signs that the bulb horn was at last on its way out as a piece of initial equipment, except for taxicabs, for which it was a legal requirement. As a general accessory the bulb horn still had plenty of life, especially in the East – its use was compulsory, for example, in India, where the raucous electric horn was disliked. It was lucky, therefore, that at this moment Lucas were able to take over from the Graham Amplion company the interests and manufacturing rights they had arranged with the Sparks' Withington Company of the United States, which enabled Lucas to offer British manufacturers the Sparton motor-driven electric horn. This involved periodical payments to the American company amounting to £6,000 in all. From the reception it received – Morris immediately ordered Sparton horns for his 1929 cars – the change was made only just in time for Lucas to keep in the business of supplying horns as initial equipment on a serious basis. They had been making electric horns, of course, since before World War I, starting with a King of the Road 'buzzer' model in 1911, going on to the 6- and 12-volt diaphragm models for small and large cars after the war, and in 1928 adding the King of the Road Alto electric horn, with the high-frequency note that Bosch had made all the fashion among British motorists. But none of these horns had made much headway as initial equipment, the majority being sold as accessories through the motor and retail trades.

In the autumn of 1928 the negotiations with Robert Bosch AG were carried a stage further when Bennett and Oliver Lucas met Dr Rassbach at the Berlin Motor Show. Rassbach said that, although Lucas had agreed they might be interested in co-operative manufacturing with Bosch in Britain of anything new, to avoid 'the evil of unnecessary competition', unfortunately Bosch had nothing new, and the situation in Germany now called for quicker measures than holding out for a future hope. In the Bosch view the German motor industry was not in a sound condition (it was rumoured that the German banks had seriously considered accepting an offer from the Belgian Minerva group to take over a large block of shares in Daimler-Benz), so Bosch were looking around for alternative outlets.

One idea was to develop new lines in the domestic market; another was to capitalise their reputation in the motor industry by starting manufacture in other countries. 'I believe,' Rassbach now wrote, 'that for certain classes of work such as lighting and starting equipment for large commercial vehicles, heavy-duty magnetos, aircraft magnetos, vibrator horns and perhaps a number of other things we could offer you advantages in some form of co-operation. I believe that the greater part of this class of work business is being done by you through CAV, or is not being touched at all.' His suggestion was that Lucas should sell Bosch a half-interest in CAV, but nothing was to come of this scheme for several years. Meanwhile he assured Lucas that if Bosch ever decided to manufacture in England, he would let them know.

Conversations that were later to have important results were held with various people throughout 1928, but it was not until the end of the year that the next positive step was taken, this being an extension of the selling rights of the Nife alkaline battery to motor-cycles, followed early in 1929 by the purchase of 28,850 preference shares and 12,500 of the 71,150 ordinary shares in Batteries Ltd from Svenska Ackumulator Aktiebolaget Jungner, Pritchett & Gold and the EPS Co Ltd. Bennett and Oliver Lucas joined the Batteries board. The motive behind this acquisition was to safeguard the company's investment in the lead-acid battery against the possibility (which did not materialise) of the alkaline battery becoming more popular.

So far all the expansion had taken place at home; now the scene moved to the other side of the world, where Jack Masterton was at grips with a difficult situation about the supply of replacement batteries. The batteries sent out in new vehicles to Australia did not last long, and the demand for replacements was so heavy that they were continually in short supply. This had encouraged a certain amount of local manufacture, which in turn led to the imposition of a 45 per cent duty on imported batteries. The two leading importers, Lucas and Chloride (the British subsidiary of the American Electrical Storage Company), decided to meet the situation by going into local manufacture together. The 'Best Buy' was Masse Batteries, Ltd, of Sydney, but instead of negotiating a joint purchase, Chloride went ahead and bought Masse outright at the end of 1928. What was intended to be a joint Lucas/Chloride company, Associated Battery Makers of Australia Pty Ltd, to run the Masse factory was formed in 1930, but the arrangement for Lucas to have a share in this company was never completed. Chloride UK formed two selling companies, Exide

Batteries of Australia Pty Ltd./Masse Batteries Pty Ltd, and Willard Batteries of Australia Pty Ltd, which, with Joseph Lucas (Australia) Pty Ltd, became known as the Associated Selling Companies and drew all their supplies of Exide, Masse, Willard and Lucas batteries from ABMAL at factory cost plus 7 per cent for sale through distributors appointed by each selling company in each state.

This was not exactly what Lucas had intended by joint manufacture by Lucas and Chloride, but it did ensure that Lucas batteries were for sale on the same terms as their competitors'. The importance of this aspect can be judged by the fact that in 1929 more replacement batteries were sold in Australia than in the United Kingdom. In that year a power of attorney was given to Masterton to enable him to form a Lucas Australian subsidiary company to handle the sale of batteries as original equipment for vehicles arriving from Britain. This called for an ingenious and simple accounting procedure, which Masterton has recorded in one of his Historical Notes:

> In those days Lucas prices for original equipment varied between different cars and vehicle manufacturers due to special bargains made, special rebates and concessions, and different split-up prices. Obviously the deletion allowances (whatever they were) would be questioned and would give rise to suspicions that Lucas were not treating all their customers on the same basis. It was therefore decided to introduce a voucher system, and Lucas persuaded the UK car manufacturers to continue to charge their distributors in Australia for a complete vehicle or chassis and send them a battery voucher with each vehicle or chassis entitling them to draw a battery from Lucas in Australia at the net extra cost only to Lucas of manufacture in Australia and the transportation of the battery from the factory to the required Australian destination.

In May 1929 negotiations that had been going on for some time with a small company in East Anglia finally came to a head. (They were to lead to something very much bigger.) D. A. V. Rist had approached Lucas with the suggestion that they should take a controlling interest in the company that had been formed to take over the business he had built up in the manufacture of various motor accessories. Rist had started as an apprentice in a new company making miners' lamps in Upper Holloway, London, in 1902. Then the growing motor-car trade attracted them, and as the Prested Battery Company they turned to making accumulators and ignition coils. In 1910 he left the company after a receiver was appointed and in 1912 returned to manage it under a new name, Vulco Accessories, at the request of the debenture holders and the workpeople. In 1916 the owner died and bequeathed the business to Rist. After making batteries during the war, the company returned to ignition coils, horns and lamps, and in 1919 secured a contract from Ford for the supply of flywheel magnetos for the Model T they were assembling at Manchester. This took 95 per cent of their output. In 1922 Rist's health broke down and his doctor told him he had only six months to live. He recommended the East Coast, so Rist moved his business to Lowestoft, where he eventually recovered and lived for another 40 years. Now a new company, A. Rist (1927) Ltd, had been formed and Rist was looking for an opportunity to dispose of his interest.

Lucas turned down his first approach, but now they agreed to buy the shares held by a Mr Benson for £8,696, this sum to include payment for the directors to resign. Benson's shares, together with those held by Rist (which he gave Lucas the option to purchase), gave Lucas the controlling interest. These negotiations were carried on in complete secrecy through nominees, and the connection between Lucas and Rist was not to be divulged until 34 years later. Bennett and Lucas appointed Kenneth Corley as their liaison with Rist, and for many years Corley was the only person from Great King Street to visit Lowestoft. The Rist business had fallen away since 1927, when they lost the magneto concession from Ford on the change from the Model T to the Model A, which had coil ignition, but they had managed to get some orders for electric horns. Corley now helped them to get a contract for equipping the Austin Seven. R. W. Cox took Benson's place on the board, he and Rist running the business between them.

Negotiations with other companies came thick and fast throughout 1929. In August Hermann Aron of Rotax was approached by Ernest L. Payton, who had become chairman of Powell & Hanmer, Limited, one of Lucas's old competitors in the cycle trade, on the death of its founder, Frank Hanmer, senior. (Payton had also become a director of the Austin Motor Company.) He said that the intention was to convert the private company into a public company with an enlarged capital, and that an offer for it by Joseph Lucas would be welcome. Powell & Hanmer had been started in 1893 in a small factory on the corner of Chester Street and Avenue Road, making candle and oil lamps for bicycles, and adding acetylene lamps to the range at the turn of the century. Powell put up the money and Hanmer provided the practical experience. In 1904 it was incorporated as a company, and manufacture was extended to acetylene lamps for motor-cars and motor-cycles. Just before World War I another factory was built in Rocky Lane for the design and manufacture of electric dynamo lighting sets for cars and motor-cycles. Powell thought it would be a white elephant and flew into a rage, so Hanmer, scraping up his last penny, bought him out. The dynamo lighting sets went into production after the war, and the firm also made an electric horn for Ford and some side lamps for Austin.

Payton's connection with Austin could be regarded as ominous; Lucas would not take kindly to losing the Austin lighting contract to an enlarged Powell & Hanmer. Purchase of the company would avert this. Another point in favour of the deal was that it would permit the eventual concentration of the Lucas and P & H cycle trades at Chester Street, so giving the benefits of bigger volume production, which would help to fight the severe price competition then being experienced from Germany and Japan. After a lot of discussion, it was agreed to buy the company for £500,000, the Lucas capital being increased by the issue of 200,000 shares of £1 each and a credit arranged at the bank to enable the deal to be completed in cash or shares. The P & H business continued to be run under its own name and arrangements were made for Rotax lamps to be transferred to Chester Street from Willesden (Lucas having decided that London was not the right place for the manufacture of sheet-metal work).

As with the case of Rist, Lucas decided to keep this Powell & Hanmer transaction quiet, and the notice to shareholders calling an extraordinary general meeting on 26 August 1929 for the purpose of passing a resolution to increase the capital of the company made the point that 'it is desirable for business reasons that the identity of the business we are acquiring should not be disclosed at the present time.' Of course this did not prevent questions being asked by a persistent shareholder, these being dealt with in his usual magisterial manner by Bennett, as witness the following exchanges:

Q: Is the business it is proposed to acquire an old established one?
A: It is.
Q: Is it a serious competitor?
A: Yes, but only in a comparative degree; it could more aptly be described as one whose activities run along lines of development similar to our own. We do not try to buy up all competition, nor is it the object of the directors to make Lucas a sort of octopus that just devours every business that comes its way with the sole object of becoming big.
Q: Has the company paid dividends during the last five years?
A: Yes, they have been paid regularly; the company is a private

company, its shareholders being dependent on their dividends for their income.

It was understandable that many of the P & H workpeople resented being taken over, regarding the company as a family affair and over-looking the somewhat rough conditions they had had to put up with. To their surprise they found that Lucas paid them for working over-time – something the Hanmers had always resolutely refused to do, their alternative being to send baskets of fruit to the assembly shops at exceptionally busy times. Moreover, Lucas paid pensions. The re-sentment did not last long.

CHAPTER SEVEN

IMPROVING THE PRODUCT - IN PUBLIC

While the productive strength of the company was being built up by these acquisitions and arrangements, some notable new Lucas products were introduced in the closing years of the 1920s. The most famous of these was a new Lucas car headlamp that was announced in the catalogue for 1928 (issued in October 1927).

For some time Oliver Lucas had been nettled because Rolls-Royce and the makers of luxurious coachwork fitted headlamps of Continental origin, mainly Zeiss and Marchal, instead of the biggest Lucas lamp. According to Robert Neill, this was partly due to a form of price snobbery: 'Very often they only fitted Zeiss lamps because they were charged £20 a pair for them, whereas our most expensive headlamp, which was simply a bigger edition of our normal range, might have cost £10.'

Oliver Lucas decided to do something about this, and after much experimental work produced the 'new high-power mirror projector', which was modestly described in the catalogue as 'the World's finest automobile lamp . . . designed on entirely new lines and incorporating special and exclusive features . . . In appearance the projector is particularly handsome and majestic, and the fine workmanship and finish are fully worthy of a Lucas Lamp intended for the World's leading cars.' The price was £21 finished in 'ebony black' (a Lucas finish patented by Egginton and Normansell) with plated parts, £22 nickel-plated, and £30 silver-plated. The main feature of the design was an optically ground mirror set in the centre of the parabolic reflector, the bulb being carried on a tripod extension and facing towards the mirror, which was therefore free from any central aperture.

Just before the catalogue went to press, it was realised that the lamp did not have a name or serial number. Someone put the problem to Oliver Lucas in his office. Looking up from his desk rather irritably he said after a moment's thought: 'Oh . . . call it the P100,' adding, because the questioner looked a bit puzzled: 'P for Posh . . . 100 for candle-power.'

In the following year a variant of the P100 incorporating a dipping device was added. This was called the P100DB and had an extra bulb set behind an optically ground plano-convex lens in the top half of the reflector. A change-over switch extinguished the main beam and produced a dipped (and reduced) light from the supplementary bulb. Unfortunately it also gave the image of the bulb on the ground, so experiments continued in the matter of beam control generally. Eventually, some years later, Neill was sent over to Paris and negotiated with Marchal for Lucas to use their striped reflector, which Oliver Lucas greatly admired. All other lamp-makers, including Lucas, controlled the beam by lenses in the front glass, but Marchal obtained their beam distribution by a series of flats, or semi-flats, on the reflector itself. An incidental advantage was that they could use a plain front glass.

The P100 headlamp gave Lucas the same prestige in the motor-car world as the Silver King had done – and was still doing – among cyclists. The coveted order from Rolls-Royce was at last received, but was followed by complaints that the silver-plated bodies of the lamps were found to be scratched when they arrived at Derby. It appeared that the Rolls-Royce inspectors went over them with magnifying glasses. The trouble was only cured by giving instructions for the lamps to be handled with cotton wool and put into special crates on slings in the presence of a Rolls-Royce inspector, who travelled in the lorry with them to Derby, where the World's Finest Automobile Lamps were again inspected before being mounted on the World's Best Cars. Some of them, for cars ordered by Indian maharajahs, were gold-plated. All the P100 headlamps supplied to Rolls-Royce were virtually individually made.

The subject of headlight dazzle became urgent as more and more cars took to the roads. Since shortly after World War I Lucas had sold a headlight dimmer, but this was only a compromise. A more positive solution was the mechanical headlight dipper made by Barkers, the coachbuilders, on Rolls-Royces and other cars with Barker bodies. The headlamps were mounted on a cross-bar which could be tilted downwards and up again by a Bowden cable connected to a lever beside the driver.

The first real step towards curing dazzle was the dipping reflector patented and introduced by Lucas in 1927. The effect was to turn the headlight beams downward and to the nearside of the road. This was done by pulling a knob on the end of a small pneumatic cylinder mounted on the steering column or facia and connected by tubing to an even smaller pneumatic cylinder in each of the headlamps. A piston in this cylinder was coupled to the back of the movable reflector. The reflector was kept in each position by a strong spring.

Harry Lucas told the shareholders about it at the annual meeting in November 1927:

> Everybody who has seen it has, in effect, said, 'Ah! that's done it.' The motoring correspondent of a London daily paper [the *Daily Telegraph*] who saw it at the recent Show enthusiastically and gratuitously described it, under the heading 'Dazzle Danger Overcome', a 'Device which Solves the Lighting Problem', and he concluded by saying, 'It is the neatest, most practical, and most genuinely desirable detail improvement offered to the motor world for years past, and deserves to sweep through the industry . . . I am confident', he says, 'it will do so.'

Next year the device was modified so that the offside headlight was extinguished and only the nearside headlight was dipped and turned to the nearside. At the annual meeting Oliver Lucas said:

> This new device has been very largely taken up by the manufacturers this season, and we hope it will be by the establishment of this voluntary road etiquette that the dazzle problem will be solved rather than by irksome legislation on what is admittedly a complex and difficult, if not impossible, matter, especially if the courtesy of the individual driver is eliminated. In America special headlamps of no-glare characteristics are enforced by law, with the result that the individual driver does not feel called upon to display any consideration to his fellow-travellers, and as the no-glare lamps almost entirely fail in their no-glare properties, the terrors of a night drive in the United States must be experienced to be believed.

The anti-dazzle system advocated in America and Europe was the double-filament bulb, which was then in its early stages of development. In America the night-driving situation was made worse by the inferiority of their headlamps and their use of 6-volt electrical equipment. The Lucas dipping reflector was brought to its next phase of refinement in 1929 by replacing the pneumatic cylinders with an electric solenoid method of operating the reflectors that needed only the touch of a switch on the steering wheel or column. This was followed by a foot-operated switch, as used in America.

In the same year (1928) that motorists were able to buy the P100 headlamp cyclists were offered the Lucas King of the Road Dynamo Set No 25 – 'undoubtedly the finest light-giver for pedal cyclists'. The set comprised a dynamo with a knurled wheel which engaged with the side of the tyre, a headlamp, a tail-lamp, and cables and bulbs – all for £1 5s. The clip holding the dynamo incorporated a spring so that the dynamo could be moved into or out of engagement, and the dynamo was waterproof and rustproof.

But the cycle dynamo set had a powerful rival in the battery lamp, which was made by the Ever Ready company largely as a means of selling their dry batteries, of which they were by far the leading makers. Its great attraction to the cyclist was its low initial cost, against which had to be set the recurring cost of new batteries, so that for those who did a lot of night-time riding the Lucas dynamo set was a better proposition, and it sold in large quantities at home and abroad, where it had to compete with a dynamo lighting set made by Robert Bosch. Lucas and the other principal bicycle-lamp-makers, Powell & Hanmer and Millers, were forced to go into the battery lamp business, but it was not nearly so profitable because all they made was the tin case, the reflector and the switch. The battery, bulb and glass were bought out. Another drawback was that it cost as much to package the battery lamp as it did to make it. The Lucas battery lamp, complete with a handle which enabled it to be used as a carrying lamp as well, was put on the market in 1929 at 3s 6d. Lucas tried making their own dry batteries at Formans Road for a time, but this was not a success, as they could not compete with Ever Ready and their enormous output. At the peak of the battery cycle-lamp business in the United Kingdom production by the members of the Cycle Lamp Association reached about 7 million lamps and between 30 and 40 million batteries a year.

All through the latter part of the 1920s the Lucas suction windscreen-wiper, which had been introduced together with a hand-operated model in 1925, was the subject of a difficult and prolonged marketing struggle. The Lucas wiper was made on the lines of the American Trico model by arrangement with the British concessionaire, C. G. Vokes. The parent Trico-Folberth Company did not like this arrangement, and tried to end it by a series of price cuts in the Trico model that eventually made it completely unprofitable to compete with on the British market. Lucas were not put off, because they believed they could break the Trico patent if it came to an outright clash; but they preferred to avoid this contingency, since the result would have been to throw the suction-wiper market wide open to all comers, in which case it would be worth nothing.

This running battle went on for nearly five years, until the Americans broke the stalemate by taking Lucas to Court, chiefly to test whether the agreement between Lucas and Vokes was binding on the Trico-Folberth company. Unhappily Vokes himself was not an ideal witness and the judge felt bound to award the case against Lucas on the facts. But the case cleared the air and the two principals came together to work out a new basis of agreement, Trico conceding that the line Lucas had adopted, while causing them considerable irritation, had at any rate resulted in there being only themselves and Lucas to consider in supplying the market in future.

But Oliver Lucas was not satisfied with the suction windscreen-wiper, with its fluctuation in speed according to the opening of the throttle, so while the arguments with Trico-Folberth were going on he developed an electric wiper with an inductor type motor which he patented in 1927 in conjunction with E. O. Turner and S. A. Mason. This was introduced in the 1929 catalogue as 'the most silent electric wiper yet produced', and had fixing bolts that made it interchangeable at the top of the windscreen with the suction model, which continued to be made. This first Lucas electric screen wiper was not self-starting – it had to be started by spinning a knob, several attempts having to be made sometimes before the motor took over, which was infuriating when the wiper was needed instantly. In the following year a 12-volt model was added, which was strong enough to drive a second arm and blade on the passenger's side.

There were two Turners in the company at this time – Dr E. O., the technical head of the Electrical Company, and D. C., who was a works engineer. Dr Turner, as I have already noted, came to Lucas from BLIC when that company was taken over in 1927 and was a curious mixture. By nature and training he was a musician (he had qualifications) and was a capable electrical engineer only by necessity. He had charm and human qualities but no idea of organising. He could not stand his namesake, who reciprocated the feeling – in fact they hated each other – with the result that they would not work together in the slightest degree. This made life very difficult, because they were jointly responsible for technical development and research; yet they were always at loggerheads. It must have been a relief, not least to Oliver Lucas, when Dr Watson arrived on the scene from ML and was appointed chief engineer, which gave him overriding powers. Dr E. O. Turner became chief of the technical department and D. C. Turner general production manager.

By 1929 Lucas were able to establish the manufacture of another motor-car component, the shock absorber, which they have continued to supply (in a different form) to the present day. Some years previously they had made a near-copy of the Hartford friction-type shock absorber which was so popular with sports-car owners in the 1920s. The effect of this device was to stiffen the reaction to road shocks and the rebound of the laminated springs normally used in those days, giving a firm but very bumpy ride. Indeed when the Lucas friction-type shock absorber was tried on a Morris Cowley, the chassis frame cracked in several places. In normal service the friction discs wore out quickly, and it was decided to drop the Hartford-type in favour of another French shock absorber, the Houdaille, which used hydraulic vanes displacing rape seed oil instead of wooden discs as the damping medium. The concession for the Houdaille in England was held by Colonel Colin Defries, operating as the Houdaille Hydraulic Suspension Co Ltd of Drayton Gardens, Kensington, London, and the licence for Lucas to manufacture an English version was arranged with him in 1927 by Arthur Benstead, the general manager of Rotax. Lucas called their shock absorber the Luvax, a name that condensed Lucas, CAV and Rotax in one word.

A company with that name was registered in 1927 and a corner of the CAV works at Acton was allocated to it. The first manager, H. W. Pitt, was reputed to have designed the last motor-car made by the Napier Company (presumably the 30/35hp model in 1914–15). The Napier factory was also at Acton, so Pitt would almost certainly have known Charles Vandervell. Meanwhile the Houdaille had been chosen as original equipment on the new Model A Ford, and in March 1929 Bennett was able to report that arrangements had been made by Benstead with Defries for Lucas to manufacture them. Furthermore it was agreed that Lucas were to become Defries's sole source of supply of Houdaille shock absorbers, instead of the parent factory in France, and £10,000 was advanced to him on account of royalties to enable him to develop any demand there might be for them, on condition that they were manufactured by Lucas. At the same time Lucas were free to exploit the Luvax, and promises had already been obtained from several manufacturers to fit it on their next season's cars. 'In this way,' Peter Bennett summed up, 'we shall control both the Luvax and the Houdaille.' A sum of between £60,000 and £70,000 was spent on the plant and buildings at Acton.

The original Luvax shock absorber gave a good deal of trouble. A trial batch was sent along to the Lucas depot at Acton for testing. Roy Harrison, the manager, had recently spent a holiday in North Wales and remembered that the road in the Festiniog Valley was atrocious, so he fitted a car with the Luvax dampers and sent it there to be tested.

'We wrecked them very quickly on those pot-holes,' he recalls, 'and I was very unpopular for having chosen such a rough test.' A year later Harrison was sent out to Australia to take charge of the new Australian subsidiary company established by Masterton (he was to stay there for the next 30 years), and he arrived in time to receive the brunt of the complaints about the early examples of the Luvax being unable to withstand Australian road conditions.

The trouble with the Luvax was partly due to the light alloy back plate, which bulged when the oil was cold, but the main reason was that the British car manufacturers economised on springs and shock absorbers (and other components) in those days, and the Luvax shock absorber they ordered was too small for its job. Larger shock absorbers would have been more efficient and able to stand up to rough roads, but they would have cost more, which made them unacceptable as original equipment. In 1930 the Luvax received some favourable publicity when it was used by the team of Austin Sevens in the RAC Tourist Trophy Race in Ulster, and again in the 500-mile Race at Brooklands, where the little car averaged 83.41mph on the bumpy concrete track.

In contrast to these new products, a famous Lucas component lost its best customer as the Twenties gave way to the Thirties: in February 1929 Morris Motors told Lucas that they were redesigning their engines to use a dynamo and a separate self-starter instead of the combined dynamotor they had taken since 1922.

Starting still gave motorists a lot of trouble, especially in the winter, and in 1929 Oliver Lucas decided to tackle the whole subject on a scientific basis. A cold room capable of taking a complete car was constructed and put in charge of a bright young engineer named Ralph Barrington from the laboratory in Well Street (where he had worked with Herbert Astbury on the development of a new moulding powder in conjunction with Bakelite). Originally the starting tests were carried out with the car inside the cold room and an electric motor with reduction gear outside, measurements being made of the torque in the connecting shaft. Barrington and his assistants found that the engines of cars were invariably assembled much too tightly, and on one occasion, when a James Handy-Van was being tested, the motor turned the whole vehicle over in its efforts to rotate the engine. This technique of testing was replaced by a calibrated starter motor, and the unnecessary stiffness of engine assembly was pointed out to the motor manufacturers. Another lesson passed on as a result of the cold room testing was that much thinner lubricants could be used, which would greatly help starting without ill-effects as regards cylinder wear. In this work Barrington received great assistance from some of the oil companies, particularly from O. T. Jones of the Vacuum company, who then marketed a thinner Mobil Arctic which set a new fashion. As it was the only cold room available to the motor industry at the time, Oliver placed it at the disposal of all Lucas customers free of charge, a gesture that paid handsomely in goodwill.

Before the 1920s ended, Lucas started a new branch of its business in such secrecy that no word about its progress was to be heard for some 25 years. Jack Masterton has recounted the background in one of his invaluable Historical Notes about the company's activities:

> When financial accounts were prepared for the operations of Lucas depots they showed bad results. This was mainly due to the rather generous service given to the public and the trade in dealing with guarantee claims and other troubles in connection with Lucas electrical equipment. Lucas depots were also built rather extravagantly at the time to improve the public image of the company, causing the overheads to be considerably higher than was really necessary for the business transacted. They also had to employ skilled personnel for diagnosis and workshops, and to distribute service information and educate the trade generally in maintenance and service of Lucas equipment.
>
> Independent agents, on the other hand, were apparently making money although operating in smaller districts and with smaller turnover. Many applications for Lucas agencies were being received and Lucas competitors were busy appointing agents in smaller towns. These independent agents were taking local trade away from the Lucas depots while using the Lucas depots for guarantee work. They did not appear to get as much guarantee work or have to give the free service to the same degree as Lucas depots.
>
> With the growth of the motor trade and the necessity for quick service, more establishments were needed and competitors were making headway through their agents in districts away from main Lucas depots. It was also felt that the generous service given at Lucas depots was attracting complaints and claims and giving a false picture as to the reliability of Lucas equipment. The private motorists and traders tended to emphasise the trouble with Lucas equipment to obtain replacement items free of charge or at reduced prices even when the trouble was due to abuse, accident, or fair wear and tear.

This was the problem that confronted Henry Urquhart, the Service Manager, and his suggestion for solving it was that Lucas should start a chain of apparently independent small trading companies acting as

Lucas agents. Their freedom from the handicaps of the Lucas depots, and their consequent profitability, should compensate for the unavoidably poor financial returns from the depots. Urquhart's suggestion was accepted and the first of these companies, County Electrical Services, started operations about 1929 with a depot at Hanley, trading as an independent Lucas agent. It was an immediate success, so the signal was given for more 'County' depots to be opened in the smaller towns where there were no existing independent Lucas agents. In order to keep the whole thing dark and prevent any discoveries being made through the Somerset House files, a 'cover' holding company called Robert Guthrie, Limited, was formed to hold the shares in County Electrical Services and other trading companies as and when they were established. Lucas held its shares in Robert Guthrie through nominees.

Before we turn to the events of the 1930s, let us pause and take a closer look at the two men under whose direction – if not dictatorship – the company was growing so rapidly.

'A WONDERFUL PAIR...
A DIABOLICAL PAIR'

Peter Bennett and Oliver Lucas, joint managing directors of Joseph Lucas, Limited, from 1922 onwards, were one of the most remarkable partnerships the British motor industry has ever seen. Dissimilar in most respects – they had no intellectual or social interests in common – they nevertheless worked together in extraordinary harmony, and their complementary qualities added up to a formidable team. Both had curiously mixed characters. Peter Bennett was at the same time religious and aggressive, hard-faced and kind-hearted, loud-voiced and sympathetic – the archetypal Birmingham man. Oliver Lucas was not formally religious in the way that Bennett was but set himself exceptional standards of integrity; he could be sarcastic to the point of rudeness, yet was basically gentle; and though as a rule he much preferred to talk to men who could design things and make things, he was patient in explaining technical details to non-technical people, especially if they were young and enterprising. He had not much time for others.

Both were autocratic, but in their behaviour this took completely different forms. Someone who knew them well said that Peter Bennett fought his battles with a bludgeon while Oliver's weapon was a rapier, the one using tough language to hammer his opponent into defeat, the other sitting quietly until – *jab* – the point was driven home with paralysing effect. And they had different – and complementary – powers of leadership. Oliver Lucas was the brilliant engineer who could inspire a small team of young men and individual craftsmen; Peter Bennett was the father-figure of the entire company, and his annual 'progress' round the various factories was a great tonic to the whole organisation. It was an apparently informal occasion but in reality it was carefully rehearsed, with a card of details about each person he was scheduled to talk to. He never referred to the cards but would put an arm round a man's shoulders and ask after his wife. When Oliver Lucas made a grand tour, each factory was cleaned and painted up for his benefit; he was well liked, but Bennett's boisterous *bonhomie* was not in his nature and the result was not nearly so effective *en masse*.

To say that Peter Bennett was the commercial man and Oliver Lucas the born technician does not tell the whole story. Bennett had not spent his early working years in magneto production without acquiring some superficial technical knowledge, but he never did any practical work on developing electrical equipment – his prime interest lay in expanding the company's business and negotiating acquisitions. Oliver Lucas, for all his devotion to the technical side and his ability as an engineer, had no technical training; like Sir Henry Royce, he was an instinctive engineer, with innate engineering judgement. But he had his feet firmly on the ground, and Peter Bennett – although 10 years his senior – relied heavily on him not only for his technical judgement but for his commercial judgement as well.

This aspect of Oliver Lucas was confirmed by someone outside the company, Sir William Lyons, who knew both men well from the time he himself moved his embryonic Jaguar company (then Swallow Coachbuilding) from Blackpool to Coventry in 1928. We were talking about Oliver Lucas's technical flair and its importance in the development of the company when Sir William sounded a note of caution: 'Don't underrate his commercial sense,' he said. 'From my dealings with them both I would say that Oliver Lucas held his own with Peter Bennett in all their decision-making discussions.' Others go so far as to say that Peter Bennett was to some extent the mouthpiece of Oliver's decisions. For his part Oliver certainly had a wholehearted admiration for Peter Bennett's financial and negotiating skills. Oliver Lucas was not an organisational man, and he tended to become immersed in the details of an engineering development at the expense of seeing it as a complete project. Charles Marcus, vice-president of the Bendix Aviation Corporation, who came to know him closely, once said: 'Oliver has a wonderful brain, but he doesn't know how to direct it.'

Although so different in temperament and ability, 'PFB' and 'OL' invariably came to the same conclusion over any problem. They instinctively understood the working of each other's very different minds; it was as if they could hear each other thinking. Sir Kenneth Corley has told me that on at least one occasion Bennett said to Lucas: 'While you were away X came to see me and asked what we were going to do about the problem he has been discussing with you, so I said Y.' Oliver was silent for a moment, then he said: 'Funny you should say that, Peter. When I got home last night he rang me up about the same thing. My answer was Y too.' They had both reached the same conclusion separately from their own points of view. For Joseph

Lucas, Limited, the fact that every decision on a financial or commercial problem was the combined judgement of two such strong yet different people was of enormous value. Never was there a more striking example of the old saying that two heads are better than one.

I have said that Peter Bennett was loud-voiced, this being particularly evident when he got into a temper – which he frequently did. Sir Kenneth Corley has described what happened on these occasions:

> I've never known a man who could get into such a rage. He would fling his arms in the air and would roar and rage up and down the passages in the office. He would literally shout and bawl and hollow until the windows shook and people outside would stop – they wouldn't know what on earth was going on. He would create the hell of a storm – but the storm would pass and all would be calm an hour later or the next day.

And Bernard Scott has told me about the time he was walking along the corridor as a young man when double doors burst open and the burly figure of 'PFB' appeared. 'He seized me by the coat and shouted "What do you know about fog lamps?" I replied: "Oh, there's the FT 37, sir, and the FT 37P. And then there's the one we're struggling to get right, the FT 57, and that also has a P version . . ." He roared: "No, you bloody fool, why aren't we making any?" "Well, I don't know", I began to murmur, and he bellowed: "Well, bloody well go and find out." '

A likeable part about Peter Bennett was that he could make fun of himself. One day the young Kenneth Corley went into Bennett's office and found him with his ear pressed against the door communicating with Oliver's adjoining room. 'Come here and listen to this,' he beckoned to Corley. Oliver Lucas, normally the quietest-spoken of men, was yelling down the telephone on a long-distance line. Bennett was convulsed with laughter, and kept on saying: 'And they say I shout . . .'

Many stories were told about the two adjoining offices with the communicating door – often open – between them. It was obviously the most convenient arrangement, because they could stroll into each other's offices and keep up a running dialogue, but it also had the effect that a visitor to one of them would more often than not find himself confronted with their combined opposition when the occupant of the other room joined them after a time. Whether this was by accident or design was never established, but they were certainly crafty enough to have pre-arranged such apparently casual interruptions. When the visitor was a member of the staff summoned to answer for some shortcoming, the combined onslaught could be devastating. Senior executives were sometimes treated like erring schoolboys and deprived of any trace of their status.

Indeed status was not encouraged at Joseph Lucas in those days, and no one was left in any doubt that the people who really ran the business were Peter Bennett and Oliver Lucas. This went for the board of directors as well. At foremen and factory-floor level their policy was to divide and conquer, and they accomplished this by deliberately leaving positions ill-defined (someone described them to me as 'a wonderful pair – a diabolical pair'). Even managers were never too sure of the actual title of their appointments. When Ernest Watson was appointed Chief Engineer in 1931, he found on his arrival at Great King Street that none of his future staff had been told about it, which made his task of reorganising the various engineering sections that much more difficult. Time after time I have been told by retired executives: 'I suppose I was assistant manager, sales manager, or something; positions were always rather vague in those days and we never quite knew what we were.' This was mainly Peter Bennett's doing, for he was always reluctant to allocate responsibility. He even carried this to the point of forbidding people's names being put on office doors. Oliver Lucas had his own abomination, which was for anyone to be called an 'expert'.

But it must not be thought that this intensely autocratic behaviour on the part of the joint managing directors was resented (among the supervisory staff they were affectionately called 'The Bing Boys'). It was tempered with just as much genuine concern for the welfare of everyone in the company, not least in the matter of minimising the seasonal lay-offs that were a black feature of the motor industry before the war. As in the days of the founder, Lucas were regarded as good, considerate employers, and both Bennett and Lucas did many individual acts of kindness behind the scenes. Most mornings they would do a quick tour of the Great King Street shops together, stopping for a word here and there with the men and women at work.

Their attitude to the staff and workpeople was summed up by Oliver when he paid tribute to them at an annual shareholders' meeting. What he said then is worth quoting in full:

We work them hard, very hard indeed, but no harder than we are prepared to work ourselves. We believe there is nothing like hard work, that is if the work is productive, to give a man a contented mind, and I think we have been able to show once again that their work in every sense of the word has been highly productive. We have, therefore, a lot of happy people working together, and that makes for the good team spirit we enjoy in our organization to a unique extent. Now that is something we value very dearly, and I am sure you will join with me most heartily in paying tribute to our splendid staff.

Above all, there was pride in working for Joseph Lucas, Limited, because by the early 1930s Peter Bennett and Oliver Lucas had brought the company to the forefront of Birmingham technology. Lucas was the progressive place, the 'new frontier' of technology.

Directly he was appointed joint managing director, Oliver Lucas started a policy of selecting and training young men for future management positions. That he was more concerned about this problem than Peter Bennett was due no doubt to the responsibility he felt in having his name, his family name, attached to the company and its products, and the consequent need to safeguard their reputation. As a direct contribution to this policy he began to employ a series of personal assistants, carefully choosing young men who impressed him for reasons they did not always suspect at the time.

The first to be selected for this treatment was Robert Neill, who was working as assistant to Paterson at the newly opened Formans Road battery factory when Oliver visited it one day in 1923. Neill had found out something rather peculiar about the double-filament bulb in the Lucas headlamp of his motor-cycle. It was made by GEC, who were the main suppliers of bulbs to Lucas at that time, and Neill discovered that when the main filament broke, the reserve filament, even if it stayed intact, became unserviceable. The reason, he worked out, was because it was earthed through the main filament. He remarked on this, very diffidently, in conversation with Oliver Lucas, adding a suggestion for curing it by wiring the lamp in a different way. For Oliver Lucas this was just the kind of attitude of mind that marked the possessor down as a young man to encourage.

It was in fact no coincidence that a month or two later Neill was sent by Walker, the commercial manager of the Electrical Company, on the tricky assignment of taking away the Lucas agency from the Italian who held it in Florence and appointing another one in his place, before going on from Italy to inspect the Lucas agent in Prague. For a young man of 21 with no knowledge of Italian, talking through an interpreter about contact breakers and platinum points as they checked the Italian's stock was a tall order (today a team would be given the job), and the whole exercise was of course a deliberate test. On his

(above) Men and women working side by side making car lamps in the 1920s. At that time Lucas employed more women than men, and labour intensity was high
(below) the Great King Street head offices and works in 1953. Since then the street between the factory buildings has become private property and has security gates each end

The Lucas P.100 headlamp was produced primarily for luxury cars like this Rolls-Royce with Park Ward coachwork *(F. N. Birkett)*, but it was equally successful for motor racing and was used by the winning Bentleys at Le Mans in 1929 *(Autocar)*

return he was sent round the motor-car and motor-cycle factories for a while until he was brought back to Great King Street as Oliver Lucas's first personal assistant.

'This was a terribly interesting and formative time in my life,' Neill has told me. 'Oliver Lucas was an exacting man to work for, pedantic in the extreme in the correct use of English. If you said the wrong thing or used the wrong phrase you were very firmly told about it.' He had no time for superfluous words in a business conversation, and could not stand the custom of starting a report with a paragraph of generalisations before getting down to the facts. People who worked for him only made that mistake once.

Neill was followed by Kenneth Corley, who came to Lucas's attention in a quite different way. He had joined the company in 1927 at the age of 19, being sent to the Leyton service depot to begin with in order to learn about the product and to understand the business. Back in Birmingham he was put under Walker 'as a sort of office boy or runabout' to learn something of the commercial side. In 1933 Morris Motors held one of their dealers' conventions over which William Morris himself presided with W. M. W. Thomas (later Sir Miles and later still Lord Thomas) sitting alongside as his sales director. The theme of the convention, paraphrased by Corley, was 'Why the hell can't we sell more cars?' – to which the dealers replied: 'Well, because the cars aren't very good anyway and in particular there is this lousy electrical equipment which you fit on them.' Lucas, as always, were the convenient whipping-boy on these occasions. The dealers concluded: 'Why don't you put some decent electrical equipment on them and then they'll be saleable,' at which there was a round of applause.

This got back to the Lucas board at Great King Street, and it was decided to dispatch Walker round a selection of the Morris main distributors in England and Scotland to find out exactly what went on at the convention. Walker took young Corley with him, visiting such firms as Hewins of Maidenhead, Appleyards of Leeds, Beatties of Newcastle, and Watsons of Liverpool, in each case seeing the managing director. The scene moved to the Motor Show at Olympia a few weeks later. Walker and Corley had prepared a brief for Oliver Lucas, and he took Corley along with him to the Morris stand, where they were to meet Miles Thomas. Corley had never met Oliver Lucas before, and was accordingly in awe of the great man as Oliver put over his story to Thomas, not daring to interpose anything himself. Corley felt that his boss was winning, so when Oliver called on him to add his own comment, he said: 'Really Mr. Thomas, what is in their minds is your back axles; if you only get the back axles right it might be different' – to which 'Tommy' replied: 'You're absolutely right.'

On the way back to the Lucas stand Oliver, after a thoughtful silence, said quietly: 'Well done, Corley.' It was only as he got to know him better that Corley understood how much those words meant; Oliver Lucas seldom said things like that. This was one of those rare moments, for he had just decided that Corley was to be his next personal assistant. And Corley does not forget to add: 'I always thank "Tommy" for helping me to get my job' – for that was the first step on his road to the chairmanship of the company.

And so we come to Oliver Lucas's third personal assistant, Bernard Scott, who was destined to follow the same path. Bernard Scott does not properly enter this history until the next chapter, but the manner of his appointment to Oliver Lucas's staff belongs to this study of the joint managing directors. Scott maintains he joined Joseph Lucas by accident; he was meant to be a doctor but found himself 'a failed schoolboy' – he had not matriculated – when he had to leave school early because his father got into financial difficulties (the year was 1931, and times were hard). It was his mother who suggested, after many fruitless interviews, that he should try and join 'a decent Birmingham firm like Joseph Lucas.' He was interviewed by Bertram Waring, the secretary, whose courtesy made a lasting impression on the 16-year-old boy. 'He called me Mr. Scott, and ended the interview by asking me would I like to give the company a trial for say three weeks?'

Like Corley before him, Scott spent his early days in London, for, although a true Brummy, his family were living temporarily in the South. He started in the old Wandsworth service depot (now no more – in fact Scott sold it 40 years later when he was general manager at CAV) – and after two years, first at Acton and then at CAV, he was brought back to Birmingham to complete his training. After a spell in the service department he went to production, and while he was there he took out a couple of patents in his own name, paying 15s for the provisional specifications. He was encouraged by his father, who was a compulsive inventor ('always taking up patents, father was'). One of the patents was for traffic control by means of a strip in the road (which was, of course, anticipated) and the other was sparked off in Scott's mind by the new regulation that forbade the use of motor-car hooters after 11 o'clock at night. His invention was a device which, when switched on at that hour, caused the horn button to flash the headlights instead of sounding the horn.

Scott continues the story:

I got these two provisionals under my own name, stuffed them in an envelope at my digs in Handsworth and addressed them to the managing director, saying I hereby present to the company what I think are a couple of good ideas. The next thing that happened was that I was sent for in Well Street, where I was working in time-study (the whizz-kid department of those days) and told to go over to Great King Street and see a chap named Corley. He had got my letter in his hand and said: 'The managing director is most displeased'. I said why should he be displeased? 'Didn't you know that any ideas that you have in relation to the company's business belong to the company? What do you mean by taking out patents?' I said: 'I took them out certainly, but I'm giving them to the company . . .' 'Well, don't you do it again'.

It was very nicely done, but I got the great big tick-off. Corley was personal assistant to Oliver Lucas and to cut a long story short about two months later I was sent for again and I thought well, this is the final chop, but Corley then said: 'Mr. Lucas is going to America and I'm going with him (on a previous visit he had taken Robert Neill) and we thought there ought to be someone in the office to answer the telephone and read the magazines.' While he was saying this a head appeared round the door (yes, it was Mr. Lucas) and said 'Ha!' And that was that. Anyway they eventually came back from America and Mr. Lucas talked to me for the first time and then Kenneth Corley went off to work for Mr. Walker.

Once again a young man of individual character and evident initiative had attracted Oliver Lucas. He appointed Scott to take Corley's place.

What impressed Bernard Scott most, perhaps, about his new chief was that he knew more about the design of the product than anybody else and, what was even more important, he knew how to make it. As we have seen, he had always been intensely interested in production engineering, and he kept himself right up-to-date by his regular visits to the States, the fountain of knowledge on the subject. To accompany him on a tour of the shops – his own or those of another manufacturer – to listen to his comments on the scope for production engineering, and to hear his appraisal of a factory, these were experiences that his fortunate young personal assistants were never to forget.

Oliver Lucas was always on the look-out – especially when he was in America – for new ideas, new methods, new products, and he urged all the young men at the factory, wherever they found themselves, to follow his example. Herbert Astbury has told me how he used to emphasise: 'Although we may think we are very bright and the leaders in the industry, it is as well to remember that we can't have all the best people and all the best ideas in the world all the time.' He often said how frequently, and yet how willingly, he paid to look into the BLACK BAG submitted by often over-enthusiastic inventors; he felt 'it was always worth while because you never knew when you would come across something novel which could play a major part in the future of the company.' In Astbury's case these words were to bear particularly valuable fruit, as we shall discover in due course.

To the members of his personal staff Oliver Lucas could sometimes seem more like a machine than a human being. The company – especially the product – was the overriding interest in his life, and he expected others to feel the same. His devoted secretary for many years, Miss Parkes, has told me how she cheerfully accepted the un-spoken decree that she could have no life of her own; apart from a strictly punctual 9 o'clock start, there was no such thing as normal working hours. Oliver himself never showed any signs of fatigue, and his energy was boundless – he was fond of reminding laggards that 'the footprints in the sands of time were not made by sitting down.' Every winter he went ski-ing, usually with John Black, the head of Standard Motors, and on one occasion he came back with a broken leg. At the factory he terrified the Commissionaire by throwing his crutch down the staircase at the Directors' entrance and hopping down on one leg. He was on close terms with the leaders of all the big car companies – Pat Hennessy, Spen Wilks, Billy and Reggie Rootes, John Black, Bill Lyons – who valued the first-hand knowledge of the American motor-component industry he gained on his regular visits to the States. They asked him to drive and comment on their proto-type new models.

On one of these American trips he got on exceptionally good terms with Henry Ford – a considerable achievement – who thereafter re-garded him as a personal friend. The incident throws an interesting light on Oliver Lucas's business technique. It began with his finding out that Fords, who had previously used their own equipment on the cars made in Britain, were going to change their model. Oliver Lucas determined to try and use this opportunity to get some Lucas equip-ment on the new car. He decided that the best approach would be through Henry Ford himself. But first he made a study of the great man's interests and hobbies and found out that he was interested in music, in old machinery, and in old clocks and watches particularly.

So he studied these subjects over a period of months before asking Charles Sorensen, Ford's Chief Engineer, to arrange a luncheon appointment with Henry Ford at the Rouge on his next visit to America. He found an old watch with an unusual escapement, he swotted up Morris dancing, and he learnt to play the saw with a bow.

At last the word came through that the luncheon had been arranged. As they sat at the round table, Oliver talked mostly to Sorensen. Half-way through luncheon he produced his watch, looked at it casually and replaced it in his pocket. From the pause that followed he sensed that it had not escaped Henry's attention. Then he took it out again and said it was time for him to go. Ford's reply was: 'What's that watch you've got there, Lucas?' Oliver quietly passed it over for him to examine. Talk of his leaving was forgotten. After lunch Henry said, 'Are you interested in music?' to which Oliver replied: 'Not much. I fiddle about with a saw and a bow. I've got an ear for music. In the Cotswolds where I live we do a bit of dancing.'

'Come into the ballroom', said Henry Ford. There, one of the two orchestras constantly on duty was instructed to play appropriate music and soon Oliver Lucas was demonstrating Morris dancing to Henry Ford and Henry Ford was dancing back at him. This went on for about an hour; then Ford said: 'Nice to have seen you, Lucas, come back to the office for a minute.' And there he said: 'I'll autograph one of my photographs for you.' Which he did, but not without the difficulty which this extraordinary man found in writing even his own name.

That photograph, signed 'Sincerely, Henry Ford', was as good as an open cheque for Lucas when Oliver got back to England. It meant that he had actually spoken to and received a photograph from Henry, and Henry had agreed that Oliver was the right kind of guy.

The final difference between Peter Bennett and Oliver Lucas was in their attitude to the outside world. Oliver Lucas was completely introverted as far as Joseph Lucas, Limited, was concerned; his only desire was to concentrate on the success of the company, and he had no time to spare for the wider affairs of the city of Birmingham, the motor industry, or British industry as a whole. He could be fiercely patriotic, though, and in 1929 made a furious attack on Austen Chamberlain, the MP for West Birmingham, because he bought an American-made Chrysler instead of a British car. In this he got full support from Sir Ernest Canning, an old friend and supplier of equipment, who happened to be chairman of the Birmingham Commonwealth Association at the time. Oliver continued the theme at the Lucas annual meeting, when he praised the big steps forward made by the British manufacturers at the Motor Show. 'There is now no excuse for anyone buying a foreign car,' he said. 'I would go even further and say it is a disgrace, especially in view of the present unemployment, to buy anything but British.'

Peter Bennett on the other hand, the born extrovert, was attracted by all these outside issues and in his lifetime was to engage himself in the affairs of the Birmingham Chamber of Commerce, the Society of Motor Manufacturers & Traders, the Federation of British Industries, the House of Commons and the House of Lords – as well as many minor local associations. He was a natural choice as delegate for any important conference concerning the British motor industry, as, for instance, the Imperial Economic Conference at Ottawa in 1932. (The many Government posts he was to hold during World War II will be dealt with in their proper place.) He was able to take on all these extra activities partly because the company had by now reached an assured position in industry, partly because Oliver Lucas (with the growing support of Bertram Waring) was willing to bear an even greater share of running the show, and partly because an exceptionally efficient management team had been forged and was producing people capable of bearing the highest responsibility.

Some of these new managers and managers-to-be have already appeared in these pages. More will emerge as we now go on to follow the company's history in the 1930s.

PART FIVE

THE NINETEEN-THIRTIES

CHAPTER ONE

THE LINK WITH BOSCH - AND BEDAUX

The New Year of 1930 brought with it an atmosphere of economic gloom. On top of the uncertainty surrounding the Chancellor's intensions about the McKenna duties there was the undermining of confidence at home by the Hatry crash in the City and world-wide anxiety about the effects of the American Stock Exchange collapse. The company braced itself for a slack period until the end of the season, while in Parliament a new Road Traffic Act was passed which abolished the 20mph speed limit, made third-party insurance compulsory and introduced the *Highway Code*.

On the factory front the prevention of industrial accidents received a good deal of attention about this time and was taken up by the Employers Federation. Lucas were able to tell them that they had already appointed their own safety inspector, with the result that other manufacturers were pressed to follow their example in order to stave off any further legislation. Although the Lucas safety inspector normally worked through the works manager, he had the right of direct approach to the managing director if he felt dissatisfied. The company took a leading part in the formation of a local committee to keep the subject alive. The inspector's report for the whole of 1930 covered fifty-nine accidents due to power-driven plant, causing the loss of 39,348 hours of working time among the 8,380 employees (who worked on average 197 hours each per month). On top of this it was estimated that 20,000 hours were lost in attending the ambulance rooms for dressings and treatment of minor injuries and ailments. One employee died from septicaemia, but it turned out that he was a youth in such poor condition that a trivial scratch took a bad turn and his death was in no way connected with his work. Fifteen people suffered some permanent partial disability, but no permanent total disability cases were recorded. Certifying surgeons visited the factory on forty-four occasions and examined 428 young people. They also investigated four cases of alleged industrial diseases, but as no comment was made about working conditions, it was assumed that they satisfied the surgeons.

The appointed surgeon for the Formans Road battery factory made fifty-nine visits and 5,419 examinations of lead workers, as a result of which 104 were transferred from lead work but no certificates permitting resumption of work in lead were issued. One employee was certified as suffering from lead-poisoning.

The safety inspector's report gives an idea of the amount of production plant in use at Great King Street in 1930. He stated that the power-driven plant included 365 power presses, 342 milling machines, 528 drilling machines, 303 polishing spindles, 512 lathes, 278 capstan lathes and 285 automatics.

In May, after six months of discussion, an agreement was reached with S. Smith & Sons (Motor Accessories) that gave Lucas an even stronger hold on the electrical equipment market. Smiths had built up a modest connection with some of the small motor manufacturers for the supply of lighting, starting and ignition equipment as a side-line to their main business in instruments and sparking plugs. They supplied the equipment for Bentleys, which may have been partly due to their being close neighbours in Cricklewood, in North London, and for a short time Morris took a supply of dynamotors from them as a dual source. Smiths had found difficulty in providing adequate service facilities for such a small output of electrical equipment, which became dispersed on motor-cars all over the country. For 10 years they had sold car batteries obtained from Peto & Radford under their own name. In 1927 they had bought 75 per cent of the share capital of Ed Jaeger (London) Ltd, the Franco-Swiss instrument firm for which Rotax were agents for a time. (Ed Jaeger offered the shares to Lucas, who declined to buy them, since it was their policy at that time not to get involved in any business outside their established line of products.) And since 1919 they had owned the issued share capital of ML Magneto Syndicate, Ltd.

Lucas now acquired the Smith lighting, starting and ignition department (excluding sparking plugs), the stock being paid for at two-thirds the book value and £5,000 being paid for the tools, dies, patterns and plant. This business was transferred to the Rotax works at Willesden. From the Lucas point of view the most important item in the 'package deal' with Smiths was the purchase of the whole £93,000 share capital of the ML Magneto Syndicate in exchange for 31,000 fully paid Lucas ordinary shares, the consideration for the sale amounting to £116,250. ML had a good reputation and a first-class technical staff led by Ernest Watson. Finally, the agreement removed any possibility of Lucas and Smiths treading on each other's toes in future by including three lists prepared by Peter Bennett and Gordon Smith. The first was a list of Smith products which Lucas undertook not to manufacture or supply without their consent; the second was a list of Lucas products with the same conditions for Smiths; and the third was called the outstanding list, because it contained products not in the first two lists which were reserved for future discussion.

It was decided to run the ML magneto business as a separate entity until the relative positions of magneto and coil ignition had become clearer, though Oliver Lucas was of the opinion that the magneto would eventually disappear entirely from motor-cars. As well as magnetos and coil ignition, ML were making 80-watt permanent magnet rotary transformers for military aircraft radio transmitters and dual output hand-driven generators complete with coding discs for emergency radio transmission, in both cases for the Air Ministry. (The hand-driven generator had become essential equipment for aircraft after the crew of the 'Southern Cross' spent seven days vainly trying to rig up a hand drive for the wireless generator when they were forced down on a lonely part of the Australian coast in April 1929; all attempts at transmission failed and it was only by chance that they were rescued.) ML were also making rotary transformers and anode converters to provide high tension power for home radio before the advent of all-mains sets. As exercises in diversification they made pneumatically powered and controlled miners' lamps for use in the presence of fire damp, and Bakelite mouldings. They had also started manufacturing diesel injection pumps in a small way under licence from the REF Apparatgebau of Stuttgart. All this was done at the Victoria works in Coventry.

Lucas thought that the manufacture of ML magnetos, especially for agricultural and stationary engines, was worth continuing, so this was moved to a new building on the corner of Great King Street and Bridge Street, which was also needed to handle a useful order from Ford for Lucas dynamos and starters. (In the longer term a similar extension would be required at the other end of Great King Street where it met Farm Street in order to concentrate in Birmingham the motor-car business then being done by CAV and Rotax in London.) The remaining electrical business and the miners' lamp were moved to Rotax at Willesden, but the Bakelite moulding section stayed in Coventry. The manufacture of ML fuel-injection equipment, such as it was, was transferred to CAV at Acton.

The man who took the ML electrical components and miners' lamps down to Rotax at Willesden was Raymond Woodall, who had started as an apprentice at ML under Ernest Watson in 1918, and in the years to come was going to play a major part in building up Rotax as a leading aviation-component company. At that time the

Rotax aircraft business consisted of 12-volt 150-watt wind-driven generators (mostly for de Havilland Moths) which were modified versions of automotive generators of the Leitner third-brush type driven by small wooden propellers made by Airscrews Limited, of Weybridge.

An unexpected benefit from the acquisition of ML was the recruitment of a bright young cost accountant named Frederick Coleman, whom Bertram Waring immediately took a liking to and decided to train as a sort of administrative consultant or troubleshooter. To begin with, Waring got Coleman to go through the whole system of costing and works procedures at Great King Street. Coleman found them antiquated, long-handed and individually carried out instead of being co-ordinated. Then he was moved on to Formans Road, where his recommendations helped to set the pattern for the decentralised reorganisation of autonomous companies within the Lucas group that was to take place in later years.

The acquisition of ML also resulted in an amusing incident in a minor key – the annoyance that was felt by the Lucas managing directors when they heard that ML had lost the Rudge-Whitworth motor-cycle ignition business to the long-standing Lucas rivals, Millers. Their irritation was out of all proportion, of course, to the size of the order, and so too was their delight when the Lucas Electrical people took their revenge just before Christmas by securing the Veloce motor-cycle company business (1,000 coil ignition sets), which had formerly gone to Millers.

The reader may remember that at the last meeting with the representatives of Robert Bosch AG the Germans had said that if they ever decided to manufacture in England, they would let Lucas know. During the summer of 1930 Lucas got to hear independently that Bosch had bought a site, so when they met Wild and Felmett at the Motor Show and the Germans confirmed this information, adding that they were working on the plans for a factory, Peter Bennett and Oliver Lucas showed no very great concern. As Peter Bennett explained afterwards:

> We made it clear that while we should remain personally friendly, they would have to fight their way in, and it would probably cost them a million or two to establish themselves here. Whether they expected a different approach we never knew, but they seemed unhappy and when we suggested we should no doubt see them at the following Motor Cycle Show they jumped at the idea, particularly as Dr. Rassbach would be back from the United States and would join us.

When we met a few weeks later, Rassbach asked if there was any way we could avoid a dog fight. Could they turn over this new factory to something else, and join us in a joint enterprise? Their idea was that we might allow them to take up a shareholding in Joseph Lucas. We were not very keen on this, but we did work out a scheme, and they went back to Stuttgart to submit it to Mr. Robert Bosch, who had the last word. As it was their own idea, we were somewhat surprised to receive a letter declining the suggestion.

Sensing that there was something we did not understand, we offered to extend to Stuttgart a trip we were shortly making to Paris. When we arrived they explained that Mr. Bosch felt they could not cut themselves off from direct contact with commercial vehicle development in this country, as they placed great value on this for the future, and asked whether they could join us at CAV. This suited us much better than any direct connection with Joseph Lucas, and so we were able to work out a scheme by which they secured a 49% interest in CAV, gave up the idea of making in England and placed all their experience at our disposal. The value of the last point was very great as they had developed the fuel injection system while CAV had only just started work on this, and had a long way to go.

The world was in fact on the threshold of an engineering development which was to give Joseph Lucas yet another opportunity – after the evolution of the bicycle and the growth of the motor-car – to expand their range of manufacture to a marked extent. It seems difficult to realise nowadays, when the diesel-engined lorry and bus are in universal use, that in 1930 diesel power for vehicles was in its infancy. Since the first experimental engines had been produced by Hornsby-Akroyd (to the patent of the Yorkshire engineer, Herbert Akroyd Stewart) in 1892 and by Rudolf Diesel, working for MAN in Germany, the practical development of the compression-ignition engine had been confined to large engines for power stations, ships and railways. It was not until 1924 that the first successful diesel-engined road vehicles made by two German companies, Daimler-Benz and MAN, were exhibited at the Amsterdam and Berlin motor shows respectively. But the fuel injection pump essential for the full-scale production of a diesel engine for road vehicles did not arrive until 1926, when Robert Bosch produced a pump based on Karl Pieper's patent of 1892. The first British diesel-engined bus did not run until March 1930, when a Lancia was converted from petrol to diesel power by the installation of an early Gardner engine. That CAV were working on a fuel-injection pump in the same year shows that Peter Bennett and Oliver Lucas were fully alive to the potentialities of the diesel engine, especially for commercial vehicles, and the opportunity that now presented itself to learn from Bosch, the pioneers in this field, was therefore of the highest value.

Bennett made the arrangement look quite simple, but there was a good deal more in it than that. In addition to the sale to Bosch of 49 per cent of the issued capital of C. A. Vandervell, which changed its name to CAV-Bosch, Limited, the agreement provided for the exchange of patents and technical information in which Lucas as well as CAV were to participate; for the sharing of markets; and for transferring to the new joint company the shares in Bosch, Ltd, the company formed in England in 1924 by Robert Bosch AG to distribute Bosch sparking plugs and starting, lighting and ignition equipment imported from Germany. The shares in the Bosch service agency, J. & A. Stevens, were transferred to Bosch, Ltd, at the same time and the Bosch service business was operated thenceforth from Acton. The Robert Bosch shares in Bosch, Ltd, had been held by the Bosch associated company in Switzerland, Industria Kontor, and it was to this company that the Robert Bosch shares in CAV-Bosch were transferred in accordance with a supplemental agreement.

The exchange of patents and know-how meant that Joseph Lucas/CAV-Bosch and Robert Bosch were able to manufacture each other's products as defined in schedules without any further licence, and this applied to equipment for cars, motor-cycles and cycles as well as for heavy commercial vehicles. But they were restricted by the market-sharing arrangement as to where they could make and sell them. For Lucas and CAV-Bosch the agreed area was the United Kingdom and the Dominions (except Canada and Newfoundland) and the British Empire and Mandates (except Palestine and Iraq).

In this area Lucas were given the manufacture and sale of equipment for cars and the manufacture of all lamps, horns and batteries for commercial vehicles; CAV-Bosch were given the manufacture of other equipment for commercial vehicles and the sale of all commercial-vehicle equipment. Lucas agreed not to manufacture car equipment outside the area (except in the United States and Canada) and not to sell in competition with Robert Bosch in any part of the world outside the agreed area (except in the USA and Canada) beyond what they had sold in relation to Bosch in 1930. CAV-Bosch were not to manufacture or sell commercial-vehicle equipment outside the agreed area.

For their part Robert Bosch undertook not to manufacture equipment for cars and light commercial vehicles in the agreed area and not to sell any products in the agreed area except through Bosch, Ltd, which now became a subsidiary of CAV-Bosch. (It is worth noting that similar agreements were made before the war by Robert Bosch with the American Bosch Corporation in the United States, Ateliers de Construction Lavalette in France and Fabbrica Italiana Magneti Marelli in Italy, thus establishing a multi-national interest in fuel-injection equipment production.)

In fact the whole affair was extremely complex, involving other companies (Bosch, Ltd, and Industria Kontor) as well as the main parties, the valuation of the assets of Charles A. Vandervell, and altering the articles of association. Consequently the agreement was not signed until July 1931, but co-operation between the two companies proceeded quite happily meanwhile. A number of Bosch people visited Lucas and CAV, while Waring, on the management side, Dr Watson, D. C. Turner, who was in charge of electrical production, and R. A. Jones, who controlled costs and planning, went over to Stuttgart to gather and exchange information.

Dr Watson has described in his *Memoirs* how the association with Bosch was planned:

> The liaison presented three facets: that with the Electrical Company in Birmingham, that with the electrical side of CAV at Acton, and that with the diesel side of the latter company. The first was purely an interchange of knowledge and experience from which each firm was free to benefit if they thought fit; the second involved joint control of design, development and manufacture of electrical products made by CAV; while the third covered manufacture of fuel injection equipment at Acton under immediate control of Stuttgart. With this latter I had nothing to do, and Bosch made it perfectly clear that although they welcomed my views and suggestions in other directions, in this particular line no opinions or comments were called for. The Bosch organisation were quite justly proud of their position in the diesel field and of their products and naturally felt that any other firm must be technically inferior to themselves. This tended to colour some of their views and formed one of the problems to be met with in discussion.

Although it went against the grain, the Lucas people involved were often forced to accept the Bosch attitude without demur, because of the long-term need to master the technique of producing the Bosch injection pump in quantity. Astbury, who by that time had moved to CAV and was largely responsible for the engineering sales side, was one who had first-hand experience both of the desire to retaliate and of the restraining hand of the Lucas senior management: 'I recall on one occasion I wanted to dig my heels in because they were patently wrong about something we wanted to do to suit our customers, and Oliver Lucas agreed they were wrong. But he said, "Look, Herbert, we want to get along with these chaps. You may have to swallow your pride a bit, but don't fall out with them. It isn't going to ruin us. We want to make sure we get all we can out of them, and then if there is any bother we have got the know-how." '

Astbury continued:

On the diesel side it was quite clear-cut. We were a pure licensee making to German designs, and any decisions regarding design and design policy were taken by the Germans and written down – instruction and specification. I went to Stuttgart several times before the war to discuss various points and found them reasonably open in discussions but totally inflexible in accepting ideas that came from our side. They just listened. We said: 'Here are our troubles; we thought we should do so-and-so and we are going to try it', and we showed them the details and that was the last we heard of them. We never had any reply to any letters about design changes or recommendations. But sometimes these changes would appear in their products, without any announcement, six months later.

One immediate result of the link with Bosch was that manufacture of ML fuel-injection equipment had to be stopped and all concerned with it at Acton had to leave the company. The parent manufacturers of the pump, REF, were competitors of Bosch in the same town, Stuttgart, and Bosch would not permit anyone engaged on making the rival pump at Acton to have any part in making Bosch equipment in the same factory. As we have seen, even Dr Watson, who was probably closer to Bosch than anyone else at Lucas or CAV, was under a Bosch injunction (doubtless on account of his ML/REF background) not to have anything to do with CAV-Bosch activities in the fuel-injection field, although they had no objection to his being involved in the electrical side of the arrangement. The effect was to drive the CAV technical staff into two camps, injection equipment and electrical, which had very little contact with each other.

In the next few years, apart from the major benefit of CAV-Bosch being able to make the Bosch fuel-injection equipment, Lucas were to make use of Bosch patents and technical knowledge of voltage-regulator dynamos (as will be described later), electric horns for cars and motor-cycles (which CAV-Bosch also found useful for com-

(above) Long service certificates have always been an important feature of Lucas employment. Alice Bosworth joined the company as a solderer in 1909 and helped to make OL signalling lamps during the Great War. She received her 25 years certificate in 1934 and went on to complete 46 years' service before retiring in 1954

(right) Ambulance rooms were started by Joseph Lucas in the early 1920s. This picture, taken in 1929, shows the relaxed and reassuring atmosphere that pervaded these first-aid centres

The first royal visit – 1 March 1939. Queen Elizabeth, accompanied by Viscountess Halifax, was given a great welcome as she was shown round the factories by Sir Peter Bennett, the chairman, and Oliver Lucas *(Taylor's Press Service)*. Six months later Britain was at war. Demonstrations of Lucas loyalty did not depend upon the royal presence; the workshops were splendidly decorated by the workpeople at their own expense to celebrate the coronation of King George VI on 12 May 1937

mercial vehicles) and electric windscreen-wipers. CAV-Bosch also started to produce Blue Spot radio sets and Mary Ann vacuum cleaners to the designs of Robert Bosch, the marketing being done through the British Blue Spot Company and BEDA. (Once again the business in radio receiving sets was to prove disappointing and for the second time in their history CAV stopped making them in 1932. The vacuum cleaner showed little profit but production continued spasmodically up to the outbreak of World War II.)

The agreement with Bosch came at a time when motorists were taking an increasing interest in the type of electric horn fitted to their cars. Bosch had always been a front runner in this field and now Lucas were able to take full advantage of their knowledge, especially of the high-frequency horn. New models graded H1, H2, H3 and L1, L2, L3, according to their degrees of high or low notes, were introduced, followed in 1932 by twin Alto and Altette horns giving various combinations of sound. The car manufacturers generally supplied only one low-note horn, but an extra horn tuned to a higher note to give a blended tone could be added as an accessory. As time went on there was a public reaction to the noise of motor horns and eventually the Government persuaded the SMMT to put a voluntary limit of 100 phons on high-frequency horns and 105 on wind-tone horns. (The Lucas wind-tone horn, the Mellotone, was introduced in 1934.) Lucas introduced a two-way horn control, 'soft' for built-up areas and 'loud' for the open road, as a palliative, but they had to accept the voluntary limits in the end. Some export markets, however – Egypt and South America were examples – still demanded loud horns, so Lucas continued to supply them. Then the Government made it an offence to sound the horn after 11 o'clock in built-up areas. As we have seen, this prompted Bernard Scott's invention, which Lucas put on the market, of a switch that converted the horn button into a headlight flasher. (The anti-noise agitation eventually made motorists lose interest in the distinctive notes of their electric horns, and the demand for special high-frequency horns fell away to such an extent that Lucas were content to let Bosch and other Continental makers capture the market with imported horns.)

The agreement with Bosch in 1931 also made available the Bosch electric windscreen-wiper, which Lucas were now free to import, copy or borrow from as they wished. It was decided to manufacture it entirely at Great King Street and put it on the market in 1933 as a new Lucas model, additional to the Lucas patented electric wiper, which had been in production since 1929. The Bosch design had the advantage of being self-starting but the three-pole armature was small and 'finicky' (as Dr Watson described it), and difficulties arose from fluctuating torques and forces on the armature which Bosch warned Lucas about in advance. Up till now electric wipers, which were mounted at the top of the screen, had only one arm, on the driver's side, and to meet the demand for an extra blade on the passenger's side, a 'slave' arm driven by means of a coupling bar was provided. But this arrangement was clumsy and noisy – apart from being unsightly – so a *de luxe* model was also offered, with the motor mounted on the inside of the screen and a gear and rack system for operating both arms on the outside. This did away with the coupling bar, and the external mounting of the gearbox cut down the noise.

John Morley told me how this gear and rack system came to be used. 'Sir Herbert Austin said to Oliver Lucas one day: "Let me have a little motor, show me the smallest motor you make", and he went away and mounted the motor on a model windscreen with a rack and pinion system for operating the second arm. He gave it back to us and said: "How much would you sell that for?" He had made the first decent wiper, made up of our parts, and he did it himself – yes, he probably used his own hands because he was a practical mechanic.' Even so, it was really only a compromise and the answer to the whole problem was seen in the following year when Lucas moved the motor and driving gear out of sight and sound underneath the scuttle at the bottom of the windscreen. The more powerful motor was mounted on rubber and the wiper arm spindles were coupled by concealed link couplings.

Shortly before the successful conclusion of the agreement with Bosch, Arthur Benstead of Rotax had proposed to the Lucas board that the company should make parts of a German windscreen-wiper which was being sold in England as the British Berkshire, sending them to London to be assembled by the concessionaire, Colonel Defries, with whom Benstead had arranged the Houdaille/Luvax shock absorber deal a few years earlier. The Lucas directors were not keen on the idea, especially in view of the possibility of being able to manufacture the Bosch wiper, but Benstead drove home the point that if Lucas did not accept the job, Defries would get it done elsewhere, and this might encourage the company who took it on to go into serious competition with Lucas for the electric windscreen-wiper market. Eventually he got his way and Lucas agreed to make certain parts of the British Berkshire for Defries. By incorporating more than 50 per cent local content Defries was able to avoid paying import duty on the complete wiper, and at the same time justify calling the wiper the 'British' Berkshire. He succeeded in getting it fitted to a few cars, including the Talbot and the Riley, before giving up the project.

Meanwhile two new car lamps had been introduced in 1931. A new approach to the problem of dazzle was made in the form of a three-lamp high-power projector set comprising two normal P100 headlamps and a new PL40 centre lamp which was aimed towards the nearside of the road. A foot switch was provided to turn off the headlights and switch on the centre light when meeting other traffic. This was fitted as special equipment on various cars. In the same year a simple fog-lamp with an amber glass was marketed. Fuses for lamps and other accessories had been introduced generally in 1930.

While the Bosch affair was going forward, Oliver Lucas had something else that was also occupying his attention. It had begun at Christmas 1930, when Mr Minch of Auto-Lite came over from the States to study the prospects of starting manufacture in Britain. Oliver Lucas spent a lot of time with him and found out that what they were really interested in was satisfying the requirements of Ford. He offered to go to America to discuss ways of helping Auto-Lite and a few weeks later received an invitation to do so.

The background to this development needs to be borne in mind. Faced with a $33\frac{1}{3}$ per cent import duty on cars in Britain and preferential duties for vehicles sold within the Dominions and Commonwealth, some American and Continental companies turned to manufacturing or assembling cars in England both for sale here and for export to the preferential Empire markets. And the Americans were quick to realise the advantages to be enjoyed from manufacturing or assembling in Canada. General Motors had already established themselves in Britain by acquiring Vauxhall Motors and were soon to start making Bedford trucks at Luton. So far Vauxhall had been content to buy much of their car electrical equipment from Lucas, and the General Motors manufacturing subsidiary, Delco-Remy, confined itself to spare parts and service problems in the United Kingdom. Now Ford had built a great plant at Dagenham as the British base for supplying the United Kingdom, Europe, and the British Empire with small cars, and they naturally wanted to get their electrical equipment from the same company, Auto-Lite, that they dealt with in America. Lucas feared that if Auto-Lite established their own factory in Britain, they might get some business from Vauxhall as well as from the 100 per cent British car manufacturers in order to increase their volume of production. All this could mean smaller sales for Lucas unless the situation was handled very carefully.

Before leaving for the USA, Oliver Lucas got a letter of introduction to Charles Sorensen, the Chief Engineer of Ford at Detroit, from Sir Percival Perry, the head of the British Ford Company. He took Robert Neill, his personal assistant, with him. His aim was to try and buy off Auto-Lite, and a cable from him reported that they would be prepared not to establish themselves in England for a payment of not less than £20,000. In return, they would help Lucas to secure the whole of the Ford business in Britain and give them full manufacturing assistance. But agreement was to be neither as cheap nor as quick as that, and though the terms of an agreement on these lines were drafted after much consulting on the telephone with Peter Bennett in Birmingham, nothing definite was arranged. It was clear that Auto-Lite could not proceed without Ford's approval. Sorensen listened carefully to what Oliver had to say about the Lucas/Auto-Lite scheme but was obviously only interested in it as far as it affected the Ford company and Dagenham.

This was Oliver's second visit to the United States, and once more he was impressed by the time speeds of the operators and the fact that what the American car manufacturers considered a very small model run, 500 cars a week, was the largest Lucas order in Britain – for the Austin Seven. Before leaving America Oliver Lucas fitted in a visit to the Electric Storage Battery Company at Philadelphia, parent of the Chloride company in Britain and makers of the Exide battery. There he picked up useful tips about an automatic plate-casting machine and a method of forming the plates after the battery had been assembled complete that he took back to Formans Road.

But the most significant technique that Oliver Lucas learned on that American visit was not so easy to adopt in Birmingham. He found out that Auto-Lite were one of many leading companies which owed part of their astonishing productivity to a wages incentive scheme worked out by a consultant named Bedaux. Born in Paris in 1887, Charles Eugène Bedaux had emigrated to America when he was about 20 and had become a naturalised American citizen in 1917. He built up an engineering consultancy business on both sides of the Atlantic based on the 'Bedaux Plan'. This was a wage incentive scheme which used 'Bedaux Units' as a measurement of human productivity, one unit equalling the work that should be done by one man in one minute. The incentive took the form of a bonus for accomplishing more than 60 units in an hour. To Oliver Lucas the scheme had the attraction of being a way of using American methods without depending upon a volume of production that Lucas could not expect to enjoy in Britain, and on his return to Great King Street he had no difficulty in getting Peter Bennett's agreement to trying it in a section of the works. The arrangements were made through two Americans, C. J. ('Merch') Carney and Frank Mead, to whom Oliver had been introduced by Auto-Lite and who had come over to London to organise the Bedaux system in England.

Bennett explained the system to the directors at their meeting in November 1931: it was a method by which careful study was made of the whole situation in the shop by Bedaux engineers before a rate was finally settled. He went on: 'Enormous changes are made in procedure to enable them to obtain the best results and this, combined with the security the worker feels, results in a very greatly increased output per worker. It brings to light many deficiencies that would otherwise remain unnoticed. The Bedaux engineers are highly trained men and we pay for their service at a fixed rate per hour.' Bennett concluded: 'The trial in a part of the Electrical Works has been so successful that we are extending it as rapidly as possible.'

He spoke too soon. In January the 140 workers, mostly girls, who had so far been satisfied, suddenly refused to go on with the scheme. (There were exceptions. Mrs Lloyd, now a pensioner, who was working at the time in the winding shop, where the girls regarded themselves as rather superior to the others, has told me that they did not want to go on strike but their foreman told them they had better do so because 'they're coming to fetch you'.) Albert Siddall, one of the first engineering graduates recruited in a recent move by Waring to remedy the company's deficiency in qualified staff, had been chosen with a few others by the Bedaux engineers to do the pick-and-shovel work of putting the Plan into operation. They were in the preliminary stages of assessing the work in the screw machine shop and Siddall has a very distinct memory of being almost literally chased out of it. Another man engaged on this advance work, Horace Millward, swears that he was in fact chased on to the roof and would have been thrown into the street below if he had not managed to escape from his pursuers.

From the management point of view Bertram Waring, who had just been appointed joint general manager with F. H. Walker, watched what was being achieved by the Bedaux Plan with his accountant's eye to costs. He said afterwards:

I realised that despite increases in workpeople's pay, labour costs were being reduced by at least one third. When resistance started to rise I was dismayed and looked round for someone to explain to the workpeople how advantageous to them this new scheme was. None of the factory supervision were ready to take on the task and, in fact, they were secretly pleased at the turn of events, but eventually I got Normansell, who had just been promoted to general works manager, to come and help me. The two of us addressed groups of workpeople in small batches because we were afraid of talking to a large group at one time. From these small groups I learnt enough to fill a book of what not to do when introducing a new wages scheme. We were too late in our endeavours, the tide swept over us, emotions swelled and burst out as the first strike the company had ever experienced.

Waring made a last-minute attempt to prevent the strike spreading to the Luvax works at Acton, where the Bedaux plan had been started on a small scale. He set off about midnight with the Bedaux chief supervisor in the latter's Mercedes (Waring himself owned an Austin Seven). The American mystified Waring by producing a revolver, loading it, and putting it on the seat beside him. After three hours' sleep at Grosvenor House, they went along to the factory at 8 o'clock to find the workpeople assembled in the canteen and singing *Land of Hope and Glory*.

It appeared that before we arrived they had appointed representatives, so off we went for the first discussion while the workpeople resumed their sing-song. This time it was ... *Britons never never shall be Slaves*. We got the committee to agree to an extended trial of the Bedaux system. They returned to the gathering of workpeople and told them of their decision. This was received in icy silence, and the crowd drifted away. A week later the head of the committee wrote to say that the whole committee had been repudiated by the workpeople and they could do nothing more. So we went ahead without any consultation and it never looked back. The workpeople, having repudiated their leaders, had no one to organise resistance.

There was a very different situation at Great King Street, where opposition to the scheme was highly organised and spread to the whole factory. As Waring had realised, the scheme had been badly introduced – it was not properly explained in advance. But other circumstances combined to fan the smouldering resentment caused by the presence of 'imported' engineers who were said to be paid enormous wages (they were in fact paid £47 a week). Up to that time the supervisors enjoyed an excessive amount of control in their shops, and they were consequently bitterly opposed to the Bedaux engineers' recommendations for grouping machine tools. Then the work-people did not take kindly to the extensive stopwatch timing of their movements – the girls complained that they were even timed when they went to the lavatory – and the speeding-up of work and re-organisation entailed some redundancies at first. On top of all this was the feeling of insecurity brought on by the slump which was affecting the whole country. (Great King Street had been on short time earlier in the year, and in 1932 unemployment was to reach a peak of 2.8 million.)

The whole scene was ripe for exploitation by Tom Roberts, a militant Communist in the works, who set up a rank-and-file committee of forty, representing ten departments, to prepare action against the 'slavery system'. According to the *Daily Worker*, the Lucas workers refused to leave their fight in the hands of 'reformist' trade union officials: 'The workers, following the lead of the Communist organisers, realised they must *act themselves*, and they must build up their own *revolutionary leadership*.' Lunchtime meetings outside the factory quickly grew from a few dozen people to several hundreds, helped by unusually mild weather for January. The National Unemployed Workers Movement joined the Communists in keeping up the agitation. The trouble at Lucas was only one expression of the antipathy to the Bedaux system in the Midlands. Several thousand workers at the Wolsey hosiery factory at Leicester had rebelled against its introduction six weeks before, and had been on strike ever since; there were rumblings about its use at Kynochs, and its proposed introduction at the Moss Gear factory in Birmingham.

The Lucas directors did not waste time in reaching a decision. Notices were posted in the shops:

It has been brought to the notice of the Directors that dissatisfaction exists regarding the application of the Bedaux wages payment system. The Directors have always prided themselves on their good relationship with the Lucas workers. They do not desire to impose a system of payment that will not have the full co-operation of the workers. In these circumstances the Bedaux system of wages payment will be discontinued and a return will be made to the ordinary Lucas system of piecework payment. The changes will be made as soon as the necessary Lucas piecework prices can be fixed.

Peter Bennett noted that the effect on the girls brought back memories of Mafeking and Armistice Day. The *Daily Worker* was exultant, its banner headline for Friday, 29 January 1932, reading:

VICTORY! BEDAUX SYSTEM SMASHED!

Lucas Employers Completely Beaten

Ten Thousand Lucas Workers Cheer Communist

Inspiration to Smash Bedaux Everywhere

The paper went on to describe how Comrade Roberts was raised on the shoulders of the workers at the dinner-hour meeting after the notice was read.

An attempt was made to hold a victory march on the following day, but the police intervened and banned the demonstration. The Chief Constable went on the platform and was duly booed by the 5,000 people estimated (by the *Daily Worker*) to be present. A further mass meeting was held that night at the Farm Street schools, at which Comrade Roberts declared: 'The victory is a victory for the policy of organised working-class struggle, as against the union officials' policy of co-operating with the employers.' On the same day several letters of thanks were received by the management from groups of work-people, one of them reading: 'We, the employees of G Block, wish the Management to accept our appreciation of their decision to discontinue the Bedaux system and assure them of our continued support.'

The investigations carried out for the Bedaux plan, and its results while it lasted, had opened the eyes of the Lucas management to the savings and benefits that could be achieved by workshop reorganisation coupled with some form of incentive payment scheme. Put another way, the experience had substantiated Oliver Lucas's advocacy of the plan as he had seen it operating in America. The benefits – to the workpeople as well as to the company – were too valuable to be discarded. The policy agreed upon was to move quietly and systematically, avoiding the pitfalls of the past and achieving the same results. It would be necessary to carry the staff with them, and it would be easier to do that now that they had a better appreciation of the mentality of the workpeople in the face of the prevailing economic conditions.

Although it would be necessary to obtain privately some outside advice, it would be made perfectly clear that the scheme they were going to introduce was a Lucas scheme, operated by Lucas officials, and not an outside policy imposed on them by an unknown force emanating from some mysterious quarter. All this would take many months to work out; meanwhile there were other affairs that demanded urgent attention.

CHAPTER TWO

AN HISTORIC VISIT

Immediately after the Bedaux affair was over Oliver Lucas and Bertram Waring sailed to America to see the Bendix Corporation at the invitation of Charles Marcus, the vice-president, who had suggested when they met in London recently that 'Bendix and Lucas should lay their heads together.' Rotax and CAV had continued to make Bendix starter drives after the take-over, but Lucas had made them change the name to 'American-type drive'. For some reason of Bendix internal administration Rotax and CAV had not been asked to pay any royalties, so Lucas had made a financial reserve against a royalty claim from Bendix, the figures at 31 March 1931 being CAV 189,987 drives to 21 February 1931, and Rotax 13,040 drives to 31 December 1930. Bendix had a British company, Bendix-Perrot Brakes, Ltd, making Bendix brakes and Stromberg carburettors in the old Bowden brake factory at King's Road, Tyseley. The brake business was just approaching the paying stage. They also had a number of other ideas in connection with automatic starting (Startix) and clutch control.

Bendix had now decided to concentrate all their interests in the United Kingdom in the hands of a single British company, and they invited Joseph Lucas to enter into an arrangement on these lines. Lucas made it clear to Marcus from the start that they would not touch the carburettor business on any account, but were willing to discuss the rest of the proposition. (In the event Bendix sold the Stromberg business in England to Zenith.)

Although his name does not appear in any of the relevant records, there are grounds for believing that Arthur Benstead played the part of *éminence grise* in these negotiations. Some years before Lucas acquired Rotax he had made arrangements for the use of the Bendix drive in Rotax starters. He was a close friend of Charles Marcus (who thought the world of him) and Marcus was the Bendix vice-president, engineering, at the time. It is more than likely that Benstead arranged the meeting between Marcus and Oliver Lucas in London which started the ball rolling.

In the United States Oliver Lucas and Waring saw Vincent Bendix, the head of the organisation, with various executives – Marcus, McGrath and Ferguson. Bendix offered Lucas participation in the

Bendix company in England to the extent of 33⅓ per cent, and at their option up to 51 per cent after a year. Bendix had invested half-a-million dollars in the English company and they made it a condition that Lucas should become definite partners in the brake and clutch business in England, while all other items could be operated on a paid royalty basis without any minimum guarantee. A 5 per cent royalty would be payable to Bendix for development work, manufacturing information, and maintaining the patents. The Startix automatic starting device would carry a royalty of 10 per cent. In return, Lucas would receive a management fee. Finally, arrangements could be made for Lucas to use the Bendix starter drive, which would result in a considerable saving in cost, on payment of a small royalty to clear the arrears due. Oliver Lucas undertook to discuss this comprehensive offer with his colleagues on his return to Birmingham.

While he was in the States, he drove several cars and buses fitted with the latest brakes, finding them a distinct improvement on the brakes at present offered by the Bendix company in Britain. He particularly liked a simple vacuum booster they had developed that seemed to give all the advantages of powered braking at its best without the disadvantages of the type then widely used in Britain. He was also shown the clutch control, which provided two-pedal driving. He did not see anything of the Lockheed hydraulic brake, which was not made at South Bend, although it was still at that time controlled by Bendix. Bendix anticipated, he reported, that the mechanically operated brake, either with or without power assistance, would become supreme.

Before he came home, Oliver Lucas spent a few days at the Bendix aviation plant at East Orange, and in some ways this was the most significant part of what was undoubtedly an historic visit. He was astonished by the wide range of equipment made there – starters of all type, voltage control dynamos, constant speed dynamos for radio communication, pressure vacuum pumps, variable pitch propellers, variable speed superchargers, and several other items under development. He got the impression that Bendix made practically all the electrical equipment for the American aeroplane industry, and he confirmed that this was true when he visited the Detroit Aero Show. He summed it up by saying that Bendix enjoyed a position in the aeroplane world comparable with that of Lucas in the motor-car field in Britain. In fact Bendix were so convinced of the great possibilities in the aeroplane industry that they had changed the name of their holding company to the Bendix Aviation Corporation. Oliver Lucas found that Bendix were most anxious to have Lucas as partners in this area, too, in spite of the difficulties of their association with Bosch through CAV, which were explained and appreciated. In his report on this part of his visit he told the Lucas board: 'It is the writer's belief that there must inevitably be a considerable business in aeroplane equipment of a profitable nature in the reasonably near future which will be done by someone in England. As the Bendix Aviation Corporation have undoubtedly the most highly developed equipment, it would seem desirable that it should not be allowed to go elsewhere.'

The whole project was considered at the Lucas board meeting in May 1932 and was approved as a basis of negotiation. But it was not until six months later that agreement was finally reached, whereby Lucas were to purchase a two-thirds share interest (instead of the one-third originally proposed) in the Bendix-Perrot Brake Company at Tyseley for the sum of £91,363 6s 8d, and would also be given sub-licences of various motor-car products of the Bendix Aviation Corporation. They were also to have the benefit of the licence of the aviation equipment made by the corporation, and it was decided to exploit this equipment under the name of and in the factory of Rotax.

The board meeting of 23 November 1932 can therefore be said to mark the birth (perhaps conception would be more accurate) of Lucas Aerospace, with all the beneficial consequences that this was to hold for the company, the aviation industry, and the nation. The meeting was also an important stage in the gradual orientation of the Joseph Lucas business into three industrial groups – the Lucas factories supplying the motor-car, motor-cycle and bicycle industries, CAV-Bosch concentrating on the commercial vehicle industry, and now Rotax being chosen to supply the aircraft business (still barely worth calling an industry).

In the 12 months or so since he had brought the ML products down to Willesden Ray Woodall had been round the aeroplane firms and the airlines, so he was ready to exploit the Bendix products now made available, above all the Eclipse inertia engine starter. This used energy stored in a flywheel which was wound up to speed by hand to provide power to start the engine through an epicyclic gear reduction, a multi-plate clutch and Bendix gear engaging mechanism. It was fitted to the Hawker Hart biplane. Up till then aero-engines had been started by 'swinging the prop' or by the old Hucks starter (a motor-car engine mounted on a truck which reversed up to the aircraft propeller), but these methods were unsuitable for the bigger engines which were being introduced at the time. The inertia starters designed and produced by Bendix were therefore just what the British aero-engine manufacturers needed, and, by taking the Bendix licence, Rotax were able to supply them with little delay. It would have taken several years and a lot of money to produce an equivalent starter of their own. Bendix had the advantage of US Government financial support which Rotax were able to benefit from indirectly.

But Rotax still had other work to do, and while the Bendix deal was being negotiated, the factory at Willesden was being reorganised, its products at this time including motor-car dynamos and starters for such companies as Clement-Talbot, Sunbeam, Daimler and Riley, where the quantities were small, and special panels for switchboxes which were not suitable for production in the main Lucas works. They had also started to make electric tools – mostly drills and grinding machines – when Lucas took over the power tool division of Alfred Graham, of Slough, makers of Amplion loudspeakers and of the Amplion horn, which had already been transferred to Lucas in 1928. And when it was decided that Newtons of Taunton should produce mercury arc rectifiers, they were manufactured at Willesden under Newtons' name. In the following April the old company, Rotax (Motor Accessories), was put into voluntary liquidation and the whole of the assets were taken over by Joseph Lucas, Limited, a new company, Rotax Ltd, being registered to take over the sales side; but in fact it was only a department of the parent company and had no separate existence.

Once again Lucas made as little fuss as possible about an important extension of their business. They decided to keep their own name from being too prominently associated with the Bendix brake company at first 'because they did not want the trade to feel they were spreading their energies over too wide a field.' J. Albert Thomson and Bertram Waring were appointed to the board of Bendix-Perrot Brakes, Ltd. Captain J. S. Irving, who had joined the company as chief engineer shortly before Lucas had taken it over, was put in charge. He was the designer of the Irving-Napier Special – the Golden Arrow – with which Henry De Hane Segrave set up a new world speed record of 231.44mph at Daytona Beach, Florida, in March 1929.

Looking back on this visit of Oliver Lucas to the United States, one cannot fail to be struck by two features of it. First there is the respect for Joseph Lucas as engineers and manufacturers that was implicit in the invitation from the Bendix Corporation to join them in so many of their activities. (The same might be said of the approach by Robert Bosch AG in the previous year.) The second is the extraordinary *rapport* which evidently developed between Oliver Lucas and American executives and engineers in the automobile and aviation industries. For his part, the combination of engineering originality and industrial enterprise he found in the big American factories was entirely congenial; he felt completely at ease and at the same time stimulated. On their side, the Americans saw in him a man of brilliant intelligence, acute perception, and with a freshness of outlook that made him a valuable contributor to any discussion they had with him. As Sir Kenneth Corley put it recently: 'They felt they got as much from Oliver Lucas as they gave.'

Before 1932 was out the country at last emerged from the dark days of the depression. 'October was the most remarkable month the company has ever experienced,' said Peter Bennett in his monthly report to the board in November. 'Not only did it soar above anything we have ever known at this time of the year but equally it exceeded any demand we have previously experienced in the company's history.'

The actual increase in demand was 40 per cent, yet somehow they succeeded in keeping pace with deliveries. 'Had we failed the makers,' Bennett added, 'the result might have been disastrous as it would have tempted them to look round for alternative sources of supply to guard against a repetition of the same trouble in the future.' He himself was sure that the car-makers would not have got any better results elsewhere, because it was only by their own policy of concentration that they had been able to meet the demand; but even if it might not benefit the manufacturer to try a new supplier, it would certainly hurt Lucas. Bennett added: 'At the slightest suspicion of a shortage the various car manufacturers telephone Oliver Lucas or myself, or if we are not available one of our general managers (Waring and Walker). They are good enough to tell us that we are among the best of their suppliers, and we feel that they believe they have only to mention the matter to get immediate attention.'

Indeed the relations between Joseph Lucas and the car manufacturers could hardly have been better, the latter having a profound respect for the solid financial and commercial success of Great King Street, as witnessed by the annual company reports. Bertram Waring was always ready to advise ailing companies on how to improve their management and administrative techniques, and he sent Coleman to Rovers (among others) for a time to help them in this way.

Lucas had come through the great depression – the 'economic blizzard' as Peter Bennett used to call it – relatively unscathed, and now they faced the prospect of a new and prosperous phase in the development of motoring. Before World War I motor-cars had been strictly for the rich people; in the 1920s they came within reach of the middle classes; now it was becoming possible for many working men to buy a reliable and comparatively cheap form of personal transport in the small cars offered by the big motor manufacturers.

Relations between Lucas and the two great American firms in the same line of business, Delco-Remy and Auto-Lite, took a new turn in 1932-3. First an agreement was reached with Delco-Remy & Hyatt Ltd for the right to manufacture in the United Kingdom a vacuum control unit for distributors to a design patented by General Motors (the company was the English subsidiary of GM and was concerned primarily with spares and service problems for imported cars). The royalty was 3 cents a unit for the first 50,000 and 2 cents thereafter. The device consisted of a pressure-conscious diaphragm operating a linkage which rotated the entire distributor body about the cam to suit variations in load, thus providing an improved form of automatic timing control. It was added to the Lucas distributor in 1933. (In 1939 a new model distributor was produced with the vacuum-operated timing control built into it.) Masterton followed this up by arranging for Lucas to make certain ignition parts for Delco-Remy in order to avoid having them as competing manufacturers in Britain. (A few years later the Delco-Remy office in London asked Oliver Lucas if he would make a rectangular fog-lamp for them which they could sell in Britain under the Delco brand name. Oliver agreed and the specified lamp was produced. It worked fairly well, with the aid of a fluted glass, but the precision pressing techniques required for the reflectors, and a suitable device for checking them, were not yet available. However Delco were happy to have the lamp, though it was not a big seller.)

Then the negotiations with Auto-Lite, which had been dragging on for more than a year, suddenly rose to a climax. It will be recalled that the terms of a working arrangement by which Auto-Lite would help Lucas to get all the Ford business in England had been drafted, but no agreement had been signed because of opposition from Ford in America, who took most of their electrical equipment from Auto-Lite and would have preferred to see the British Ford company being supplied by a local Auto-Lite factory in England. Now the situation changed overnight with the news that Auto-Lite had lost the Ford business in America, because Ford had decided to make their own electrical equipment. Arthur Benstead, the Rotax general manager, who had very valuable connections and travelled extensively, happened to be in the States at the time. He immediately got in touch with Auto-Lite and reopened the question of a deal with Lucas. The negotiations were carried on by Mr Kelly, vice-president of Auto-Lite, when he came over to England a few weeks later. Agreement in principle was reached in May 1933, whereby Auto-Lite undertook not to manufacture in England and Lucas, of course, agreed not to go into America; Auto-Lite placed all their manufacturing experience at Lucas's disposal and Lucas were to pay, not the £20,000 originally discussed, but £12,000 for the first year, £15,000 for the second, and £17,000 for the third year. The agreement would make it obligatory for Auto-Lite to send over their production engineers every year to assist in improving the Lucas layout. Their chief engineer, Charlie Francis, came over to Great King Street immediately and was described by Peter Bennett as 'the most valuable production engineer we could possibly have.' Francis was a very good practical man and could make press tools. Lucas engineers were invited to go over to Auto-Lite and see how they made dynamos and starters. This was valuable, because, as Robert Neill remarked, 'You can't walk round someone else's plant without seeing something which is of interest or help – in the words of the Chinese proverb: "One look is worth a thousand words".' But once again the negotiations petered out and a formal agreement was not signed.

The Lucas engineers sent back the disturbing news that a five-man team of Ford engineers from Dagenham was at Auto-Lite picking up as much knowledge as they could about production and engineering before going on to do the same thing at the Ford electrical plant at Ypsilanti. The reason for their visit, they said, was that Ford were planning to make their own electrical equipment at Dagenham.

This would mean a serious loss for Lucas, who supplied coils and distributors, dynamos and starters for the British-made cars, so Oliver Lucas rang up Dagenham and was put on to a newcomer, Patrick Hennessy, who had come over from the Ford plant at Cork in the previous year (1932) to take up the position of purchase manager at the new Dagenham plant. Since he had arrived, none of the Lucas top brass had been in touch with him, and he not unnaturally resented it. Sir Patrick Hennessy (chairman of the Ford Motor Company from 1956 until his retirement in 1968) told me recently what happened:

Oliver Lucas asked if he could come and see me and I said I was too busy – getting my own back if you like in a small-minded way. When he eventually came down to Dagenham I said, 'Well, Mr. Lucas, this is a great honour. You have never previously taken the slightest interest in the Ford Motor Company or what you supply to us, and we're satisfied neither with the quality or anything else.'

He did not know then that Oliver Lucas saw Sir Percival Perry, the Ford chairman, from time to time and had had a letter of introduction from him to Charles Sorensen, who virtually ran Ford world-wide, in 1931.

Oliver replied, 'I understand you have got a plan to make your own electrical equipment – but of course you'll never have the volume to compete.' I told him we might get the Vauxhall volume and perhaps some others too, because the stuff we made would be good. He then apologised for not having come to see me before and asked, 'What can I do now?' I said, 'Frankly, I don't think it's in my power to do anything because I'm committed: we're on the point of ordering all the equipment, providing the space, and everything else.' He said, 'Can you tell me what's wrong with our equipment from the technical point of view and from the quality point of view?' I told him I had a complete list of it, and his people had had it every month, and there was also the question of price. But anyhow it had gone too far.

This is where Oliver did a really first-class job on me. He said, 'Would you give me the opportunity of bringing along every piece of equipment you buy from us so that we can go over them together?' I said, 'All right, if you want to do that we'll set aside a room for you and a big table, and you bring the equipment down all labelled up. Incidentally you had better have price tags on it because we're not paying these prices for all the years ahead, and it's no use putting yourself in a monopoly position because we're strong enough to break it.' He came down and did a wonderful job, a wonderful selling job, and of course he knew the technical stuff too, Oliver did.

I didn't know what to do, to be honest with you, I was committed, and the big terrifying boss in America whom everybody in the world knew – 'Cast Iron' Charlie Sorensen – they all shook when he walked around – he made it a terrifying situation. I told Oliver, 'I think it's probably impossible for me to change, but you had better make the best case possible. I promise you one thing, I'll try.'

Sorensen came over just then by accident, and when I told him about what I could do with Lucas and the kind of deal I had made – that we couldn't actually compete with the new situation – of course he abused me up hill and down dale and got very rough indeed. He had provided all the information for us to go into manufacture ourselves and had put a gang of people on to it for a long time. I said, 'We've got enough to do without all this, and we can buy better now than we can make.' In the end he agreed.

This started a friendship with Oliver Lucas; we became the closest friends, it worked out and he benefited from it. We taught him better ways of buying the bits and pieces he had to buy, and better ways of production because we had access to the American techniques – I was doing this sort of thing with the other suppliers too, and they all said 'No' at first. One of the most enjoyable associations I had with anybody for years afterwards, until he died, was with Oliver Lucas. There was never any argument about prices. He said, 'All right, we'll fix it when we see how it works out – if it doesn't work out in your case we'll pay you, if it doesn't work out in my case you will pay me,' and it was a very good deal. I used to go up to Birmingham fairly often anyhow in those days. I always went round to see Oliver and he had always saved up something interesting to show me. I was not the technician he was, though I had a good working knowledge, and we had the most fascinating discussions about everything. He was outstanding.

The Startix device licensed from Bendix went into production in 1932. In theory this had several advantages: it automatically started the engine when the ignition key was turned (instead of having the usual separate switch for the starter); it restarted the engine automatically when it stalled; and it incorporated a time-delay system which cut out the starter if the engine refused to fire. Lucas were assured that it had been quite satisfactory in America. The Startix was particularly suitable for cars fitted with free-wheels, and Rover were one of the first to order it. Wolseley, Morris, Armstrong-Siddeley and Standard all showed interest. Dr Watson has described what happened:

> We went into production on quite a large scale but soon hit trouble, largely due to the difference in characteristics of the British 12-volt and American 6-volt starters. Even after certain modifications to the Startix and the starters had been made, service troubles were still severe, and the climax was probably reached when cases occurred of cars in showrooms proceeding through plate-glass windows when a prospective customer turned the ignition switch. This led to the demise of Startix and no one – least of all the Lucas engineers – lamented its passing.

Actually the failure rate of the Startix was never more than 2 per cent, but on the volume produced this meant that everybody got to hear about it and its withdrawal was inevitable.

The Lucas dipping-reflector method of solving the headlight dazzle problem was now firmly established in Great Britain, but everywhere else the answer was found in the double-filament bulb, which had been developed to a very effective pitch. To keep their options open, Lucas had investigated the possibility of making a double-filament bulb of their own, and in 1932 they announced the introduction of 'an additional anti-dazzle device to the range of Lucas anti-dazzle systems' in the form of the Lucas-Graves 'Blue Star' gas-filled anti-dazzle bulb. This had two filaments, the main filament being located at the focus of the reflector and providing the normal driving beam, while the secondary filament, slightly in advance of the main filament, had a shield underneath which cut off all the rays that ordinarily would be reflected upwards and so cause dazzle. Instead, the secondary filament gave a downward flood of light with a flat-top driving beam, which was non-dazzling. In order to spread the beam sideways and illuminate the full width of the road, a special headlamp glass with a series of vertical lenses of correct optical curvature had to be used, and the light was diffused by the shape of the front glass and the satin finish of the bulb. Without these measures the beam from the Lucas-Graves bulb was too concentrated.

The events leading up to the introduction of the Lucas-Graves bulb have been described to me by Dr Harvey Nelson, who joined Lucas in 1936 after getting a PhD in physics at the Royal College of Science (he went on to become chief lighting engineer of the company in 1947, chief engineer, Joseph Lucas (Electrical), in 1961, and technical director of the same company in 1970). He said:

> We think of the Lucas-Graves bulb as something that originated in the early 1930s. In fact I believe the original patent was taken out in about 1911 by a French concern. Major A. Graves devised his double-filament bulb in 1924, and Philips produced a bulb of the same type. As happens with many inventions, this rediscovery of the original French idea occurred to two people at the same time, but quite separately. The Philips organisation used it as a means of getting uniformity of lighting in Europe. I believe they did the right thing because there were a large number of small lamp manufacturers operating in Europe at that time, with very little in common. In this country we had already gone into the dipping reflector, followed by dip-and-switch. The result of that, applied uniformly in Britain – because we had got nearly all the market by then – was the same sort of thing that Philips had achieved in Europe with the twin-filament Duplo bulb. We had a possibly less scientific solution, but from the point of view of nasty seeing conditions, if anything a slightly better solution. The dazzle was greater but the light on

the road was greater, and that has been an argument between ourselves and the Europeans ever since.

Robert Neill, who succeeded W. H. Egginton as head of the lighting design and engineering team, recalls an incident when this argument took a direct turn:

Bosch couldn't understand how we got away with dipping reflectors in this country because they were so bad from the anti-dazzle angle, while we couldn't understand how they got away with their double-filament bulbs in Germany because they gave such little light in the dipped position in those days. So they asked us to go over to Stuttgart to talk about it, as they were trying hard to persuade us to use the Duplo bulb. Watson and I went over to Germany and they laid on a demonstration of their lamps and our lamps. I always remember it because it was in the winter and there was a hard frost and we went on winding roads round Stuttgart. The roads were white, the trees were white – it was ideal from the point of illumination, you see – and their dipping bulbs worked quite well. They'd got enough light when they were dipped and they weren't worried too much about the oncoming car because theirs was a better anti-dazzle device than ours, but it didn't give enough light to our way of thinking to deal with the conditions in England. So we arranged for them to pay us a return visit and we'd give them a demonstration. We took them round Coventry one night. It was raining, everybody was dazzling us (I remember one of the Germans muttering 'We'd shoot a man who made as much dazzle as this') but we'd got our dipped reflectors right down in the gutter so we could see where we were going and they could understand a little better our way of thinking after that.

There was a basic difference of opinion about the right method of headlamp research at this time between the British and Americans on the one hand and the Continentals on the other. The British and Americans did practically no static work in testing headlamps; they preferred to drive and find out whether the headlamps were effective in all conditions. The Continentals were devoted to static tests, which showed off to the best advantage the hard cut-off when the lights were dipped. (In time both sides modified their ideas; certainly the old static test dogma gradually disappeared.) The Lucas-Graves double-filament bulb did not catch on in Britain, only Vauxhall taking it for a time as original equipment, but it continued to be fitted to cars for certain export markets where the Philips Duplo and American Bilux bulbs were the accepted form of anti-dazzle lighting.

Although cars fitted with Lucas dipping reflectors or double-filament bulbs managed quite well in fog, an auxiliary fog-lamp was found to be more effective. The first Lucas fog-lamp, produced in 1931, had been a simple amber-glassed lamp, which conformed to the current thinking that a yellow or amber light was better in fog than a white one. In fact, as Neill reminded me, 'It only reduced the glare in proportion to the extent that it reduced the total amount of illumination. The real consideration in making a fog-lamp is that it must not give any top scatter.'

In 1933 the Lucas engineers got to work and produced a new fog-lamp called the FT37, a very sophisticated optical design with a normal parabolic reflector split in half which together with a bulb shield gave a strong flat-topped beam without any upward glare. It had a single-filament bulb and a clear glass. At first the body of the lamp was the same as one of the Lucas motor-cycle headlamps, with a bulge at the back into which a switch and ammeter were normally fitted; on the fog-lamp this bulge was used for giving access to the bulb mounting, so that it could be adjusted for focusing and altering the length and concentration of the beam. The FT37 was an instant success and more than 140,000 were sold in the first year. But its success was spoilt by the high cost of manufacture. It was too expensive to cut the reflectors in half and join them together again, so the reflectors were pressed with a step in them to give a similar effect. Unhappily these one-piece reflectors were not quite as good, because the step obtained with pressure could not be as sharp as with a split reflector joined together. Against this, the pressed reflector enabled the body of the lamp to be made symmetrical, which pleased the car manufacturers' stylists. Nevertheless the FT37 continued to sell well for a few years, and in 1934 was called a pass-light as well as a fog-lamp.

A different kind of auxiliary lamp, the spotlight mounted on the windscreen pillar, was introduced by Lucas in 1933. Spotlights had been widely sold for some years by American and Continental makers, being especially useful in country districts for reading signposts and road numbers, but in England they were illegal unless they incorporated some means of making it impossible to use them while the car was moving. Now, in response to a strong demand, notably from trials and rally drivers, Lucas produced two spotlights, one with a handle at the back for swivelling the lamp and the other with a driving mirror at the back instead.

Improved driving vision of a different kind was also provided in 1933 by the Panoram and Panoramette saloon mirrors, which gave an undistorted view to the rear through an angle of 160 degrees; in other words, the driver could see through the side windows as well as behind the car. The larger model was just over 12in wide. Lucas had, of course, supplied a wide range of observation mirrors since the growth of motoring in the 1920s. The exterior ones were fitted either to the windscreen pillar or on to the side of the body by means of various brackets, including a triangular one called the Girderscope, which was patented by two Birmingham brothers named Griffiths, from whom Lucas had acquired the manufacturing rights in 1925 (they paid a royalty of 3d a bracket to start with but this was quickly cancelled by an outright payment of £2,500). An interior mirror was produced for the first time in the same year.

The positioning of exterior observation mirrors continued on the windscreen pillar or body side in the 1930s, until the increasing use of all-steel monocoque bodies made it more difficult to fix brackets on the body. In 1935 Lucas changed over almost completely to a new convex mirror mounted on the front wing. Just before the war a rival company (Harris & Sheldon, makers of Desmo accessories) produced a wing mirror with a patented joint which enabled the mirror to be returned to its original setting if it was accidentally moved out of position, whereas the Lucas mirror had to be readjusted and tightened up again. Lucas tried to produce an alternative but the Desmo device was closely patented and the Lucas mirror inevitably lost sales.

The recovery from the slump was confirmed by the figures for the 1932–3 financial year ending August 1933. For the first time sales topped £5 million for the whole group, including CAV-Bosch. Exports were still puny at £167,169. The car and motor-cycle business represented two-thirds of the total sales, while the cycle trade was worth £192,517. Luvax brought in £225,825 and 'other trades' £115,495, these including Newtons' production of garage equipment and industrial motors, electric tools made by Rotax, and the Powell & Hanmer sundries like Coronet cameras and odds-and-ends made specially for Woolworths, which they had taken on to keep the factory busy during the slump. These P & H items were sub-contracts given to Frank Hanmer, junior, by W. Elliott, who was the Austrian consul in Birmingham and had a small works in Great Hampton Row. The Woolworth orders were a mixed bag and included fire-tongs, spectacle cases of various designs and finishes, splashers for taps and perforated spoons for vegetables (an echo of Joseph Lucas's vegetable press). P & H also made Ever Ready Lamps as a sub-contract. Lucas themselves were producing Beetleware (plastic cups and saucers for airlines), which they had inherited from the mouldings section of ML, while Lucas and CAV were both making Mary Ann vacuum-cleaners. Rotax were making mine lamps and Newtons were still doing train lighting as well as industrial motors.

In the motor contract business, Austin with £479,795 were slightly ahead of Morris Motors (£449,251) at the top of the list, but Morris also had contracts for Morris Engines, Morris Bodies, the MG Car Co, Morris Commercial Cars and Wolseley which brought his overall total up to £746,101. Humber and Hillman, together with Commer Cars, were in third place (£225,185), followed by Ford (£220,723), Daimler/BSA (£220,707), Standard (£215,482) and Vauxhall (£118,056).

The number of British cars equipped by Lucas and Rotax was 247,653 for home and export. These included 34,557 Ford Eights, for which Lucas supplied the dynamos, starters and distributors but not the lights, batteries and cables. They also equipped 26,879 light commercial vehicles and 40,314 motor-cycles. Such was the scale of operations of Joseph Lucas and the motor industry in the early 1930s.

Most of the contract business was for lighting, starting and ignition equipment, but Lucas were also supplying observation mirrors, door handles, window winders, hub caps for wheels, illuminated instrument panels and number-plate boxes, switches, interior lamps, and auxiliary lamps. A minor development in 1933 was the provision of a battery master switch. This multiplicity of items prominently marked 'Lucas', with its indication of what critics liked to call 'the monopolistic grip of Joseph Lucas on the British motor industry', brought a backlash which Masterton has described:

Service failures were over-emphasised both to the owner and the manufacturer. If the failure rate was 1 per cent and there was only one Lucas item on a car, then Lucas equipment would be considered very good with only one car in a hundred having a Lucas equipment failure during the guarantee period. If there were 50 Lucas items on a car and the failure rate per item was the same, there could be 50 per cent of cars with a Lucas item failure during the guarantee period – which was obviously intolerable.

Apart from the normal occasional troubles with the main equipment – batteries, ignition, and starting – Lucas began to have very much more trouble with the additional items like electric windscreen wipers and shock absorbers.

There was consequently a change of policy and the prominence of the name 'Lucas' on items under the continual gaze of the car driver was reduced. At the same time Lucas tried to cut down the range of items supplied to car manufacturers. They stopped making plated hub-caps when the existing contract expired and a few years later (in 1936) gave up the manufacture of window winders and sold the tools to Wilmot Breeden, for whom they made them.

Lucas continued to hold their major share of the original equipment battery business, but now the competition in the replacement battery market became intense. The Chloride Electrical Storage Company, makers of Exide batteries, who supplied Ford, Vauxhall, Rolls-Royce and a number of car importers with original equipment batteries, had always taken the lion's share of replacement sales, and had been in agreement with Lucas about discounts since 1927. They had also acquired several medium-sized battery manufacturers of repute. But there were many small makers and assemblers whose products were often of poor quality and whose price-cutting policy was playing havoc with the whole replacement battery trade.

In May 1933 the Motor Agents Association asked the leading battery firms for help in regulating the distribution of starter batteries. Jack Masterton has described the background: 'The MAA were alarmed at the growth of tyre and battery shops selling direct to the public. They wanted the distribution of tyres and batteries to be confined to garages (their members) and an undertaking to be given by the manufacturers not to supply the objectionable shops with batteries either directly or indirectly under other names. At the same time the garages insisted on being free to buy cheap batteries for used cars in their own stock.'

In the end a compromise was reached. The garages were prepared to enter into exclusive selling agreements and the manufacturers undertook to supply them with a cheaper range of batteries under other names. To give effect to this decision, the manufacturers held a meeting at which representatives of Lucas, Chloride, Oldham, Tungstone and Young agreed to form the British Starter Battery Association. The BSBA then entered into individual contracts with MAA members, who agreed not to buy or sell any batteries except those made by BSBA members, including the cheaper range of batteries which they would supply for used cars.

To provide this cheap range of batteries, the Jewel Battery Company, Limited, was formed with an authorised capital of £5,000. Lucas and Chloride each held 1,000 preference shares and 200 ordinary shares and Oldham held 200 ordinaries, making up the issued capital of £600 ordinary and £2,000 preference shares. Any of the members of the BSBA could make the Jewel battery, calling it by some distinctive name, but they were not to advertise it or give any indication of its origin or of the other parties concerned. It was Peter Bennett who suggested that the jewel names should be taken from those described in the Bible as decorating the Gates of Heaven. Lucas chose Sapphire, Chloride took Emerald, and Oldham and other members of the BSBA decided on Ruby, Onyx and Pearl. Prices for the various types of customer were laid down. To save costs, the Jewel battery had thinner and shorter plates with separators made of Douglas fir instead of the Port Orford cedar separators used in standard batteries. The containers were also of a cheaper grade. But the main reason for their lower selling price was that everybody concerned took a smaller margin of profit.

The impact of the Jewel battery extended over the next 10 years, but it deserves to be told here. In time it became the leading seller. Instead of being fitted only to used cars, as originally intended, it was sold to motorists by agents and the trade generally in place of the higher priced standard battery of better quality. When the war put an end to normal motoring, Lucas took the opportunity to stop selling the Jewel battery in 1942. The Jewel Battery Company was finally liquidated in 1960.

From its introduction the lower price of the Jewel battery obviously had dangerous implications for the sale of the standard battery, selling at a higher price, so in January 1934 the company introduced the Lucas Insured Life Scheme for their standard battery range. Every battery was guaranteed for 12 months from the date it was put into service and was replaced by a new one if it failed during that time because of faulty workmanship or defective material. During the 12 months after the expiry of the guarantee a new battery was supplied in exchange for a defective one at a price depending on the length of time the original battery was used.

Batteries were not the only components that were the subject of discussion with the factors and specialist stockists of electrical equipment at this time. The sale of 'pirate' spare parts of all kinds had reached such proportions that Lucas were forced to take some defensive measure against it, and this took the form of a Preferential Spares Discount Agreement which provided for reciprocal action. Lucas would give better discounts on spares, provided the signatories would undertake to buy, whether for resale or use in repairs, only 'genuine' (made by Lucas) spare parts for electrical equipment and would send all armatures for rewinding to the factory.

Towards the end of 1933 the annual meeting of shareholders approved the capitalisation of £975,000 on a share basis. This script issue of bonus £1 shares was made possible by the amount of money standing to the credit of the reserve, premiums on shares issued, and accumulated profits. At the same time it was felt that the workpeople should have the opportunity of sharing in the prosperity of the company, so the meeting was also asked to empower the directors to form the Lucas Workers Shares Bank, which they did. The possibility of issuing workers' shares was considered, but as Peter Bennett explained to the shareholders:

> We have come to the conclusion that anything of the nature of issuing Workers' Shares is impracticable. It is a matter on which there is general agreement that in all cases of small capital absolute security is of more importance than interest. Happy as we may feel about the position of Joseph Lucas, Limited, at the present time we cannot guarantee its permanent prosperity, and therefore we should not feel content nor would it be wise to provide the workers with an opportunity of securing shares which would have to be subject to the risks of good and bad trade with all that might mean for the future.

Instead it was planned that the company would issue to the bank redeemable preference shares up to a limit of £100,000, ranking after the existing shares and bearing the same rate of dividend as the ordinary shareholders received. The bank's function would be to act solely as a savings bank in which the workpeople could make deposits. The plan was for it to invest its funds in the redeemable preference shares and in trustee securities, and the money received by the company in payment of the shares would be reinvested in the bank at a small fixed rate of interest to provide extra security for the depositors. The object was to obtain a higher rate of interest for the depositors than they would be able to obtain elsewhere. (For various reasons the formation of the Lucas Workers Shares Bank was put off. Then the war caused a further postponement, and it was not until 1949 that the bank finally came into operation.) Meanwhile, in 1932, the Work People's Old Age Fund had been started with a donation of £10,000 from the company's profits.

Towards the end of 1933 Joseph Lucas acquired a small business which was to be of considerable value both commercially and technically in the years ahead. Four years earlier, when the working agreement with S. Smith & Sons was first mooted, Peter Bennett had discussed with Gordon Smith the possibility of Lucas buying a Smith subsidiary, North & Son Limited, who made Watford magnetos, speedometers and other instruments. The company had been formed before World War I by a Yorkshireman, Robert Benson North, who began life as a watchmaker and could claim to have been the initiator of the speedometer and the revolution counter. Thousands of these instruments were made in a little factory at Watford. Much against their will (because they insisted that electricity was not in their line), North & Sons were persuaded to make magnetos during the war. They continued afterwards and the Watford magneto achieved a fine reputation, being fitted to the Rolls-Royce-engined Vickers Vimy that made the first Atlantic flight in 1919 and the Vickers Super-marine S6B seaplane with Rolls-Royce 'R' engine that broke the world air speed record at 407.5mph in 1931. It was also used in Bristol and Napier aero-engines. North died in 1929, and the great depression put the company in the hands of the receiver. The business was acquired by Smiths, who offered it to Lucas, but the price was not regarded as sufficiently attractive for them to purchase it.

Now, after struggling on for four years, the company was again on offer, and Lucas bought the assets and goodwill from the receiver for £22,547. Half this purchase price was recovered from Smiths in payment for the speedometer and instrument side, while Lucas kept the magneto, which was all they were interested in. The story behind this transaction was that Lucas, in acquiring the Watford magneto side of Norths, were acting at the behest of the Government. The financial failure of Norths left BTH as the only British source of magnetos for aero-engines, and the Government were determined to have an alternative manufacturer. Apart from an order for 100 three-cylinder magnetos from the Bristol Aeroplane Co in 1926, Lucas had virtually given up making aero-engine magnetos after the war, as the turnover was so small, but now they found themselves back in the business again. The stock and goodwill of Norths were transferred to Rotax at Willesden. Once again, as they did with ML, Lucas acquired not only a fine product in the Watford magneto but a talented designer in the person of A. M. (Tubby) Allen, their chief engineer.

With the Watford magneto added to the Bendix starter and other items at Willesden at the end of 1933, Lucas decided to form a Rotax aero department in which to concentrate the manufacture of aviation equipment.

CHAPTER THREE

ENGINEERING CHANGES GEAR

At the January 1934 board meeting, following the formation of the Rotax aero department at the end of the previous year, Peter Bennett had this to say about it: 'Although the turnover is small, they are making steady progress and account for £5,000 of the £15,000 sales of Rotax general sundries last month. We are not regarding this as profitable, but we feel it is essential that we should keep in on this side ready for any developments that may occur later.'

When Bennett spoke these words, the swing from the disarmament hopes of the 1920s to the decision to rearm that followed the resurgence of Germany in the early 1930s was just about to begin. Hitler had become Chancellor 12 months earlier, but the British Air Estimates in March 1933 did not provide for a single new squadron. The 10-year programme had been suspended for another year, and Churchill thundered that Britain was now only the fifth air power. In October Hitler showed what he thought of the 'Macdonald Plan' by walking out of the Disarmament Conference and withdrawing from the League of Nations. Churchill's bitter comment was 'Thank God for the French Army!'

The March 1934 British Air Estimates provided for four new squadrons, but the Prime Minister, Stanley Baldwin, was at last becoming shaken by Germany's aggressive attitude. In July the Government decided to enlarge the Royal Air Force by forty-one squadrons, or some 820 aeroplanes – though this would be spread over the next five years. Bennett's 'any developments that may occur' were already beginning to happen.

Meanwhile, at Great King Street, a minor but important technical development was engrossing the attention of Oliver Lucas, Ernest Watson, and the staff of the electrical laboratory. Up to this time Lucas and the American manufacturers were alike in using the third-brush control dynamo, whereas voltage control was general on the Continent. With third-brush control the dynamo had an intermediate brush short-circuited to one of the other brushes, with the result that, as the load increased, it caused armature reaction which shifted the flux across the pole face and automatically limited the current flowing to the battery, thus preventing the bulbs burning out. But it also resulted in overcharging in the daytime and loss of electrolyte. Lucas had overcome this as long ago as 1927 by a switch which put a resistance in the circuit, providing a two-charge rate – one rate for the daytime and another at night – but the Americans were slow to adopt this. In 1932 Lucas introduced a three-charge rate system. Bosch, on the other hand, had gone to the heart of the matter in obtaining voltage control by limiting the excitation of the main field. They offered their constant voltage controller to Lucas as a part of the CAV-Bosch agreement, but on examination it proved to be what Dr Watson has described to me as

... a typical Bosch product, something only they could make. It was a beautifully made thing, enclosed in a circular container, very neat and compact to look at, but the adjustment was completely blind. You merely turned a nut, but you couldn't see what it was it was doing. Bosch had also realised that it wasn't the right thing and were bringing out a much bigger regulator on a simpler principle, completely open so that you could see what you were doing, but it was intended only for their bigger commercial vehicle dynamos.

Well, under the Bosch agreement we made a few thousand of the small ones, the very complicated ones, to begin with but we soon dropped them. Instead, we designed a smaller version of the bigger Bosch one for passenger cars and brought it out in the mid-1930s. I must confess that it was with great fear and trepidation that we launched this new regulator, fully expecting on a new and comparatively untried design to have endless service troubles. Fortunately this was not the case and on the whole the regulator gave good service, only giving rise to spasmodic outbreaks of trouble when ill-considered attempts were made to cheapen it, when certain guiding principles were discarded, and when stabilising processes were omitted. It became universal in this country, and we modified it a bit. The original Bosch design put a limit on voltage but not on current, which meant that although your battery voltage couldn't rise above a certain limit in value, you could pass a very heavy current into a discharged battery, which might damage the dynamo. So in 1934 we added some compensating winding to put a controller on both voltage and current so that you couldn't burn out the dynamo. We called that the 'compensated voltage control', CVC, and that in turn became universal on all British cars from that time until the electronic control came in recently. That was one thing that Lucas Electrical – as distinct from CAV – were able to take from Bosch.

The introduction of voltage control dynamos had begun in a very tentative way in 1933, and that was the position when Oliver Lucas took Kenneth Corley with him on his annual visit to the States in January 1934. One of his main objects was to study car design trends and their influence on equipment and accessories, the other being to establish better contacts with General Motors, particularly with Delco-Remy. He began by seeing C. E. Wilson, joint head of the GM Accessories Division, who gave him an introduction to visit the Delco-Remy electrical equipment plant at Anderson, to which he had previously been officially refused admission. There he was freely given all the information he wanted, together with samples of parts and complete articles. In conversation with F. C. Kroeger, the general manager, and S. H. Prescott, general manager of the Guide Lamp division, he brought up the question of a closer association with Delco-Remy, at which they referred him back to Wilson. By this time Wilson had gone to Florida for three weeks, so Oliver Lucas followed him there. Wilson, while friendly and helpful, referred him to his senior colleague, D. L. Pratt, in New York, but he pointed out that any arrangement would have to be acceptable to the Vauxhall company, who represented their chief interest in England. Oliver Lucas cabled Charles Bartlett, the Vauxhall managing director, who was quite responsive, before going to New York to see Pratt and Mooney, the head of GM Overseas Operations.

Although Oliver Lucas emphasised to Bartlett that his purpose was to get as much information as possible from Delco-Remy, through some form of association, in order to get Lucas's manufacturing costs nearer to the American figures and so be able to supply Vauxhall (among others) with equipment at the lowest prices, what he also had in mind, of course, was that by so doing he would make it unnecessary for Delco-Remy to start manufacturing motor electrical equipment for Vauxhall (among others) in England.

Oliver Lucas called on the Sparks, Withington Company, whose Sparton horns Lucas had been making under an agreement with the British licensee, Graham Amplion, since 1928. Captain Sparks gave him an 'overwhelming' welcome, and then they discussed the terms of an agreement which was later signed by the two companies. Sparks, Withington undertook to give Lucas the complete know-how and patents of their horn manufacture for the sum of 25,000 dollars, in return for which Lucas undertook to supply horns made to their designs only in the United Kingdom and Ireland, where Sparks, Withington would only supply horns as already fitted to imported American cars. Before he left, Oliver was shown round the old-established plant by Captain Sparks, who gave him full details of operating times so that he could compare them with those at Great King Street.

At Bendix, his next port of call, he was relieved to find that a new and better brake was nearing the end of its development. The present brake was admitted to be more suitable for the large American car than the British. At the Elmira plant they had developed a new type of drive for the motor-car starter, which cured the overstressing of the spring, with resultant breakage, that had been a fault of the original Bendix drive. He rounded off the trip with a visit to the Bendix Aviation plant at East Orange, where the executives told him how delighted they were with their association with Rotax, who were now making aviation starters under licence at Willesden. Benstead had sent them a report suggesting various improvements in the starter and Bendix were adopting six of the recommendations themselves.

On this United States visit Oliver Lucas obtained more precise information than on previous visits about the sales prices of electrical components to large car manufacturers, and this confirmed his view that Lucas were nearer to American production costs for their type of goods than the British car manufacturers were for the motor-car as a whole. The Americans employed superior production techniques and enjoyed the benefit of much longer runs, but they had to pay more for their labour. The net effect was that their productivity was three or four times as high.

Nevertheless, American competition continued to be a thorn in Oliver's side. No sooner had he returned to the works than word came through that they had lost the order for shock absorbers from Ford, who had taken 65,000 last year. Then Vauxhall, who had previously taken 11,000 shock absorbers a year, decided to exercise their right to manufacture the Lovejoy device, a General Motors product, having shortly before cancelled their Bendix brakes order so that they could make their own. Lucas were anxious lest this should lead to an extension of the process to the electrical equipment. Although there were frequent rumours at this time of other British firms wanting to start up in competition, Lucas knew that their business required so much capital, combined with detailed knowledge, that intending competitors could never decide how to begin. The real danger lay with fully established and experienced organisations in America deciding to come over to Britain, above all Delco-Remy (now that Auto-Lite were no longer being urged to do so by Ford). Oliver Lucas admired Delco-Remy enormously and regarded them as the pattern for Lucas to follow. Unhappily no real progress had been made towards forming an 'association' with them.

The answer was to be sought in improving their own production efficiency. The plant and equipment were already under continuous review, but there were possibilities of making better use of manpower. Work on an alternative to the Bedaux Plan had now reached the stage when it was thought that, with adequate explanation to the workpeople in advance, it could safely be brought into operation. A series of meetings was held at which Oliver Lucas went over the scheme in detail, without incurring any apparent opposition. It was called the Lucas Point Plan System, and many years later Sir Bertram Waring told me: 'Roughly how it turned out was that people got a third more pay for half as much extra work. We were really back to piece-work – but on a proper valuation instead of a hit-or-miss valuation.' It was piece-work converted into points, or as Coleman (perhaps unconsciously borrowing from Proust) called it, 'Time Earned.' The formula was exactly the same as Bedaux, but the word Bedaux was never used. Indeed, so unpopular had the word become that the Bedaux operation in Britain was now carried on by Mead, Carney in the name of Associated Industrial Consultants, a deliberately verbose title that did not lend itself to slogan shouting.

I asked Sir Bertram where the outside advice had come from. 'We got rid of the original Bedaux engineers', he said, 'but we got another lot from Bedaux who were not called Bedaux engineers. They were called Lucas Point Plan System engineers – and that solved all our problems.'

That was true in the long run, but there were in fact some local difficulties – including stoppages in some departments – which took a little time and patience to settle before the Lucas Point Plan System was completely accepted in the summer of 1934. Great care was taken to ensure that the Bedaux men who were brought in to supervise the Lucas teams operating the system concealed their true identity. Lucas paid a third of their salary, so they could be said to be 'on the staff', but they were wholly responsible to Bedaux.

This is the last we shall hear of Charles Bedaux in this history of Lucas, but his name was to appear in the headlines two years later as a close friend of King Edward VIII. It was at Bedaux's château in France that the Duke of Windsor and Mrs Simpson were married and spent their honeymoon after the abdication. Soon afterwards Bedaux, who by now had strong Nazi/Fascist sympathies, arranged for them to visit Germany on the pretext of studying housing conditions, a subject the Duke was thought to be interested in because of his bitter comments on the housing conditions of Welsh miners. The proposed visit alarmed his British friends (Lord Beaverbrook flew to Paris to urge him not to go) but the Duke used the argument that, since he now had no formal position in England, he could go where he liked. In Germany Bedaux arranged for him to see Hitler, Hess, Goering and Himmler. His next plan was for the Windsors to visit the United States, but after the German visit American union opposition was so vociferous and menacing that the Duke himself cancelled the idea. In World War II Bedaux, who had given up his American business in 1937, worked for the Vichy Government and co-operated with the Germans. He was arrested in Algiers when the Allies landed there in 1942 and was sent back to America to stand trial for treason. He committed suicide in Miami in February 1944.

One of the Bedaux supervisors of the Lucas Point Plan System was Frederick Garner, who was eventually to join the company properly in 1943 and to go on to become managing director. Garner had started life at Rolls-Royce, working in the experimental department with Ernest Hives. After a spell with W. H. Allen of Bedford on heavy mechanical and electrical machinery, diesel engines, steam turbines, pumps and generators, he went to Napiers because he thought he would have a better future there. Realising his mistake, he moved once more to Brunner, Mond (later ICI), and spent an adventurous seven years in Africa as a prospector and engineer, becoming chief engineer and deputy general manager. He returned to Europe to join the Bedaux organisation and was sent to Philips at Eindhoven, where he saw mass production in action for the first time, to learn the technique of applying the Plan.

Lucas was Garner's first Bedaux assignment, and he was given a team of six young work-study engineers to reorganise the manufacture of cable harness for motor-cars at the Rocky Lane factory in Birmingham. The object was to increase labour productivity. 'I had a marvellous team,' Garner has told me. 'They were all Lucas men – one a mathematician, another a designer of equipment, another good at time and motion study, and so on – between us we raised productivity by over 300 per cent in one fell swoop, largely through improving methods of production.'

This was in keeping with Garner's personal philosophy – he preferred studying ways of improving production to working stopwatches. He was also an advocate of making things accurately by measuring dimensions precisely, and as time went on he was responsible for putting in a lot of measuring equipment in the factory. He noticed that his views were shared by Albert Siddall, one of his young assistants, 'who seemed to be the only person to query the existing production methods.' (He later made Siddall his deputy.)

The Lucas Point Plan System and the Time Study Department, which was really part of it, stimulated by the fresh thinking of Garner and another Bedaux man, a trouble-shooter named Cavanagh who had been in the Navy – all under the co-ordination and direction of Oliver Lucas – brought about a fundamental change that found its expression in a new body, the Process Planning Department. Siddall recalls:

This was the beginning of a modern management system distinct from the old Lucas system. The technology, instead of being organised on the shop floor, was decided by people working outside the shop who determined how things should be made and what equipment should be used for making them. The previous system was based on the shop foremen or superintendents. They were the manufacturing management, men of all work – and some of them were damn good, I must say – they decided how the job should be done, they decided what equipment would be needed, in many cases they actually made the equipment themselves in their own small toolroom or they told the main toolroom what they wanted; they fixed a time for the job, and dealt with the social problems of the people – they dealt with every aspect of the manufacturing scene. The Process Planning Department started with two or three people, and gradually built up until it became quite powerful. It really made decisions on how things should be made and what equipment should be used, and that had quite a revolutionary effect on the manufacturing times and the overall efficiency of the plant and its profitability. In the early stages manufacturing times were reduced by half on a big scale, and the tools were made differently (they were designed on the drawing board instead of *ad hoc*, as it were). By introducing a professional body of engineers to look after the technology of manufacture, the process planning system was really the beginning of a modern production engineering system. It also had a big effect on the overall management structure, because you couldn't make a change like that without taking in the whole of the manufacturing system, which grew from a complete line management to a line-and-staff management.

All this was not accomplished without tremendous resistance from the old guard, but it was gradually worn down as the beneficial results became clear for all to see. With the total payroll for the whole group now reaching 20,000 for the first time, modernisation of engineering management was vital for the company to keep itself at the peak of efficiency. The training of their intake of boys now entered the company's plans and the first Lucas Engineering School was opened in 1934 for the training of craft and technician apprentices, the initial course being attended by seventeen boys.

Certain improvements in manufacturing technique, started a few years earlier by Jock Miller, were taking on a wider significance. In his experimental work in the Electrical Company's laboratory Miller had developed a new method of brazing the tungsten contacts in coil ignition distributors and magnetos to mild steel rivets, followed by a technique for grinding a domed contact face; and a new department for this work had been started. Dr Watson adds: 'His greatest contribution was, I think, the introduction to the Lucas organisation of the copper brazing process in a hydrogen atmosphere. Neither Miller nor Lucas can claim to have invented this. It actually started, I believe, in this country and I myself saw something of it in a little laboratory in Wolverhampton in 1913, but it was dropped during the 1914–1918 War and started up afterwards in the United States, whence it returned to this country in the 1930s.'

Lucas in fact became the first company in Britain to make large-scale use of this process, which now plays an important part in Lucas manufacturing both in Birmingham and Burnley. From this, Miller and E. V. Beatson went on to develop resistance brazing, which was later to be of great value in the Burnley factories.

For some time Miller had realised that one of the most important processes involved in the manufacture of any component was not so much the formation of a piece by machining, stamping or drawing as in the assembly of the pieces to form a whole. Moreover it was in these assembly operations that the skill of the operator became of great importance. One could dimensionally check a machined or punched part, but it was hard to check properly on assembly operations. Miller therefore set out to make the assembly operation as far as possible independent of the operator's skill. He turned his attention to the use of controlled spot-welding as a substitute for soldering with the help of the Chemical and Metallurgical Department. The evolution of the welding machine built like a machine tool with adequate rigidity and precise guidance of the moving hand, and with the factors which control the weld, pressure, time and current value automatically controlled, owed much to Miller and Beatson working together with the welding machine manufacturers. For Jock Miller this represented a gradual but complete change from the electrical work to what he called 'the art of sticking things together.' In the eyes of his chief, Dr Watson, it was a far more rewarding and important job.

On the selling side a new procedure was adopted in June 1934 in fixing contracts with manufacturers, Lucas undertaking that their prices would stand as long as the motor manufacturers did not increase their prices to the public. The current trend was actually in the other direction, towards reducing car prices, but a close understanding with the motor industry on these matters was an essential part of the Lucas policy. As the chairman, Alderman Sayer, put it: 'The motor manufacturers' good will is not shown on the balance sheet, but it remains the outstanding asset of the business.' A few months later the battle between the big manufacturers for the small car market reached a new pitch at the time of the Motor Show. Austin – now Lucas's largest individual customer – reduced the price of the Seven to meet the competition of the Ford Eight, while Morris were having great success with a new version of the Morris Eight, which they were making at the rate of 1,000 a week. Ford introduced a second string, the Ten, at their own motor show at the Royal Albert Hall. Peter Bennett remarked: 'The struggle between these firms will be very carefully watched, as we are very interested parties.'

In turn, the manufacturers took advantage of Lucas's objective viewpoint to ask their opinion on how their cars compared with those of their rivals. Bernard Scott (who shared a Morris Eight with his sister at the time) was sent for one day by Oliver Lucas and found him talking to Rowland Smith, the head of Fords. 'Don't be nervous, don't be worried,' Oliver said, 'but tell Mr. Smith what you don't like about the Ford Eight.'

Scott took his cue and said: 'It's not as good as the Morris Eight. It's got no flair about it – it's got no feeling of quality. It wants a bit of styling.' Mr Smith looked at him thoughtfully and said: 'What would you do about it?'

'It's the little things. Take the door handles, for instance. Now the Morris Eight . . . that's got some quality, some dignity, about it. The dashboard's nice — '

' — Well, I'll send you an Eight and a Ten and you can do what you like with them, Mr. Scott, and you can keep them for as long as you like and draw sketches and so on, and you can say what you think.' 'Oliver Lucas said: "Fine!" and I had got a Ford Eight and a Ford Ten all to myself,' added Scott. 'I got the Styling Department to work, and we re-styled all sorts of details.'

A New Traffic Act in 1934 introduced the 30mph speed limit in built-up areas, which is still with us 40 years later, and driving tests were made compulsory. Joseph Lucas made their own contribution to road safety by bringing out the Trafficator, a less equivocal and more comfortable method of signalling changes in direction than the driver's arm, especially at night and in the rain. The Trafficator was an illuminated semaphore direction indicator with a self-cancelling switch operated by the steering wheel, available either as a black box fitted to the side of the car or recessed into the door pillar so that it was flush-fitting when not in use. Unhappily, if for some reason the self-cancelling switch did not work, the signal arm was vulnerable to being wiped off. The name bore the unmistakeable stamp of Harry Lucas and was registered. The Trafficator was a German invention for which Lucas had obtained the patent rights for the British Commonwealth from A. H. Hunt (Safetisigns) Ltd in 1932. A royalty of 6d a pair was payable on Trafficators sold to car manufacturers as initial equipment and 2s 6d on those sold as accessories (up to 50,000). There had of course been previous attempts to provide direction signalling for motorists, and Lucas had produced rear number-plates incorporating illuminated arrows. But these were limited in their effectiveness and the Trafficator was the first popular direction indicator used in Britain.

The increase in business brought by the Trafficator was particularly welcome, because profits from two other Lucas products were being undermined by an unexpected development in the cycle industry. The Hercules company had introduced mass-production methods to such good effect that they were able to sell over a million bicycles a year at a very low price, and now they added to the value of their machines by fitting a bell as standard equipment. Up to this time bicycle bells had been bought separately as accessories. Hercules also decided to fit dynamo lighting sets to their *de luxe* models. This presented Lucas with the dilemma of choosing between quoting for the Hercules orders at prices which meant little or no profit, or letting the business go to a competitor. They chose the former, and Masterton takes up the story: 'I remember while on holiday being called to the telephone by the buyer of Hercules to tell me that it had been decided to give Lucas the order for 1,000,000 bells and 50,000 dynamo sets for which a quotation had recently been submitted.' Lucas were not the only people to be worried by Hercules. Raleigh gave up making motor-cycles so they could concentrate their resources on competing with Hercules in the bicycle trade.

Before the end of 1934 there were several more changes in the overall composition of the group. First the goodwill and stock of industrial motors made by Newtons at Taunton were sold to Cromp-

ton, Parkinson (the garage equipment and similar work being transferred to Rotax at Willesden), and then a 40 per cent interest in the
Wilmot Manufacturing Company was purchased from Carl Breeden
in exchange for 10,000 ordinary Lucas shares at £3 a share.

But the most far-reaching transaction of this kind was the reorganisation of A. Rist (1927) Ltd, in which the company had had the
controlling interest since 1929 and had subsequently increased its
shareholding. During the intervening years there had been a revolution in the method of wiring motor-cars, which had previously been
done by the motor factories and body-builders with spools of cables
and wires they obtained direct from the manufacturers. (Incidentally,
the original two-wire insulated return method of wiring had been
replaced by the single-wire earth return system, the negative battery
terminal being earthed.) Lucas had often been consulted on the
specification of cables for various cars, especially whether there was
enough copper in the cable to carry the current required for lighting
and starting without too much voltage drop or without risk of fire.
They had also given advice on proper insulation to avoid short-
circuits or damage. When several wires or cables ran alongside one
another, they were simply bound together with insulation tape. The
logical development was a complete harness for each model, braided
up and laid out so that it could go straight on to the car. This method
would save a lot of time in wiring the car and would also be much
more reliable, because the work would not be left to semi-trained individuals to carry out. Lucas had been asked by several car manufacturers to supply such a complete harness, but when they went to
buy stocks of cable and wire, they discovered that the main suppliers
were in a 'ring' and they had to pay their controlled prices.

The ingenious Rist found a way round this by buying the Flexible
Electric Cord Company, a small concern making electric wires, and
moving it to Lowestoft. He offered it to Lucas, who declined to buy
it, but although they did not want to acquire the company, Lucas certainly had good use for the motor-car cables it was now producing,
and they purchased large quantities of cable from Lowestoft. The
success of Rist's little company angered the cable ring, which tried to
squeeze it by cutting prices down to an uneconomic level. Rist then
brought two other companies to Lucas, and in order to safeguard
their position in case the ring succeeded in their squeeze, Lucas decided to buy them. Armoury Wire & Tinsel Company made fine
copper wire on a small scale and Scott Insulated Wire Company made
enamelled wire. The latter had been established by a German com-

pany which had to withdraw because of the Nazi decree concentrating German manufacturing interests within Germany.

In November 1934 Lucas decided to reorganise the whole Rist operation – including Flexible Electric Cord – as a self-contained independent company which would supply them with a large amount of their cable requirements at the same price that the ring would supply them. Earlier they had invested £27,571 in the concern, and now they had to pay a further £47,300 to complete the purchases and provide working capital. The name of the Flexible Electric Cord Company was changed to Rists Wires & Cables, Ltd. Two years later A. Rist (1927) was wound up and its business in ignition coils and other goods transferred to the new company. Lucas's part in all these Rist affairs was still kept absolutely secret.

Rist himself was delighted with this secrecy. He loved intrigue, and was always full of business scandals which he liked to impart by sidling up with a conspiratorial air and saying very quietly: 'Have you heard so-and-so . . .' Some time after Lucas had taken control of his company he made this cloak-and-dagger approach to Peter Bennett one day (or it may have been Oliver Lucas) and murmured: 'I think we ought to make bulbs.'

This was a very shrewd remark, because it was just what was in the Lucas managing directors' minds. The reason was that the supply of bulbs was controlled by another ring, and it was characteristic of the individualist in Rist that he should be keen to make an undercover attack on it. The ring was called the Electrical Lamp Manufacturing Association – ELMA for short – and they had all the bulb manufacturers tied up. Lucas found that it was impossible to get individual prices from any of them; the same prices were quoted everywhere. They made the best of the situation by specialising with GEC and getting the benefit of their service. This was all the better because Oliver Lucas had a personal contact there in George Chelioti, the managing director of GEC Lamps at Hammersmith. George Chelioti was of Greek origin; he and Oliver were sympathetic characters and understood each other. Nevertheless, the ELMA people used to come down to Birmingham every year and Lucas had to sign their agreement – otherwise they had no bulbs.

The company were therefore ripe for Rist's suggestion, and plans went ahead in the greatest secrecy to manufacture bulbs at Lowestoft. Kenneth Corley was still the confidential liaison between the Lucas managing directors and Albert Rist, and the bulbs were referred to as 'heat units' in his reports, so that nobody would guess what was afoot. ELMA could normally detect anyone starting to manufacture bulbs in this country because they knew where the particular lead glass lead-ins were produced on the Continent. They had to be made of a special alloy which enabled a seal to be made between the glass and the electrode filament that went up inside the glass. As soon as someone attempted to make lamps, ELMA were down on them either through the patent angle or by internal spying, so everything had to be done very secretly indeed. Corley recalls that ELMA also controlled the supply of the special glass tube from which bulbs were made. Rist had various contacts on the Continent and was in his element buying glass-blowing machinery from Germany and Czechoslovakia. Lucas started making bulbs at Lowestoft and they were quite good. In doing so, they got to know by practical experience how much it cost to make a bulb (a side-lamp bulb cost about 2d in those days).

The rest of the story took several years to unfold and did not reach its climax until 1939, but it deserves to be told here. When the plant was working satisfactorily, it was decided to market the bulbs under the innocent name of Beacon lamps. Rist had succeeded in building up a production unit making headlamp and side-lamp bulbs of proper quality and in sufficient quantity to supply the whole of Lucas's requirements. A very substantial reserve stock had also been accumulated, with the result that Lucas could be quite independent of ELMA without any anxiety at all. All this had been done without the most powerful ring in the country – and probably in Europe – realising what was going on. There came the day when ELMA arrived at Great King Street for their annual visit.

ELMA representative: 'Here is the agreement, Mr. Lucas, with our prices for next year, our discounts, and so on.'

Oliver Lucas: 'I'm not signing.'

ELMA representative: 'But where are you going to get your bulbs from, Mr. Lucas?'

Oliver Lucas: 'Oh, we've made other arrangements.' Pause. 'We're making bulbs.' Another pause. 'Didn't you know?'

Lucas then made what to some people seemed an equivocal decision. They decided to offer their Beacon lamp business to ELMA, using the argument: 'Look here, we don't really want to make bulbs. We've found out what it costs – you've been taking us for a ride. If you are prepared to work on a cost basis, using our costs as factual, we'll stop it, and won't make bulbs, and you can buy the business.'

Oliver Lucas invited the ELMA representatives down to Lowestoft to see the works. Robert Neill, who was now in charge of lighting design and engineering and had been brought into the Rist 'secret', went round with them. 'You could see in their faces what they were thinking', he told me. 'All this going on – and they knew nothing about it, they literally hadn't a clue. They could hardly believe it.'

George Chelioti's comment on the affair was: 'Lucas were the first people to hit ELMA over the head with a bludgeon – and sell them the bludgeon afterwards.' This was a typical George Chelioti witticism – it appealed to Oliver Lucas and he was fond of quoting it.

The terms were that Lucas sold the whole of the shares in the Beacon Lamp Co Ltd for the sum of £100,000 to the General Electric Company, British Thomson-Houston and Siemens Electric Lamps & Supplies, acting jointly for ELMA, who agreed to supply Lucas with electric bulbs at prices which were considerably lower than those in the previous purchasing agreement, for a period of 10 years. Lucas had no doubt in their own minds that selling outright in this way, on such exceptionally favourable terms, was better than trying to carry on the bulb business themselves.

CHAPTER FOUR

ROTAX TAKES OFF

During the 1930s the Lucas board continued to be dominated by the two joint managing directors, Peter Bennett (also deputy chairman) and Oliver Lucas, who were at first the only executive directors. The other members of the board – Alderman J. Sayer, chairman, Harry Lucas, and J. Albert Thomson – had no executive functions. But Bertram Waring, the secretary, was in many ways like another executive director, for the managing directors were happy to leave more and more of the administration of the 20,000-strong company in his capable and humane hands.

Peter Bennett, without relaxing his grip on the business of the company, was taking on more outside duties: he became President of the Birmingham Chamber of Commerce in 1932, a Justice of the Peace in 1933, and was elected President of the Society of Motor Manufacturers & Traders, the highest honour in the industry, in 1935, being followed by his Lucas colleague, J. Albert Thomson, in 1936. Oliver Lucas, on the other hand, devoted his whole time, if not his whole life, to ensuring that the technical basis of the company, in production as well as product, was maintained at the highest level. Luckily Bertram Waring was ideally suited by temperament and experience to follow through the policies within the company that Bennett and Lucas laid down, and they gladly left the job to him. Moreover, they found Waring's strength as an accountant invaluable in assessing and shaping the company's financial policy and procedures.

Waring's position had thus become rather more than anomalous by the mid-1930s, but justice was done at last when, at the board meeting on 23 July 1935, on the recommendation of the managing directors, he was appointed an additional director. The same meeting recorded the death of Bernard Steeley, Harry Lucas's brother-in-law, who had worked with Joseph and Harry in the early days and was one of the original directors of the company when it was formed in 1898, until he retired in 1921.

Two examples of Waring's constant thought for the well-being of the workpeople occurred immediately after his elevation. He realised that many of them were never able to take a holiday of any sort (there were no paid holidays in those days) simply because they had not saved up any money when August arrived. So the Workpeople's Holiday Fund was started on a contributory basis, the company adding a 50 per cent bonus to the contributions paid by the workpeople, which were £2 for men and £1 for women, girls and youths. Men paid their contributions at the rate of 1s a week and the women, girls and youths 6d a week. The holiday fund applied only to August. The second innovation was the appointment of a full-time company medical officer, who was installed in a new first-aid and medical treatment department on the second floor of a new building that was being put up on the corner of Great King Street and Well Street. This arrangement was a vast improvement on the old ambulance rooms, which had become inadequate and congested.

The annual expedition to the United States in November 1935 was unusually strong. Oliver Lucas took with him Dr Watson, the chief engineer, and Arthur Benstead, general manager of Rotax. At this time Fred Coleman was attached to Rotax and Waring arranged for him to accompany Benstead to the United States, where he used his experience of estimating at Lucas to assess the cost of American products as they visited various factories. Coleman benefited enormously from the trip, as the Americans allowed him to look into their costing, accounting and financial systems. Waring, in fact, was doing for his side of the business what Oliver Lucas was doing in terms of technology.

'OL' spent a valuable $2\frac{1}{2}$ hours with Kettering, head of General Motors Research, who gave him detailed drawings of the fuel-injection pumps they were using on diesel-electric locomotives made for the big American railroads. At Delco-Remy he found confirmation of the Lucas advanced theories on ignition and voltage control: at some points Lucas were ahead of Delco-Remy on the development side, but the American superiority in manufacturing technique – only partly due to their larger quantities – held many lessons for Lucas. The question of quantity and the amount of specialised production equipment it permitted to be used cropped up again at the Ford dynamo and starter plant at Ypsilanti, where only one type of each was made and the output was about 5,000 a day. In his report on this factory he noted: 'Unfortunately these extremely low costs are taken as a basis of comparison for our quotation which we put into Dagenham, England, and although we are not expecting to get down to these very low American figures the differences are quite difficult to explain away.' Charles Sorensen gave him the whole production information and costs of the Ypsilanti plant.

He naturally called on Auto-Lite, who were now working for Chrysler, to see if the projected agreement could be brought any closer to finality, and extracted a draft letter from them for further discussion in Birmingham. At this time Auto-Lite were making 8,000 sets of dynamos and starters a day, which was the Lucas output for a week. Coleman noted that this was the scope for the economies of scale that had such an attraction for Oliver Lucas.

The arrangement Lucas had with Trico for making suction wind-screen-wipers was due to run out next year, so Oliver went to see them at Buffalo. He found that technical development of the suction wiper had not reached a sufficiently advanced state for a basis of further co-operation to be worked out. Lucas were by now firmly convinced of the superiority of the electric windscreen-wiper, though they would continue to sell a suction-operated model (with more power to deal with full-throttle conditions) until the agreement with Trico ran out. As there had been a good deal of argument about wiper arms and blades, which Trico had covered with many patents, Lucas decided to give up making them and to buy them in future from Trico.

At Bendix Aviation Oliver Lucas found that Rotax at Willesden were more advanced than Bendix at East Orange in developing light-weight high-speed magnetos for aeroplane engines. (The Rotax lead probably owed something to the pioneer work on magneto design – reducing the size of aero-engine magnetos to 60 per cent of their normal size – carried on by Dr Watson at ML during World War I, for which he received the OBE.)

At South Bend, having seen the state of Bendix brake development, he was more than ever convinced that Lucas would have to work out their own salvation if they were to carry on successfully at Tyseley. A few months earlier Peter Bennett had warned Vincent Bendix that he would rather wind up the business than drift on year after year with such little progress. He told him bluntly: 'The trouble is we do not have a saleable product.' All their best customers except Hillman and Standard had changed to Lockheed (to whom Bendix had given their hydraulic brake licence) or the newcomer, Girling. Bendix had suggested that Lucas might be able to get into the hydraulic brake field by selling Bendix brakes with hydraulic actuation bought from Automotive Products, the Lockheed licencees.

Ernest Watson took advantage of this United States tour to discuss with various American engineers their attitude to the controversy about the relative merits of the 6-volt electrical equipment which was universally used in the United States and the 12-volt system pioneered by Oliver Lucas in Britain. The argument, he has told me, ran like this:

The pros of the 12-volt system we put forward were: (a) lighter and cheaper wiring, or less voltage drop and loss; the voltage drop at the brushes totalling about one volt is independent of the voltage used and is a smaller percentage of the whole on a 12-volt system; (b) more efficient dynamos and starters; 12-volts enabled the starter to accelerate much more rapidly when the engine fired and prevented the pinion being thrown out of engagement, as was prone to happen on a 4-cylinder engine with a 6-volt system, and (c) more uniform temperature distribution in the filament of the headlamp bulb; with the short filament of the 6-volt system there is an appreciable loss of heat to the filament supports.

Against these points the Americans (and Bosch) claimed for 6-volts (a) the ability to use a slightly cheaper battery (less labour and parts in inter-cell divisions and terminal posts and welding), and (b) possibly a longer life for the smaller bulbs used in sidelights etc., owing to the thicker filaments. It was often claimed that American cars with 6-volts were as good at starting as British cars with 12-volts, but this was due to other factors, chiefly larger bearing clearances and possibly the use of thinner oils. There was a craze in this country for the use of relatively high viscosity oils which were supposed to give better lubrication when the engine was warm.

The position in Britain was that Lucas supplied 12-volt equipment for all medium-sized and larger cars, including the Vauxhall, but 6-volt equipment for small cars, including the Ford (the Ford dynamos and starters were made by Lucas to Ford USA drawings and were stamped FORD). Lucas also made 6-volt equipment for the Bedford trucks produced by Vauxhall under General Motors auspices. Considerable pressure was put on Lucas from various quarters, including the SMMT, to go over to 6-volts entirely, but Oliver Lucas stuck to his guns and in the end the Americans had to admit defeat, though the argument was to linger on for years. The efficiency of the Lucas dynamo was considerably improved in 1935 by the introduction of the 'ventilated' type of machine, which gave an increase in output of 25 per cent over a non-ventilated machine of equal physical size, owing to the improved cooling.

In his report to the board on his return Oliver Lucas set out his admiration for the American motor industry in terms that, read with hindsight, deserved to have been more widely publicised in 1935:

The value offered by the motor industry is quite outstanding, and though this is my fifth trip I am still quite unable to understand exactly how it is possible to produce such a lot of motor-car for so little money – and it must be remembered that the American motor-car is not a thing which can be laughed at from any point of view. The workmanship, care in design, and the terrific research organisations behind the three important manufacturers make the industry a very formidable competitor, and unfortunately there is not enough evidence to indicate that this state of affairs is fully appreciated by the manufacturers in England. I am not suggesting that the English manufacturers could successfully copy an American car for this market, but it does seem to me that the extent and thoroughness of the American organisations is insufficiently appreciated. As a result of this trip I shall be sending out some other engineers to follow up specialised lines of manufacture or design.

There was certainly one British car on the market at this time which caused people to wonder 'how it was possible to produce such a lot of motor-car for so little money,' and that of course was the Jaguar. It was William Lyons's policy to make his car look like a Rolls-Bentley and sell it for half the price. An essential ingredient of this formula was a pair of Lucas P100 headlamps as used by Rolls-Royce (for which Rolls-Royce paid the full price), and the negotiations that went on with Lucas to get them at the price Lyons could afford were long and intricate. A part of the compromise eventually reached was that they would carry a different medallion, which would distinguish them from the Rolls-Royce headlamps – if you looked close enough. Shortly after they appeared on the 1937 Jaguar saloon, Lyons was invited by Rolls-Royce to go up to Derby. Over lunch at the famous round table Ernie Hives quizzed Bill Lyons on how he made his Jaguar at the price. At the end of Lyons's explanation of his production costs and overheads Hives asked him with his twinkling smile: 'And what about the Lucas P100s?'

For some time Oliver Lucas had been campaigning for a change in the earthing of electrical systems on British cars from negative to positive, and in June 1935 he received powerful support in a report issued by the Institute of Automobile Engineers. The reasons they gave were that (a) battery terminal corrosion could be greatly reduced by earthing the positive instead of the negative battery terminal, and (b) a high-tension ignition spark of negative polarity would result in reduced wear (due to the burning of the spark central electrode and of the distributor rotating electrode), and also a lowering of plug gap breakdown voltage, with consequent less strain on

ignition components. At that time positive spark polarity was produced on a negative earth system by the coil design in use, and a
reversal to negative spark polarity could most easily be achieved by
changing to an earthed positive battery terminal.

Dr Watson told me: 'With negative earth we also had trouble with
corrosion in switchboxes and fittings due to the liberation under damp
conditions of nascent oxygen at the positive pole. The Americans, I
think, were divided, some negative, some positive – probably the
trouble was not so bad with 6-volts. The Continent generally earthed
the negative – certainly Bosch did. When we had the working agreement with Bosch in the early 1930s we discussed it with them but
they refused to change over. A lot of their cars were 6-volt, I remember.' Watson added that positive earth had another small advantage in
that the discharge voltage of a sparking plug was slightly lower when
the central electrode was negative, and as the primary and secondary
windings of the coil were in series, the conditions at the plug were
more favourable.

As a result of the combined onslaught of Oliver and the IAE, the
British motor industry adopted positive battery earthing in 1936. But
this was not to be the end of the story, as we shall see later.

At the Lucas board meeting in February 1936 Peter Bennett had
remarked that the increase in business which had lasted for three
years had 'temporarily come to a standstill.' A feeling of slackness
throughout the country had spread to most of the motor industry.
He pinpointed the Hoare-Laval pact to partition Abyssinia between
Italy and the Emperor as the event which had led to 'hesitancy in
certain quarters,' and he added: 'It is the feeling of uncertainty as to
what will happen in Europe that is much more responsible than either
the weather or the King's death for the hold-up we are now experiencing.'

The hold-up did not apply to the aero department at Rotax, which
was making rapid progress. By August 1936 its sales for the 1935–6
financial year had reached £188,308, compared with £88,784 in the
previous year and only £20,422 in 1933–4, when aircraft equipment
was included among the 'general sundries' made at Willesden. In
addition to continuing to make the Watford magneto for the Rolls-
Royce Kestrel and Bristol Jupiter aero-engines, Rotax had now developed new magnetos for the Rolls-Royce Merlin, the Bristol
Mercury, Pegasus, and Perseus, and certain smaller engines, such as
the Pobjoy Niagara V. Most of these magnetos embodied new
features – new magnetic circuits utilising the latest permanent magnets

of aluminium-nickel, such as Alneco and Alcomex, improved contact breakers and cams (tungsten contacts instead of platinum), and better lubrication of the cams and lever pivots.

So far wind-driven generators had been adequate for supplying electric power in aircraft, but they were inefficient and obstructed the smooth airflow over the airframe. This did not matter so much with biplanes like the DH84 and DH86 transports, but it became very important when designers turned to the monoplane. The time had therefore come to drive the generator from the engine instead of by a 'windmill', and the first engine-driven generator used in an aeroplane in Britain – and as far as is known in the world – was produced by Rotax in 1936 for the Pobjoy Niagara V engine, two of which powered the Monospar built by General Aircraft. It was the work of Ray Woodall, who was *de facto* chief designer as well as chief sales-man, such was the exiguous size of the Rotax staff at that time. Pobjoy provided a pad and a shaft running at the right speed to suit the generator, the gearbox for the drive being integral with the engine. The N2AO engine-driven generator of 150 watts output at 12 volts dispensed with the third-brush regulator and used the Tirrell, or vibrating contact regulator, so providing a constant voltage system.

The monoplane had shown its potentialities in 1934, when the de Havilland Comet, a racing aeroplane, had won the England–Australia air race. De Havilland had tried hard to get the Air Ministry to support the construction of a civil airliner incorporating the design philosophy of the Comet, but it was not until 1936 that the aircraft was ordered. It was called the Albatross, and five were put into service by Imperial Airways in 1938. Rotax did a substantial amount of work on the electrical system. In that year the Cadman Committee reported on the Empire's air transport policy, a subject which was causing much concern because of the Government's concentration on military aircraft for the rearmament programme and the consequent neglect of civil aircraft manufacture. The report recommended in-creasing subsidies for civil aviation from £1·5 million to £3 million, which encouraged de Havilland to put forward a project for a metal airliner that would be smaller than and complementary to the Alba-tross. (They had been chagrined to see British Airways buying American twin-engined airliners in the absence of any suitable British machine.)

The DH95, called the Flamingo because Captain de Havilland had admired flocks of these birds on a sales flight he had made recently to Kenya, was powered by two Bristol Pegasus 890hp sleeve-valve radial engines, and could seat up to twenty passengers with a crew of three. Rotax provided a comprehensive range of equipment for the Flamingo, including the first 500-watt air-cooled generator with voltage control by Tirrill regulator. (This became the standard generator in RAF fighters during the war, and was ultimately up-rated to 750 watts.) Another 'first' by Rotax in the DH95 was a landing lamp fitted to the underside of the wing and electrically extended and retracted. Rotax also played an important part in developing the control system of the de Havilland constant-speed propellers made under licence from the Hamilton company of the United States. Rotax starting and ignition equipment was used in the Bristol engines. Work on the Flamingo was begun early in 1938; it made its first flight on 28 December that year and was put into service by Jersey Airways in mid-July 1939, only 6½ months later – and two months before the outbreak of war.

Only sixteen Flamingoes were built. They were used by 24 Squadron RAF for transporting 'very important people' and by the newly formed British Overseas Airways Corporation. One of them was specially furnished and delivered to the King's Flight at Benson airfield.

Meanwhile Rotax had been supplying electrical equipment for the Handley-Page Hercules and Armstrong-Whitworth Atalanta airliners, used by Imperial Airways during the 1930s. Their most significant achievement in those pre-war years, however, was the engineering of the first high-capacity electrical system used in a British transport aircraft, the Short C-class four-engine flying boat, which entered service on the Empire routes of Imperial Airways in November 1937. The equipment was certainly the first complex installation in which Rotax took something like a systems responsibility, and comprised generators, magnetos, starters, batteries and other equipment. The demands for electrical power were far higher than anything previously experienced, and Ray Woodall designed a 1,000-watt 24-volt engine-driven generator with air-cooling to increase the power-to-weight ratio. (This was later uprated to 1·5kw at Farnborough and became the Rotax KX generator, which was used on most of the Bomber Command aircraft during the war. It was made by several sub-contractors, including GEC, using Rotax drawings.) The total value of business for the Air Ministry in the year ended August 1937 was £235,903.

The Eclipse hand and electric inertia starters were now being superseded by another product made under Bendix licence, the direct cranking electric starter, which was made in two types. The first was supplied in two sizes, a small one for the range of de Havilland Gypsy engines (and later the Alvis Leonides) and a larger one for the Bristol Pegasus. The second type was much bigger and was to be used on the Bristol Hercules sleeve-valve engine, which appeared in 1936. The Rotax engineers had now had time to develop an electric starter of their own design, the first engine to be fitted with it being the Pobjoy Niagara.

Rotax were also making under Bendix licence a small vacuum pump to operate gyro instruments, which enabled aircraft designers to dispense with the Venturi that was normally used for this purpose. And when several aircraft manufacturers decided to fit the Goodrich de-icing system, Bendix licensed Rotax to make a larger version of the pump, together with valves and other parts for the system, which consisted of rubber inflatable overshoes on the leading edge of the wing that broke up the ice when it had formed. (Later, during the war, porous metal overshoes were substituted to provide cable cutters to deal with barrage balloons, and these in turn gave way to electrical heating for de-icing and anti-icing.)

It might be asked why Rotax drew so heavily on Bendix licences. The reason was that they had a comparatively small aircraft design and development team at this period (though it was soon to be expanded), and it would have been impossible to finalise all the products for which licences had been taken in time to meet the needs of the aircraft industry if they had tried to design and manufacture them on their own. In that case the industry would have been forced to order the equipment direct from America. Besides, the engineering team were fully occupied in the design and development of generator systems and ignition work, and, as this resulted in most of the generator business and a large proportion of the ignition business being obtained by the company in the future, Rotax were able to enjoy the best of both worlds.

Rotax were called upon by Bristol to help cure the cooling troubles they were experiencing with their air-cooled Pegasus engine. It was proving difficult to balance the cooling requirements of stationary ground running and in-flight running, and it was proposed to make the louvres adjustable by means of an electric actuator. Rotax designed a small 3in motor driving into a 360:1 epicyclyic reduction, with its angular travel controlled by cam-operated limit switches. This marked the introduction of the electric actuator as a control mechanism. The British industry did not accept the relative complexity of this device to begin with, and it was left to Fokker in Holland to be the first to use it on their Pegasus-powered aircraft. The early switch mechanism did in fact give some trouble, and one of the company's first overseas service calls was made to Holland in June 1938.

Looking at all this work in progress, Lucas came to the conclusion that the time had come for Rotax to concentrate on aircraft equipment and be relieved of the miscellany of products they were still responsible for. Arrangements were made for the ex-ML mine-lighting equipment to be taken over by Davis of Derby and for the manufacture of electric tools to be done by CAV. The garage equipment and tools business was sold to Lancashire Dynamo and Crypto, who later formed the Crypton company, which continued to run it. The electric tools and the garage equipment were in highly competitive fields and did not mix easily with the more expensive and sophisticated aircraft equipment, which was not unnaturally given higher priority (more especially as the need for rearmament was being increasingly recognised). Not being allocated their own machine tools, the electric tools and garage equipment showed a loss. Most of the staff on the garage equipment side had become discontented, and they left to join the new owners in Somerset when the business was sold.

With hindsight it is possible to criticise the decision to dispose of this garage equipment business, which would have been useful after World War II to balance the ups-and-downs of the aircraft industry, but the circumstances of the sale, when the delayed expansion of British air strength was at last being given the highest priority, doubtless fully justified the decision taken at the time. The effect of these moves was that the aero department of Rotax became the whole of Rotax.

The tidying-up process was extended to other spheres of the Lucas business. In October 1936 the company's interest in Scott Insulated Wire was disposed of, and in the following month (as has been mentioned earlier) the manufacture of window-winding mechanism for Wilmot-Breeden was transferred to that company. The dual operation had never been very satisfactory, and, although there was a theoretical profit, it was generally thought that the company would be better off without this particular part of its turnover.

Down at Acton important changes in the Luvax business took place in 1936. Pitt had realised for some time that, although the original shock absorber had sold well (in the year ended 7 August 1933 sales had amounted to £225,825), the Houdaille hydraulic vane design was not ideal. He therefore designed an entirely different shock absorber, with horizontally opposed pistons displacing high viscosity oil and acting as an integral part of the suspension, which he patented jointly with the parent company in May 1936, along with an improved version of the vane type with a separate pump.

This was followed in 1936 by Oliver Lucas sending for John Morley, who had been Lucas's assistant service manager since 1930, and telling him: 'You've had plenty to say about our shock-absorber business from the service point of view; well, we're going to give you the opportunity of running the business and getting it right.' Morley was at once surprised, delighted and a little disconcerted at being imposed on a man who was much older than himself. In the event there was no friction, indeed the reverse, and Morley enthusiastically supported Pitt's new plans because he had seen the horizontally opposed piston-type shock absorber made by Delco-Remy in America, in which they went so far as to ensure the accurate fit of the pistons by using piston rings. In the next few years the old vane-type Luvax was phased out and the new model was fitted to most of the British volume-produced cars (except the small Fords, which had Armstrongs, and the Morris 8), most of the luxury cars (except the Rolls-Royce), and nearly all the commercial vehicles and buses.

In October 1936 a decisive point was reached in a lengthy investigation by Bendix at Birmingham to find a constant velocity joint which they could offer to the British Government for equipping four-wheel drive military vehicles. It had started a couple of years earlier when Charles Marcus of the Bendix Aviation Corporation in America had sent Oliver Lucas the drawings and details of the Weiss constant velocity ball joint, which they had bought, adding the suggestion that Lucas might be able to sell it to the British Government, who were believed to be contemplating building 4 × 4 vehicles for the Services. The Russians were also expected to be potential customers, because they were planning to build 10,000 four-wheel-drive vehicles a year for military and road construction work. 'OL' was not satisfied that the Weiss was the right answer, in spite of the US Government having chosen it in preference to the rival Rzeppa joint, which was even more expensive to make than the Weiss and did not provide for rolling end motion.

Captain J. S. Irving, the Bendix manager at Tyseley, reported to Oliver Lucas in October 1936 that the War Department, as well as Strassler and other vehicle manufacturers working with them, were all in favour of the Tracta joint, which had the same characteristics as the Weiss and could be made quite easily on machines already installed at the factory, whereas considerable investment would be required to make the Weiss. 'I have very thoroughly investigated the technical aspect of this particular unit,' he wrote, 'and consider it will meet the present requirements and will probably prove remunerative almost from the start. I am meeting M. Gregoire, the inventor, tomorrow for a preliminary discussion on his terms in the event of our finally deciding to take up the English rights for it.'

The situation was not without irony for Gregoire, because he had appointed the French Bendix company the exclusive licencee for the Tracta joint in France in 1933 and had tried to get the parent Bendix company in the United States to take up the licence there in 1934. But Bendix had just committed themselves to the Weiss joint, and would have nothing to do with the Tracta in America. Now Gregoire found himself doing a deal with Bendix in England. In his autobiography, *Best Wheel Forward*, he records: 'I was made most welcome by the chief, Captain Irving, and his commercial director Lane, and I signed a most satisfactory contract with them in 1937. They immediately contacted those British designers who were busy developing prototype cross-country vehicles.'

Dr Watson, who was spending 20 per cent of his time with Bosch at Stuttgart, noticed that there was no sign in Germany of 'the uncertainty as to what will happen in Europe' which Peter Bennett had referred to in February 1936. But he did notice a change in the atmosphere in which he and his other Lucas liaison colleagues were now working. In his *Memoirs* he records:

Initially we were free to visit all departments and talk to all and sundry. Later, as war work, particularly in the form of aircraft magnetos, took up more and more of the Bosch effort we were barred from certain departments or at least our freedom of discussion and inspection was curtailed.

In the year or two before the war there was little doubt that the German Government were exercising some control over the Bosch organisation and important members of the SA and even of the SS were in responsible positions there, but the general feeling of the people was markedly evident at a very large celebration held in Stuttgart in September 1936 to mark Herr Bosch's 75th birthday and the jubilee of the founding of the firm. A number of speeches were made in the large assembly hall by various local officials but their reception was entirely overshadowed by that given to Herr Bosch himself and also to Dr. Eckner, the head of the Zeppelin firm who was well-known throughout

Germany as a bitter opponent of Hitler but was so respected by his colleagues and workpeople that even the Government did not dare to touch him.

Robert Bosch showed his disregard of the Nazis by having a picture of himself on the front of the commemorative programme, instead of the usual portrait of the Führer. The jubilee of one of Germany's most famous companies was therefore boycotted by the Party leaders.

This was the time of the Spanish Civil War, which had erupted in July 1936 and in which Germany became secretly involved in spite of subscribing to the French plan of Non-Intervention, whereby the Spaniards were to be left to settle their differences without any outside help. In the spring of 1937, when the war was at its height, Bosch suddenly informed Joseph Lucas that they would like to dispose of their interest in CAV-Bosch. (In accordance with the agreement made when the company was formed, they were bound to offer their interest first to Joseph Lucas.) The motive for the Bosch action was not disclosed. Some people thought it was due to German Government pressure in order to obtain foreign exchange to pay for military expansion, but no proof of this has been produced. (In 1943 the Economic Section of the US Department of Justice produced their *Report on the Activities of Robert Bosch GmbH in the Fuel Injection Industry*, which gave detailed information about the agreements made by Robert Bosch with their associates abroad, including CAV-Bosch, but the sale of the Bosch interest to Lucas before the war was not mentioned.) Certainly the purchase – after long negotiations – of the 147,000 'B' shares in CAV-Bosch held by Industria Kontor, the Bosch associate company in Switzerland, for £249,000 involved another associate of Bosch in Holland as a third party. The sale of the CAV-Bosch interest was thus arranged outside Germany.

The agreement was signed in June 1937, but it was not regarded as the end of the relationship, and it was agreed that the technical and engineering co-operation, with patent interchange, should be continued for a long period ahead. (This payment-for-service basis was to last till the outbreak of war, when Lucas notified Bosch that they considered the agreement null and void and the name of the British company was changed to CAV Ltd. Bosch Ltd, the company established by Robert Bosch in 1924 to distribute Bosch products and taken over by CAV-Bosch when that company was formed in 1931, stayed as a subsidiary of CAV up to and throughout the war, being eventually sold back to Robert Bosch in 1954 for £25,000.)

In fact the high-sounding technical and engineering co-operation that was supposed to be continued between the two companies was proving to be something of a fallacy as far as fuel-injection equipment was concerned. That it could even be a handicap and have serious long-term consequences for Lucas was shown by two incidents involving Leyland Motors, which occurred at this time.

In 1937 Leyland were dissatisfied with the mechanical governor then in use for diesel engines and asked CAV to make a combined governor they had designed themselves, consisting of a small mechanical governor to look after maximum speed combined with a pneumatic or vacuum governor to regulate the idling and intermediate speeds. CAV thought the design was clumsy, so they produced an alternative, which by the terms of the agreement had to be approved by Bosch. Astbury told me:

> I spent many a frustrating discussion with Bosch design and development engineers, trying to persuade them that the design we wanted to put forward to Leylands was satisfactory. I was blocked at every turn; they would come back with specious arguments, with alternative designs that were no different from ours. The result was that at the end of 1938 Leyland said to CAV: 'We want a combined governor. Either you make our design, as you seem incapable of making any alternative suggestions, or we'll make it ourselves or get it made elsewhere.' This meant we had to take it on in order to safeguard the governor business, knowing that if we lost the governors they would probably make their own pumps as well; but we would have much preferred to make our own design, which we believe Leyland would have accepted.

Much the same thing happened with injectors. Leyland wanted CAV to make an injector of their own design, which was effectively the Gardner type with the needle in the body. 'Bosch wouldn't hear of it', said Astbury. 'They had recently introduced their own long-stem nozzle, which was detachable and included the valve, so we put up all sorts of alternatives to Leyland on these lines. In the end they said, in so many words, "To hell with you – CAV, Bosch, the lot of you – we'll make our own nozzles." They did, and still are – 35 years later – to the great loss of CAV.'

The technical agreement between Bosch and Lucas, it seemed, prohibited the manufacture of fuel-injection equipment designed by CAV-Bosch or CAV. Bosch genuinely believed that as the pioneers of the diesel injection pump they were the sole possessors of its technology. Their inflexible and sometimes arrogant attitude as the parent company towards their associate company in England was not lost on the young CAV engineers involved in these incidents, and they were able to avoid falling into the same trap when CAV in turn became the parent company of overseas associates in the years ahead.

The long-drawn-out negotiations with Auto-Lite at last came to an end in July 1937, when the two companies put their signatures to an agreement. The sum to be paid by Lucas was $50,000 a year, payable in quarterly instalments during the life of the agreement, which was three years. In return they got complete knowledge of and the exclusive right to use Auto-Lite machines, processes, patents and designs for the manufacture of ignition coils, distributors, starter motors and current-voltage control units. Auto-Lite were to keep Lucas informed of research and development by visits and exchanges of engineers. There were reciprocal arrangements for Auto-Lite to use any Lucas designs they wanted. Lucas were not allowed to manufacture the goods in question in North America, or to supply those goods except when they were parts of complete exported vehicles or replacements for Lucas equipment. Auto-Lite were similarly excluded from the United Kingdom. All this added up to a satisfactory arrangement from Lucas's point of view, because they had always wanted to know how to produce a smaller volume at prices equal to or lower than those current in America. Their materials would not cost any more, but now with the benefit of Auto-Lite production technique their labour would cost less. And the threat of Auto-Lite starting a factory in England was removed. All that was well worth $50,000 a year.

Production engineering was very much in their minds at this time. Lucas were already well aware of the benefits that could be obtained if only car manufacturers could be persuaded to use standardised electrical equipment instead of every company stipulating its own sizes and specifications, but as yet the industry gave no sign of accepting the idea. Nevertheless this was the basis of the development of production engineering by Lucas in 1936-7. Albert Siddall has told me what happened:

> The next logical step was to start a completely different philosophy of design and manufacture. We decided we would have standard products – one basic distributor for all the chief motor-cars – and instead of having the old system of shops laid out by types of processes (all the screw machines in one shop, all the presses in another) we began to lay them out by products. We had what we called our standard shops. We started in Great King Street on the dynamo and starter, all the major operations being done in one shop, brackets and yokes and so on right through on

line flow. Each manufacturing line was not completely automatic, not by far, and they weren't just devoted to one product, they worked to a range of products because people still insisted on variations from the basic design. We made three types of dynamo down one manufacturing line, making one machine one week, another machine another week, and so on. By and large it worked very well, and we were just thinking in terms of having standard shops for every product – that was our thinking at the time – when the preparations in the event of war breaking out forced us to postpone the whole idea.

What those preparations were will be told in the next chapter.

While plans were being made for the 1937 Motor Show, which was to be held at the new Earls Court exhibition hall for the first time, Oliver Lucas went off to America on 1 September on his annual visit. This time he took with him a comparative newcomer to the company, whom he thought would benefit from the experience. On leaving Cambridge University Eric Earnshaw had done a postgraduate apprenticeship with Reyrolle before joining Lucas in 1933. He was immediately singled out by Oliver Lucas and Bertram Waring as a man made for high responsibility. After a time in production control at Great King Street he was sent to Rotax in 1936 as production manager, where his enthusiasm for aviation (he was a pilot in the Auxiliary Air Force) immediately inspired the whole company. He was evidently being trained to succeed Benstead as general manager of Rotax when Benstead retired, though it is most unlikely that anything so positive was mentioned at the time.

In America Oliver Lucas and Earnshaw were able to make the most of the time available because H. E. Talbott, one of Walter P. Chrysler's right-hand men, placed his personal twin-engined Lockheed aeroplane at Oliver's disposal. They went first to the Bendix plant at Sydney, New York, where the Scintilla magneto was made; then to Trico, at Buffalo, where they found the suction screen-wiper still dominant; and on to Detroit to visit General Motors, whom Oliver described to Earnshaw as 'primarily engineers'. Fords were 'primarily manufacturers', and Chryslers 'primarily salesmen'.

What interested Oliver most at GM was that they had just gone over entirely to day work, which was a big change for them, as they had built their business on various forms of payment by results. The change had been introduced by the new president, Knudsen, who was originally with Ford, where day work had always been preferred to any method of payment by results. At Ford, where some preliminary work by Patrick Hennessy, the chief buyer at Dagenham, smoothed the Lucas path considerably, Oliver had a long talk with Edsel Ford about general conditions in America and England. Unfortunately Henry Ford was unable to see him because he had, ironically, fallen off his bicycle on the previous day and was rather badly shaken.

About his visit to Auto-Lite at Toledo, Ohio, Oliver remarked: 'This contact has become of increasing value to us as they have stepped right ahead in their development work and are now supplying most of the independent people including Chrysler.' His next call was at the Monroe Shock Absorber Company, Monroe, Michigan, where he saw the new telescopic direct-acting shock absorber they were making for Chrysler and others, and confirmed the arrangement they had recently made whereby Lucas became entitled to their designs and manufacturing information. In his report he added: 'Whether or not we shall be successful in introducing this type to the English market is somewhat doubtful, the reason being the difficulty of adapting this somewhat long shock-absorber to our small English cars. However, it has always been our policy to have as many associations and rights as is reasonably possible so that we are prepared whichever way the fashion or trend of design goes.' He then went on to Delco-Remy, where he was not sure of his reception because there had been a slight coolness (which will be explained later) between the two companies, only to find that this appeared to have been quite forgotten. 'I am at the moment,' he reported, 'trying to negotiate a licence with them for a special form of armature winding which I think will be to our advantage.'

At the Bendix factory at South Bend he had been preceded by a letter from Peter Bennett to Vincent Bendix stating firmly that the British company really ought to be offered back to Bendix (or to one of its licencees) or wound up. The Cowdray brake, for which some hopes had been held, was not a success, and they had had to fall back on the old Bendix servo brake 'with all its known defects'. Lockheed (Automotive Products) and Girling were outselling them, a position Lucas were not prepared to accept indefinitely. Oliver had a talk with Marcus, during which the idea of coming to some arrangement with Automotive Products was revived. As a result Marcus came over to England in December and meetings were held with Automotive Products to discuss an amalgamation of braking interests. Agreement was reached between Lucas and Automotive Products, and Marcus took the details back to America for Bendix Aviation Corporation to confirm them. Nothing more was to happen until the following spring.

Oliver Lucas took advantage of this trip to call at the laboratories of the Polaroid Company at Boston, with whom he had already reached an understanding for the sole rights of this material in Great Britain for use in motor-cars. With its property of converting ordinary light which is vibrating in all planes into light vibrating in one plane only, Polaroid seemed to be a potential answer to the dazzle problem, but in the words of his report, 'the practical means of carrying it into effect have not up to the present been available.' Meanwhile he was considering taking up the manufacture of a non-glare desk-lamp which Polaroid were developing.

The Lucas company put a lot of work into the idea of using polarised light for headlamps at this time. It had all started when Oliver Lucas met Professor Land, the brains behind Polaroid, and was immediately attracted by its possibilities. It seemed that it might enable cars to be driven with headlights full on without dazzling oncoming vehicles, and everybody would be able to see where they were going without any dipping or reduction in driving light. Bernard Scott, at that time his personal assistant, was told to organise some practical experiments with Dr Nelson, who had recently joined the company, and Nicholls the chief chemist. They fitted up two cars with Polaroid headlights, which gave a perfect anti-dazzle light when approaching each other, in spite of some fears that the effect would be spoiled when bumps deflected the beam. Just at that moment it was announced that Wheelwright, one of Professor Land's earlier associates, was to give a paper on polarised light at the 1937 annual meeting of the British Association for the Advancement of Science at Blackpool, so it was arranged for Scott, Nelson and Nicholls to go to the meeting and supplement the paper with a demonstration. Dr Watson also took Nelson to Stuttgart to see the experiments being conducted by Bosch, which turned out to be much the same as those at Birmingham, though on a larger scale. Both Bosch and Lucas were worried about the loss of light involved – in those days they had no means of getting a lot more power.

Oliver Lucas himself never gave up trying to sell the idea of polarised headlights. Bernard Scott recalls:

I had a little kit made up which pleased him enormously; it was a suit-case with all the necessary tricks and toys in it. We went to see the Minister of Transport, Alfred Barnes (this was a bit later, just after the War), and I was produced and told the story and did the demonstration. I can see Oliver now watching me like a hawk, waiting for the slightest pause or faltering on my part, when he would take up the thread and carry on. It was marvellous training for a young man.

To make the system less critical in operation, Lucas experimented with circular, or rotary, instead of linear polarised light, but this raised two questions. As Dr Nelson put it: 'What do you do with the filter? If you've got a toughened glass windscreen you've got to put the filter outside the screen, and a fixed filter doesn't appear to be the most satisfactory arrangement. Then, if you use spectacles, you have got to have a laminated windscreen.'

In the end it all proved abortive because of what Nelson called 'the politics of introduction.' Polarised headlights for cars would only work if everybody had them, so what would happen to the drivers of cars made before the system came into force? And then there was the dazzle that polarised headlights would cause to pedestrians, unless everybody wore spectacles.

The year 1937 was to prove eventful for Joseph Lucas on several fronts. The first development involved such widely different aspects of the company's business as Lucas service and the supply of carbon brushes for electrical equipment, and culminated in March in the acquisition of a promising Lucas agency called Globe & Simpson (Sheffield), Limited, which had five branches in the North of England. The firm had started in 1921 as small wholesalers of motor parts, including some electrical items. In the course of building up the business they began to distribute carbon brushes under their own trade name of 'Jumbo'. This would have been all right except for the fact that they described them in their catalogue as being made to Lucas specifications and identical to the brushes used in Lucas equipment. These 'genuine' brushes were offered at lower trade prices than the Lucas prices. The truth came out when Oliver Lucas challenged the suppliers, the Morgan Crucible Company, who admitted that they were supplying other firms in addition to Globe & Simpson with carbon brushes identical to the Lucas brushes at prices that enabled them to compete for the spare parts trade. Their defence was that this extra turnover allowed them to quote lower prices for the brushes used by Lucas for initial equipment, to which Lucas naturally retorted that it was unfair that the price advantage they enjoyed because of their volume should be used against them by 'pirate' spare parts competitors – and that in any case it was hardly the thing to supply brushes made as a result of their experience to other people.

On the face of it Morgan Crucible should have had the last word, because they were the sole suppliers of carbon brushes and Lucas could not get them anywhere else. Oliver Lucas's reaction was characteristic: he arranged for carbon brushes to be made in the electrical laboratory in Well Street. As soon as Morgan Crucible got to know this, they agreed not to supply Lucas-specification carbon brushes to the spare parts trade except through Lucas, unless special arrangements were made on price and conditions, both at home and abroad. This spelt the end of the 'Jumbo' carbon brush business for Globe & Simson, who very sensibly decided that 'if you can't beat them, join them' – and applied for a Lucas agency, giving up all 'pirate' parts activity in return. The move paid handsomely and they became enthusiastic Lucas agents. After a time they needed bigger premises with workshops and service facilities, and they found the extra capital required to build them in West Street, Sheffield, on the latest Lucas main depot lines.

Jack Masterton represented Lucas at the trade lunch following the official opening, at which the directors said they hoped their new premises would make it unnecessary for Lucas to open their own depot in Sheffield. Masterton agreed that this might indeed be un-necessary, because they could perhaps buy Globe & Simpson instead. Mr Duffy, the managing director, and his colleagues seized on the suggestion, provided they could continue to run the business. And so, very quietly and entirely through nominees, so that no one should get to know about it, the deal went through, Lucas buying the 29,671 £1 shares in Globe & Simpson at 43s 7d a share for £64,768. In November 1937 Lucas transferred the shares of County Electrical Services (which by now had thirteen depots) into Globe & Simpson, which became the holding company of the various subsidiaries. In order to preserve the secrecy of the operation, it was given the code name Spares Distribution within the Lucas organisation, though it was in fact a part of the Sales & Service Company, which controlled the Lucas depots and official agents. Spares Distribution continued to expand because of a clause in the Lucas agency agreement which prevented the Lucas agency being sold with an agent's business except with Lucas's approval. When agents got into difficulties, or wanted to retire, they approached Lucas about their agency, and Globe & Simp-son were given the chance to acquire the whole business. Between 1937 and 1939 Express Magneto (Repairs) and Electrical Co (later Express Electrical Services) and Irvine Electrical Services, both with several branches, were acquired in this way.

Another radical change in Lucas service arrangements – this time widely publicised instead of being kept secret – occurred when a solution was found to the long-standing dissatisfaction about the charges for repairing Lucas electrical units, whether by the factory or by electrical specialists. The trouble was caused partly by the basis of assessing the charges of repairs and partly by the time taken to get reports on defects and estimates of the cost of repairs. A flat rate was tried without success, and in 1937 Lucas were approached by the Motor Agents' Association to see whether some remedy could be found. Discussions went on for the rest of the year, and it was not until January 1938 that the Lucas B.90 Factory Exchange Service was introduced (B.90 stood for the section of the ledgers and the page number in which the scheme was recorded). Lucas supplied a range of factory-rebuilt units in exchange for worn or damaged units handed in by users at fixed nett prices for wholesalers, retailers and users. This put an end to all argument about individual repairs and saved an enormous amount of correspondence. The items covered by the scheme were distributors, magnetos, dynamos, starter motors, current-voltage control units, horns, direction indicators and armatures for dynamos and starter motors. A special discount was later introduced for fleet operators. The B.90 scheme, including the work of reconditioning the worn or damaged units, was carried out by the Sales & Service Company, whose main business continued to be selling equipment and accessories for the replacement market.

Alderman Sayer told the August 1937 board meeting that this was the last time he would preside, as he would be retiring at the end of the month after 17 years' service. And so, on 23 December, Peter Bennett was elected chairman, Oliver Lucas became deputy chairman, and Alderman S. J. Grey was elected a director to fill the vacancy caused by Sayer's retirement. (In 1914, when Thomson-Bennett was purchased, Peter Bennett had confided to Jack Smith, his foreman at the little works in Cheapside, that he would never be happy till he was head of Joseph Lucas. Now, after 23 years, he had realised his ambition.) Peter Bennett marked his appointment as chairman by starting a Hard Luck Fund for the workpeople, with a personal contribution. This fund was to prove a great benefit to those suffering from hardships beyond their control, and was always associated with his name. In 1937, too, a pension scheme for the men in the works was drafted, using as a basis of the fund the £90,000 that had accumulated over the years from amounts voted by the board for staff welfare purposes. The same year saw the start of holiday pay being paid entirely by the employers as the result of an agreement between the employers' federation and the trade unions, so the Lucas August Holiday Fund was converted into a fund for pay-outs at Christmas, Easter and Whitsun provided by the workpeople's contributions.

At Formans Road, where by 1937 extensions to the battery factory had reached the point when the fields and allotments surrounding the original works had almost disappeared, health was always a major concern. But the medical arrangements kept pace with the bigger scale of operations. The one (old) visiting doctor was replaced by a full-time (young) doctor, and the one VAD nurse by a day and night shift of state registered nurses. A dental surgery was provided, with free dentistry for all the lead workers, and regular blood-tests were started. This enabled any cases of lead-absorption by the workpeople to be discovered before any harm was done to their health, and they were immediately transferred to non-lead work. Consequently lead-poisoning was practically unknown. The latest car battery now had an improved container, with reinforced partitions and a prismatic acid level indicator, both introduced in 1936.

And now an altogether novel sound – music – began to be heard in a Lucas factory for the first time during working hours. The idea was put forward from various quarters and Bertram Waring took it up. But he acted very cautiously: it was to be tried out first in F6, where the workpeople were mostly women, who were to be asked if they would like it for, say, half-an-hour in the morning and afternoon, and he insisted that it was not to be put over as a management idea. Podbury was told to wire up the shop, and records were obtained from the canteen. Waring, ever the accountant, also gave instructions that output statistics were to be compiled before the idea was put into effect, and comparative figures taken afterwards, all this being done confidentially. In this way 'music at work' arrived at Great King Street in the closing months of 1937. (It was not until nearly three years later, on 23 June 1940, that the BBC began to broadcast their 'Music while you work' radio programme as a war-time stimulus to productivity.)

CHAPTER FIVE

THE RUN-UP TO WAR

For many people in the Lucas organisation life became somewhat ambivalent in 1938 and 1939 as the company strove to maintain its peacetime business in the face of the recession caused by the increasing threat of war, which nevertheless brought with it the possibility of big orders from the Government. At the board meeting held on 21 June 1938 Bennett reported that: (a) sales were down to the level of 1934–5, (b) the total number of employees had dropped to 17,031, compared with 20,026 at the beginning of the year, (c) the Luvax factory was in the throes of introducing the Monroe-design piston-type shock absorber (the first customer being the Citroen assembly plant at Slough), and (d) 'Needless to say, if the present European crisis continues much longer the figures will be affected much more seriously, and in the event of war, car production at least will come to a stand-still temporarily.'

In these circumstances a statement by Oliver Lucas at the same meeting did not make the impact it might have done in normal times. It was that the time had come when the resignation of his father should be placed in the hands of the board, to take effect from the end of the current financial year in August. Even then Harry Lucas, now aged 83, was not to lose all contact with the company, and at the August meeting he was duly retained as consultant. His place on the board was filled by F. H. Walker, joint general manager, who brought the number of executive directors up to four.

In July a new aircraft department was started at Great King Street to carry out sub-contract work for Austin. This was primarily for an order for 450 sets of equipment for the Fairey Battle single-engined bomber, each set comprising instrument, lighting, starting and bomb panels, ammunition box and crate for accumulator and dynamo, and wireless trays. Perhaps it should be explained that this order was undertaken by Lucas, instead of being given to Rotax, because the metal-work it entailed was more suited to the Great King Street factory. Rotax were now beginning to produce several components for the new Bristol Hercules engine, designed for the big bombers that were on the way for the RAF. These were an electric starter based on a Bendix design, a geared 24-volt motor to operate the opening and closing movement of the cowl gills, and various new types of switchgear.

At the end of July 1938 Lord Halifax said in Parliament: 'I do not believe that those responsible for the Government of any country in Europe today want war,' whereas a month later Winston Churchill was warning his constituents: 'I must tell you that the whole state of Europe and of the world is moving steadily towards a climax which cannot long be delayed.' The climax – and the anti-climax – came at the end of September with the tragedy of Czechoslovakia, Munich and Chamberlain's 'peace with honour – I believe it is peace in our time.'

For Lucas that period of emergency (mobilisation orders were issued by the Admiralty to the Fleet on 28 September) meant no more than a slight drop in output while everyone concentrated on air-raid precautions and kindred matters, including the assembly, boxing and distribution of 115,657 civilian gas masks. Under Garner's guidance preparatory work was now going on at Great King Street for making sub-assemblies of the wing sections of the Spitfire fighter, which it was intended to produce at a new 'shadow' factory being built at Castle Bromwich. This factory, which was to be managed by the Nuffield Organisation, was designed for making aircraft with semi-skilled labour by batch production methods, instead of using highly skilled individuals making single aircraft, as had been the practice up till now. The Lucas process planning department was ideally suited to this project, as Albert Siddall has told me: 'We tackled this quite big job with confidence basically on the same lines that we had developed for our own products. It was the first example of modern press shop methods and techniques being used for aircraft manufacture, so much so that eventually we were up to 100 sets of wings a week, which would be fantastic even by today's standards.'

The combination of Fred Garner and Albert Siddall now began to have a greater influence on the development of the company than was perhaps realised at the time. Garner, still part Bedaux/part Lucas, had virtually become Oliver Lucas's adviser on process planning and its consequences, which meant what processes should be used, what machinery should be bought, even what type of buildings should be built. He confined himself to policy and planning, leaving the execution to Siddall, who by now had become head of the process planning department. These two worked in perfect concert, Garner encouraging Siddall in all his executive decisions and Siddall being

able to lean on Garner to get Oliver Lucas's support for his manufacturing plans, for 'OL' was by this time deeply preoccupied with the
wider issues of company policy.

The incident that perhaps did more for Garner's reputation in the
eyes of Oliver Lucas than anything else had recently occurred. Oliver
was worried about the battery factory at Formans Road. From what
he knew of American methods, it was still backward in manufacturing
technique, in spite of the steps taken over the years to improve it. So
on 16 February 1938 he asked Garner to suggest what should be done,
adding that anything less than doubling the productivity (though he
did not use the word productivity, because it had not yet come into
fashion) would be regarded as failure. Garner recalls:

I went and looked at it all, and I must say it looked very Ancient Britain-
ish. And oh, the health hazards, I thought they were shocking. I saw
people working over lead dust, and I thought these people ought to be
remote, they ought not to be there. And then when I saw them with
asbestos, shredded asbestos, and they were tipping it out of bags ...
One section reminded me of the *sakias* I'd seen in Egypt where camels
go round and round and pump water for irrigation, only here men
mixed tons of lead oxide paste with shovels and then pushed it round
with their shoulders.

After that I walked across the road into a little park, sat down on a
bench and thought about it for a bit, running my shoes over the bare
earth where the grass had worn away. I thought I'll have to resign from
Bedaux – certainly withdraw from Lucas – because I can't possibly do
what Oliver Lucas wants me to do.

And then I thought of all that tonnage and the way it was being
handled and I thought well now, back at Brunner Mond we wouldn't
have seen this stuff, in the heavy chemical industry you don't see people
handling all this tonnage – hundreds of tons of lead a week – it would
have been mechanised. That was the ICI approach. It was only common
sense.

I went into that park every day for about a week and in the end I decided I'm damned if I'm going to resign – I'm not going to give in to
this one. What I did was to work out how many men it should take to
make so many batteries. You see, I was no good at work study – I
never could work out time and a third at 4½d. an hour. At the end of
about three months I said if we did this, that and the other we could make
a 6-volt, 11-plate battery equivalent (that was the standard in those days)
in 23 minutes direct time. Then I asked the Lucas people to come round
and find out how long it took to make a battery at Formans Road, and
after a time they said it takes 58 minutes. And do you know for the life

322

of me I couldn't tell whether I was home and dry or not at first. Eventually I decided that 23 minutes was a bit less than half of 58 minutes, so I sent my report in to Oliver Lucas.

Of course Garner gave a copy of his report to the three Formans Road people concerned – Robert Young, Andrew Black and John Merrick – and they wrote a criticism of it. Then a deal was made. 'We'll let your report stand if you'll get it back from 'OL' and make a recommendation that we should go to America to study the latest production techniques,' they said. Fortunately Oliver Lucas was away, so Garner got the report back from Miss Parks, attached a memorandum with the agreed request – and was summoned to 'OL's' presence. He had the report in his hand as Garner entered. 'Why do I have to read down to the third line before I get the answer I want?' he snapped. But he went on to agree with Garner's recommendation for the three from Formans Road to go to America – 'providing you go with them.'

At the factories they visited they developed a team technique of getting the information they wanted. Merrick would ask about production figures, expressing such incredulity that he was given details of the weekly output. Garner would follow up with innocent comments about the number of people employed, in this way extracting the exact payroll from the proud Americans. By dividing one set of figures into the other and averaging the number of 13, 11 and 9 plate batteries, they found that at the first factory the answer was 58 minutes – exactly the same as at Formans Road. Another was 57, others a little lower, but when they got to Exide, the really big company, the figure dropped to the twenties and was repeated at the Ford Motor Company's battery factory. Their last visit was to the General Motors battery factory at Delco-Remy, and there the time taken to make the equivalent battery was found to be 23 minutes – much to Garner's relief. On their return to England the reorganisation of battery manufacture at Formans Road was put in hand.

As the main suppliers of fuel-injection equipment for diesel-engined vehicles, CAV were called upon by the vehicle manufacturers and the Service Ministries to tackle the problem of starting them in extremely cold conditions – a problem that had been an anxiety for some time. (It was later to become acute in 1941, when Germany invaded Russia and Winston Churchill promised every possible aid – including trucks – to the hard-pressed Soviet army.) The fuel-injection equipment engineers at Acton gradually built up a technique of cold starting which worked satisfactorily in temperatures as low as minus 40 degrees. It was based on the use of ether stored in sealed capsules like soda-water Sparklet bulbs (in fact they were made by the same company and were called Etherlets), in conjunction with a special carburettor made by the Zenith and Solex companies. The starting procedure began with puncturing the capsule with a simple piercing drill that allowed the ether to flow to the carburettor, which then metered the amount of the flow of ether to the engine as it was simultaneously cranked. Initial firing took place, and then, by means of a butterfly in the air intake, it was possible to control the engine until it could accelerate and take off on its own fuel injection.

Until a cold room could be built at Acton, the experiments were made in a cold room at the Institution of Automobile Engineers' research laboratory at Brentford (the forerunner of the MIRA research centre at Nuneaton), and in the cold room at Great King Street, where Ralph Barrington's long experience of cold starting petrol engines was invaluable. An essential part of the whole programme was to produce a starter motor and a battery that could crank the big truck engines at these extremely low temperatures. From 1935 onwards John Merrick and his men at Formans Road had spent most of their time working for the War Office, and in the end they produced a battery that was superior in performance to the batteries of the other suppliers.

By the summer of 1939 Merrick realised that the battery manufacturers would be in a much better position to meet the demands that were likely to be made on them in the event of war breaking out – as seemed almost certain by now – if they combined their technical resources. He put the idea to Oliver Lucas, who replied without hesitation: 'All right, if you know the Chloride boys well enough see if you can form a technical committee.' And so Chloride (Exide), Oldham, and Pritchard & Gold (Dagenite) joined with Joseph Lucas in starting a technical committee which, as Merrick recalls, 'produced a really marvellous battery, so much so that in the early part of the war when the Americans were becoming quite involved they asked for our technique and we gave it to them.'

While these warlike activities were going on, the new factory at Shaftmoor Lane, Birmingham, where all lamp manufacture was to be concentrated, got into production. Planning the layout of this new plant gave the Lucas engineering staff the opportunity to put into practice the latest ideas on production engineering, including the use of overhead conveyers on a really comprehensive scale for the first time. Headlamp design had just taken an entirely new turn in the United States, but it was still too early to say whether the change would spread to Europe. On his visit to America in 1937 Oliver Lucas had brought back with him an experimental 5¾in headlamp called a sealed beam, in which the glass reflector (incorporating the filaments) was fused with the front lens to make an all-glass sealed unit. This device had been developed by General Electric, who held the master patents. At that time American cars had annual model changes and a special headlamp for each model; the lamps were expensive and they were bad, because they were made to an old specification and the various States interpreted them differently. The cost of service was appalling – there were plenty of bulbs but headlamp lenses were expensive to replace and the whole lamp (after a crash) even more so.

A co-operative engineering exercise was put in hand between the leading car manufacturers and the bulb-makers (chiefly General Electric, who had a big headlight division). The advantages of the sealed beam unit were standardisation of the product from the purchasing point of view, standardisation of the light pattern, and of course the economy of production resulting from standardisation. The Americans had another more subtle reason for wanting to change their headlamp design: it would enable them to move from the specification which had controlled their headlights for some 10 years. The sealed beam unit allowed a specification to be used that could not be achieved with a replacement bulb unit, so they would be able to upgrade the specification in a very big step.

The Americans intended that the use of the sealed beam unit should be tried out at first on the expensive cars – the Cadillac, the Lincoln, and the Chrysler Imperial – which seemed to be a logical move. Then the Chevrolet division of General Motors – the biggest selling make – upset the plan by announcing that they too wanted the sealed beam headlamp and were determined to have it. That meant that nobody could be left out, so the new unit went more or less right across the board in the model changes for 1939. There was barely time for Joseph Lucas and the British car manufacturers to realise the implications of this change before more serious events intervened.

The car market was holding up quite well, the Lucas share of the business being mostly dynamos and starters, which accounted for 56 per cent of the profit of the total contract sales of equipment for cars and light commercial vehicles. New machinery was ordered to make the latest type of two-leading-shoe Bendix brake at Tyseley. Free-of-charge service was now costing the company much less, largely due to a welcome improvement in the quality and performance of its products as a result of the measures taken in recent years. Service was highly organised, with four area headquarters operating in London, Glasgow, Sheffield and Manchester. Sales Distribution alone had thirty-three depots under its control.

The motor-cycle business had gone down heavily, but it began to pick up again in the spring of 1939, when BSA and Norton started getting orders from the Government for service machines. Before that, Jack Sangster's two companies, Ariel and Triumph, were between them taking over a third of Lucas's total motor-cycle component deliveries, and together with BSA (who were making a 250cc model with coil ignition) accounted for 65 per cent of the business.

Unhappily the cycle trade was doing badly, the Lucas business being only £108,911 for the nine months to May 1939, compared with £207,428 three years previously. Sales of the cycle dynamo set had suffered a blow from the decision of Raleigh, the cycle manufacturers, to produce a hub-dynamo set of their own. The idea of incorporating a dynamo in the hub was not new; Bosch had made one several years earlier and Lucas had considered it; but both had turned it down because it cost more to do less than the tyre-driven dynamo, though the latter was admittedly noisy and was liable to be stolen. The subsequent story of the hub dynamo, as told by Masterton, finds a convenient place here:

> The Miller company decided to make hub dynamos but the Raleigh company promptly took action for infringement of the patent, which action went right through to the House of Lords and Millers lost. It is interesting to recall that Lucas produced a few hub dynamos at the request of BSA (this was in 1940) and although neither Lucas nor BSA intended to go on with the scheme, some bicycles with Lucas hub-dynamo sets were sold to the public so that the invoices could be given to Raleigh who had made some rather objectionable threats, and it was decided to call their bluff. They were however too wary to get drawn into conflict with Lucas and pursued Millers alone.

Lucas refused to join in a price-cutting war with Ever Ready and Millers over the price of cycle lamp batteries, which they cut from 2s 6d to 1s 9d for a time, until they realised their folly and put them back again to half-a-crown. Lucas were still selling oil and acetylene lamps for bicycles, but mostly from stock as the models were withdrawn or exhausted. Bells, cyclometers and reflectors were the other

main cycle accessories, but bells had never recovered from the
Hercules decision to fit them as initial equipment. Masterton's
Historical Note on the subject reads:

> It caused dealers to sell other makes of bicycles with a bell, and they were
> in the market for the cheapest bells they could buy. This caused an influx
> of cheap bells from Germany and Japan, and eventually Woolworths
> were selling bicycle bells at 6d. each retail, from which it was obvious
> the Japanese must be selling bells below the cost of the basic materials.
> They also started selling cheap dynamo sets. This was having an effect on
> the Lucas cycle business, so the writer decided to apply to the Govern-
> ment for tariff protection, in which he was successful.

The duties, which were alternative to the existing duty of $33\frac{1}{3}$ per
cent, were 3d on each bell, 2s 6d on dynamo sets and 2s on dynamos.
By this time it was estimated that the organised British national and
regional cycling clubs had about 120,000 members.

But the emphasis was continually shifting to Government work in
all the group's companies. The Lucas factories were supplying electrical equipment for Morris and Commer military vehicles, batteries for
the RAF, signalling lamps, landing lamps for the Air Ministry, and
engine parts for Armstrong-Siddeley, while preliminary arrangements were being made to produce the centre section of a Westland
fighter and aeroplane gun-turrets for Boulton & Paul. Rotax, already
making magnetos, starters, generators and other aircraft equipment,
were producing vacuum pumps for instrument operation and air
compressors which had previously been imported from Eclipse in
America. CAV were making most of the electrical and/or fuel-
injection equipment for heavy military vehicles, tanks, troop and Bren
carriers, scout cars, tank landing craft, rescue launches, submarines,
and a large variety of marine and stationary engine applications.
Rist Wires & Cables were turning out vast quantities of telephone
cord, and Bendix were producing brakes for military vehicles.

On 1 March 1939 Joseph Lucas, Limited, were honoured by their
first visit from Royalty. By now the threat of war had drawn so close
that every royal occasion became an outlet for expressions of fervent
patriotism, and the visit of Queen Elizabeth to the main Lucas factory
was no exception. The buildings were lavishly draped with banners
and streamers; the columns at the entrance to Great King Street were
decorated with portraits of the King and Queen; and the bridge was
surmounted by a huge replica of the crown, orb and sceptre above
the words 'In Loyal Tribute'. The shops were profusely decorated by

the workpeople themselves and transformed into what a local news-paper inevitably described as 'a veritable fairyland'.

Arrangements for the manufacture of war equipment in 'shadow' factories were now being made on a large scale, and in May it was the turn of Lucas to be approached by the Government. It had become urgently necessary to duplicate the supply of fundamental aircraft equipment being produced by Rotax at Willesden (where the factory had been rebuilt and enlarged) but the Lucas factories at Birmingham were considered to be unsuitable as an alternative because of their vulnerability to air attack. A new, partly equipped factory built by the British Sewing Machine Company at Merthyr Tydfil in South Wales had become available, and Lucas agreed to take it over on a rental basis, any capital expenditure being safeguarded by Govern-ment guarantee. The factory was to be run by Rotax and was ex-pected to get into a reasonable flow of production by February or March 1940. The full production capacity would be about three-quarters of the present Rotax capacity, with an approximate sales value of between £500,000 and £600,000 a year. Meanwhile a con-siderable amount of experimental work was being done by Rotax on aircraft components, including a 24-cylinder magneto suitable for new Rolls-Royce and Napier aero-engines and a cartridge starter which the Air Ministry were showing some interest in – an interest that was not shared by the aero-engine manufacturers. De-icer equip-ment, with all its technical difficulties, was also being investigated. The electric tool business transferred from Rotax to CAV was now being run by a new subsidiary called the Acton Tool Company.

But the peacetime development of the company still had to go forward. By the summer of 1939 the Bendix brake business at Tyseley had reached the end of the road. Communication on the Lockheed project had been resumed in the spring of 1938, but while letters and cables were crossing the Atlantic a new Bendix hydro-mech-anical brake had been produced at Tyseley and was shown at the London Motor Show in October 1938. This was followed by an offer from Rover to exploit an improvement to hydraulic brakes which Lucas were anxious to adopt. An argument then broke out about Lucas having to pay royalties on their new brakes to Bendix Aviation Corporation in America. Finally, in a letter to Marcus on 8 May 1939, Oliver Lucas agreed that there were only two choices worth con-sidering: 'We sell out or, alternatively, buy your present holding.' Rather to Lucas's surprise Bendix accepted the alternative in June. (As Masterton wrote later in his Note on the subject: 'Possibly Bendix were influenced by the imminence of war. Many Americans believed England would lose and were anxious to realise any assets in England.') It was not until November, two months after the outbreak of war, that the Bendix Aviation Corporation actually sold their 40,000 £1 shares in Bendix, Ltd, to Joseph Lucas for £108,266.

The talks with Bendix were carried on by Oliver Lucas in an atmosphere of gathering storm. Peter Bennett, as a member of the National Advisory Council on Rearmament, had become wholly occupied with Government work in London and was not even able to spare the time to attend the monthly board meetings. This council had been formed in 1938 to advise the Prime Minister on whether they were satisfied that rearmament was being pushed forward as fast as possible. It was a high-powered team of eminent and competent men, and Peter Bennett was invited to join it both as chairman of Joseph Lucas and chairman of the Federation of British Industries (the forerunner of the present-day Confederation of British Industries). The other members were Mr Marquis of Lewis's (later Lord Woolton), Sir Andrew Duncan and Sir Cecil Weir.

Then, on the fine Sunday morning of 3 September, the Member of Parliament for the Edgbaston division of Birmingham broadcast on the radio the announcement that 'this country is at war with Germany'.

*   *   *

When the sombre words of the Prime Minister, Neville Chamberlain, brought the 20 years of peace between the wars to a close, Joseph Lucas, Limited, were very different from what they had been at the beginning, and so too was the motor industry, which was by far their largest customer.

The 100 or so British car manufacturers who exhibited at the 1920 Motor Show had dwindled to about twenty in 1939, and of these the 'Big Six' – Austin, Ford, Morris, Rootes, Standard and Vauxhall – were producing nearly 90 per cent of all the cars made. The 100,000 cars on the road after World War I had grown to about 2,000,000 by the time World War II broke out.

As for Lucas, their growth can best be summarised by comparing the figures in 1920 and 1939 for various aspects of their activity, disregarding any minor variations in between – for the trend was always upwards:

	1920	1930	1939
Issued Capital	£700,000	£1,222,800	£2,208,100
Profit	£57,844	£232,995	£352,480
Sales	£1,331,658	£4,828,363	£9,104,138
Dividend (Ordinary)	10% plus 5%	15% plus 2s	15%
Employment (approx)	3,000	8,000	20,000

To sum up, with three times the amount of issued capital, the sales had increased sevenfold and the profit was sixfold. The number of people employed had grown at roughly the same rate as the sales and profit. Only the rate of dividend remained virtually unchanged.

The company's position as the leading makers of motor-car lighting, starting and ignition equipment was unchallenged, being firmly based on the supply of these items as initial equipment for the vast majority of cars produced in Britain (during the peak period of 1937-8 Lucas's average output of this initial equipment was 9,100 sets a week). In the much smaller commercial vehicle field Lucas, with their CAV subsidiary, were the predominant suppliers of lighting, starting, ignition and fuel-injection equipment, while Rotax were making great strides in the supply of components to the growing aircraft industry as the Government belatedly made its preparations against the event of war.

HARRY LUCAS PASSES ON

The minutes of the board meeting held on 24 March 1939 began with a simple underlined statement:

Mr. Harry Lucas died 12th March

Although he was retained as consultant after his resignation from the board in the previous August, the old man's contacts with the company had become increasingly tenuous. His death at the age of 84 was a solemn moment in the company's history, for it severed the last direct link with the founder and the company's formative years as Joseph Lucas & Son.

Since his retirement from executive service in 1923, 'Mr Harry' – 'The Guvnor' – had not failed to attend the factory regularly in his position as consultant director. He had a small office, always with a coal fire burning, winter and summer, next to Slade the registrar, who looked after him generally and kept him supplied with pens, which he always lost. He spent much of his time wandering round the offices and shops, talking to people with the help of a pencil and writing pad for their replies. Herbert Astbury remembers the day when, as a young man, he was working in the electrical laboratory in Well Street and Harry Lucas came over to him as he was testing one of the first Lucas high-frequency horns, which was under development at that time (this was the Alto, so the date must have been 1927). 'He asked me what I was doing, so I gave him my written answer. He smiled, touched his ears, shook his head and then patted his tummy, indicating that he could feel the sound there.' It was unsafe to take advantage of his deafness, however, because he was an expert lip-reader and had a disconcerting habit of taking up remarks that people assumed he had not heard.

Harry's deafness could be quite alarming to young people who were not used to the technique of conversing with him. Bill Shaw (who later became chief buyer) remembers a Tuesday morning soon after he joined the company as a boy after World War I when Harry Lucas, whom he had not seen before and did not know, came into the office where Shaw was sitting on a high stool. Harry asked, 'Where's Barnes?' (his boss) and Shaw said he had gone to the Mint.

From the look on the old man's face Shaw immediately sensed that he had not heard him.

> I went up, put my two hands by his ear, and got my fingers in his whiskers. He grabbed my wrists and pushed them down with a growl. 'Don't do that, speak to me properly', he said, so I shouted out my reply again at the top of my voice. He went out and I asked my immediate chief, 'Who's the old chap with a beard?' When he told me, 'That's Harry Lucas' I thought that's finished me for a start.
>
> Well, on the Thursday morning I'm coming down the old office (before F Block was built) with a letter under my arm, and being in a cheerful mood I walked with a bit of a roll. At that moment I saw the old boy coming through the door towards me and imitating my roll exactly. Do you know, he was my man from that moment, and I never altered my opinion – I often said he set the spirit of Lucas.

On one of his walks he beckoned Coe, the general office manager, and said, 'Who's that chap standing there?' 'That's Mr. Casson, the stationery buyer,' answered Coe. 'Tell Mr. Waring he ought to be sacked straight away', Harry Lucas said. 'Whenever I see him he's just lounging about talking.' Coe explained on the writing pad that this was because they had no waiting room and the top of the stairs was the only place Casson could interview travellers. Harry Lucas grunted and marched off to Waring's office. Within a fortnight they had their waiting room. As a good Victorian, he deplored the wasteful habits of modern times, and on his walks round the factory and offices he used to encourage people to untie the knots of parcels instead of cutting the string, and save paper and envelopes so that they could be used again.

Having built up the finances of the early business for his father, Harry continued to keep a close watch on the money. For many years he insisted on signing all the company's cheques, batches of several hundred at a time being taken to his office by a lad named Tooze. Mr Tooze, now retired, has told me how he had to wait for two or three days until they were all signed. Signing the cheques gave him a picture of what was going on in the factory. One day he paused at a cheque in payment for a supply of wood-wool and asked Tooze where the wood-wool was kept. 'In the new packing department, sir,' replied Tooze. 'Right, let's go and see it,' said Harry. Tooze has told me what ensued:

> In the packing department he asked the manager to open several bales of

the stuff on the floor. He then gave him and his staff a long and what they thought was a boring lecture on the danger of fire, fiddling all the time with a little silver matchbox on the end of his watch chain. Suddenly he struck a match and dropped it in the wood-wool, which immediately went up in flames. But he had taken good care to do this in a place where the surrounding floor was empty, so there was no real danger. Everybody dashed for the fire buckets, while Mr. Harry took my arm and said, 'Come along, young man, that's better than all the talking.'

Occasionally he would wander into Bertram Waring's office and ask how things were going. 'I used to say, "Oh, we did a turnover of so much last week",' Sir Bertram recalled. 'No, that's not what I mean,' the old man would mutter. 'What have we got in the bank?' – this with a trace of 'Brummagem' in his voice. 'And if it was less than a million pounds he didn't think much of it,' Sir Bertram added. 'If it was over a million we could go on for another week.'

He also liked to know about the cash, as well as what was in the bank, as Fred Coleman remembers:

On Monday mornings Harry Lucas used to walk very slowly down to the far office, the cashier's office, and ask for the cash balances as at the week-end of CAV, Rotax and other subsidiary companies and outlying departments that handled cash. This was given to him on a single half-page of quarto paper. He then used to chat about the smallness or largeness of the balances. It was his way of knowing what the state of the company was, and was a relic of the early days when he ran the business more or less single-handed at Great King Street. It didn't matter that it had no relevance in modern times.

Peter Bennett had a very high regard for Harry's financial judgement, while Oliver depended on his father's long experience in handling the problems of patent registration and validity, until Dr Watson took this task over in the 1930s as a part of his duties as chief engineer.

Harry inherited Joseph's love of the apt quotation or saying, and he used to copy them out and send them to Waring (himself a collector of texts and extracts) in the form of little hand-written notes. Sir Bertram showed me one dated July 1936 which he kept under the glass top of an office table. It read: 'An unbroken course of good fortune is always suspicious, prosperity is more secure when it is sometimes interrupted – Gracian (Spanish). About 1584-1658 AD.'

In the true Birmingham tradition Harry Lucas never lost the feeling that the workpeople were a kind of family, for whom he was responsible, having to educate them, chastise them, and care for them as though they were his own. This patriarchal attitude persisted even when the payroll had grown to some 20,000, to most of whom he was no more than a rather quaint old figure – if they were aware of his existence at all. He would turn down every other engagement in order not to miss an annual sports day, saying with some pride, 'I am going to see my people enjoy themselves.'

Remarkably tough himself, even when he was elderly, he depised any sign of laziness or softness in his staff. Seeing a crowd waiting to go up in a lift in a six-storey building, he told them: 'I'll carry you up on my back.'

He had always been fond of lectures as a young man, and in his semi-retirement he organised a series of talks for the workpeople, roping in the other directors as speakers. Harry himself talked about his early motoring experiences (no transcript, unhappily, has survived), Oliver gave a lecture on Venice and another about his infantry signalling lamp in the war, Waring recounted his reminiscences of the Gallipoli campaign, while Peter Bennett described his first winter sports holiday in Switzerland. (It is a startling reminder of the disparity between social groups that existed in those days to read that Bennett said, 'This is a bit of cheek my talking to you about all this, because you'll never have the chance to see it for yourselves'.) And Harry got his old friend, George Lanchester, to give a talk one evening.

Harry Lucas undertook few outside duties, his interest being centred very much on the company to the end of his life. Perhaps the most important was the Rowton House hostel for the poor, which he helped to found, becoming chairman of the Birmingham board. He carried on Joseph Lucas's participation in the Birmingham Temperance Society, but not with the same zeal.

Having driven a motor-car since the very beginning, Harry Lucas was reluctant to give it up when his increasing deafness cut him off from the world of sound. To guard against the lack of noise from adjacent traffic, he had his Daimler fitted with mirrors that gave him as nearly as possible an all-round view. Someone who used to drive with him reported that the only indication of his deafness was that he was quite oblivious to the occasional grating of a badly timed gear-change (which itself was no doubt largely attributable to his not hearing the sound of the engine). In his later years he forsook the Daimler for an elderly little Calcott, for which he had a great affection.

He died in 1939 at 'Hilver', the house in St Agnes Road, Moseley, where he had lived serenely with his wife Kate since the beginning of the century. The funeral took place two days after his death at Perry Bar Crematorium (in which he was a shareholder) with the minimum of fuss, for as Oliver Lucas put it to someone who approached him on behalf of the workpeople, who wanted to pay some last tribute to 'The Guvnor': 'It was no mere whim when he specified "no flowers," as he was one of the very earliest and staunchest advocates of funeral reform, having seen so many examples where money which could be ill afforded was spent on a display of last rites.' It was decided that flowers, if insisted upon, should be sent to hospitals, but this did not prevent a group of Birmingham artists, for whom Harry had been a sympathetic patron, bringing their flowers to the Crematorium.

At the Lucas factories in Birmingham 10,000 workpeople stood in silence for two minutes as the hour of the funeral struck.

TELEGRAMS & CABLES.
"LUCAS, BIRMINGHAM"

TELEPHONES:
NORTHERN 5201 (12 LINES)

HEAD OFFICES
GREAT KING ST.
BIRMINGHAM, 19

YOUR REF _____
OUR REF OL/JAP

MANAGING DIRECTORS' OFFICE

13th March 1939

Dear Mr. Pacy,

My Mother has asked me to say how very deeply she appreciates the kindly thought and deep regard which has inspired the various members of the organisation who have approached you with a request to pay some last tribute to "the Guvnor".

I feel that some explanation of his viewpoint will help those interested to realise that it was no mere whim when he specified "no flowers", as he was one of the very earliest and staunchest advocates of funeral reform, having seen so many examples where money which could be ill afforded was spent on a display of last rites.

You know my father was, a man of strong views and Mother and I feel it is the least we can do now that he has gone, to set an example in the present instance, but the gesture which has just been conveyed to us, viz. that a tribute of flowers should be sent to the Hospitals we think will be a means of bringing joy to the sick and we are sure would not run contrary to his views.

On behalf of my Mother, therefore, I would like to accept the suggestion in a deeply heartfelt manner.

With kindest personal regards,

Yours sincerely,

Oliver Lucas

S. Arrol Pacy, Esq.

ACKNOWLEDGEMENTS

No author leans more heavily on other people than the industrial biographer, for it is only by talking to countless members of the company, past and present – as well as to people outside – that he can fill in the bare bones of the minutes, the reports and the statistics that form the framework of the story.

In starting by acknowledging the help and counsel I received from Bernard Scott, I do so not simply out of deference to his position as the present chairman of Lucas, but because the idea of recording the history of the company came from him in the first place. That he gave me the privilege of being the author is something for which I shall always be grateful. He saw to it that I was given every possible facility, including many hours of his own valuable time while he 'thought aloud' about his forty-odd years with the company.

Sir Kenneth Corley was the chairman when I started to write the book (Bernard Scott was managing director) and he too gave me tremendous support with his personal reminiscences, especially of his years as general manager of the Electrical Company and commercial director of the group. Sir Bertram Waring was the company's honorary president, going into Great King Street for a few hours most days of the week. He took a kindly interest in what I was doing, and I was more fortunate than I realised to be able to draw on his memories of the five-fold growth of Lucas during his eighteen years of chairmanship, to say nothing of the earlier years. During our talks in his office, he often said, 'I shall look forward to reading your book . . .' and it was sad that he did not live to see the publication of this first volume.

The same can be said of two other directors whose deaths were lamented before my work was finished, but not before they had given me the benefit of their long experience. Dr Ernest Watson took the project of the history under his wing, talking to me by the hour in his old Cotswolds house under the watchful care of his devoted and hospitable wife. He had so much to tell – he had a marvellous memory – above all about Lucas's great contribution to the development of the gas turbine engine. Then there was John Morley, who translated Watson's technology into the production of Lucas gas turbine equipment at Burnley. He had joined Lucas as a youth and he told many a fascinating tale of a lifetime spent with the company. Henry Urquhart and Fred Coe were two retired managers who also unhappily died before they could see the results of my talks with them in print.

Manufacturing efficiency has been one of the key factors in Lucas history, and I am grateful to Fred Garner and Albert Siddall, who were largely responsible, for talking to me so freely and vividly.

I am indebted to Alec Nicol for making available to me two vital documents. The first was the Harry Lucas letter book of the 1880s, which gives such an intimate picture of the little firm of Joseph Lucas & Son in its early struggles. The second was the draft of a short history of the company prepared some years ago by Mrs Oriana Shaw, together with her supporting notes and interviews with old employees, many of whom, of course, have since passed on. Although her work never got beyond the typescript stage, Mrs Shaw's painstaking investigations have not been wasted in the long run, and I gladly acknowledge the help they gave me. I also obtained much useful material from the series of grey-covered papers in which Jack Masterton recorded his impressions of many Lucas events before and since the war. As the commercial director for many years he had been at the centre of Lucas affairs.

The biographer of a big company would be lost without a cicerone to guide his steps in meeting and talking to people who can help him in specific areas. As my official link with the company, Harold Neville played this part admirably, being able to brief me about people and policies from his own 40-plus years' Lucas service. I would like to thank him now for all his kindness and co-operation.

With so much help from so many people, it may seem invidious to pick out some for special thanks, but it would be churlish not to mention a few more – at all levels – who gave generously of their time in tape-recorded conversations. I am thinking particularly of Robert Neill, Herbert Astbury, Harvey Nelson, John Merrick, Fred Thacker, Bill Shaw, Roy Harrison, Bill Robinson, Henry Mayer, Fred Coleman, Ben Morris, Arthur Gregg, Arnold Egginton, Reg Tooze and Len Boughton – not forgetting a party of lively pensioners at the Social Club who were so eager to tell me their experiences over a cup of tea that they quite overwhelmed the capacity of the tape-recorder. The unique Jack Orme deserves a place all on his own, because I called on his remarkable memory in many letters after our first meeting. I valued his help as much as I admired his character.

To Jessie Parkes, for so long Oliver Lucas's secretary, I am grateful for giving me a view of him that supplemented the memories of his three personal assistants, Neill, Corley and Scott, and completed the picture of this important figure in Lucas history. And from his brother-in-law, Charles Filter, I received some interesting photographs of Oliver Lucas taken during the Great War.

For the pre-war CAV story, both before and after Lucas took over the company in 1926, my thanks are due to Geoffrey Savill for giving me a comprehensive chronology of events and to Leslie Johnston for much factual information about the company in its early years, and later. The origin and growth of Rotax before the war were set out for me in the historical notes of the company written by Ronald Legg, who also gave me his personal memories. Ray Woodall then filled in the picture from his own experience of building up the aero side of the business from scratch in the 1930s.

Then I come to those who provided information from the records at Great King Street, Park Street and elsewhere, on whose help I was dependent. Norman Partridge, who had worked for Dr Watson, was an unfailing source of facts about Lucas electrical products; Ray Pettigrew, the group patents manager, placed his most valuable documents at my disposal; Andrew Willis, the company registrar, was always willing to delve into his files about Lucas companies (their number is legion); while Roger Pattison at Park Street patiently answered my calls for financial details about Lucas over the years. Much information was hidden away in old catalogues and advertisements, and here Barry Homer was my enthusiastic informant. Gwyn Jenkins, the editor, was always helful in tracing information from the pages of *Reflections*, the Lucas house magazine.

As a regular visitor to the Great King Street headquarters, I naturally had to look to the administration for some help, and this was given in full measure (until her retirement) by Nancy Barr, the impressive head of the secretariat. It was she who personally supervised the loan of the precious minute books from the strong room – and made sure they were safely returned under lock and key!

Turning to the assistance I received from outside the company, in my research into the origins of Joseph Lucas, the man, I received wholehearted help from Dorothy McCulla, head of studies at the Birmingham Reference Library, and from Dr R. J. Hetherington, research associate of the Birmingham branch of the Victorian Society, who sent me long letters containing a mass of useful information about George Dawson, Joseph's schoolmaster and minister, and early nineteenth-century Birmingham generally. C. J. Simmons, secretary of the Birmingham Temperance Society, helpfully enabled me to have access to documents relating to the time when Joseph Lucas was the Society's chief benefactor. And I would like to thank the ministers of the various Birmingham churches for checking their baptismal registers to find a record of Joseph Lucas's baptism.

So little was known in the company about Joseph Lucas's early life that it was most welcome to be able to talk to Mrs E. L. Thomas, whose late husband was Joseph's grandson (he was the son of Emily, Joseph's eldest daughter). Mrs Thomas supplied the portraits of Joseph and Emily Stevens, his first wife, which are reproduced in this work, and she very kindly presented the original daguerreotypes, mounted in dark green velvet frames, to the company's archives. I was also privileged to meet another of Joseph's grandsons, Felix Lucas (the son of Christopher, Joseph's second son), with whom I had a useful talk.

Lucas cycle lamps have become collectors' items, and I was glad to discuss them in correspondence with Peter Shirtcliffe, who has made a study of the subject. Another cycle lamp connoisseur, Dr Christopher Brooks, opened his unique collection of early catalogues to my inspection when I visited him at Newthorpe.

Three great figures in the motor industry – Lord (Miles) Thomas, Sir Patrick Hennessy and Sir William Lyons – were good enough to give me their views of Lucas as seen from the outside in the years when Peter Bennett and Oliver Lucas ruled the roost, and for their courtesy I am most grateful. And to Alick Dick I am indebted for the story of how the agreement between Harry Ferguson and John Black came to be signed on the back of Claridge's menu and was witnessed by Oliver Lucas and Henry Tiarks.

But above all, I suppose, I am most grateful to the shade of Joseph Lucas for providing the story – at any rate the essential beginning of it. He wrought better than he knew, and by the end of this first volume the company has outgrown anything that he could have imagined when he formed it in 1897. In tracing his early progress I came to have a warm regard for 'Old Joe', and I humbly dedicate this history to his memory.

BIBLIOGRAPHY

The following were the principal works consulted in the preparation of Volume 1. They are given in chronological order of publication.

Birmingham and District Hardware, by S. Timmins, 1864

The Resources, Products and Industrial History of Birmingham, by S. Timmins, 1866

Old and New Birmingham, by Robert K. Dent, 1880

The Making of Birmingham, by Robert K. Dent, 1894

The Bartleet Bicycle Book, 1931

Report on the Activities of Robert Bosch, GmbH in the Fuel Injection Industry, by the Economic Section of the US Department of Justice, 1943

RAC Golden Jubilee Book, 1947

Horseless Carriage, by L. T. C. Rolt, 1950

History of Birmingham, by Conrad Gill and Asa Briggs, 1952

Motoring Cavalcade, by W. J. Bentley, 1953

The Vintage Motor-Car, by Cecil Clutton and John Stanford, 1954

Veterans of the Road, by Elizabeth Nagle, 1955

The Observer's Book of Automobiles, by Richard T. Parsons, 1955

Edwardian Cars, by Ernest F. Carter, 1955

The Life of Lord Nuffield, by P. W. S. Andrews and E. Brunner, 1955

Veteran and Edwardian Cars, by D. Scott-Moncrieff, 1955

Golden Milestone, by the Automobile Association, 1955

From Veteran to Vintage, by Kent Karslake and Laurence Pomeroy, 1956

40 Years of Motoring, 1919–1959, by Edward Young, 1959

The Motor Industry, by G. Maxcy and A. Silberston, 1959

Commercial Road Vehicles, by E. L. Cornwall, 1960

Jaguar, a Biography, by Lord Montagu of Beaulieu, 1961

The World's Automobiles, 1862–1962, by G. R. Doyle, revised by G. Georgano, 1963

Lanchester Motor Cars, by A. Bird and F. Hutton-Scott, 1965

The Bull-Nose Morris, by Lytton P. Jarman and R. Barraclough, 1965; new edition *The Bullnose and Flatnose Morris*, 1976

Wheels Within Wheels, by Geoffrey Williamson, 1966

Milestones in a Motoring Life, by Dudley Noble, 1969

Bicycling, a history, by Frederick Alderson, 1972

How Your Birmingham Grows, by John Whybrow, 1972

Rudolf Diesel and the Diesel Engine, by John Moon, 1974

Index